JUN 1 9 2014

Die in Paris

The true story of France's most notorious serial killer

Marilyn Z. Tomlins

Published by Raven Crest Books

ISBN-13: 978-0-9926700-0-9
ISBN-10: 0992670004

to jt

CONTENTS

Author's note   1

Prologue: Saturday, May 25, 1946   3

Part One: Horror   5

Chapter 1: Saturday, March 11, 1944   7

Chapter 2: Sunday, March 12, 1944   33

Chapter 3: Monday, March 13, 1944   41

Chapter 4: Tuesday, March 14, 1944   51

Chapter 5: Wednesday, March 15, 1944   61

Chapter 6: Thursday, March 16, 1944   77

Chapter 7: Friday, March 17, 1944   89

Chapter 8: Saturday, March 18, 1944   103

Part Two: Child, Soldier, Doctor And Mayor   105

Chapter 1: Child   107

Chapter 2: Soldier   117

Chapter 3: Doctor   127

Chapter 4: Mayor   143

Part Three: Murder 169

Chapter 1: Paris 171
Chapter 2: Good Neighbour 189
Chapter 3: Angel Maker 199
Chapter 4: Killing Jews 201
Chapter 5: Killing Gangsters 217
Chapter 6: Killing Jews Again 223
Chapter 7: Looking For Dr Eugène 231
Chapter 8: Gestapo Prisoner 241
Chapter 9: Release And Destroying Evidence 251

Part Four: Justice 263

Chapter 1: Slow But Certain Progress 265
Chapter 2: Arrest 271
Chapter 3: Interrogation 283
Chapter 4: Facing Justice 309
Chapter 5: The Trial Continues 341
Chapter 6: Innocent Or Guilty 363
Chapter 7: Death 407

Bibliography 416
Contact Details 421

AUTHOR'S NOTE

Dr Marcel Petiot existed in the basement of the human spirit in a time and place that struggled, like everywhere touched by the Nazi poison, to find the light; in Paris in the years of the Second World War.

I am not a macabre person, but, when I first came across this man, I found him ghoulishly fascinating. As I began to learn more about him, he drew me down into him, and I use the word 'down' consciously. I had to know more and still more about him.

In this book, I do not analyse or judge him, because I never analyse or judge the murderers I write about. I will allow you, the reader, to make up your own mind about him.

In the years that I researched his life and his crimes and wrote this book, I got to know him well. For this reason I call him Marcel throughout the book. I do so despite that no one ever calls him anything but Dr Petiot.

I wish to explain the French Franc (FF) amounts I mention in the book.

From 1940 to 1945 the French Franc/U.S. Dollar exchanged at the rate of FF48.02/$1, and the U.S. Dollar/British Pound at the rate of $4.03/£1.

This means that 50,000 French francs equalled just over 260 British pounds or a thousand U.S. dollars. A man's suit would have cost £2.75 in the United Kingdom and a house £550, and in the USA a man's suit would have cost $24 and a house $3,920.

MARILYN Z. TOMLINS - PARIS, FRANCE

PROLOGUE

Saturday, May 25, 1946

In the predawn hours of Saturday, May 25, 1946, the residents of Rue de la Santé in Paris's fourteenth *arrondissement* – district - were awakened by car doors slamming and men's voices. Accustomed as they were to early morning noise coming from the large triangular building that dominated the street - La Santé Prison - they still jumped from their beds and rushed to their windows. Something was wrong.

They could see dozens of 'swallows' - policemen in black uniforms, capes and *képis* - brandishing batons to stop an excited crowd of journalists, photographers and Parisians from reaching the prison gate.

At 6 A.M. the first rays of a late spring sun reflecting off the broken glass on top of the wall enclosing the building, the prison gate swung open, and a black Citroën box-shaped police patrol van drove out. Cameras started to flash, and cries of 'death to him' rang out.

The vehicle was taking a beheaded man to his final resting place in an unmarked grave south of the capital.

'Louisette' had had her revenge.

PART ONE

HORROR

CHAPTER ONE

Saturday, March 11, 1944

In the early evening of Saturday, March 11, 1944, the telephone rang on the desk of the duty officer at the Porte Maillot police station. Until that moment, Rue le Sueur in Paris's elegant sixteenth *arrondissement* had made it into the news just once. That was in April 1912. That month, the French singer and actress, Léontine Pauline Aubart, from Number 17, had set sail from Southampton for New York with her lover, Benjamin Guggenheim, but she had returned to Rue le Sueur, alone and grieving. The ship she and her Ben had boarded in Southampton for the Atlantic crossing was the Titanic. Guggenheim had gone down with the ship.

Rue le Sueur would yet again be in the news.

On the phone was Jacques Marçais, a retired clerk.

Jacques and Andrée, his wife, lived in an apartment at Number 22 Rue le Sueur. He was calling to report that for the past six days pestilential smoke has been pouring from the chimney of a townhouse across the street.

The duty officer did not understand why someone would think that a smoking chimney needed investigating. In 1939, world war had broken out and France had capitulated to the enemy - Nazi Germany - and, since June 1940, when the Germans had occupied northern France, which included Paris, they had been imposing frequent power cuts on the Parisians. That night, it might have been spring, but it was still cold in Paris, and the Parisians had to light fires for heat. Consequently, in just about every Paris living room, a fire was roaring, and, from every Paris chimney, poured smoke.

Jacques explained.

It was the chimney of an uninhabited house, and that was certainly not normal.

The duty officer promised to send a patrolman over as soon as possible.

* * *

In pre-war days, on a Saturday evening at six - it was six sharp when Jacques stepped outside to wait for the patrolman - the narrow, one-way, Rue le Sueur would have been buzzing. Some of its residents would have been coming home with last-minute purchases from the family-owned shops on neighbouring Rue Pergolèse. Others would have been setting off for a night of fun in Paris's multitude of cabarets and music halls.

On that night, almost four years into the German Occupation, Rue le Sueur was dark, deserted and silent. Not only had wartime food rationing and shortages emptied the shelves of Rue Pergolèse's shops, but a blackout and curfew were in force. The blackout siren had sounded at six, but though the curfew would not commence until ten, all the street's residents were already indoors.

Jacques would also have been indoors.

Approaching the townhouse with the smoking chimney, he very much wished he were.

* * *

Today, Rue le Sueur is what real estate agents describe as prime location.

A street of handsome six or seven storey buildings with boutiques or offices on the ground and lower floors and apartments on the upper floors, it runs between Avenue Foch and Avenue de la Grande-Armée. Avenue Foch enjoys the reputation of being the Paris street with the most expensive properties, and Avenue de la Grande-Armée is one of the twelve avenues opening onto Place de l'Étoile at the upper end of Avenue des Champs-Élysées. Therefore, 'Étoile', with its Arc de Triomphe monument, is but a stone's throw from Rue le Sueur. The Eiffel Tower standing in the public garden of Champs-de-Mars is also close by; at night the tower glitters beyond the Avenue Foch end of the street.

In 1944, four or five storey turn of the century residential buildings lined the street, the traffic moving from Avenue de la Grande-Armée towards Avenue Foch. There were, in fact, only two businesses on the street. One was a tiny *bougnat*-bistro. The other was a garage. The *bougnat*-bistro - a coal merchant, who also sold wine, something one no longer comes across in Paris - was at Number 19. The garage took up all of the ground floor at Number 22 where Jacques and Andrée lived. From the top of the building fluttered the Nazis' red, white and black Swastika; in June 1940, at the fall of France and the commencement of the wartime Occupation, the Germans had requisitioned the garage for TODT, the Wehrmacht's Supply Service.

The townhouse with the smoking chimney, built in 1834 on 323 square metres of land, the only *hôtel particulier* - individual house - was at Number 21. It was four storeys high, which, in present day French architectural terms, means that it had a *rez-de-chaussée* (ground), *premier* (first), *deuzième* (second), and *troisième* (third) floor.

Once the home of a prince and princess, the Prince and Princess Colloredo de Mansfeld - he was Czech and she French - and the most elegant property on the street, the townhouse was in a state of utter dilapidation. Its façade was black with grime and dust, pigeon droppings covered the metal window shutters - there were four windows to a storey - and paint peeled from its large double front door, a *porte cochère* - a gateway - through which horse-drawn carriages had once passed.

The townhouse's decline had begun on the death of the prince in the 1930s when the princess had moved out, leaving the upkeep of the magnificent house to tenants. One tenant had been the French actress Cécile Sorel who had used the townhouse as a warehouse for stage props. What had further contributed to the state of the property's dilapidation was that the princess had sold it at just about the same time TODT had requisitioned the garage across the street, and that the property's new proprietor had not moved in. He had, instead, also used the townhouse as a place of storage. Or so Jacques and Andrée had thought.

* * *

The story that the couple would tell about the townhouse after that March night, was that the goings on at the property after the princess had sold it, had intrigued them.

They said that the new owner, a youngish man - they thought that he was in his thirties - used to come to the townhouse quite often, but that he had never remained for long, just for a few hours, and such visits were either at a very early hour of the morning or at nightfall.

They said that he had arrived either on foot or on a bicycle, always approaching the townhouse from Avenue de la Grande-Armée. When he was on his bike - it was painted green - he was dressed in *bleu de travail*, the blue overalls and cloth cap of a French worker, but when on foot, he looked the Paris *gentilhomme*; he wore a suit, shirt with starched cuffs and collar, a fedora and a brightly-coloured bow tie. Often, when on his bike and dressed like a French worker, he pulled a small cart behind him; bikes and *vélo-rickshaws* had become the primary modes of transport in Paris, because, along with rationing food, the Germans were also rationing petrol. His cart was always packed high. They had wondered what he was carting to the house. Whatever it was, it was hidden under a stained sheet of canvas.

When on foot and looking the Paris *gentilhomme*, he frequently had another person, male or female, with him. They always carried suitcases - always two suitcases - and should the person with him be a woman, he carried one of her suitcases for her. Those visitors had puzzled the couple as much as the man; whereas he had set off again after a while, they had remained at the house, and no sooner had he disappeared around the Avenue de la Grande Armée corner than sounds of banging drifted from the townhouse. The banging had often continued deep into the night. There had once even been banging on a Christmas Eve; it had been interminable.

On other nights, other noises, too, had drifted from the house: a child's crying, a woman groaning as if in pain, a man shouting angrily.

One night, one of the street's residents walking by long after the curfew had sounded, had even heard a man's voice calling out for help from somewhere deep inside the house.

"*Au secours! Au secours! S'il vous plaît, au secours!*"

Help! Help! Please help!

The couple would say that around May or June of the previous year they had noticed that the man had stopped coming to the townhouse.

The townhouse had obviously been abandoned.

The months had passed and 1943 had ended, and there still had been

10

no evidence of activity at the property.

Then, on Monday, March 6, the townhouse's chimney had started to spew smoke.

The couple would say that, at first, the smoke had risen in thin, white coils, which the early spring wind had swept into their kitchen; they lived on the top floor. Around midnight, that night, the smoking had stopped, but only to recommence the following morning.

All of the Tuesday, the smoke had risen into the sky, and, again, at around midnight, it had stopped, only to begin again in the morning.

The smoke had by then turned black and a pestilential stench clung to it, as well as to everything else; their furniture, their clothes, their hair. Even the food they ate.

As Andrée would continue with the story, on that third day, she had started to feel queasy and soon she was vomiting. She wanted Jacques to summon the police or the fire service, whichever would get to the townhouse quicker, but he had refused. He wanted to know from her whether she had forgotten that France had lost the war and that the victorious *Boches* - the Germans - had become their new masters. Having 'swallows' swarming all over the street was bound to draw the *Boches'* attention and that would have been most undesirable, he had told her. He knew that contact with the police was contact with the Germans. At the start of the Occupation the police force had been given the choice of resigning or working under German orders. It had chosen the latter. The Germans, therefore, knew whatever the police were doing.

"But I insisted and he had no choice but to summon the police," Andrée would end her story.

"And just as well I did," Jacques would say, nodding.

On reaching the townhouse, he had seen that someone had left a note pinned to the gateway. The note had obviously been there for some time because rain had smudged the message: 'Absent for a month. Forward mail to 18 Rue des Lombards, Auxerre.'

The townhouse had indeed been abandoned.

Its chimney should not have been spewing smoke.

* * *

About fifteen minutes after Jacques reached the townhouse, two faint strips of bicycle headlights came around the corner of Avenue de la Grande–Armée. 'Swallows' patrolled by bike and Porte Maillot had sent over not one, but two. Because of the blackout, the bike's headlights were painted blue as those of all vehicles had to be.

Patrolmen Joseph Teyssier and Emile Fillion's shift was about to end. The call to Rue le Sueur would be the last of the day. They wanted to get it over with so that they could go home.

Wasting no time, they wanted to know from Jacques what was going on.

He showed them the note.

Several of the street's residents, including Andrée, had stepped out on to the street and the *concierge* - supervisor - from the apartment building at Number 23, the building next door to the townhouse, walked up.

"The proprietor's name is Petiot," she said.

He was a family doctor.

"He lives at Number 66 Rue de Caumartin in the ninth *arrondissement*."

The patrolman knew that Rue de Caumartin was close to 'Printemps' department store and Saint Lazare railway station.

The *concierge* had more information she wanted to pass on.

The doctor had bought the townhouse two years previously, at which time he had building work done. He left a set of keys with her to let the workmen into the house in the mornings and to lock up after them at night.

"He is an attractive man. Charming, too. Real gentleman, if you ask me," she said.

He never talked down to her because he was a doctor, and she, the supervisor of a building.

"But the house does not look all that great inside, if you ask me," she added. "Not for a doctor's place, *alors*."

She had the doctor's telephone number.

"PIGalle 77-11."

She suggested that the patrolmen telephone him and summon him to his townhouse.

The two patrolmen decided that they would.

***

On the corner of Avenue de la Grande-Armée was a bistro, Le Crocodile.

Patrolman Teyssier, more extrovert than his colleague, decided to walk there to make the call.

The bistro was already shuttered for the night. The Germans were also imposing three 'dry' days on the Parisians and that Saturday was such a day. There had been no reason to keep the bistro open.

At Teyssier's first knock, the owner hastily rolled up the metal shutter. Having heard noise on the street, and having been concerned like all his neighbours about the smoke and the stench, he had been watching from an upstairs window, pleased that the police have been summoned. He had wanted to do so himself, but like Jacques, he, too, had not wanted to draw the attention of the Germans.

A couple of minutes later a telephone exchange operator put Patrolman Teyssier through to PIGalle 77-11.

A woman's voice was heard on the line.

"*Bonsoir. Qui est à l'appareil?*"

Who is speaking?

"*Bonsoir Madame*, it's the police," replied Patrolman Teyssier into the mouthpiece.

He asked to speak to Dr Petiot.

"I will call him, *Monsieur l'agent*," replied the woman.

A man's voice came on the line.

"*Bonsoir, Monsieur*, it's the police," repeated the patrolman.

He apologised for calling in the evening; it was dinner time and, despite the food rationing and shortages, it was still a sacred moment for a Frenchman.

"A fire has broken out at Number 21 Rue le Sueur, and I've been told the property belongs to you," he explained.

There was a slight hesitation on the other end of the line.

"Have you gone in?"

Patrolman Teyssier said he had not.

"Don't, and don't touch anything," cautioned the voice. "I'll be right there. In fifteen minutes at the most; that's how long it will take me to cycle over. I'll be bringing the key. But don't go in! Wait for me."

Before the patrolman hung up, he asked the doctor - he presumed he was speaking to *the* Dr Petiot, proprietor of the townhouse - to hurry.

"It's urgent. The smoke stinks, and everyone feels sick!" he said.

13

For half an hour, the two patrolmen waited for the doctor to materialise, and, after having waited for another fifteen minutes with still no sign of him, Patrolman Teyssier returned to Le Crocodile to make another telephone call. The owner, having changed to his working clothes of black trousers, white short-sleeved shirt, black waistcoat and a white, ankle-length, cloth apron tied around his waist, was busy opening up. He sensed it was going to be a busy night on the street and he was willing to break the law; if anyone wanted something stronger than a cup of ersatz coffee, he was their man.

Patrolman Teyssier called Porte Maillot again. He asked for the fire service to be sent over. He wanted them to hurry because something awfully rotten was burning.

Ten minutes later, a fire engine, headlights also painted blue, raced around the Avenue de la Grande-Armée corner and up Rue le Sueur and came to a halt in front of Number 21, its tires screeching.

* * *

Like everything else in wartime Paris, locks were hard to replace.

For this reason, *Caporal* Avilla Boudringhim of Porte Maillot fire service, having been told by the two patrolmen that the townhouse's owner was not just anyone, but a doctor, was reluctant to smash the one on the gateway. Therefore, he and his crew of three entered the property through one of the shuttered ground floor windows: neither the old shutter nor the cracked window pane behind it had offered their hammers much resistance.

Inside the house, they found themselves in a large salon.

They saw by flashlight - a switch in a wall had failed to produce light - that the room was in a state of great disarray. Several items of furniture, some broken, others covered in old blankets, were piled against the walls. Cardboard boxes, hat boxes and suitcases lay all over the floor. Some of the suitcases were open: an incredible array of goods spilt from them. There lay men's jackets, ties, socks, a woman's gold lamé dress, a large feathered hat, handbags, numerous pairs of shoes. Also, pots of face cream, boxes of pills, tubes of ointment, some razors, pairs of eyeglasses, some cutlery and crockery, several army-issue blankets and several sheets. Price tags were attached to several of the items and some suitcases bore labels of Orient Express trains, Cunard cruise liners, and luxury hotels in London, Nice, Venice, Istanbul and New York. It was as if someone had abandoned moving in or had been disturbed while moving out.

Boudringhim and his men made their way from the room to an oval-shaped hallway. It was in perfect order; it was even elegant. The walls were covered in tapestry fabric. On the floor lay a carpet, which looked expensive, and brocaded *Louis Quinze* chairs were arranged in a semicircle in front of a marble fireplace adorned with two harp-playing porcelain cherubim. A large still life hung on one of the walls.

A red-carpeted staircase led from the hallway to the upper floors, and the fire chief motioned to his men that they were going to see what was upstairs.

The stairs led to a corridor, doors on both sides. The men opened each and flashed their lights into the rooms in front of them. All, but one of the rooms, were in a similar state of disorder to the salon. The exception looked like it was being turned into a study, perhaps a library. Its walls were lined with glass-fronted cases, all filled with books. More books lay in piles on the floor.

The firefighters went up another staircase, that one narrow and uncarpeted, their footsteps deafening in the darkness. Again, they pushed open doors and flashed their lights into rooms, all cluttered with boxes, suitcases and old dusty furniture.

Down the men went again.

Upstairs, they had counted the rooms; there were ten.

Nowhere up there had they found any signs of fire. The stench that was out on the street had been present, yes, and they had had to cover their noses with large woollen handkerchiefs they carried around especially for that purpose, but they had not even seen a match or a cigarette butt anywhere.

The house had a basement. A second staircase in the hallway led down to it. The firefighters were going to go down to see what was there, but a glass door drew their attention. The door was closed, but not locked.

It opened onto a small, dark, oblong courtyard. The locked gateway was at one end of the courtyard. At the other was an archway. A second larger courtyard could be seen beyond it. A narrow metal door also led off the courtyard. The door was ajar. Behind it was a set of narrow, cracked stone steps. The men knew that those would lead down to the townhouse's basement. They started to descend, stepping carefully so as not to trip in the semi-darkness.

It had been chilly in the courtyard; going down the steps, the air turned hot and foul, fouler than what it had been in the house.

There was a door at the bottom of the steps. It, too, stood ajar. Judging by all the open doors, the house's proprietor seemed to have left the townhouse in a great hurry.

In the excitement of that moment the firefighters did not think of looking for the electrical mains to switch the electricity back on; in Paris townhouses, the mains were always in the basement.

By flashlight they saw that the basement consisted of a short, narrow, low-ceilinged corridor. Several doors led from it. Those were closed. The men opened one after the other; again not one was locked. Behind each was a tiny roughly-cemented room. The rooms were all empty. Flashing their lights into the last room on the corridor, they knew they had found the source of the stench.

The room in front of them was approximately four metres wide and three metres deep. Rusty water pipes and flyspecked electrical wires ran up its walls and into a ceiling blackened with soot and blistered with damp. Two old and dented coal and wood burners stood against one of the walls. One was much larger than the other. The smaller was rusted and it had neither door nor chimney; it was obvious it would never work again. Coal was smouldering in the furnace of the larger one. A burnt log, or what looked like one, protruded from the coal. The firefighters covered their noses; the air was really foul. They stepped into the room, Boudringhim leading. They had to have a closer look at the burner; they wanted to see if there might be something else in its furnace. Boudringhim poked at the log with his flashlight; he wanted to free it, but only ash scattered to the floor.

He groaned.

What was protruding from the coals was indeed not a log; it was an arm. The hand was still intact: the fingers, swollen and black, were clearly discernible. They were pointing at him. It was as if they were beckoning him to come closer; to come and see what was going on and to do something about it. To help.

He leant forward and another groan escaped him.

In the furnace, flames were devouring a human skull, its eye sockets

16

empty and its mouth agape. It was as if the skull, too, was making a final effort to call for help, to yell for help.

There was more horror.

In a corner of the room lay a pile of human remains.

The firefighters flashed their lights at it. They saw a foot, a rib cage, a jawbone, another arm, another skull; the complete torso of a woman.

"What could I have done in such a place?" Boudringhim would later ask.

He motioned his men to get the hell out.

Terror speeds the legs.

Within moments, the four put their hammers to the gateway's precious lock.

The lock, smashed, they staggered on to the pavement.

The two patrolmen were waiting.

"*Messieurs...* you have some work ahead of you!" stammered Boudringhim.

The fire chief wanted to say more, tell the two what he and his men had seen, but the words would not come. One of his men was vomiting against TODT's garage. The other two had sunk to their knees in the gutter.

In the morning, in his statement to the police, Boudringhim would say: 'After exploring the ground and upper floors of the house, we went down to the basement and, guided by the smell, we came to a room with the two burners. There we saw human flesh burning in one of them. We also saw some human remains lying on the floor. A fleshless arm stuck from the lit furnace. I think it was the arm of a woman'.

* * *

The two patrolmen braced themselves for what was to come and disappeared into the house.

Their noses led them to the basement.

Having seen what no one should have to see, they too turned on their heels and fled.

Outside, Patrolman Fillion collapsed against the house. His colleague continued running. He ran to Le Crocodile to make his third telephone call of the night. He again called Porte Maillot.

"We need help over here!" he shouted into the mouthpiece. "We've found bodies burning... lots of them."

The duty officer said that he would immediately send more men over.

* * *

Patrolman Teyssier had hardly returned from Le Crocodile to join his colleague in front of the townhouse when a bike sped around the corner at Avenue de la Grande-Armée. The cyclist - a man - wore a grey tweed overcoat and black fedora. Reaching the townhouse, he leant the bike against TODT's garage; next, he walked over to the two patrolmen. His breathing coming in rapid gasps, he greeted Patrolman Teyssier, ignoring Patrolman Fillion.

"Good evening, *Monsieur l'agent.*"

The two patrolmen, still trying to gather their wits, gave a sigh of relief; they thought Dr Petiot had finally arrived.

"No. I am the doctor's brother," said the man, and added: "My brother will be over shortly."

"We want to show you something," said Patrolman Teyssier. "Do you mind coming with us?"

"I take it that you are French?" asked the man.

Later, Patrolman Teyssier would say that he and his colleague had found the question puzzling and they had not replied. He described the man as in his mid-thirties; about 1.70 metres in height, and, despite a yellow complexion and dark half-moons under his eyes, good-looking. The man's eyes, he said, were strange. One moment they were a very deep black and sparkled, yet the next they were as dull as an onyx stone.

The man dashed past the two patrolmen into the courtyard and, unhindered by the darkness, and apparently also by the stench - he seemed unaware of it - over to the glass door. He obviously wanted to get inside the house quickly.

"No, this way *Monsieur*, if you please," Patrolman Teyssier called out, running after him.

The French consider it impolite to omit *monsieur*, *madame* or *mademoiselle* when addressing a stranger, and despite the night's bizarre circumstances, the patrolman was doing his best to remain polite.

It was to the basement that the two patrolmen wanted the man to go.

18

Down in the basement, knowing what was waiting there, the two did not want to go into the last room on the corridor. They stood back and motioned to the man that they wanted him to step into the room. Without hesitation he did, and they watched, not taking their eyes off him for a second. Pensively, he looked at the larger burner. The arm no longer stuck from the coal; it lay on the floor. The hand had been ripped away and there were few fingers left on it. In the furnace, the head had cracked lengthwise. He turned to look at the pile of human remains. He had started to sweat; glistening beads of perspiration clung to his forehead. He had also started to rub his hands together; he was doing so vigorously as if he were washing them under a tap.

He cleared his throat.

"*Monsieur l'agent*, my head is on the block here," he murmured.

He had again addressed only Patrolman Teyssier, but he had not looked at him, but down at the floor.

He spoke again, his eyes still on the floor.

"What you see here, *Monsieur l'agent*, concerns the Resistance. I am, you understand, in the Resistance. These... these here... these bodies here... they are the bodies of Germans and of French traitors. They arrested and tortured me."

The two patrolmen would recall later that they had seen him sweep something off the floor; he had closed his hands over whatever it was. Next, he had dropped the object into one of the pockets of his overcoat. They would not ask him what he had picked up. They would explain that they had been too mesmerised by his hands. Those were large, red and calloused, and his fingernails were rimmed with dirt. "Not the hands of a doctor," they would say. "Rather those of a worker; someone who laid bricks or worked the land."

The man looked up and wanted to know whether the two had notified their superiors.

They nodded in unison.

"They are on their way, *Monsieur*," said Patrolman Teyssier.

"In that case, I have no choice but to go," replied the man.

He explained that he had hundreds of documents at his home which he would have to destroy because they identified members of the Resistance.

"If these documents fall into the hands of the Germans, all these brave blokes will be shot," he said.

Again, the two patrolmen nodded.

Back on the street, they started to blow their whistles. They wanted those gathering outside - by then there was a crowd - to stand aside to enable the man to get to his bike.

"*Vive la France!*" whispered the man to the two 'swallows' when back on his bike.

They nodded.

"*Vive la France!*"

They too had whispered: there were informers everywhere and only a fool manifested patriotism.

Yet, they had removed their *képis*, and were holding those over their hearts: down in the basement they had seen that some of the man's molars had been drilled down. They knew that drilling teeth was one of the Gestapo's favourite tortures. It had decided them that he had, indeed, been truthful in claiming that he was a resistant, and that the bodies in the basement were those of Germans and their French supporters; in other words, traitors.

* * *

The two patrolmen, still holding their képis over their hearts, watched the man and his bike disappear into the darkness of the blacked-out Parisian wartime night. They were honouring not only the hero on the bike, but also their poor martyred country, occupied as she was by the German Nazis.

They had not asked the hero on the bike whether his brother, Dr Petiot, proprietor of the townhouse, was also a resistant and whether the doctor was aware of what was going on in the house's basement. Neither had they asked him where he lived or what his telephone number was so that the police could get in touch with him.

The man's bicycle was green.

* * *

No sooner had the bike disappeared around the corner of Avenue de la Grande-Armée than a black *traction-avant* Citroën, the standard front-wheel drive service vehicle of a police officer drove up the street.

A few minutes later, Inspectors Chevalier, Gauthèrie and Lainé, and a captain named Déforeit, followed the two patrolmen and the fire chief down to the basement. They saw that the larger burner was still alight and asked why no one had thought of extinguishing the fire. The fire chief called his men to do so. The fire, extinguished, the four officers told him that he and his men could return to their depot; their work was done.

Alone with the two patrolmen, the four wanted to be briefed on the night's discovery.

They heard that the house was the property of a Dr Petiot from Number 66 Rue de Caumartin in the ninth *arrondissement* and that the doctor had been summoned, but had not yet arrived.

They were also given the note which had been pinned to the gateway.

They were not told of the man on the green bike.

Soon afterwards, the two patrolmen having returned to Porte Maillot, Inspector Lainé also set off for the police station. He wanted reinforcement sent to the townhouse. What was going on there was too big for Porte Maillot to handle.

The Crim - *la Crim'* - should be called in. The Crim was *la Brigade Criminelle* of the Brigade Special No. 1, Paris's Criminal Investigation Department, based at Number 36 Quay des Orfèvres that forms part of the *Préfecture de Police* - police headquarters - in the Palais de Justice complex on Île de la Cité, one of the two islands in the Seine in central Paris. It is still today Paris's police headquarters.

The Palais de Justice complex stretches from Quay des Orfèvres, the southern border of the island, to Quay de l'Horloge, its northern border, and from Boulevard du Palais in the east and Place Dauphine in the west. It extends over twenty hectares and it has twenty kilometres of corridors, seven thousand doors and three thousand five hundred and fifty windows.

Those who work at Number 36 Quay des Orfèvres call it *la grande maison*, the big house. Parisians, both in fear and respect, never call it anything but *le Quay*, the Quay.

* * *

At 8.05 P.M. a telegram, numbered 100101, was sent by *pneumatique* -

underground pneumatic tube - from Porte Maillot police station to the Quay. *Pneumatique* was faster than a telegram. The addressee also received, not just a sheet of paper on which letters had been pasted, but the original correspondence in its envelope.

The telegram read:

'Towards 7:45 P.M. a smell somewhat like a gas leak led to the discovery of the remains of several partly-burnt human corpses next to a lit burner in the basement of an uninhabited private townhouse at Number 21 Rue Le Sueur. The owner appears to be Mr Piot (sic) from Number 66 Rue de Caumartin'.

It bore Captain Lainé's signature.

It arrived in the Quay's telegraphic room at 8:25 P.M.

At 9:30 P.M., an hour after its arrival and almost four hours after the discovery of the basement room's horrific secret, the Quay reacted; one of its detectives telephoned the home of the head of the Crim - Commissioner Georges-Victor Massu.

* * *

Mrs Massu, the archetypal stoic policeman's wife, was still up and washing the dinner dishes when the telephone rang. She ran to answer. A call at that time of the night meant that there was trouble somewhere in Paris.

Because it was a Saturday night, Massu, in his early fifties, well-built with pitch-black hair and a fine moustache, and an ego to match his exalted position - the rumour in the force was that crime writer Georges Simenon had based his pipe-smoking Inspector Maigret on him - had hoped for a full night's sleep and was already in bed.

"*Allô, j'écoute*," he muttered grumpily on taking the receiver.

The Quay's detective refused to say what was going on, but asked Massu to come to headquarters immediately. A car was already on the way to pick him up.

The commissioner dressed hastily.

He put on a grey suit, black double-breasted overcoat and grey fedora just as he would on a weekday morning, and when his front door bell rang, he was at the door. Waiting with him was Bernard, his 19-year-old son. The latter was a law student. He accompanied his father whenever a

22

night call seemed interesting. The mystery surrounding that call certainly made it so.

It was a short drive from the Massu apartment to Île de la Cité and it was not long before the commissioner learnt of the night's grisly discovery. He heard that several bodies had been found burning in the furnace of a burner in a basement room of a townhouse at Number 21 Rue le Sueur in the sixteenth *arrondissement* and that a neighbour had reported that the house's proprietor was a Dr Piot (sic) from Number 66 Rue de Caumartin in the ninth *arrondissement*. The doctor had been summoned to the property, but had, as yet, not made an appearance. He also listened to a warning to be careful; he knew the caveat was the Quay's way of telling him the Gestapo might have been responsible for what had been going on at the townhouse. The probability had already crossed his mind. He knew Rue le Sueur. He knew TODT had a garage at Number 22. He knew the street was off Avenue Foch where the Germans' security and intelligence service, the *Sicherheitsdients* or SD occupied Numbers 82, 84 and 86. He also knew that the feared Gestapo - Secret State Police - used Number 84 for imprisonment, interrogation and torture. Everyone in Paris knew.

The name Piot (sic) meant nothing to him.

* * *

It was through a deserted Paris that Massu and Bernard drove a few minutes later, the commissioner behind the wheel of his own service *traction-avant*. Even the capital's pavements were deserted; an *ausweis* - night pass - issued by the Germans was required for excursions after the curfew had sounded and the Germans were not generous with those.

Rue le Sueur itself was calm; the curfew and the 'swallows' who had replaced Teyssier and Fillion had sent the neighbours home. The only evidence that it was not just another blacked-out wartime night was the presence of the men in uniform and of a *panier à salade* - a salad basket, as the French call a patrol van - parked in front of the townhouse.

Told that Dr Piot (sic) had not yet arrived, Massu began his inspection of the property, accompanied by Bernard and several 'swallows'. He started with the basement. Battery-operated lamps had been set up; 'swallows' had found that the house's electricity had not just been switched off at the mains, it had been disconnected altogether. The doctor had obviously not been paying his electricity bills.

Massu and Bernard spent several minutes in the last room off the corridor; because the room was tiny, the 'swallows' remained in the corridor.

In a book the commissioner was to write, and which was published in 1959, 'L'Enquête Petiot' - The Petiot Investigation - he described what he saw down there.

'My son walked ahead of me, a flashlight in his hand. Its white and trembling beam lit up the basement with the two burners, revealing visions of Hell. Here, a partly burnt skull, with the gaping holes of its eye sockets and its aggressive-looking teeth, seemed to have come straight out of Dante's Inferno; over there, a stiff hand was curled up as if its owner had, at the moment of death, desperately tried to hold onto thin air; there, the torso of a woman, its chest gnawed away to show splinters of bones, which were the ribs; further away, a foot, blackened like a log of wood that had smouldered, without flame; everywhere, strewn around in a shapeless magma, tibias, femurs, bits of arms, jawbones... And over this horrendous charnel house floated the awful smell of charred flesh, a sinister stench of grilled human flesh'.

After Massu and Bernard had seen the burners, the 'swallows' took them to a scullery. It was also in the basement. It was bare but for two stone sinks built into a wall. One sink was large and deep and had a sloping bottom. The other was an ordinary kitchen sink. A stone draining board, long enough for a man to stretch out on, ran between the two. A damp and greasy mark was on the board. Bernard put his nose to it: he said he could smell soap. Underneath the board was an opening to a drain. The drain was rusty, yet clear and odourless. Three barred, blackened, pavement-level windows faced the sinks. Blackened windows were not odd or unusual in Paris. Today, Parisians still blacken pavement-level windows for privacy and security.

Going up the stone steps to return to the house's hallway, Massu noticed a sack under the steps. He flipped it open with his feet. It contained the headless left side of a human body. He could not tell whether the body was male or female. It was in too advanced a state of decomposition.

Upstairs more battery operated lamps had been set up and 'swallows' were hanging the obligatory blackout curtains. The doctor had not taken the trouble to do so.

Massu stared in disbelief at the disorder he witnessed around him. He and Bernard walked through rooms of which the floors were strewn with bicycle wheels, car tires, gardening tools, pots, pans, kettles, lampshades, toys, old yellowed newspapers and magazines. There were also some exquisite objects lying about; Sevres, Limoges, Dresden and Baccarat vases, Gobelin tapestries and numerous original paintings in gilded frames. He knew his wife would have loved the latter objects. He also knew he couldn't buy them for her.

There were five bedrooms, a bathroom and toilet on the house's second storey. A cracked tub stood in the bathroom. In the toilet, the bowl was blocked with what looked like kitchen waste. In one of the bedrooms an enormous canopied bed stood behind a lacquered Chinese screen; it would not have been out of place in the Château of Versailles. There was no mattress on the bed and a family of rats nested under the floorboards in front of it. It was obvious that no one had used that bathroom and toilet or had slept in that bed for a very long time.

Massu studied the books in the library room. Those in the bookcases were perfectly alphabetised. The subject of many was crime. He saw some of Conan Doyle's books, and those of Dashiell Hammett and Maurice Leblanc, creator of Arsène Lupin, the gentleman thief. Georges Simenon's 'Inspector Maigret' books were on the shelves too; finding those amused him.

There were also many books about Jack the Ripper and Henri Désiré Landru, called the Modern Bluebeard, guillotined in France in 1922 for the murder of ten women and a 19-year-old man whose bodies he had disposed of in the furnace of his kitchen stove, and about doctors who had killed: Dr Harvey Hawley Crippen, Dr H.H. Holmes, Dr Thomas Neill Cream.

The other side of the law was represented too; complete sets of the books about and by Jean Alexandre Eugène Lacassagne, founder of the Department of Forensic Science of Lyon University, known as the 'father of forensic science' for his pioneer work regarding blood patterns in a human body after death and for matching bullets to guns. Also, complete sets of books about and by Edmond Locard, the forensic science pioneer and one time assistant to Lacassagne at Lyon University and creator of

Locard's Exchange Principle that established that every contact leaves behind a trace. Also, books about and by Cesare Lombroso, the Verona-born criminologist and founder of the Italian School of Positivist Criminology, who, in his 1876 book, 'Criminal Man', stated that there was a link between one's appearance and one's character. All murderers, therefore, have the same facial, anatomical and psychological traits. From Lombroso's theory had developed the first national identity card. In 1912, a law had been passed in France that made it compulsory for all 'nomads and itinerants' to carry a document that bore their photograph, name, date and place of birth and their anthropometric details, as well as their parents' names and their date and place of birth and death if applicable.

So too books about and by Alphonse Bertillon, policeman and biometrics researcher who had developed a system, 'anthropometrical signalment' or 'Bertillonage' - measurement of the human body that included the middle finger - to identify recidivist criminals, and which led to both fingerprinting and the mugshot.

The house inspected, Massu, Bernard and the 'swallows' went out into the back courtyard. Unlike the smaller front courtyard, the back one was uncovered, yet enclosed; on three sides by the house itself and on the fourth by a wall. The wall was as high as the house, but its brickwork was of a different colour, and trellis panels to which withered ivy clung, covered the wall up to the house's second storey. The differences told Massu that the wall had been raised and that it had been done not all that long ago, and obviously to shield the courtyard from prying eyes in the neighbouring apartment buildings.

There were three adjoining outhouses in the courtyard. Since the 'swallows' had not yet inspected these, Massu said he would do so. He started with the one on the furthest right. Its unlocked door opened into what looked like the consulting room of an unsuccessful doctor. In the room stood a desk, a sofa covered in a shabby velvet cloth, a coffee table and a glass-fronted cabinet. The cabinet was filled with medical books. Some old magazines lay on the coffee table. Several instruments of the kind with which doctors carried out uncomplicated routine medical examinations lay on the desk.

Two doors led from the consulting room. Behind one was another flight of stone steps that led down into another area of the basement; the 'swallows' had already discovered that a labyrinth of corridors made it possible to move around underneath the property without being seen by someone who might be looking down from a neighbouring building.

The other door opened into an odd corridor of about two and a half metres in length and a metre in width. At the corridor's furthest end was yet another door. A chain and padlock hung from the knob.

The door opened into a small, triangular room.

In the room, Massu's attention was immediately drawn to eight large iron rings embedded in one of the walls at a height of approximately 1.70 metres. A metal hospital cot stood against the facing wall. A padded door with an electric bell beside it took up most of the third wall. The walls were, like those of the basement, roughly cemented, but brown wallpaper covered the one behind the cot. The wallpaper was lumpy. The paper had obviously been applied hastily. He ripped it off and found that underneath one of the lumps was a glass peephole. The peephole was approximately ten centimetres in diameter. It was at a height of 1.70 metres. Therefore, similar to the rings. Like the canopied bed upstairs, the cot was without a mattress. An army-issue blanket hung over its headrest. The electric bell beside the padded door did not work, and the door was a fake; it was a padded panel of wood nailed to the wall.

Massu, on leaving the room to inspect the other two outhouses, made another bewildering discovery. The door that led out into the corridor did not have a knob on the room side. Should the door slam or someone deliberately close it from the corridor side, whoever was in the room, was trapped.

The second outhouse was a storage room. Its door was also not locked. It contained another metal cot without a mattress, but nothing else.

The third outhouse had a sliding door; it suggested its use was once as a stable. A padlock hung from the door. The outhouse was L-shaped and the door was on the short leg of the L. A stained wheelbarrow stood near to the door and what looked like soggy plaster lay on the floor. White footprints led from the soggy plaster to the long leg of the L.

Massu decided to follow the footsteps.

Bernard would do so too.

A few of the 'swallows' followed.

Massu and Bernard made sure not to step in the soggy plaster.

After a few steps, they stopped walking. Ahead of them the floor was covered in quicklime, bubbling, steaming quicklime, and from it stuck slivers of bone and what looked like chunks of meat. From what they had already seen down in the basement, they knew that what they were looking at were not the bones and meat of an animal, but human bones and human flesh.

There were two large paving stones lying on the floor further ahead. Two of the 'swallows' helped Bernard push those out of the way. They concealed a pit. It was about 6 metres deep. A pulley with a cord and noose dangled from the ceiling above it. The noose was large enough to fit around a man's waist. Tiny morsels of flesh clung to it.

A ladder led down into the pit. No one volunteered to go down to see what was at its bottom.

"I'll do so," said Massu.

He removed his overcoat and hat and started the climb down. Within seconds, he scrambled back up, unsteady on his feet. The pit, as he would write, was worse than anything he had seen in all the years of his career. 'At the bottom of the pit, I could only guess the depth of the quicklime into which my feet disappeared. The stench was atrocious. It strangled me. The crumbling of bones under my feet left me without any doubt that the real horror of the house could be found down there. What we had seen in the basement was nothing compared to what was down in that pit'.

After having pulled himself together, he started to search for another room with a hole in one of its walls, a hole at the height of approximately 1.70 metres; he had to know what the hole in the triangular room was all about.

He found the room, the wall and the hole.

The hole was in one of the walls of the short L section of the stable.

An old electric heater stood in front of it.

He wanted to look through the hole to see what was on the other side of the wall. At 1.67 metres in height he needed to step onto the heater to be able to do so. Putting an eye to the hole, he looked straight into the triangular room, onto the wall with the rings. So the hole had been made in order to spy on whoever was in the triangular room or to watch what was going on in the room. Plus, whoever had been doing the spying had also needed something to stand on to be able to put an eye to the hole;

he and that person must be the same height.

* * *

Other inspectors arrived at the property.

The most notable was Detective Chief Inspector Marius Battut. He arrived at the same time as Paris's Chief Medical Examiner, Dr Albert Paul. In his forties, DCI Battut was Massu's deputy. He was known at the Quay as a *flic's flic* - a copper's copper - and in the underworld as a meticulous investigator who always got his man. Dr Albert Paul was a wispy-haired man in his late fifties. He was not only Paris's chief medical examiner and post-mortem surgeon, but also head of France's Institut Médico-Légal, Paris's institute of forensic medicine and main mortuary, on Quai de la Rapée in the twelfth *arrondissement*.

Despite his reputation as a tough man, Battut refused to go down into the pit.

Dr Paul could not wait to do so; cadavers did not upset him. Known at both the institute and the Quay as 'the man of the hundred thousand autopsies', he had, in the previous 18 months, performed post-mortems on 327 bodies, either fished from the Seine or found in Paris's many parks and dark alleys. Of those, most had been headless or dismembered, yet he had successfully identified two hundred and forty-two. The remaining 85 still lay in refrigerated cupboards at the institute. Thirty-five were female. There was, however, a dark side to him. As Paris's CME he assisted at each execution the Germans carried out in the capital; he had to confirm that death had taken place. To some French, those who opposed the German Occupation, that made him a *collabo* - a collaborator.

He had arrived at the house dressed in a dark suit, dark overcoat and fedora.

He removed neither the overcoat nor the hat to climb down into the pit. He re-emerged after what seemed a long time to Massu and Battut. He held a skull. The victim had been scalped, and the ears, nose and lips had been cut from the face, he explained. The work had been done with a surgeon's scalpel and it had been done most skilfully. There were more such scalped and mutilated skulls down in the pit, he said. He had not counted them, but, judging by the amount of human remains he had seen down there, someone had been making an effort to destroy the bodies of at least twenty people, male and female.

He added that he found it difficult to believe it was the work of just one man, but one of those responsible for the carnage knew that mutilating the face made identification difficult, if not impossible.

* * *

At 2 A.M. Dr Paul left and Massu and Battut also wanted to return home - the night had been long, far too long - but they still waited, and hoped, that the townhouse's proprietor would turn up.

Briefly, they discussed whether Battut should go to the address the *concierge* had supplied earlier - Number 66 Rue de Caumartin - to hear what the doctor had to say for himself.

There was a hitch.

Both knew, even every rookie policeman knew, a Frenchman's home was sacrosanct during the hours of darkness. Article 76 of Frimaire 22 of the Revolutionary Year VIII (December 13, 1799) of the French Constitution made it so. The Article stipulated: 'The home of any person living on the French territory is an inviolable sanctuary. During the night no one has the right to enter it unless for reasons of a fire, flooding, or if summoned from the interior of the home. During the day, one can enter it for a specific reason, or by law, or on the order of a public authority'.

Calling in on the doctor would be breaking the law and that they were reluctant to do; reluctant, despite that the Germans broke France's laws every minute of every day, and night.

There was also another reason why they thought that Dr Piot (sic) should not yet be visited. They suspected that he was a Gestapo torturer and neither wanted to become involved with anything that concerned the Germans.

"So, I'll be off home," said Massu to Battut.

"I'll call it a day, too. Or, rather, I'll call it a night," replied the DCI.

At the gateway, the 'swallow' standing guard recognised Massu and stopped him. He told the commissioner that Porte Maillot had sent over a messenger with a *pneumatique* - he was holding an unsealed, white envelope in his hand - and he did not know what to do with it because it was not addressed to anyone in particular. Or, rather, it had originally been sent by the Quay to Porte Maillot, which now wanted someone at the townhouse to act on it. Would the commissioner accept the *pneumatique*?

Massu took the envelope, showed Battut that the seal had been broken, which meant that Porte Maillot, the original recipient, had read the message.

After reading it himself, he handed it to Battut to read, too.

'Order from German authorities. Stop. Arrest Dr Petiot. Stop. Dangerous lunatic. Stop'.

"Confirms our suspicion," said the DCI.

So, what was he to do Massu wondered?

Rush to the doctor's apartment as the occupying Germans had ordered the Quay to do or wait until daybreak as his country's constitution demanded?

He opted to wait until daybreak; he did not want anyone to say that he had broken Article 76 of 22 Frimaire of the Revolutionary Year VIII.

"First thing in the morning, go see what the good doctor has to say for himself, but do be careful. Take some men with you," he told Battut.

***

As Massu and Bernard drove home, the politically-appointed *préfet* - prefect - Amédée Bussière, in his capacity as Chief of Police and Fire Service of the *département* - the prefectural subdivision of Île de France, in other words of Greater Paris, occupied by the Germans, issued a statement to the media about the night's discovery. He said that two gas technicians trying to locate a leak in the basement of an uninhabited house at Number 21 Rue le Sueur in the sixteenth *arrondissement* of the capital had found the charred remains of two vagrants. A police investigation had established that the vagrants had been sleeping in the basement and that one had accidentally set his clothes alight, which had started a small blaze.

Had the Gestapo ordered him to issue such a statement or had he acted on his own initiative suspecting that the police had inadvertently discovered a secret Gestapo torture house? No one would have dared ask him, but there was not a person in France who did not know on whose side he stood; that he was, indeed, a *collabo*. He had been appointed by

31

Maréchal Philippe Pétain, France's puppet head-of-state. Pétain and his government were based in the spa-town of Vichy, 406 kilometres south of Paris, in the part of France the Germans had not occupied and which was known as Vichy-France. Northern France was known as Occupied France.

The morning papers printed the statement. The Second World War raging, and death and destruction the order of the day, the statement attracted no attention.

-0-

CHAPTER TWO

Sunday, March 12, 1944

Massu had the habit of standing at the window of his third storey office each morning on his arrival.

Sunday morning, he did so again.

In front of him was Place Dauphine. The square was lined with horse chestnut trees covered in spring shoots. According to legend, a horse chestnut on the Avenue des Champs-Elysées was always the first to turn green in spring, and always on March 20. He knew that each year Place Dauphine's trees were green long before.

To his left was the Seine and to his right, Rue de Rivoli.

Most of the *bouquinistes*— bookstalls— on the Seine's quays were closed. The Germans were also censoring the Parisians, so most of the booksellers' stocks had been confiscated. Not that the Parisians minded. They had more essential things to buy than books.

On Rue de Rivoli, the Hotel Meurice, at Number 228, served as headquarters for General Otto von Stülpnagel, the German Military Commander of Occupied France. From the street drifted voices speaking German, the slamming of car doors and the rumble of tanks. There were always tanks on the street to guard the general and his staff.

Behind the commissioner was the giant Palais de Justice complex. The Conciergerie, a building with two Tudor towers, formed part of the complex. It was at the Conciergerie where Queen Marie Antoinette had been held prisoner during the French Revolution. From there, she was taken on a horse-drawn cart to be guillotined. He still had no idea whether Dr Petiot was responsible for what had gone on at the townhouse, but he knew that, if so, in normal times, the guillotine would also have awaited the doctor. However, France was occupied, and he was not even sure that he would be allowed to continue the investigation he

33

had begun the previous night; he had even asked DCI Battut not to set off for Dr Petiot's apartment after all, not until the Quay had confirmation that the Germans indeed wanted the doctor to be arrested. If, as he and the DCI suspected, the doctor was a Gestapo agent, then the Germans would call them off to deal with the doctor themselves by means of a bullet in the back of his head as punishment for his negligence. Negligence for leaving the house without having extinguished the fire in the furnace.

Standing there at the window, he knew that the Quay had that morning asked Prefect Bussière to ask the Germans whether they still wanted an investigation to be launched. The prefect, respecting the Nazis' strict hierarchy, would have had to approach General von Stülpnagel through the office of Count Ferdinand de Brinon, the General Delegate or Ambassador of Vichy-France to Occupied France. The Count was, like the Prefect, a collaborator; as Vichy-France's 'man in Paris', he and the Germans worked closely together because the civil jurisdiction of the Vichy government extended over Occupied France.

Waiting thus for the two collaborators to liaise with the Germans, Massu contemplated the legal procedure that would follow should the Germans want an investigation.

He would have to report his team's findings to a *juge d'instruction* - an examining magistrate - who would have to compile a dossier for the public prosecutor's office where a team of advocates would decide whether there was sufficient evidence to take the case to court. In court, an *avocat général* - a chief prosecution counsel - would argue the state's case. A junior counsel would assist him. A judge who would be addressed as *Monsieur le Président* - Mr President - would preside over the court, and two magistrates would assist him. Deliberating in the presence of the judge and the two magistrates, six jurors would decide whether the doctor was guilty. If guilty, the guillotine awaited him. A *bourreau* - executioner - known to the public only as *Monsieur Paris*, would do the job.

* * *

Just before 10 A.M. Prefect Bussière signalled to the Quay that the Germans wanted a full investigation launched immediately, and Massu

34

ordered Battut to Dr Petiot's apartment. As before, he asked him to be careful.

* * *

Number 66 Rue de Caumartin was a five-storey building. A bistro, La Chope du Printemps, and a hairdressing salon, Gaston Coiffure, were on the ground floor. When Battut drove up just after ten, both were closed. Before the Occupation at least the bistro would have been open. Those days were long gone; Hitler had made sure of that.

An *abri* sign hung to the left of the building's front door; in the event of an air raid, people could shelter in the basement. Britain and the United States had started to bomb Berlin, and the Parisians were expecting they would also bomb Paris. Because of the Occupation, France was enemy territory.

Dr Petiot's shingle hung to the right of the front door. It described him as a graduate of the Paris Faculty of Medicine, and informed that he received patients every weekday. From Tuesday through to Thursday he received them from 1 P.M. to 3 P.M. and from 6 P.M. to 10 P.M. On Fridays he received them only until 3 P.M. He also received patients on Saturdays, 1 P.M. to 7 P.M., but only by appointment.

Inside the building, a ground floor door marked '*Concierge*' swung open almost immediately on Battut's knock. A little girl stood in the doorway. Accustomed to postmen and tradesmen knocking at the door, she was not taken aback at the sight of three men outside in the hallway; two Crim investigators were with Battut. Outside, half a dozen 'swallows' waited in a police patrol van in case Dr Petiot proved difficult. Massu's instruction to Battut was that he should ask the doctor to accompany him to the Quay. He was not to say anything to him about arresting him or to provoke him in any way.

The little girl said her name was Alice Denis. She was 12 years old and she was the *concierge's* granddaughter. Her grandmother had gone out and she was looking after her gran's *loge* - booth. She knew the Petiots, she said. They lived on the first floor. There were three of them: father, mother and son. Mrs Petiot's name was Georgette and the son's name was Gerhardt. The doctor's name was Marcel.

Battut and his two colleagues climbed the bare wooden stairs to the first storey. The DCI knocked several times at the Petiots' door. It remained closed. He tried the knob and it turned in his hand; he was not surprised. He pushed the door open. He could not enter; Prefect Bussière issued search and arrest warrants and he had not yet issued any for the doctor's family residence.

From what Battut could see of the place from the door - its hallway, and it was dark - he reckoned the Petiots were not home.

Back at the *concierge's* booth, Alice Denis said she had last seen *Monsieur le docteur* Petiot the previous day. It was in the evening, around half past eight. He was walking away from the building. She hadn't seen Mrs Petiot for days. She hadn't seen Gerhardt for several months; his parents sent him to live with an uncle and aunt somewhere in the countryside.

Deciding there was no point hanging around in the hope the Petiots would return, Battut and the two detectives drove back to the Quay.

* * *

Not waiting for the DCI's return from Rue de Caumartin, Massu set off for Rue le Sueur.

The street was closed off to all non-police vehicles and non-resident pedestrians, yet, a noisy crowd of Parisians gathered in front of the townhouse. News of a massacre at the property had spread through the neighbourhood and many had turned up to watch.

Le Crocodile was open. Normally on a Sunday it would not have been. It was packed; it was a warm and sunny morning and the owner had hastily retrieved chairs and tables stored away for winter. Those were set up under horse chestnut trees. Like Place Dauphine's trees, they were in glorious bloom.

The *bougnat*-bistro— Le Rendez-vous des Chauffeurs was its name— was also open and the patrons were drinking wine. Although the street swarmed with 'swallows', none of the patrons had bought coal as French law required they should in order to be served alcohol.

At the townhouse, Massu found Dr Paul had arrived. Two of the CME's colleagues from the Médico-Légal Institute, Dr Léon Dérobert and Dr René Piedelièvre, were with him. So were four gravediggers in *bleu de travail*. They had been recruited earlier in the morning at nearby Passy Cemetery. They were sifting through the quicklime and putting the bones and other human remains they found into cheap, wooden coffins. It was work 'swallows' or firefighters would normally have done, but not a single 'swallow' or firefighter had wanted to do it on that occasion. The remains were to be taken to the institute for examination.

Dr Paul told Massu he already knew his estimate of the night before of around twenty victims was incorrect. There were more, many more. He also said he and his two colleagues had not found any blood or internal organs among the remains. That meant the murderers - he still thought there had to be several - disembowelled the bodies. Perhaps they knew doing so would reduce the odour of decomposition. The disembowelment had probably been done in the scullery in the basement, on the wooden board that ran between the two sinks. The blood and organs would have dropped straight into the drain below the board and into the sewer. Detectives had checked with the Paris municipality; there was a sewer directly underneath the scullery. It emptied into the Usine de Clichy water processing plant. From the plant, the stuff would have been carried by the Seine into the ocean and forever out of sight.

The CME also pointed out that although the limbs had been cut from the bodies with an orthopaedic surgeon's skill, afterwards they had been crushed with something like a hammer or a metal rod and it had been done in an extremely amateurish, perhaps frenetic manner.

Elsewhere in the townhouse detectives were gathering evidence. Some were meticulously powdering the doorknobs and light switches in search of fingerprints; others were tagging and listing each and every object. An initial search of the property had revealed, a cane; pocket knife; nail brush; cigarette lighter; toothpick; a pair of woman's trousers; a man's three-piece suit of trousers, jacket and waistcoat; an evening gown; a man's white shirt; a woman's hat with a peacock feather; a woman's nightgown; a black and white photograph of a man; a rubber name stamp; a box of visiting cards; a birth certificate; 2 women's umbrellas; 2 necklaces; 3 shaving brushes; 3 razors; 4 pipes; 4 tweezers; 4 men's umbrellas; 5 gas masks; 5 cigarette holders; 5 books of cigarette paper; 6 hairbrushes; 6 toilet bags; 6 powder puffs; 6 medicine cases; 7 pocket combs; 7 pairs of eyeglasses; 8 boxes of soap; 8 handheld mirrors; 9 nail files; 9 boxes of mascara, 10 clothes brushes; 11 powder puffs; 12 pots of body cream; 15 decorative hair combs; 15 boxes of face powder; 16 tubes of salve; 16 lipsticks; 22 used toothbrushes; 22 flacons of Eau de Cologne and 27 tubes of face cream.

The evening gown was of black satin with golden swallows embroidered on its bodice. A label on the gown identified its designer as Sylvie Rosa of Rue Estelle, a street in the Mediterranean port city of Marseilles. The woman's hat was of brown suede. Its label identified the milliner as Suzanne Talbot from Number 143 Rue Royale in Paris. The rubber name stamp and visiting cards bore the name L. Duplan of Number 185 Rue Belliard in the eighteenth *arrondissement*. The birth certificate had been issued in Paris on June 9, 1931. It was that of a man named Max Wolkowitz, born in Paris on July 2, 1902. Efforts had been made to remove a monogram from the white shirt. From the few shreds of cotton that remained, it looked like the monogram had been KK or RR.

Another item on the detectives' list of objects was human hair. Several kilograms of it had been found in cardboard boxes. Not a strand was grey.

Meanwhile, another team of detectives was calling on each and every of the street's residents. At first, none wanted to talk; they had heard that the Germans had something to do with what had gone on at the townhouse, and they did not want to become involved. After some spirited persuasion from the detectives, a few decided that they did after all have something to say about the townhouse, and its proprietor.

The resident who had heard the call for help on passing one night was a Victor Avenell. He was a professor of literature. He lived at Number 24, across from the murder house. He confirmed that yes, he had heard a man's voice call for help. His next door neighbour, a count named Saunis, confirmed the Professor had told him about it.

An aged couple admitted they had been watching the house, and they had seen its proprietor. The couple ran a guesthouse at Number 18 and their surname was Petiot.

Eugène was a sprightly 85-year-old. Marie, his 82-year-old wife, was equally alert. They were adamant they were not related to the doctor; they hadn't even known that his surname was Petiot.

Three *concierges* also confessed knowledge about the house and its proprietor.

The *concierge*, who had told Teyssier and Fillion that the doctor had left a set of the townhouse's keys with her, remembered the doctor had a prominent black beauty spot on his right cheek. He was about 1.70 metres in height, and he had the habit of rubbing his hands together, she said.

Her two colleagues said the doctor had a brother; they had seen him. One said she had even spoken to him. She explained how that had happened. She had found an envelope addressed to the doctor in her letter box and on seeing a man entering the townhouse, she had gone to hand it over. The man who had opened to her knock had told her he was not the doctor, but the doctor's brother. She had seen that man for a second time. He and two men had delivered large, heavy sacks to the townhouse. The delivery had taken place not that long into the past, she said. In fact, it had been during the previous month of February.

The third *concierge* said she had also seen Dr Petiot's brother that February day; she remembered the exact date. It had been on Saturday, February 19. Her story was that she was sweeping the pavement when she saw a truck pull up. Three men had then carried some heavy sacks from the truck into the house. Knowing that building work had been carried out at the property she thought the three were delivering some cement or bricks for further construction work. One of the three, she said, she had seen before; he had visited the house before. It had been the year before, during the month of May. He had come to the property by truck then also and had come to pick up some suitcases, forty-nine of them, perhaps forty-six or fifty, she could not remember. The driver of the truck had helped him to carry those from the house to the truck. The truck was grey and not in a roadworthy condition. She could not remember the number on the licence plate, but it was a number registered in Paris; that she could remember. She could also remember she had seen the words 'Avenue Daumesnil' on one of the truck's side panels.

Asked how she knew that the man was the doctor's brother, she said that she had described him to her colleagues, and they had told her that he was the brother of the townhouse's proprietor.

Deciding there was nothing more for him to do at the townhouse, Massu set off for Porte Maillot police station for a word with the two patrolmen, Teyssier and Fillion. The two were not at the station; they had failed to report for duty and a colleague sent to their apartments had found no one at home and the window shutters closed. It was presumed that they had made a runner. So they had. They were to remain missing until after the war. The explanation they would then give the Quay for their disappearance on the morning after the discovery of the human remains at the townhouse was that after a night of reflection they had come to the conclusion that the man on the green bike was not a brave resistant, but a Gestapo torturer, and, as they were the ones who had discovered what he had been up to, the Germans would surely have been after them. They had feared, as they would explain, not what their superiors could have done to them, but what the Germans would have.

* * *

Before the day ended, Prefect Bussière issued arrest warrants for both Dr Petiot and Georgette, his wife. He also began preparing a 'Wanted' poster for the two. It was to be distributed throughout both Occupied-France and Vichy-France.

L'Affaire Petiot - the Petiot Case - had begun.

-0-

CHAPTER THREE

Monday, March 13, 1944

Massu's first act of Monday was to visit the Petiots' apartment. He set off from the Quay in his *traction-avant*, his secretary, Jean Canitrot, behind the wheel. A team of four Crim detectives followed in another *traction-avant*; they were to start searching the apartment immediately.

A 'salad basket' completed the convoy; Massu was taking several 'swallows' along. The Petiots, had they returned during the night, were to be arrested and taken to the Quay. Should the doctor resist arrest, then the 'swallows' would be needed.

* * *

Rue de Caumartin was just a little livelier than on the previous morning.

Gaston Coiffure was still closed, but La Chope du Printemps was open. On the pavement, underneath a torn tarpaulin, flapping in a sudden breeze, stood a few small, round wicker tables and chairs. The name 'Bézayrie', obviously the owner's name, was written in faded lettering across the tarpaulin. So, too, the words *plat du jour* despite the fact that such a thing as a dish of the day no longer existed in wartime Paris.

In the bistro, behind a zinc-topped bar stood a tall, thin waiter dressed in black and white. There were no patrons, so he was reading a newspaper, the morning's *L'OEuvre*.

The daily was reporting a new Landru Case. Fifty-five women had been murdered in a Paris townhouse. The women, while still alive, had been thrown into a pit filled with quicklime. The newspaper gave the address of the crime scene as well as the address of the residence of the owner of the townhouse - Rue de Caumartin. The owner's name was also

41

given - Dr Marcel Petiot. Prudently, the newspaper did not accuse the doctor of having committed the murders.

Massu decided he might as well step into the bistro to ask the waiter what he knew of the Petiots.

Yes, said the waiter, he knew the doctor. He also knew the doctor's wife, a charming lady. He even knew the couple's young son. The boy has not been seen around for a while. Someone said he has been sent to live with a relative in the countryside. The doctor has a bike and a cart, but not a car. Often, the doctor needed help to lift the cart over the building's threshold; it was always heavily loaded, overloaded, in fact. He used to help the doctor with the cart. No, he regularly helped the doctor with the cart. The first time he had done so, the doctor had come into the bistro to ask if someone could lend him a hand. After that it had kind of become routine. Once, a bad smell had emanated from something on the cart. The waiter said he had not thought it bizarre at the time. Parisians being compelled to buy on the black market, one did sometimes buy meat which was no longer fresh.

Asked when he had last seen the doctor, the waiter said he had seen him only 48 hours previously, on Saturday night. The doctor had rushed into the bistro to make a telephone call; it was at half past nine. He did think it strange that the doctor would want to make a call from the bistro, rather than from his own home. The doctor had asked the operator for a number in the town of Auxerre in the Burgundy region, south-east from Paris. The doctor's call had not been long.

"I heard the doctor say, 'burn the papers' to whoever was on the other end of the line," said the waiter.

Mr Bézayrie was out of town, but Mrs Denis, the *concierge* of the Petiots' building, was home.

The Petiots, said Mrs Denis, have gone away. She thought they might have left on Saturday night; she hadn't seen them since Saturday afternoon. She had been up to the apartment and had knocked several times, but the door had remained closed. She could have gone in knowing that the door would not be locked, but she thought it better not to. She knew the door would not be locked because the doctor never locked a door; he always said that a lock would not keep a determined burglar out, and why should he have to replace, at great cost, a smashed lock?

She could not believe what *L'OEuvre* had written was true.

"Dr Petiot," she said, "is the most courteous of men and a loving husband and father. He's always bringing home gifts for *Madame* and Gerhardt, and the three of them often go out to the cinema and theatre."

* * *

The Petiot apartment was, unlike Number 21 Rue le Sueur, in perfect order.

Massu stepped into a hallway; from it led a corridor with doors on both sides.

The doors on the right side of the corridor opened into rooms overlooking the street. One room was a doctor's consulting room. Another, a doctor's waiting room. He opened the shutters in front of the window and looked down onto a church, the Saint-Louis d'Antin, a massive stone building. A furrier shop was on the ground floor of a narrow apartment building beside the church. The shop was open; a man stood in the doorway. He was looking up; up at the Petiots' building. He swung round and disappeared into the shop. The shop's display windows were bare.

The doors on the left side of the corridor opened into a kitchen, five bedrooms, a bathroom and a toilet. Two dirty coffee mugs stood in the sink in the kitchen. A loaf of bread lay on the kitchen table. A slice was cut from the loaf.

A quick inspection of the apartment revealed a large quantity of drugs. There were certainly more drugs than a family doctor would need or could buy legally in bulk to cut costs or as a precaution in case of a shortage of medication caused by the war. The drugs were stored, or were hidden more likely, in a metal cupboard in a washroom off the consulting room. There were ouabaine and digitalis, both used for the treatment of heart disease; the sedative scopolamine; very many vials of morphine - detectives counted them later, and there were five hundred - and a large supply of chloroform, heroin and strychnine. Why a family doctor would need heroin and strychnine was a mystery. Another mystery was half of a banknote. It lay on top of one of the boxes of drugs, as if carefully placed there. It was not a French banknote; Massu did not know from which country it was.

Apart from the presence of the drugs, the apartment appeared a normal family home. The furniture looked elegant: tapestries hung on the walls; the floors were carpeted; on a white marble fireplace in the living room stood two porcelain cherubim which matched those found at the townhouse. What was not all that normal was a wooden sculpture of a half human, half beast creature. It had large genital organs. The statue was found in a cupboard in the consulting room; also perhaps hidden there.

Massu and the detectives went down to the apartment building's basement. They wanted to see what the Petiots had in their cellar.

Although she would not be required to open the unlocked door to the cellar, Mrs Denis accompanied them, carrying a large bunch of keys. Perished bike tires, black market smoked hams, straw-lined boxes filled with cheese, a bucket filled with eggs, bags of flour, bags of dried fruit and tins filled with real coffee whereas Parisians had to drink ersatz made of chick peas were piled high on the cellar's shelves. The Petiots had obviously been living well.

There was no sign of a green bike or of a cart. Those would never be found.

* * *

Leaving the building to return to the Quay, Massu saw that quite a crowd was gathered outside on Rue de Caumartin. Word had spread throughout the neighbourhood that the police were at the apartment of the proprietor of the Rue le Sueur murder house and that they had found bodies at the apartment too. La Chope du Printemps was packed; the waiter was running from table to table with cups of steaming ersatz coffee and glasses of red wine on a round tray balanced on the palm of one hand. In the other he held some coasters advertising beer, leaving one on each table to help him keep track of who had ordered what and how many of it.

A woman stepped towards Massu from the crowd. She was crying. Through her tears she explained her name was Marie-Jeanne Leroux. She was the Petiots' maid. She had come to the apartment to see whether Mrs Petiot needed assistance. She said she could swear on the heads of her children that Dr Petiot could never have murdered anyone - let alone 55 women. His only fault was that he was a little on the frugal side. He paid her a very low wage and he always shopped at auction houses to save a few *sous*. He even bought clothes for himself, his wife and son at auction.

Back at the Quay, Massu gave orders that the telephone call Dr Petiot had made from La Chope du Printemps to Auxerre be traced. He also told Battut to find the townhouse's previous owner, the Princess Colloredo de Mansfeld. He feared that she might be dead, her remains with those at the townhouse.

* * *

The princess was still very much alive; the Crim found her quickly through questioning Rue le Sueur's residents.

Battut called on her.

Marie Colloredo de Mansfeld was born Marie-Sidonie Desmit, a commoner, 67 years previously. She lived at Number 125 Rue de la Faisanderie. The street was not far from Rue le Sueur. She said she would certainly tell Battut everything she knew about Dr Petiot.

The princess began by saying she and her husband, the late Prince Joseph Marie Rodolph, had lived at Number 21 Rue le Sueur from 1924 to 1930. Widowhood had forced her to move somewhere more manageable. Manageable meant an apartment on Avenue Friedland, another of the avenues which run into Place de l'Étoile. She had remained living in that apartment until the Occupation when the Secretary of the French Navy had requisitioned the building. She then moved to her present apartment. On leaving the townhouse, she had at first allowed friends to stay there rent free. Later, she had let it to the actress Cécile Sorel as a warehouse. Use of the property as such had been a very bad idea, because the townhouse had quickly fallen into disrepair, she admitted. To halt the house's decline she had decided that it would be best to sell it. She sold it in 1941. The buyer was a Dr Marcel Petiot. She had not met the doctor; all transactions had been done through her notaries, Robert Sens-Olive and Ernest Champetier de Ribes, as well as a real estate agency, the Simon Agency. The agency's owner, Joseph Simon, was no longer in France; he fled in 1942 when the Nazis forbade Jews to own businesses. She did not know his present whereabouts.

She showed Battut the *Act de Vente* - the sale and purchase agreement.

Described as 'living in Seignelay', Petiot bought the house in the name of his son, Gerhardt Claude Georges Félix Petiot, born on April 19, 1928 in the village of Villeneuve-sur-Yonne. That meant the son was still a minor when his father had bought him the townhouse. The agreement was signed on Friday, May 23, 1941. She sold the house for 495,000 francs. Dr Petiot made a down payment of 373,000 francs. They agreed that he would pay the balance of 122,000 francs in annual instalments of approximately 17,000 francs to one of her late husband's relatives. The doctor hadn't yet defaulted on a payment.

In the agreement, the property was described as 'a building fronting the street - a townhouse with basement, ground floor, a square first storey, a partly panelled second storey and an attic; there is also a courtyard'.

She showed Battut some other documents. Those revealed that, since the house's construction in 1834, it had had nine proprietors.

Battut asked the princess whether the names Duplan and Wolkowitz meant anything to her. She said they did not.

Asked whether she had heard the name Suzanne Talbot before, she said she had, indeed. Miss Talbot was a milliner on Paris's Rue Royale and Miss Talbot had made several hats for her. Asked whether one of the hats was of brown suede with a peacock feather, she said that was correct. She had lost the hat. Hearing the hat had been found at the townhouse, she threw her ring-bedecked hands up in the air.

As the DCI prepared to leave, the princess gave him one more item of information. The notaries had told her that Dr Petiot planned to have alteration work done at the property; he wanted to use the townhouse as a clinic. The doctor had asked the two notaries whether they knew of a trustworthy construction company that could do the work.

They had told him they did not.

* * *

The rest of the day's investigations were straightforward.

A receipt found at the townhouse led detectives to the construction company that had done the alteration work. The Etablissement Laborderie et Minaud was based in Marnes-la-Coquette, a commune 12 kilometres southwest of Paris.

Two of the establishment's masons remembered Dr Petiot well. Louis and Gaston Dethève, brothers, immediately said they had been wondering whether they should contact the police.

They described Dr Petiot as quite an ordinary man.

"Just like you and us."

When they had first arrived at the townhouse, they found the doctor dressed in *bleu de travail,* changing the lock on the gateway. He wanted them to make several alterations. He wanted a wall on the back courtyard heightened and an extra room to be fitted into the outhouses. He gave them a sketch detailing the extra room's design. They followed his instructions although the room he wanted was to be triangular.

The doctor told them that since the house was going to be a mental clinic, the walls of the triangular room were to be soundproofed; they were to use cork to do so. They were not able to find cork because of the war. He agreed they could use plaster. He also asked them to fix a fake door to one of the walls. The door had to be padded in order to further soundproof the room. He explained he was going to give his patients electro-shock treatment and he did not want to disturb the neighbours with patients crying out during such treatment.

Asked about the wall they had heightened, the two masons said Dr Petiot wanted it done because, as he told them, mental patients were often noisy and would, without doubt, disturb the neighbours when exercising in the courtyard. The wall would serve another purpose too; it would protect his patients. During the previous summer, children from the surrounding buildings had thrown peach and apricot stones into his courtyard. If they were to do so again, one of his patients might be injured.

The doctor had also asked them to drill a hole in one of the walls of the triangular room and to fasten several rings to another of its walls. His explanation for the hole was that he had to be able to see whether his patients took the electro-shock treatment well. The rings he needed for hanging equipment.

They started the work on Thursday, October 2, 1941 and finished on October 28, a Tuesday.

The cost of the work had come to 18,000 francs. The doctor paid 10,000 francs on commencement of the work and, although he had promised to pay the balance on completion, he had failed to do so. After many reminders, a man had come to the office and settled the bill. He had paid in cash. He did not give them his name.

The two masons also told the detectives they thought the façade and the front part of the house were dilapidated and needed repairs.

Strangely, the doctor had not wanted any repair work done to it.

* * *

The name 'Avenue Daumesnil' the *concierge* of Number 22 Rue le Sueur had seen on the truck which had come to pick up suitcases from the townhouse had to be found.

Then, still as today, there were many transport companies on Avenue Daumesnil in the twelfth *arrondissement* because the street runs past both Gare de Lyon and Gare de Bercy, the two railway stations from where trains set off east into Europe. Massu wanted all the transport companies checked out and detectives began calling in on each. They failed to find the truck in question, but they found a truck driver who recalled that a colleague had done some *travail au noir*— moonlighting— in May of the previous year, by picking up suitcases from a townhouse in the sixteenth *arrondissement* for a man who had not introduced himself. The suitcases were to be taken to Gare de Lyon, the railway station that served southeast France, as the cases were bound for the town of Auxerre. There was, however, no train to Auxerre on that day, and the cases were left in the truck which was parked at a garage overnight.

Detectives checking bills of lading for May 1943 at Gare de Lyon railway station found that 49 suitcases were registered for dispatch on Wednesday, May 26. Their total weight came to 680 kilograms and their destination was Auxerre.

* * *

Late in the afternoon, Dr Petiot's biography landed on Massu's desk.

The doctor was born in Auxerre on Sunday, January 17, 1897. It made him 47 years old. His full name was Marcel André Henri Félix Petiot. On Saturday, June 4, 1927, he had married Georgette Valentine Lablais, born on Friday, July 15, 1904, in Seignelay, 16 kilometres from Auxerre, which made her 44 years old. Georgette was an only child. On Thursday, April

48

19, 1928, the couple's only child, a son named Gerhardt Claude Georges Félix was born in Villeneuve-sur-Yonne, 43 kilometres from Auxerre. He was 16 years old. Dr Petiot was mayor of Villeneuve-sur-Yonne at the time of his son's birth.

The doctor has a brother - Maurice. He lived in Auxerre. He was the owner of a bicycle and radio shop. It was his telephone number the doctor called from La Chope du Printemps.

* * *

Believing that Dr Petiot and his wife would be found in Auxerre, Massu decided he would drive to the town in the morning. Accordingly, his last task of the day was something he considered demeaning for a police chief. He put in a request to the Germans for petrol vouchers. Without a voucher no one, not even the head of the Paris Crim, could buy petrol in France.

The Germans issued the vouchers instantly.

Heartened by such unprecedented responsiveness, Massu asked the Germans what they could tell him of Dr Marcel Petiot.

Again, an instant response.

Massu was told that the Gestapo had arrested Dr Marcel Petiot on Friday, May 21 of the previous year and had held him for eight months in Fresnes Prison, 11 kilometres south of Paris. They had released him on Thursday, January 13 - two months previously.

The Germans gave no reason for the doctor's arrest and Massu did not dare question them further. He was not going to push his luck.

He telegraphed the Auxerre Crim.

He said he was on his way, but they were meanwhile to look into Maurice Petiot's life. They were also to stake out the railway station in case Maurice made a run for it, as his brother and sister-in-law had already done.

* * *

At the end of the day, Massu could say that he had suffered only one disappointment. A handwritten note had been found at the townhouse and briefly he had believed that he was on the verge of cracking the case.

The note was addressed to 'Camille', and its sender was a carpenter named Raymond Léon. The latter wrote to Camille that a cart he had made for him was ready, and could be picked up. The Crim had quickly found Léon. His story was that he had never heard of Dr Marcel Petiot until he had read of him in *L'OEuvre*. Camille, he said, was a Camille Vanderheyden who lived at Number 20 Rue le Sueur. Detectives had immediately rushed to the apartment building. Its concierge had taken them up to Vanderheyden's apartment where they had knocked for several minutes before the door swung open. Vanderheyden was in bed with influenza. Shaking both from fever and from fear of the police, he had confirmed that he had ordered a cart from Léon. He needed the cart to do deliveries. Asked what he delivered, he had replied, "Who can be choosy in wartime?"

He had not, however, ever delivered anything to Dr Petiot's townhouse.

Neither had he made any deliveries for the doctor.

Vanderheyden had been unable to explain how Léon's note had ended up with Dr Petiot, but experience told Massu that neither the delivery man nor the carpenter was a murderer.

At least, not the murderer of Number 21 Rue le Sueur.

-0-

CHAPTER FOUR

Tuesday, March 14, 1944

As Massu set off from the Quay for Auxerre in his *traction-avant*, Paris woke up to another day of German occupation.

Jean Canitrot, Massu's secretary, was again behind the wheel and beside him sat Battut's deputy, Detective Schmidt. Battut sat beside the commissioner in the rear.

Canitrot steered the car through the Big House's main gate on Quay des Orfèvres into Paris's Latin Quarter. To the left was the massive stone structure of the capital's oldest hospital, Hotel Dieu. Beside the hospital was Notre Dame Cathedral. Before the Occupation the cathedral's bells rang at that hour. Like all the capital's church bells, the Germans had silenced them.

At the southern end of Boul'Miche - Boulevard Saint-Michel - Canitrot turned into Boulevard Saint-Germain; he continued on to the narrow Rue Monge. The sun had hardly risen yet women dressed in drab wartime clothes, were already queuing for food in front of small, family-owned shops. There might not be anything to buy.

From Rue Monge it was a few minutes drive to Porte d'Italie, Paris's southern periphery. There, black and white boards indicated, in German, the highway to the city of Lyon, south-east of Paris. Auxerre was that way, too.

Twenty-six thousand souls, the *Auxerroises* and the *Auxerrois*, lived in the town in timber-framed terraced houses built on cobbled streets that ran from the River Yonne which cut through the town to vine-covered hills.

In Auxerre, the four Paris detectives' first port of call was the police station. They heard from their colleagues that there was not to be a train to Paris until late afternoon, but, as Massu had requested, detectives were staking out the railway station. As the River Yonne was navigational it was possible to reach the neighbouring towns and villages by boat, so detectives were also staking out the boarding jetties on the quays. Still other detectives were making discreet enquiries about Maurice Petiot at the town hall, at banks and at the post office.

Number 56 Rue du Pont, a long and narrow street running from the river into the old medieval part of town, was the Paris four's next port of call. A two storey building with a red-tiled roof, a red-brick chimney, a wrought iron balcony on the top floor, and a small adjoining garden behind a high wrought iron gate, it was Maurice's bike and radio shop, as well as where he, Monique, his wife, and Daniel, their teenage son, lived.

Two men were in the shop. One was dark-eyed and dark-haired and it was not difficult to identify him as Maurice Petiot. Prefect Bussière had issued the 'Wanted' poster for the Petiot couple and the bike and radio shop owner bore a remarkable resemblance to the dark-eyed, dark-haired man on the poster.

The other man, one hardly out of his teens, said his name was Robert Maxime, and that he helped Mr Petiot out in the shop and with bike and radio repairs.

* * *

Maurice Petiot seemed surprised at the police's visit; surprised and rather annoyed.

"I fail to understand why the Paris police would be interested in me, but, if you have anything to discuss, we can go upstairs, and my assistant will mind the shop," he said.

Upstairs, in the family apartment, they would not be disturbed: his wife was out and his son was at school. So, too, was the boy who lived with them. The boy was his brother's son: 16-year-old Gerhardt. A few months previously, his brother and sister-in-law had decided it would be safer for the boy to live in the countryside than in a Paris overrun with nasty *Boches*. He and his wife loved the boy, he said; they did not mind having him stay.

Upstairs, Maurice started to speak of his brother.

He had, he said, last heard of him and his sister-in-law, in the previous month. He knew his brother had bought a townhouse in the sixteenth *arrondissement* of Paris; he had not been to the house. He had not even known its address. He had learnt it from newspaper reports. His brother had nothing to do with what had gone at the house; he was the kindest, gentlest man on earth, and a member of the Resistance. In other words, his brother was a hero.

Massu showed Maurice a search warrant. He explained that the local police would be over to search the place, but he would like to look around himself.

Maurice did not object.

The property was a typical French country home. Rooms that looked down onto the street were small, dark and filled with shabby furniture of various epochs. A loft was crammed with black market food, bicycle spare parts and radio sets. So was a cellar.

Local detectives arrived and Massu told Maurice that while they were looking round he would like him to escort him and his Paris colleagues to another Auxerre address. He wanted to be taken to Number 18 Rue des Lombards. That was the address which was on the note which had been pinned to the townhouse's gateway.

Maurice jerked on hearing the address mentioned.

"Why do you want to go there? It's just an old house. No one lives there... or has lived there for a long time," he said.

Asked who the house belonged to, he said it had belonged to his father, Félix Petiot. His father had died in August of 1942, and had left him the house.

"It's just an old house," he repeated. "There's nothing to see there."

Following Maurice from the shop, Massu noticed that Dr Petiot's brother's shoulders had started to twitch, a sure sign, as the commissioner had learnt in his years with the Crim, of nervousness.

Staying behind to mind the shop, an ashen young Maxime kept on shaking his head as if he could not believe what was happening to him.

* * *

Three blocks from Rue du Pont, Rue des Lombards was a short, narrow, curved street.

Because of walls higher than the height of a man, tiled roofs and chimneys were all that could be seen of the street's houses.

There were no shops on the street.

Maurice unlocked a narrow metal gate at the street's curve.

The two-storey house behind it looked like a small fortress, or as if someone wanted to make sure it was impenetrable. Some of its windows were bricked up. Metal grills barred those that were not. A metal grill also protected the front door.

Maurice walked the Paris men through the house.

They saw it was as dilapidated as the Paris townhouse. Each door led into a room with missing floorboards, a stained ceiling and cracked walls. Thick drapes cast a profound gloom over sepia photographs hanging on the walls. Dust and cobwebs covered the furniture.

Massu wanted to know if the house had a cellar.

Maurice said it did.

The commissioner said he wanted to see it.

The house had two cellars. The lower of the two was cut deep into the earth: it reeked of damp. Bats hung from niches in its walls. Maurice switched on a light and a rat scurried across the floor.

Both cellars were empty.

Back in the kitchen, Massu pointed to a door he had not noticed before. He wanted to know what was behind it; he thought it was a cupboard.

The door opened into a tiny room.

A single bed and small bedside table were the only items of furniture.

The bed had been slept in, but it had not been remade: two blankets lay on the floor, the sheets were crumpled and the pillow bore the indentation of a head.

"Who slept here?" asked Massu.

"No one," replied Maurice.

"Don't talk nonsense. Someone slept here last night, and I want to know who it was," snapped Massu.

"It... ah ... it was a friend," mumbled Maurice.

His shoulders had begun to twitch yet again.

The friend, he said, was named Albert Neuhausen.

Like him, Neuhausen was a bike and radio trader. The two of them often did business. Albert's wife's name was Simone.

She and Albert lived in the nearby village of Courson-les-Carrières.

"I'm going to get the police to verify your claim with Mr Neuhausen. Until they've spoken to him, I'm going to keep you somewhere I'll be able to find you," Massu told Maurice.

The place Massu had in mind was a cell at Auxerre police station.

* * *

Courson-les-Carrières had two hundred inhabitants.

It was not a copper who called on the Neuhausens, but a *pandore*, a member of the Gendarmerie Nationale, the militarised police. They were, and are still today, responsible for keeping law and order in countryside areas and towns with fewer than 20,000 inhabitants.

Albert and Simone were both in their shop. She was large with dark, frizzy hair. He was short and thin with large protruding ears.

Like Maurice, the two were surprised and angry that the Paris Crim would be interested in them.

They did not know Dr Petiot, only his brother, they stated. They used to do business with Maurice in the past; had not done so for some time. Albert was adamant he had not spent the previous night at the Rue des Lombards house in Auxerre; the house was derelict, anyway, he said.

He had he spent the night at home.

Simone confirmed he did.

Back at Auxerre police station, Massu learnt that Maurice did not have a criminal record, but that his financial situation puzzled the town's business community. Having left school with no certificates, he had first worked as an electrician. Next, he had opened an electrical repair business. The business, as the one which had replaced it, had gone bankrupt. On having been rehabilitated financially for a second time, he had opened the current bicycle shop: *le vélo* had been a passion since his childhood. At the outbreak of war, he had also started to stock radio sets. Everyone knew that he had bought his first batch of radio sets cheaply from Jewish shop owners who had to flee France or who had to close their businesses because of anti-Jewish legislation. He was apparently doing well. The French wanted to listen to the BBC, and the Germans to German broadcasts, and to the BBC, too. There was, therefore, a steady demand for radio sets.

Massu also learnt that Maurice was an aspiring landowner. Over the past few years, he had bought several local properties, one of which was Number 18 Rue des Lombards. He had not inherited it from his father. He had paid 130,000 francs for it. The title deeds of some of his properties were in the names of his wife and son. He also did business in Paris. What the business was Auxerre's Crim had been unable to discover, but he spent a night or two in Paris at the end of every month. He always went down to the capital by train. He had also dashed off the previous day: he cycled to the town of Joigny, 26 kilometres north. He had left town at 1 P.M. and returned at 5:30 P.M. In Joigny he had called on Father Paillot, the local seminary's bursar. The purpose of the visit to the priest was to discuss Gerhardt Petiot's enrolment. The visit had lasted only five minutes: Father Paillot had refused to admit the boy.

Massu went to speak to Maurice.

Ensconced in a small cell in the basement of the police station, Dr Petiot's brother was a little more forthcoming than earlier.

He said that on the previous day Neuhausen had come to Auxerre to pick up bicycle parts. He could show the commissioner a copy of Neuhausen's bill. The two of them had chatted too long and Neuhausen had stayed overnight at Rue des Lombards.

"Good! Now think about it a little longer," said Massu angrily. "Who knows - you might suddenly remember that you're talking about some other night entirely, and that it was your brother and sister-in-law who slept in that bed last night."

* * *

The detective staking out the railway station called in.

A woman resembling the photograph of Georgette Petiot on the 'Wanted' poster had arrived at the station; she was standing on the platform that served the Paris-bound trains.

Massu looked at his watch. The train was bound to depart for the capital in 15 minutes. He ran to his car.

Canitrot, having heard the news, was already behind the wheel, and Battut and Schmidt in the rear.

"Tell your colleague at the station not to allow the woman to board the train!" shouted Massu to the duty officer who was still holding the telephone.

The detective at the railway station, although he did not have an arrest warrant, was to arrest the woman should she try to board the train.

As the Paris train pulled in, Massu and his Paris colleagues ran onto the platform. It was crowded. Porters in *bleu de travail* began lifting suitcases onto the train. Men in overcoats and fedoras searched in their pockets for some *sous* with which to tip the porters, while women ran around frantically searching for children who had wandered off.

One woman stood and watched the scene passively. She was *petite* and *mignonne*— fine boned and cute. She wore a black astrakhan coat, a hat and black high-heel ankle-strap shoes. An expensive yellow leather suitcase stood at her feet. Yes, she looked like a twin sister of the woman on the 'Wanted' poster.

"Mrs Petiot?" asked Massu from beside her.

She turned to look at him and nodded.

The commissioner lifted his fedora.

"Commissioner Massu. Paris Crim."

Georgette Petiot sighed deeply.

"Yes, Mr Commissioner," she said wearily.

"I have no choice, *Madame*, but to request that you accompany me."

Massu was still holding his hat.

Georgette gave another deep sigh.

"Yes, Mr Commissioner," she repeated.

Massu, holding her firmly by the arm, left the station at the same time as the Paris train.

Whispers swept through the departing train that the wife of 'Dr Satan' has just been arrested.

The newspapers had begun to call Dr Petiot 'Dr Satan'.

* * *

At the police station, Massu told Georgette that he was taking her to Paris. Her brother-in-law, having been arrested also, would accompany her.

Georgette's legs gave way and she fell down in a faint.

A few minutes later, regaining consciousness, she looked into the stunned face of her son. Gerhardt had arrived to say goodbye. Monique Petiot stood beside him. She had come to say goodbye to her husband.

Georgette, in tears, pulled both into her arms.

A detective carried a trembling Georgette to Massu's car; again looking close to fainting, she was unable to walk. He lifted her onto the rear seat.

Maurice slipped in beside Georgette. He was handcuffed.

Massu climbed in beside Canitrot.

Battut and Schmidt were to make their own way back to Paris.

Georgette leant from the window and grabbed Gerhardt's hands.

"I'll be back soon. I haven't done anything wrong, my son."

She kissed his hands.

Canitrot turned the ignition key and the car pulled away from the kerb.

"Be good! Obey your aunt!" Georgette called out.

She was leaning from the window.

Maurice tapped her on the arm with his handcuffed hands.

"Come," he said.

She pulled back and dropped her head onto his shoulder.

She was again crying.

Massu leant over the back of the front seat, rolled up the rear windows and locked the rear doors.

"Go!" he ordered.

Canitrot put his foot down on the accelerator.

For a long time, Gerhardt stood staring at the fast disappearing car. The teenager was sobbing uncontrollably.

* * *

Close to midnight the *traction-avant* arrived at the Quay. Despite the curfew and a cool wind sweeping in from the river, a small crowd of journalists, photographers and curious Parisians waited.

Georgette stepped from the car and camera flashguns started to pop.

"This way! This way!" photographers called out.

She swayed.

Massu, fearing she was going to faint again, took her by the arm and led her into the building and to his office up three flights of stairs; there were, and still are, no lifts in the building.

In Massu's office, Georgette took off her coat and hat. She wore a black skirt and a red and white sweater over a white blouse. The skirt was creased as if she had spent several nights in it. Her dark curls were held up with a sequined comb, but a few rebel strands of hair were falling over her face.

A clock on the wall showed a new day had begun.

"Mrs Petiot, we'll speak in the morning," said Massu.

Canitrot led Georgette, she, carrying her coat over an arm, to a cell in the basement. Maurice was already locked in another cell.

As could be heard, he was protesting loudly that no one had the right to hold an innocent man.

-0-

CHAPTER FIVE

Wednesday, March 15, 1944

'I tidied up the few papers scattered on my desk; I went to the window once again to look down on the Quay des Orfèvres and the Pont-Neuf Bridge at the opposite end. It was dull weather, and the sky was dirty. *Vélo-taxis* jolted over the cobbles. One day, or perhaps one night, Petiot, too, had crossed the bridge on his bicycle, towing I don't know what load in his cart... I turned around. The young woman, pressing her elbows down onto my desk, was staring vacantly ahead of her. She wore a close-fitting pullover with red and white squares. A tiny handkerchief was balled up in her right hand.'

That was what Massu would write of his first interrogation of Dr Petiot's wife.

***

Georgette Valentine Lablais Petiot was the daughter of Long Arm Lablais and Georgette Villard. Both were deceased. She was four months from her fortieth birthday, and her seventeenth wedding anniversary was less than three months away.

Long Arm had started life as Georges Nestor Lablais. Friends had nicknamed him Long Arm because he used to boast *j'ai le bras long* - my arm is long. In other words; he had clout.

He had first worked as a porter at the railway station of Seignelay. Next, also in Seignelay, as a *charcutier*; a butcher who sold only pork, raw or cooked. Georgette Villard had been a chambermaid before her marriage. Soon after the two met, they had started sleeping together. The intimacy had resulted in the birth of a daughter also named Georgette.

The child was two years and four months old before her parents were married.

In 1918, Long Arm and the two Georgettes had left Seignelay to settle in Paris. Long Arm had opened a restaurant, Chez Marius, on the capital's Rue de Bourgogne. The street, bordering the *Chambres des Députés*, the French seat of parliament, the majority of his patrons were Members of Parliament and it pleased him to believe that they had become his friends. In 1936, a widower, he had sold the restaurant and had returned to Seignelay. He had obviously done well in Paris because back in the village he had started to buy properties. With what was to become an impressive real estate portfolio, had come a common-law wife, Léone Arnoux. Like his first wife, she too had once worked as a chambermaid. He was fully thirty years older than her.

Long Arm had been delighted and greatly proud that his only child had married a doctor. He considered it proof that he had done the right thing moving his family to Paris. He believed that he had given his daughter, fourteen at the time of the move, a better life than the one he had known in Seignelay as a railway porter and a pork butcher.

* * *

Massu offered Georgette something to drink.

"No, thank you, Mr Commissioner, I will be fine; at least, I hope I will," she replied.

Her eyes were red. Detectives who had checked on her during the night had reported to Massu that she had spent it lying on her bunk, crying quietly.

"Mrs Petiot, what can you tell us?" began Massu.

Georgette crossed and uncrossed her legs, and shrugged.

"Please. Take your time. Don't hurry. We've got all the time in the world. Start where and with whom you want," said Massu.

Georgette said there was little she could tell about the townhouse; certainly nothing about what the newspapers claimed had been found there. She's been to the place only once. It was shortly after her husband had bought it. She had taken an instant dislike to it; she still did not like it. It was too big; too grand. She also disliked it for another reason. Her husband had plans to convert it into a clinic. He had enough work as it was; his Rue de Caumartin practice was successful and he was kept busy.

She did not know the name of the person from whom he had bought the townhouse, but she knew the asking price was around half a million francs. He was paying the amount off in annual instalments of 17,000 francs.

"Didn't half a million francs seem enormous to you?" asked Massu.

Georgette admitted it did.

"But I do not interfere with my husband's affairs."

In France, in 1944, women were, by law, subservient to their spouses.

She had gone to Auxerre not to flee, but to be with her son, said Georgette.

"He's never been to the townhouse."

She had also hoped that she would find her husband in the town.

"The police are accusing him of something he has not done," she said, firmly.

"Where did you sleep in Auxerre last night? Rue des Lombards?" asked Massu.

He thought the mention of the street provoked the same reaction of surprise and nervousness in Georgette as it had in her brother-in-law the previous day.

"I slept at Rue du Pont last night in my son's room. I did not want him to be alone," she replied.

"Yet, now he is, *Madame*."

"But, if I had caught the train, Mr Commissioner, he would not be, as I was not planning to stay in Paris for long."

"And we, *Madame*," retorted Massu. "We would have been waiting for you on the station in Auxerre."

Georgette, ignoring the reply, resumed talking.

She said that on the previous Saturday evening, she was the one who had answered the telephone when the police called. The call had frightened her because one did not know *what* one was dealing with when one dealt with the French police. Massu understood she referred to the fact that the police force had accepted the Germans as its masters. He too had done so, obviously.

After the call, her husband had left their apartment, said Georgette.

"And you, *Madame*?" asked Massu.

She sat in an armchair all night waiting for him to return, she said.

"And he did not return?"

63

"He did not return."

"Do you always wait up for him when he goes out at night?"

"It was not my habit, no."

"But you did wait on Saturday night?"

"Saturday night was different. It was the police who called. As I've said already."

Massu ignored the remark.

She continued. She said she knew that her husband had a bike.

"What about his cart?" asked Massu.

"I know nothing about a cart."

"He had a cart. He stored it in your cellar. Your neighbours saw it, so how can you tell me that he did not have a cart?"

"Oh, *that* cart!"

Yes, he had a cart. He had bought the bike because as a doctor he had to be mobile and he had bought the cart because he liked to shop for bargains at auction houses and he had to get his purchases home.

"What did he buy at these auctions?" asked Massu.

"Whatever caught his fancy; furniture, household equipment, clothes, chess sets, books. Sometimes he bought to sell the goods later at a profit."

Where the bike and cart were, she did not know.

Massu asked her what kind of relationship she had with her husband.

She blushed.

"Relationship?"

Massu nodded.

"My husband is always tender and kind," she said.

Massu would write: 'She replied in such a low voice that I had to lean over my desk to hear her. I stood up and pushed a chair next to the armchair. Little drops of sweat were beading on Georgette Petiot's forehead'.

He allowed her to cry for a while, then, he asked her to pull herself together.

"We are not accusing you of anything, *Madame*. We are only trying to find out the truth," he said gently.

He asked her what she would say were he to ask her to describe her husband.

"I would say. Marcel is a most even-tempered, kind and gentle husband and father. His patients all hold him in high esteem. He does not charge the less fortunate among them. He's done so much good in his life. Do please believe me, Mr Commissioner ..."

Her voice faded and she dropped her eyes.

Massu wanted to know what she had done in the hours before she had left Paris for Auxerre. She explained. She said that on the Sunday morning she had walked to Gare de Lyon railway station to catch the Auxerre train. It was a ninety-minute walk. At the station, she had heard there would not be a train until Monday. She had then walked all the way back to Rue de Caumartin, but she was too scared to go into the apartment. She had a feeling it would be dangerous to do so. She had slipped into the Saint-Louis d'Antin church; she sat through several masses. In the afternoon, she had gone to sit in the waiting room at the nearby Saint-Lazare railway station; with people around her, she had felt a little less frightened. Frightened of what, she did not say. At 6 P.M. she had left the station to walk to an apartment building at Number 52 Rue de Reuilly in the twelfth *arrondissement*. Her husband was the building's proprietor. Because Rue de Reuilly was close to Gare de Lyon railway station, it was another ninety-minute walk. She had spent the night sitting on the building's stairs. No one had seen her. At the end of the curfew at daybreak, she had gone to a nearby hotel. It was Hotel Alicot on Rue de Bercy. She had taken a room. She had remained in the room until just before the Auxerre train's departure. At the station, she had bought a newspaper. She saw her name on the front page.

"Your name?" asked Massu.

"My husband's, if you wish, but his is mine... He is the father of my child."

She started to cry again.

'Could I tell this woman, this mother, all the terrible things that her husband had done? How would that help? Even if she had believed it to be true, would this revelation have advanced the investigation the slightest bit? I couldn't help admiring the woman's courage. Despite her weakness, she fought back, inch by inch. I thought she would crack at any moment. However, she resisted. For a moment, I thought of stopping the interrogation. But I continued', Massu would write.

He asked her whether she had any idea where her husband could be. She said she did not. She emphasised yet again that he could not possibly have had anything to do with what had gone on at the townhouse.

"Mr Commissioner, oh do please believe me..." she begged. "Marcel is innocent."

Of what followed, Massu would write:

'Suddenly, Georgette Petiot opened the hand that was clenching her handkerchief; the handkerchief fell to the floor; the young woman's head seemed to snap. Georgette Petiot fainted... I rushed to her and slapped her hands. Nothing'.

Canitrot came to his boss's aid and revived Georgette with a mouthful of cognac.

The interrogation was obviously over.

"Mrs Petiot," said Massu. "I am really sorry, but I would have to ask you more questions. But I'll do so later in the day."

He was going to take her to the Rue de Caumartin apartment and speak to her there.

"Unless you have something you wish to tell me now, which would make it unnecessary to go to the apartment," he said.

"No," she replied, her voice firm again. "There is nothing to tell you."

* * *

Having arrived back in Paris by train, Battut immediately set off for the twelfth *arrondissement*. He wanted to verify that Georgette Petiot had told Massu the truth by questioning both the *concierge* of the apartment building at Number 52 Rue de Reuilly and the owner or manager of Hotel Alicot.

The *concierge* confirmed Dr Petiot was the proprietor of the apartment building. She had met him, his wife and his brother. She had not seen the doctor and his wife for months, but the doctor's brother had called around at the end of the previous month; he had come to collect the rent. There were 21 tenants in the building. None of them had mentioned to her that they had seen a woman sitting on the stairs that previous Saturday night. She also told Battut that she could not believe what the newspapers were writing was true. The doctor, his wife and the doctor's brother were charming.

Hotel Alicot belonged to its manager, Henri-Casimir Alicot. He admitted to knowing Dr Petiot and his wife well. They often returned to their hometown of Auxerre for a holiday and spent the night before their departure at his hotel; they wanted to be close to the railway station - Gare de Lyon - for their early-morning departure. He liked both. They were polite and attractive people, and the doctor did not throw his weight around because he was a medical man.

Yes, Mrs Petiot had spent most of Monday at the hotel. She had arrived at 9 A.M. She wore an astrakhan coat over a black skirt and a red and white sweater. She also carried a yellow leather suitcase. She had asked him for a room; he had seen no reason to have refused. She had looked tired and stressed. He sent a meal of soup up to her room, but she had not eaten much. One of his maids had told him that when she had taken clean towels to the room she had found Mrs Petiot fast asleep. The poor woman had left the hotel at 4 P.M. She told him she wanted to catch the 5:20 P.M. train to Auxerre. She had told him that she had spent the previous night sitting on the stairs of her husband's property on Rue de Reuilly, and that she had not been able to sleep at all. She had spoken of what the newspapers were reporting, yes. The reports she had described as lies. She told him that she wanted to get to Auxerre because she had to speak to her son before she too was arrested. She was certain she would be arrested.

Alicot told Battut that he also knew Maurice.

"He's a nice, decent, quiet man, just like the doctor. He comes to stay at the end of each month because he collects the doctor's rents. The doctor has quite a number of properties here in Paris."

Asked whether Maurice had once stayed at the hotel because he had come to Paris to collect suitcases, Alicot nodded. He could remember Maurice had left the suitcases overnight at a nearby garage, Garage Muller, at Number 206 Rue de Bercy. The following morning, Charles Marlot, his receptionist, had helped Maurice carry the suitcases to the station. They were put on a train going to Auxerre.

Marlot confirmed what his employer had said. He could not remember how many suitcases there had been, but he could remember they had been heavy.

"When did you last see Maurice Petiot?" Battut wanted to know from Alicot.

"Last month."

"Tell me about it."

Maurice and two Auxerre truck drivers had turned up at the hotel. They had come to Paris to deliver something, he did not know what, but after the delivery, the truck had broken down. The three had then abandoned the truck and had returned to Auxerre by train.

Marlot remembered that one of the truck drivers had signed the register. He went in search of it. The truck driver's name was Jean Eustache.

Before Battut left the hotel, both Alicot and Marlot told him that the police were on the wrong track. Dr Petiot could not be a murderer. Dr Petiot was a most charming and cultivated man; a gentleman like one no longer found, not in German-occupied Paris anyway.

Arriving back at the Quay, Battut gave orders that Jean Eustache should be found and questioned.

It would not be necessary.

Eustache phoned in from Auxerre and he was a very talkative man.

He said that in May of the previous year he had picked up some suitcases from Maurice's shop to deliver them to an Alfred Neuhausen, owner of a bicycle and radio shop in the nearby village of Courson-les-Carrières. He did often undertake small delivery or driving jobs for Maurice. For example, the previous month he had driven Maurice to a quarry outside Aisy-sur-Armançon, sixty kilometres from Auxerre. Maurice wanted to pick up some quicklime. His mate, Robert Massonière, had gone with him and Maurice. They had picked up 270 kilograms of the stuff. They had then brought it to Paris. In Paris, they had stayed at Hotel Alicot in the twelfth *arrondissement*. The day after, Saturday, February 19, they had taken the quicklime to a townhouse in the sixteenth *arrondissement*. He could not remember the address, but he could remember it was a dilapidated place.

Asked to confirm that Maurice Petiot had accompanied him and his mate to the townhouse, Eustache laughed.

"Of course he did. He had to open up for us, and believe me, 270 kilograms of quicklime is quite a weight to shift, so we needed as many hands as possible!"

* * *

Massu decided the time had come to question Maurice some more. The latter had slept well through what had been left of the night as his creased clothes and hazy eyes confirmed.

Dr Petiot's brother claimed he knew nothing about the townhouse.

"Think!" ordered Massu.

He banged his fist on his desk.

"You may remember that you do know something of it."

"Perhaps I know a little," Maurice admitted.

What he knew, his brother had told him, he said.

It was that the townhouse was going to be converted into a clinic. His brother hoped to have a better class of patient in the sixteenth *arrondissement* than in the less elegant ninth. At the same time, the townhouse, because it was large, was going to serve as the family home.

About who had slept at the Rue des Lombards house in Auxerre, Maurice admitted it might not have been Neuhausen, but he was adamant that he really could not remember. It might even be that Neuhausen had slept at the house on some other night and the bed had not been made. He suggested Massu should send gendarmes to Courson-les-Carrières to question Neuhausen again.

"He's a weak man and he'll break down under interrogation. If you ask me, he will confess to just about anything," he said.

Questioned about Jean Eustache, Maurice readily admitted he knew him, but they did not socialise and he had not seen him for months. He certainly had not made a trip to Paris with him on February 19, or any other date.

"I was in Auxerre, and in my shop!" he said.

Told, the Crim knew about the February 19 trip to Paris with Eustache and Massonière, Maurice slapped his hands together.

"Oh, now I remember!" he said. "Jean drove. Yes, Jean drove. His truck ran on gas. Now I remember! It then went and broke down in Paris."

'It seemed to have slipped out in spite of him. When he realised that it was too late to go back on what he had said, he carried on, as if he now wanted me to believe that the detail was of no importance', Massu would write.

He asked the reason for the Paris trip.

Maurice said for him it had just been a joy ride, but Eustache and Massonière had to deliver furniture and some coal to a Paris address.

"Thirty sacks of coal," he said.

First, Eustache and Massonière had dropped him off. Next, they had delivered the furniture. The coal they had not been able to deliver, because the truck's engine played up and Eustache had thought it wiser to park the truck somewhere, which he had done. Meeting up with Eustache and Massonière later on that day and hearing about the engine trouble, he had offered to store the coal at his brother's house so that the truck could be taken to a garage. His brother had agreed to store the coal at his townhouse and had waited for them in front of the property. Eustache and Massonière had carried the sacks of coal into the house; he and his brother had remained chatting outside.

Asked about having hired Eustache to take suitcases to Neuhausen in Courson-les-Carrières, Maurice said that he had never done so.

"I know nothing about suitcases!"

Told that he was to remain locked up, he jumped to his feet.

"How long for? How long for?"

"As long as it is necessary."

"No!" Maurice shouted. "You have no right to lock up an innocent man! Be it that you realise that I have contacts and you will be reprimanded!"

Locked up, Maurice banged on the bars of his cell until Canitrot walked up and told him he was being charged with 'conspiring to commit murder'. If put on trial and convicted, he faced death by the guillotine.

"Murder! Murder!" He began to cry. "No, you can't do this... You can't. No! No! I'm not just anybody... I'm the brother of a Resistance hero... My brother's a hero... Listen to me! You can't do this! You can't!"

Canitrot walked away.

* * *

Late in the afternoon, Massu's *traction-avant* turned into Rue de Caumartin.

News that the wife of Dr Satan was to be brought to the family apartment had leaked out and the Parisians were waiting for her.

Seeing Georgette, pale and trembling on the rear seat of the car, the crowd surged forward and banged with clenched fists against the windscreen.

Massu jumped from the car and pushed his way to Georgette's side and opened the door for her.

Keeping her eyes down, Georgette slid nervously from the rear seat and grabbed the commissioner's offered arm.

"*Salope!*" a female voice shouted from the crowd.

Bitch!

Suddenly, Georgette came to life.

"You murderers!" she shouted into the crowd. "You are abusing my distress! You are all cowards!"

Upstairs in the apartment, Massu steered her towards her living room.

Once seated, her slim legs crossed at the ankles, she began to talk.

"Here we lived like the good *bourgeoisie* that we are," she said.

Her eyes welled up with tears.

She, her husband and their son had often gone to the theatre and cinema, she continued.

"It's not against the law, as far as I know, now is it, Mr Commissioner?" she wanted to know.

"No, *Madame*, it is not against the law. But other things are," replied Massu.

Georgette described her husband as a busy man. Often, he had had to leave before a film or play ended. No, he had not always told her where he was off to. But then, he did not have to; she knew that he had to leave to see a patient because he did house calls. Yes, even at night. When he had to visit a patient during the night, on leaving he always tried not to wake her and their son. He was *that* considerate a husband and father.

It did also happen when he had to visit a patient during the day that he would not tell her where he was going.

"He did not want to bother me. I would be busy in the kitchen or I would be writing letters, and he did not want to disturb me. And, as I am not inclined to peep from behind a curtain to spy on those down on the street, like some people have the habit of doing, I did not see in which direction he walked."

Her husband was generous. He had often given her his auction purchases.

Shown an engraving depicting a couple in an erotic pose and pornographic postcards and sketches detectives had found in the apartment earlier, and asked if that was the kind of thing her husband had given her, she shrugged.

"Collectors like him will buy just about anything."

Massu showed her the wooden sculpture of the beast-man with the large genitals.

"Like this?"

She shook her head.

"No, this is my husband's work. He is very artistic. He sketches, paints and sculpts."

She was proud of him, she said.

Of several valuable items of jewellery detectives had also found in the apartment, she said that some were hers; those had also been gifts from her husband. The other items were what patients had left behind in lieu of payment.

"He does not turn a needy patient away. If patients are not able to pay him, he allows them to leave jewellery with him. But he plans to return each and every item once their owners' financial situations have improved."

"Can you please pack a small suitcase, *Madame?*" Massu asked her.

"Why?" she wanted to know.

"Because I have to take you back to the police station," he replied.

"No," she said, shaking her head. "I am home now, and here I will be should you need to ask me more questions."

She gave a little gasp and slipped to the floor. She had fainted again. In coming to, again with the help of cognac which Canitrot had found in a cupboard, she said she did not want to return to the Quay.

"I want to be with my son. I want to go back to Auxerre."

Massu helped her to her feet.

"We're not accusing you of anything, Mrs Petiot, but, as we've still got to ask you a few more questions, we can't allow you to return to Auxerre," he explained gently.

Georgette, silent, but her body in spasms, was helped back to the *traction-avant*.

Massu would write: 'We had to make our way through a real flood of people to get to the car. Curious faces, of women mainly, leant down to peer into the car. The driver drove forward, sounding the car horn several times. Georgette Petiot, slumped on the rear seat between a detective and myself, hid her tear-streaked face behind her handkerchief'.

In the car, he made a quick decision not to take Georgette back to the Quay. He would take her to hospital instead. He took her to Hotel Dieu; the Quay always took prison inmates and witnesses who had fallen ill there. She was admitted to the hospital's Pavillon Cusco. As Massu knew, but which Georgette Petiot had probably not known, the Cusco Pavilion had been constructed with a donation from a certain *Mademoiselle* Camille de Maupin or La Maupin - real name Julie d'Aubigny - a seventeenth century bisexual courtesan. Books on her were among those in the townhouse's library room.

At the hospital, doctors examined Georgette. They told Massu that there was nothing seriously wrong with her; she was just in a state of nervous exhaustion. A few days rest and she would be fine.

Massu went to tell her.

She sat in a chair, dressed in a white hospital robe, her hair hanging down in damp curls as if she had been under the shower.

The commissioner touched her arm.

"Mrs Petiot, the doctors say you are in good health. You only need a few days of rest. I am afraid, however, that I also have to inform you that I have no choice but to charge you with 'having received stolen property'.

Silently, she slumped forward.

Georgette Petiot had fainted yet again.

Giving a deep sigh, Massu pressed the bell to summon the nurses. When they ran in, he picked up his coat and hat and walked from the room without looking back even once.

* * *

At the end of the day the Courson-les-Carrières gendarmes again called on the Neuhausens. Very many villagers gathered on the street to watch. They had read in the newspapers that Dr Satan's brother, Maurice Petiot from Auxerre, had removed suitcases from the murder house, suitcases which had ended up with the Neuhausens.

Only Simone was in the shop.

Her husband, she said, was in Paris on business. She wrote down the address of the hotel he was staying at. It was Hotel Alicot.

Searching the shop and the apartment above it - the couple's home -

the gendarmes found 49 suitcases. Gare de Lyon railway station dispatch labels, dated May 26, 1943, were attached to thirty-seven.

Using a pulley, the gendarmes lowered the suitcases to the street. The cases were to be taken to their headquarters. So was Simone. Told to put on her coat and hat because she was going with the suitcases, she protested very loudly that she had not broken any law. There was thus no reason to lock her up.

At their headquarters, the gendarmes opened the suitcases.

Their contents almost filled a storeroom.

A list was telegraphed to Massu.

It was a long list: 311 handkerchiefs; 115 men's shirts; 104 shirt cuffs; one hundred petticoats; 96 shirt collars; 87 bathroom towels; 79 dresses; 77 pairs of gloves; 69 pairs of men's socks; 66 pairs of shoes; 55 panties; 48 scarves; 42 blouses; 36 purses; 29 brassieres; 28 men's suits; 26 women's hats; 22 sweaters; 21 women's cloth coats; 14 men's raincoats; 13 pillowcases; 13 unused Paris bus tickets; 11 men's jackets; ten women's hats; 9 sheets, 5 fur coats - three of them mink; 5 pairs of eyeglasses; 5 nail clippers; 3 men's night shirts; 3 tablecloths; 3 cultured pearl necklaces and a hatpin.

The clothes had been worn.

After reading the list, Massu asked the gendarmes to repack the suitcases; they were to be put on the first train to Paris. He also asked the gendarmes to call on all the relatives of Dr Petiot and his wife as well as those of the Neuhausens who were living in the region and to search their homes for suitcases. Should some be found, the family member should be arrested. What was more, should any family member act suspiciously, he or she should be arrested, too.

Suitcases were found with a couple named Mourier who were Simone's parents. Also with Léone Arnoux, Long Arm's unofficial widow and Georgette's unofficial stepmother; she still lived in Long Arm's house in Seignelay. The three were arrested.

Albert Neuhausen was arrested as well. The Crim's detectives picked him up at Hotel Alicot. He protested that he had not broken any law. He had stored the suitcases at his place for Maurice Petiot only as a favour. He was taken to a cell at the Quay.

The Courson-les-Carrières and Seignelay gendarmes handed Simone Neuhausen, Léone Arnoux and the Mourier couple over to the Auxerre police. The four, like Georgette, were charged with 'having received stolen property' and locked up.

* * *

In the evening, detectives from the Quay's forensics department arrived at Hotel Dieu to fingerprint Georgette. It was an almost impossible task; nervous and agitated, she could not keep still.

Back at the Quay, the fingerprints caused consternation. The compatriots of pioneering criminologists like Lacassagne, Bertillon and Locard, understood that the flow of the pattern of the loop of a fingerprint should be towards the ulna bone, the bone on the pinkie side of the forearm; therefore, if the hand is held up with the palm facing towards the body, the loops of the fingerprints of the right hand should spiral left and those of the left hand should spiral right. The loops of Georgette's fingerprints spiralled in the opposite direction. As far as the police were concerned, such an abnormality meant only one thing; as human fingerprints were formed during the foetal stage of life and they never altered, Georgette had been born with six fingers on each hand, perhaps she had two thumbs or two pinkies on each hand. Asked, she refused to reply.

In the morning, newspapers reported the abnormality.

Immediately, palmists, clairvoyants and mediums rang editors. They said that such an anomaly of the hands was the sign of a witch.

Dr Satan was married to a witch.

-0-

CHAPTER SIX

Thursday, March 16, 1944

The Germans stepped into the frame.

A commissioner, one Robert Yodkum, sent a report to the Quay and it was passed to Massu.

Yodkum was with Sector IVB4 or the *Judenreferat*, the Jewish Affairs Department of the *Reichssicherheitshauptamt* - Reich Security main office - or RSHA, the subordinate organisation of the *Schutzstaffel* - SS. The RSHA also comprised the Gestapo and the *Kriminalpolizei* - Criminal Police - and, since June 1942, it had fallen under *SS-Obergruppenführer* - Lieutenant General - Dr Ernst Kaltenbrunner. The RSHA's various sections and agencies operated from several Paris addresses. There were the Gestapo's three buildings on Avenue Foch at Numbers 82, 84 and 86; there was a building on Rue de Bassano and another on Rue de la Pompe, both in the sixteenth *arrondissement*, and there was the Gestapo's general headquarters at Number 11 Rue des Saussaies in the eighth *arrondissement*. However, there was yet another building, Number 93 Rue Lauriston, also in the sixteenth; it was the French Gestapo's headquarters.

Sector IVB4's offices were at Gestapo General Headquarters - Number 11 Rue des Saussaies - where Commissioner Yodkum's immediate superior was *SS-Obersturmbahnführer* - Lieutenant Colonel - Heinz Röthke. The latter's superior was based in Germany; he was Adolf Eichmann.

Massu, like everyone at the Quay, knew little more about Yodkum than what he looked like - stocky, with a grey crew cut and pale-blue eyes behind glasses with thick lenses - and that his origins were dubious, some believing that he was German because he was fluent in German, yet others convinced that he was French because he was fluent in French too. Then, there were some who said that the name Jodkum was a

77

deliberate effort to misinform and that his real name was Jokum. No, said still others, his real name was Jodkuhn. Whichever it was, Massu was delighted to have heard from him.

Commissioner Yodkum reported that in April, 1943, Sector IVB4 had learnt from a *mouchard* - an informer - that a Paris-based organisation headed by a Dr Eugène was helping people to flee France. The doctor's escape route ran through Vichy-France to Spain and from there to North Africa where escapees continued by boat either to England or South America. Dr Eugène did not turn anyone away who could afford his high fee. He was about 1.67 metres tall; he was between 35 and 38 years old; he had dark brown hair and piercing black eyes, and he had a strange habit of rubbing his hands together.

Dr Eugène's *modus operandi* was as follows.

A potential escapee had to present him or herself - the doctor accepted both men and women - at a barbershop on the second storey of Number 25 Rue des Mathurins in the ninth *arrondissement*. The barbershop was owned by one of Dr Eugène's recruiting agents, Raoul Fourrier, aged sixty-one. Another recruiting agent was Edmond Marcel Pintard, a 56-year-old out-of-work cabaret singer and cinema make-up man who used the stage name Francinet.

Fourrier and Pintard were friends. They had met through their professions; Fourrier had once supplied Paris cabarets and film studios with wigs. Both were badly in need of money - war and occupation had hit the entertainment world extra hard - and Dr Eugène had promised them a percentage of his escape network's fees. A potential escapee was thoroughly questioned about his family and financial situation. Either Fourrier or Pintard asked the questions. It was, though, Dr Eugène who took the final decision as to an escapee's suitability. Since he based his decision solely on what the escapee was prepared to pay over, Fourrier and Pintard always emphasised the importance of being financially generous towards the doctor. On acceptance, an escapee paid an initial fee of 50,000 francs; then, three or four days before the departure date, he or she had to hand over a further 90,000 francs. In some cases, the escapee would meet Dr Eugène only on the day of departure when the doctor picked him or her up at the barbershop. The escapee had to wait at a safe house for the arrival of the *passeur* - the people smuggler - who would escort him or her to Spain. Dr Eugène charged the escapee a further 400 francs daily for board and lodging.

As Jodkum further reported, he had planned to arrest Dr Eugène, but another sector of the RSHA had done so before him.

On Friday, May 21, 1943, *SS Hauptstürmführer* – Captain - Dr Friedrich Berger from IVE3, the RSHA's counter-intelligence service for the occupied countries of Western Europe, had arrested not only Dr Eugène, but also Fourrier and Pintard. The latter two were taken in first in a raid on the barbershop and rapidly they had revealed that Dr Eugène was an undercover name and that the escape network's leader's real name was Marcel Petiot; he was a Dr Marcel Petiot. Immediately Berger's agents had descended on Dr Petiot's apartment and arrested him. Present at the arrest were the doctor's wife and teenage son. So too, a family friend named Gustave-René Nézondet. The latter, a Parisian, was arrested as well, but not the doctor's wife and son. Berger had interrogated Dr Petiot, Fourrier, Pintard and Nézondet first and then, once they had been handed over to him, he had interrogated them as well.

Afterwards he had locked them up in Fresnes Prison, outside Paris. He had released Nézondet after two weeks; it was clear that the latter knew nothing of an escape network. Dr Petiot, Fourrier and Pintard were held for eight months, after which he had released them without having charged them. His investigation had shown that the doctor had never run an escape network or any kind of subversive organisation. He was simply stark raving mad.

Having read the report and after discussing it with Battut and some of his other colleagues at the Crim, Massu decided that Dr Petiot was not after all a Gestapo torturer.

However, what had, in that case, gone on at the townhouse?

He thought that Fourrier, Pintard and Nézondet would know; that they and Maurice Petiot would probably be the only four people in the world who would know, and as Maurice was not talking, he would have to see whether the other three would.

Fourrier and Pintard were known to the Crim. They were down in the Crim's files as petty crooks.

Nézondet was unknown.

Prefect Bussière issued arrest warrants for the three.

* * *

Nézondet's Paris apartment was dark and silent when the detectives called round.

Pintard was at his Paris home and Fourrier was cutting hair in his barbershop. Both were taken to the Quay; the one unaware of the other's arrest.

Massu interrogated Fourrier first.

The barber was a short, tubby man. He wore a badly-cut suit and a black beret; the beret he refused to take off. He vehemently denied Dr Petiot was a friend.

"He was my doctor, but nothing more," he insisted.

Pushed, he admitted that Dr Petiot, whom he had known since 1933, had become a 'kind of friend'. As such, the doctor had told him that he was helping people flee from France to South America and asked that should some of his clients, especially the Jewish ones, express the wish to leave France, he should direct them to him. Escapees would be travelling on South American identification documents. Those would describe them as diplomats or businessmen so they did not have to fear detection.

"Dr Petiot said to me, 'Raoul, there will be a nice commission for you'. The doctor was confident he could get anyone out of France. His confidence initially scared me. I thought he was with the Gestapo and he was out to entrap me, but he assured me that he was not with the Nazis. He said he was with the Resistance. Thinking it over, I thought it would be a great idea to help young French get out of the reach of the Nazis. I then told a friend of mine about the scheme," Fourrier told Massu.

Asked the name of the friend, he said that it was Pintard.

"Edmond Marcel Pintard".

"What does he do for a living?" asked Massu.

"He's a lady's man," replied Pintard.

His face coloured a little.

"Never heard of that," pretended Massu. "What do you mean? Is he a great lover, or what?"

Fourrier's flush became a blush as red as beetroot.

"Ah... well... What I mean is... he's a pimp... Times are tough... you know, Mr Commissioner... Whatever."

Massu said that he understood.

* * *

Pintard, bony with thin grey hair and a smile that revealed broken yellow teeth, looked older than his 56 years. He sat down opposite Massu and made it clear he was piqued to have police bang at his door.

"Do you know who I am?" he asked.

"You are Edmond Pintard, a theatre make-up man currently under threat of being charged as an accomplice to a crime," Massu replied calmly.

"Me?" he asked. "Me... an accomplice to a crime? Me... the Great Francinet? Listen to me, *Monsieur le Commissaire*, there is not a music hall director in Paris who does not know me!"

Massu laughed.

Pintard spread his arms.

"My name, *Monsieur le Commissaire*, large as this, has been on every advertising column in Paris. I can tell you that, if I am today just a make-up artist, it's only because I have chosen to step gradually into the background while still at the height of my glory!"

He insisted that he had not accepted money from Dr Petiot for introducing escapees to him.

"I did it out of the goodness of my heart."

He crossed his hands over his heart.

"Don't talk rubbish!" snapped Massu.

He grabbed a folder from his desk and waved it at Pintard.

"You see this file here? In it are the names of innocent men and women who your friend, Dr Petiot, murdered, perhaps even tortured before cutting them up into pieces, which he then threw into a pit of quicklime. Now, I will ask you this. Have you ever smelt flesh burn?"

Pintard shook his head.

"So shut up!" shouted Massu.

"So, good, I will say to you that the doctor paid me! He gave me 5,000 francs per head."

"How many did you send him?"

"Fifteen or twenty, but I can't remember exactly how many."

"Men or women?"

"Both. I met most of them in bars and nightclubs. They went to a barbershop and the doctor picked them up there. The doctor always told the barber and me that the folks had arrived safely in South America. Once, he showed us half of some other country's note. He said a girl he

81

had helped to escape had sent it to her mother here in Paris as proof that she had arrived safely over there. A flaming sun was drawn on it. The doctor said the sun was Argentina's emblem. He was an educated man being a doctor and all that, so he knew such things."

"What's the barber's name?"

"He's a good man, Mr Commissioner. He wouldn't have harmed anybody."

"His name?"

"Edouard Fourrier. But, Mr Commissioner, please, it never occurred to us that the doctor was anything but a great patriot. I am a great patriot, too. I am French, after all, Mr Commissioner, and I sincerely believed that, by helping these French people escape our enemy, I was doing my duty to my country. Edouard is a great patriot, too."

Massu wanted to ask Pintard one more question. He wanted to know whether there was anything else he felt he had to get off his chest.

"Yes," replied Pintard, nodding. "I want to ask you to tell the photographers to leave me alone."

"Why would that be?"

Pintard dropped his eyes.

"*Monsieur le Commissaire*... Look... I am a famous man, and I don't like what's happening to me."

Massu did not reply.

"Frankly... Frankly, Mr Commissioner, I must admit that I am... well... I am ashamed," Pintard continued.

He had started to cry.

Massu would write in his book: 'It was a clown who came into my office a few minutes ago. It is now a poor bastard who has only one thing on his mind; how to get himself out of the sinister trap that his greed made him fall into. The Great Francinet, the so illustrious star of the music hall, bowed his head and hid his poor old ham actor's crumpled face behind his clenched fists. He was almost in collapse. A spineless character. I wouldn't like to be in his shoes. Dreaming, at night, of all those travellers who have left for the only country we never come back from ...

'He was a lean and nervous man of average height. I hadn't yet asked him to sit down when he already assumed the air of the guy who is astonished that I should dare to interrogate him; what one of my colleagues once called their air of the innocent victim of a terrible miscarriage of justice. They are not the most difficult of customers. Generally, they are talkative and verbose; and in all the jumble of their declarations, it is not unusual to find sufficient elements of confession to make them fall like a ripe fruit into the trap.

'Edmond was no exception to the rule. He went into attack like a fighting cock. Stupidly'.

Fourrier and Pintard were charged with 'concealing evidence and not reporting a crime'. It was a new law constituted by the Germans on October 7, 1941 to stop the French helping and hiding members of the Resistance.

The two were to remain in custody.

Told, they were unable to get a word out.

* * *

Telephone calls started to arrive at the Quay. People were phoning in to say that they knew Dr Petiot and that they had seen him.

Palmists, clairvoyants and mediums also telephoned.

The palmists offered to analyse Georgette's fingerprints; the clairvoyants and mediums claimed they could lead the police to the doctor's hiding place.

The Crim dismissed all but two calls as from cranks.

One of the two calls was from a man named Roland Albert Porchon. The other caller was named Jean Gouedo. The latter agreed to come to the Quay; the other one had to be picked up and brought in with a little force.

Like Fourrier and Pintard, Porchon, the owner of a second-hand furniture shop, was known to the Crim. He was one of their informers, snitching on the *milieu* - the criminal underworld - and a rapist and child molester who was living openly with an underage girl. Shaking from head to toe with anxiety, he had to be given a cognac before he could get a word out.

He was a friend of a friend of Dr Petiot, he explained.

The friend in question was René Nézondet.

He also knew Maurice Petiot.

"We all hail from Auxerre. All of us," he gave as explanation for the friendship.

He had known that there were bodies lying at the townhouse. He had known since the previous December. Nézondet had told him about them, and it was Maurice who had told Nézondet. Maurice had described the bodies to Nézondet as, 'as black as the black plague'. There were about sixty of them. They were laid out in a row. Maurice had described his brother as mentally ill and in need of treatment. He had begged Nézondet not to go to the police.

"Nézondet had asked me also not to," he added.

They were to wait until after the war and only then would they go together to the police.

Once, he had known about the bodies, he had not been able to keep such dreadful knowledge to himself. He had told two inspectors.

"Their names?" asked Massu.

"I can't remember their names. I don't think that I ever knew their names."

Nézondet had also spoken of the bodies to other people, he revealed. To two women. Their names were Aimée Lesage and Marie Turpault; Lesage was Nézondet's live-in lover and Turpault was Lesage's best friend.

Porchon was taken to a cell and locked up. Like Fourrier and Pintard, he was charged with 'concealing evidence and not reporting a crime'. He did not react when told.

* * *

Jean Gouedo was a furrier. His shop was at Number 69 Rue de Caumartin, the building facing that of the Petiots'. Massu recognised him as the man he had seen the previous Monday standing in the shop's doorway.

The furrier's story was that his business partner, a man named Joachim Guschinov, had disappeared two years previously; in January 1942. Guschinov had paid Dr Petiot to help him flee to Argentina.

"I know the War and the Occupation are making communication with the outside world difficult, but one would have thought Joachim would have found a way to send word to his wife that he was all right, but only silence," he said.

Guschinov was Jewish; he hailed from Poland.

"He feared the Germans would arrest him, kill him. He was desperate to leave France," he said.

Dr Petiot, whose patient Guschinov was, had offered to help him do so. He had paid the doctor 25,000 francs for an Argentinean passport and another 500,000 francs for safe passage to Spain and transport by boat from there to Argentina. On the doctor's orders, both sums had been paid in cash. He had also taken jewellery worth 700,000 francs with him. He had also sewn USA dollar notes to the value of a thousand dollars into the shoulder pads of the jacket he planned to wear for his journey. That was not all. He had also taken three mink pelts from the shop; the doctor had asked for them.

"Now, knowing about Dr Petiot's townhouse, I have this terrible feeling that the doctor had done him in," said Gouedo.

Massu's reply was that one should always look on the bright side of things.

Gouedo was allowed to go home, but he was told he had to remain in Paris.

* * *

Nézondet still missing, detectives set off to fetch Lesage and Turpault.

Lesage, like her lover, was nowhere to be found.

Turpault was at her apartment.

She was not surprised at finding detectives on her doorstep. A dark-haired, fashionably dressed woman, she was talkative. Nézondet, almost hysterical, had told her and Lesage over dinner the previous Christmas that many bodies were lying in the basement of a townhouse in the sixteenth *arrondissement*. The townhouse, he had told them, belonged to Dr Marcel Petiot.

"It was the doctor's brother, Maurice Petiot, who had told Nézondet about the bodies. What was more, Maurice Petiot said that there were more bodies than those in the basement lying in a pit in a stable at the back of the townhouse. He also said that he had found an exercise book in the townhouse in which his brother had noted the names of the people he had killed and the dates of their deaths. Maurice wanted Nézondet to help him seal the pit, but Nézondet wouldn't hear anything about it.

Maurice didn't want him to go to the coppers. He said that, as soon as the war was over, they could all go to the coppers together. So Nézondet asked us - Lesage and me - not to tell anyone about the bodies," she said.

The two had also been unable to keep such dreadful news to themselves.

"We told two of your guys," confessed Turpault.

"Might you remember their names?" asked Massu.

"Yes, of course. We told Inspectors René Bouygues and Lucien Doulet," she replied.

Massu told her that she could go home, but not to leave Paris.

* * *

Inspectors Bouygues and Doulet readily confirmed that not only had Turpault and Lesage - two informers - told them that there were bodies lying at a townhouse belonging to a Dr Marcel Petiot, but so had someone else. That person was Roland Albert Porchon. He was also one of their informers.

The two explained they had not reported what the three informers had told them because they suspected Dr Petiot was with the Gestapo. It was, therefore, better for everyone that they kept the news to themselves.

Massu decided no punitive action was to be taken against the two women; it was, indeed, wiser to keep away from the Germans.

* * *

Joachim Guschinov's wife, Renée, arrived at the Quay. She still lived above the furrier shop and since Gouedo's return from the Quay she had been waiting to be summoned.

Renée's most remarkable feature was a crop of bushy, shoulder-length brown hair; it tumbled over her face as she talked.

She was not Jewish.

"I was born Catholic, and I did not convert to Judaism on my marriage to Joachim," she emphasised.

Dr Petiot had been treating her husband for some time for 'a little chronic illness that wasn't at all serious'. He had told the doctor that he felt threatened by the Nazis; the doctor had told him that a friend of his, an Argentinean diplomat, could arrange for him to flee to Argentina. Her husband had business associates in Buenos Aires and had thought that it would be a good idea to go and live there. Both of them were going to go. They were going to open a furrier shop there.

Only her husband had set off.

"I was going to go later."

"Why only later?" asked the commissioner.

"We couldn't both leave the shop," she replied.

Almost immediately she changed her mind and said that she had been unwell at the time and a long sea voyage would have been too much for her.

Dr Petiot had invited her husband to the family apartment so that the two of them could discuss the flight to Argentina over a drink. She would never forget the date: Christmas day, 1941.

She confirmed the amounts Gouedo had mentioned. Her husband had also taken a gold watch and a large diamond and platinum ring with him. They had bought those especially for him to take along.

Two months after her husband's departure she had gone to Dr Petiot to ask whether he had any news of him. He had shown her a letter from her husband claiming that he had received it only that morning. Her husband had written that he had arrived safely in Buenos Aires and that he had opened a fur shop. The shop was doing well.

The doctor had refused to allow her to keep the letter. Neither had he allowed her to keep a second letter; it was written on the letterhead paper of a Buenos Aires hotel. It was the Alvear Palace.

"The handwriting looked like Joachim's, but I thought he had written the letters in great haste, because the handwriting was not as neat as his always was," she said.

She had not reported her husband missing at the time - during those two months of worry - because she wanted to believe he was safe in Argentina. Also, had she gone to the police she would have drawn attention to herself and that was one thing she would not have wished to do.

Renée Guschinov left a photograph of her missing husband with Massu.

The photograph showed a round-faced, dark-haired, smiling man.

"Mr Commissioner," she said. "I fear that Joachim didn't leave for

Argentina after all. He ended up in that house's pit."

Massu did not tell her, but he agreed.

* * *

Before going home at the end of the day, Massu listened to a man who did not want to reveal his name. He said he was Jewish and that he had planned to flee France.

His story was that one night he had met a man in a bar who had told him that he knew a doctor who could help him flee. He had met the doctor in question, but the latter had refused point blank to help him.

"He told me I did not have enough money. That the amount I was offering him would not even cover the cost of getting me to the Spanish border."

The doctor was Marcel Petiot.

* * *

Much later in the night, a young man, also refusing to reveal his name, arrived at the Quay. He wanted the police to issue a statement of clarification he had brought along.

The statement read: 'The Association of Interns and Former Interns of the hospitals and hospices of Paris wishes to point out that Dr Petiot was never an intern in any Paris hospital or hospice'.

A doctor, he said, could never ever have done what Petiot had done.

-0-

CHAPTER SEVEN

Friday, March 17, 1944

The Quay's Vice Squad revealed that they too had a file on Dr Petiot.

Two years previously - mid-February of 1942 - the doctor's name had come to their attention when they were controlling pharmacies in order to expose doctors who were supplying addicts with drugs. Pétain had initiated a drive to cleanse the country of 'immoral elements' - immoral elements such as drug dealers and addicts.

Dr Petiot, as the VS had discovered, had too frequently issued prescriptions for large amounts of drugs, drugs such as cocaine and heroin, and which one could not have described as in general medical use. Detectives had called on him and they had been satisfied with the explanation he had given them. He had, as he had told them, initiated a revolutionary method for treating addiction; he allowed addicts to continue taking their drug of choice, but he reduced their habitual dose gradually over a period of months until the addict was 'clean'. He had claimed that he had already cured several addicts in that manner and numerous Paris doctors, having heard of his success, had adopted his method.

Soon afterwards, Dr Petiot's name had cropped up again. The records of a pharmacist in the working class twentieth *arrondissement* of the capital had shown that the doctor had issued several prescriptions for heroin over a rather short period to a man named Jean-Marc Van Bever and a woman named Jeannette Gaul. The frequency and amounts had been out of kilter with his earlier explanation. The pharmacist had told the VS, Van Bever, a coal peddler, who earned a few pounds a day, lived in a seedy boarding house at Number 56 Rue Piat, also in the twentieth *arrondissement*. With him lived Gaul, his lover. Inspectors had raided the place and Van Bever was in the room; Gaul was absent. Searching the

89

room, they had found several vials of heroin and seven predated prescriptions. Dr Petiot had issued all of the prescriptions. Bills also found in the room showed that the doctor had charged Van Bever and Gaul 200 francs per prescription. The VS had arrested Van Bever there and there, and Gaul, a former prostitute and a heavy drinker, had been arrested on her return to the room. A short man with a turned-up nose, Jean-Marc Pierre Ernest Van Bever, had been born 41 years previously to a well-known and well-to-do couple. Adolphe, his late father, had been a publisher and writer. Despite a good education, fluency in several languages, and having inherited a million francs from his father a few years previously, Van Bever was penniless, and, unable even to make a living with coal peddling, he had been supplementing his income with welfare payments.

Gaul, 35, had been as unsavoury as her lover. Her sex life had started at the age of 16 and a year later she had undergone the first of many abortions. While working as a countess' maid, she had met a Dutch drug dealer and pimp who put her on the street. She had become addicted to his merchandise, and was only too willing to have him as her pimp.When that relationship had collapsed because of her indulgence, which had bitten into his profits, another pimp had taken her over. When he wanted to place her in a *maison close* - a brothel - one that catered exclusively for a German patronage, which would have turned her into a 'horizontal collaborator' - a French woman who slept with German soldiers - she had refused, and instead she had begun working the streets as an independent, albeit doing so unlawfully because she had not registered with the police as prostitutes were legally compelled to do. A streetwalker, she had met Van Bever, and despite her addictions and the ravages of drugs and alcohol-protruding eyes and thinning, straggly hair - he had fallen in love with her. Once his lover, she had quit prostitution, but not the drugs or alcohol.

As the VS reported to Massu, the Van Bever/Gaul case had been handed to an examining magistrate, Judge Achille Olmi, and on Monday, March 9 of that year, he had summoned Dr Petiot to his office at the Quay. Van Bever and Gaul had already been brought over from their respective jails.

Petiot had been asked to explain the seven predated prescriptions, of which five were in Van Bever's name, and he had replied, "I give them prescriptions, it's true, but I consider it better to give an addict a small amount of the drug he craves than to allow him to go out and steal, or even kill to get it. I was only trying to help these two unfortunates."

The judge had charged all three with drug trafficking. He had not locked up the doctor, but had warned him not to leave Paris, and to find a lawyer. As warned, the doctor had hired a lawyer, the forty-year-old *Maître* René Floriot. Van Bever had also hired a lawyer, *Maître* Michel Menard; the latter and Van Bever's late father had been friends, so the lawyer had waived his fee, but he had refused to defend Gaul. Penniless, she had accepted the lawyer the state had assigned to her, *Maître* Françoise Pavie, a novelty at the Paris Bar because she was a woman. Two weeks later, Monday, March 16, *Maître* Menard had succeeded in getting Van Bever released on bail: Gaul had remained locked up. (In France the title '*maître*' is used when addressing a lawyer.)

On March 22, a Sunday, eight days later, Van Bever had mysteriously vanished. That morning at half past eight he was enjoying breakfast in a bistro beside the boarding house where he and Gaul had been staying and to which he had returned on his release from prison. A friend, a fellow coal peddler, was with him. A man whom the friend had later described to the VS as, 'dark-haired and in his early forties', had then walked in looking for Van Bever. The latter had left the bistro with his visitor explaining to the coal peddling friend that he was going up to his room to write a letter to the imprisoned Gaul; his visitor had offered to take it to her. Van Bever had not introduced the man to his friend. Never was Van Bever's friend to see him again. *Maître* Pavie, Gaul's lawyer, had then received two letters from the missing Van Bever. One of the letters was addressed to her while the other was addressed to Gaul. Van Bever had written: '*Maître*, I am sending you a letter to please forward to Miss Jeanne Gaul. You will present my apologies to my lawyer and tell him I no longer need his services. Kindly accept my respectful salutations. Jean-Marc Van Bever'. To Gaul, he had written: 'My love, it is no longer necessary to tell any stories. You know I am an addict to the tune of one to four shots a day. You know that Dr Petiot examined me in the next room. The proof is that he saw the scabs of my hypos. If I made false statements, it was to get temporary freedom to make a new life for us somewhere else. We will meet on your release to try to make a new life together far from all this filth. I kiss you very warmly. Jean-Marc Van

Bever'.

Despite the disappearance of Van Bever, which the police had not gone to the trouble to investigate, the drug trafficking case had been heard at Paris's Palais de Justice that March 26. In absentia, Van Bever had been found guilty and he was sentenced to one year in prison and fined 2,400 francs. Gaul had also been found guilty; she was given a six-month jail sentence with the same fine. Dr Petiot had also been found guilty and he was given a one-year suspended imprisonment sentence and fined 10,000 francs. *Maître* Floriot had filed an appeal and the fine was reduced to 7,600 francs and the suspended sentence was squashed. Gaul, having already served most of her sentence while awaiting trial, had been released within two months on Wednesday, May 20. Her lover gone, she had immediately returned to the Paris streets. She had also returned to Dr Petiot for more of his revolutionary treatment for her addiction. She was no longer alive, as Massu learnt; she died in Hotel Dieu Hospital from tetanus a few weeks after her release. Hospital staff thought she had fallen victim to tetanus by injecting with a dirty needle. On her admission to hospital, she had already lost the power of speech, so she had been unable to tell the staff who had injected her and with what, and why. Informed of her death by the VS, Dr Petiot had casually remarked that she and her lover had connived against him, and justice had been done.

Massu knew *Maître* Floriot, considered one of Paris's best legal minds, well. Coming from a modest family, Floriot had started to practise law in 1923 when only twenty-one. He wore his black hair greased and cut short and parted on the left, but his trademarks were a pair of heavy, round, black, tortoise-shell glasses, and a booming voice.

As the VS reported further, there had been a second drug case against Dr Petiot.

That case had begun on Thursday, March 5, 1942. At that time the VS had already begun to investigate the Van Bever/Gaul case.

A pharmacist in Paris's Latin Quarter had reported that he had been given an altered prescription; a line had been clumsily erased and the words '14 Vials of Heroin' had been scribbled over the erasure mark. The VS had sent an Inspector Roger Gignoux, already on the Van Bever/Gaul case, to the pharmacy. The prescription was one of Dr Petiot's. It had been made out to a Raymonde Baudet; the pharmacist knew her as a 28-year-old drug addict who lived nearby. Inspector

Gignoux had raided the Petiots' apartment where he found a large number of heroin vials as well as a register logging the names of 95 people receiving drug-addiction treatment from the doctor. He had also found several items of very expensive jewellery. Taken to the Quay for questioning by Judge Olmi, Dr Petiot's explanation for the altered prescription was that he had prescribed the drug 'Soneryl' to Baudet, a patient, and that any idiot could have seen that a different hand had written the words '14 vials of heroin'. He was therefore innocent of any wrongdoing. About the jewellery in the apartment he had explained that he had either bought the items at auctions or, temporarily short of cash, patients had left them with him. As for the large number of heroin vials and the register logging the names of people he was supplying with drugs, he said that as a medical practitioner he was allowed to stock drugs and, as any doctor would confirm, a family doctor had to keep a register of who was being prescribed what drugs.

The VS also reported to Massu that Petiot had proceeded to offer Judge Olmi his services as an informer. The judge, disgusted, had replied to Petiot by asking Inspector Gignoux to go and question the doctor in another room, any room, just as long as he would not have to see his face.

Once again, Dr Petiot had been charged with drug trafficking, but he was allowed to go home; Baudet was picked up at the apartment she shared with her mother, stepfather and half-brother, and locked up.

The VS's report did not end there.

Massu learnt that a few days after Dr Petiot's interrogation at the Quay by the VS, he had turned up at the apartment of Baudet's mother and stepfather. The mother, named Marthe Khaït née Fortin, stout, dark-haired and in her late fifties, and the stepfather, named David, were home. The latter, Jewish, was Marthe's third husband; Baudet was the second husband's child. Also at home was Baudet's half-brother, born in Marthe's first marriage. The young man's name was Fernand Lavie and he was not unfamiliar with drugs and court cases and prisons: he was a clerk at the Quay.

It was Lavie who had told the VS of Dr Petiot's visit.

His story which he had told the VS on Thursday, May 7 - two months after Dr Petiot's visit because it had taken him time to work up the courage to do so as like so many French he had feared drawing the

Germans' attention not only to himself but also to his Jewish stepfather - was that his mother had disappeared the day after the doctor's visit.

Dr Petiot, Lavie told the VS, had come to the apartment because, as he had explained to him, his mother and stepfather, he had thought of an excellent way to get Baudet out of prison rapidly. He would give Marthe a series of distilled water injections into the thigh which would leave marks, and she could tell the VS that she was a drug addict herself and that some of the drugs which had been prescribed for her daughter had been for her. Marthe had refused to be injected, but the doctor had been so persuasive that she had gone into the bedroom with him and he had injected her in the right thigh. The doctor had also given her money with which she was to pay Baudet's lawyer, a *Maître* Pierre Véron; previously, the doctor had recommended the lawyer to Marthe. As soon as Dr Petiot had injected Marthe, she had had second thoughts about having more such distilled water injections, and she had gone to her family doctor to ask about their safety. The latter had told her that a doctor who made such a suggestion could only be a charlatan, an incredible charlatan; she should have nothing more to do with him. He had even told her that she should go to the police. Frightened - her husband was after all a Jew - his mother had not gone to the police. Instead, she had decided to go and have a word with Dr Petiot at his practice. Leaving washing boiling on the stove, she had set off that very evening at seven, telling him and his stepfather that she would be back home soon.

She had not returned home.

The following morning, after having spent an anxious night waiting for her return, they had found three letters from her in their letterbox. Not bearing stamps, the letters had obviously been delivered by hand.

One letter was to his stepfather, one to him, and the third was addressed to *Maître* Véron.

To his stepfather she had written: 'I'm going away until the end of this affair, to the free zone. If anyone asks where I am, say that the affair has made me ill and that I've gone to the countryside to rest. Take the first chance you can and come to me in the free zone; that will avoid any troublesome talk and you won't need to say anything... But come as soon as possible. I will be so alone and terribly bored'.

To him she had written: 'Be kind and look after your sister while I'm gone. I have to go because of her. I kiss you all'.

She had signed the letter to his stepfather, 'Affectionately, your loving wife, Marthe'. The letter to him, she had signed simply, 'Mother'.

Both he and his stepfather thought that they recognised Marthe's handwriting, although the script had appeared uneven.

In Marthe's letter to *Maître* Véron, which he and his stepfather had opened and read, she had repeated that she was fleeing to Vichy-France. She had slipped three one hundred franc notes into the envelope. The money, as she had explained in her letter, was to go towards his fee for defending her daughter.

As Lavie had also told the VS detectives, after having received the letters, his stepfather had gone to have a word with Dr Petiot. The doctor had confirmed to him that Marthe had mentioned fleeing to the free zone, and he had given her the address of a friend of his in the free zone - he had identified the friend only as Gaston - who would be able to help her. Dr Petiot had there and then written a postcard to this Gaston at an address in the town of Loupiac in the southern-central region of Cantal to ask him for news of Marthe; his stepfather was handed the postcard to drop into a pillar box. The doctor had omitted to put a stamp on the postcard; his stepfather had to do so.

Once the VS had been told of Marthe Khaït's disappearance, Judge Olmi had instructed Inspector Gignoux, who was already looking for Van Bever, to start looking for her too. Gignoux believed that Van Bever was dead, having been killed by Dr Petiot to silence him, and he had told the judge that he would not be surprised if Marthe had suffered the same fate for the same reason.

On Wednesday, July 15, 1942, the Baudet case had been heard in Paris. Baudet was found guilty of falsifying a medical prescription to obtain drugs illegally and she was sentenced to four months in prison.

Dr Petiot was also again found guilty of drug trafficking, and again he had been given a one year suspended sentence and fined 10,000 francs. *Maître* Floriot, once more defending him, had, as before, appealed successfully.

Massu, having read the report, asked for Baudet to be picked up and brought to the Quay. He also wanted to speak to David Khaït.

Baudet was nowhere to be found. She had done her time, and, after hanging around some Paris backstreets for a while, she had disappeared, just like her mother.

David Khaît also could not be found; he, too, had disappeared. As Lavie would tell Massu, he thought that the Gestapo, hunting for Jews, had pounced on his stepfather while he was out walking one pleasant warm and sunny afternoon.

* * *

There was something the VS withheld from Massu.

On the Monday after the discovery of the human remains at Dr Petiot's townhouse, *Maître* Véron, tall, athletically-built, handsome and a brilliant lawyer, had burst into Judge Olmi's office. Hammering the judge's desk with a fist, he shouted that he had told him back in 1942 that Dr Marcel Petiot had killed Van Bever and Marthe Khaît in order to stop them from giving evidence against him and that the doctor should be arrested and investigated, but he had been ignored. Olmi had stuttered a reply. He said that he had planned to arrest Dr Petiot, but that the case had been taken away from him. Who had done so and why, he had not said.

Maître Veron, but this Massu also did not know, was in the Resistance. He was holding the rank of Major.

* * *

Nézondet and Lesage were found in Paris at their apartment. The two claimed they had been there all the time; the police should have knocked louder.

The two were taken to the Quay.

The moment Aimée Josephine Lesage sat down in Massu's office, she started to talk. She and Nézondet had been together since 1936; they planned to get married, she said. They were good friends of the Petiots - the doctor, Georgette and Maurice. The two of them - she and Nézondet - often dined with the doctor and Georgette.

They've never been to the townhouse.

"I can confirm my friend Nézondet's story that Maurice Petiot told him that he had seen sixty bodies at the townhouse. Knowing something like that weighed heavily on our consciences, but, believing that Dr Petiot was killing Germans and French collaborators, our burden eased," she

96

said.

They were going to go to the police as soon as the war was over. She was allowed to go home.

* * *

At 10 P.M. Massu had Nézondet brought to his office.

René-Gustave Nézondet was 48 years old. Tall and unruly hair tumbling over his forehead, he looked surprised to find himself at Paris's police headquarters and in the office of the Crim's chief. He had a paralysed left arm; it hung limply at his side.

Earlier, Canitrot, who had unsuccessfully tried to engage him in small-talk, had warned Massu that he was going to be difficult to interrogate. "Boss," he had said, "this fellow is not going to make things easy for you. He's not just going to be short on words; he's going to clam up completely; you won't be able to get a word out of him, or it's going to be 'no' to all your questions."

Massu went to stand behind Nézondet. He was putting in overtime for which there would be no pay, but he was prepared to remain standing there for the rest of the night. After ten minutes of silence, he changed his mind; he felt a sudden pang of hunger.

"Canitrot, I'm going out for a bite to eat," he said.

"*Bon appétit,*" replied Cantirot.

Nézondet, fidgeting with a bunch of keys with his good hand, gave no indication that he had heard that Massu was going out to eat.

The curfew had of course sounded but the commissioner knew that no copper would dare arrest him. Of the Germans he was not so certain, but he was prepared to take the risk.

He went to a bistro on the nearby Boul'Miche. The bistro had already closed, but the owner was still serving drinks and meals to a clientele consisting mainly of police; some were in uniform, their capes hanging over the back of their chairs and their *képis* on the tables.

At 11:30 P.M., all Paris's lights dark, Massu walked back to the Quay. He had had a bowl of soup and a glass of red wine. Nézondet sat with his eyes closed, but looked up when the commissioner walked in; he even smiled at him.

"Now, where were we," said Massu, sitting down behind his desk.

Nézondet cleared his throat and lifted his good arm.

"*Monsieur le Commissaire.* May I speak?" he asked.

"Go ahead," said Massu.

"I want to tell you everything... I mean ... whatever I know."

Massu gave a sigh of relief and gratefully motioned for Nézondet that he was all ears.

Nézondet began with his own story.

He hailed from Migennes, also in Burgundy. At the end of his studies he had moved 31 kilometres north to Villeneuve-sur-Yonne where he started to work as an auctioneer's clerk. Dr Petiot was already practising medicine in the village. The two of them had met when the doctor one day attended an auction. The doctor, he said, loved shopping for bargains. Soon the two of them were firm friends; the fact that both of them were bachelors had bonded them. Later, because he had hurt his arm and could no longer lift heavy objects, essential if one worked for an auctioneer, he had opened a *guinguette* - a small leisure complex - where men fished for trout over the weekends and brought their girlfriends at night to eat, drink and dance. Then, both he and the doctor had taken wives. He was the first to have got married because Dr Petiot had taken a bit longer to tie the knot with Georgette.

"She ... Georgette... Mrs Petiot loves to dance. Marcel... Dr Petiot... is not such a keen dancer, but he came dancing almost every Saturday night for Georgette's sake ... for Mrs Petiot's sake," he explained.

In 1933, the Petiots had moved to Paris. Because his marriage had broken down, there had been no reason for him to stay in Villeneuve-sur-Yonne, so he had followed his friends to the capital. In Paris, he had first worked as the *concierge* at the Paris daily *Le Figaro*, then, because the paper had evacuated to Lyon at the start of the Occupation he had gone to Lyon too. Two years later he had returned to Paris and Dr Petiot had helped him get his current job; he was a travelling salesman with a pharmaceutical company.

This was the 'everything' Nézondet had wanted to tell.

Massu wanted to know more.

"Did you tell your girlfriend and her friend, Marie Turpault, and a certain Roland Albert Porchon, of bodies at Rue le Sueur?"

"Of course not!" snapped Nézondet. "What a laughable story!"

To prove his point, he laughed.

Massu signalled to Canitrot to fetch Porchon, and hardly had the latter walked in, and without him having uttered a word, Nézondet admitted he had, indeed, known of the bodies at the townhouse.

"Maurice Petiot told me, and I then told my girlfriend and Marie, and this one here about the bodies," he said.

He pointed to Porchon.

"When was this?" asked Massu. "When did Maurice Petiot tell you about the bodies?"

"Last December. Maurice was staying at Hotel Alicot. He came to Paris because the *Boches* were holding Marcel... I mean Dr Petiot ... pardon me ... at Fresnes because of the escape route he was supposed to have been running, and for which I, totally innocent, was locked up, too. Maurice was as white as a sheet when we met up. His hands shook. I asked him what was going on. He told me he had seen something terrible at Marcel's house. I thought Marcel must have some guns or a radio transmitter there, but Maurice said to me, 'there is enough in the house to have us all shot'. He told me that the escape route for which Marcel and I had been locked up by the *Boches* had both started and ended at the townhouse. I could see the struggle going on inside him. I told him his brother was my best friend and that, between friends, a secret, no matter how heavy, always remained a secret. This particular secret would remain such, too. Maurice said there were sixty bodies. They were in a pit. They were naked, and their heads had been shaved. I asked him how Marcel had killed those people. Only with great effort could he tell me. He said, 'my brother told me he injected them with poison from a distance'. I can't remember the name of the poison, but I remember Maurice told me Marcel hid the syringe in some rings in a wall. I didn't go to the police; I know I should have, but Marcel was my best friend. I was also thinking of Georgette... I mean, Mrs Petiot ... pardon me ... and young Gerhardt."

"Did Mrs Petiot know what was going on at the townhouse?" asked Massu.

Nézondet nodded.

"A month after Maurice's revelation, while Marcel was still in prison, I had dinner with her. I told her what her brother-in-law had told me. She fainted three times. Aimée was with us, and she told me afterwards she thought Georgette was just acting. Aimée's a nurse. She knows things like that. Afterwards I told Maurice I had told his sister-in-law everything, and he was very angry with me. I then asked him what he was going to do about the bodies, and he replied, 'I'm going to think about it'."

Massu told Nézondet he was under arrest.

"I'm keeping you here in a cell."

"I haven't done anything wrong," protested Nézondet.

"All the same," said the commissioner.

Nézondet was taken down to the basement to a cell.

* * *

Porchon who had been sitting in silence while Nézondet replied to Massu's questions, could not yet return to his cell.

"Maybe you've had time to remember the names of the two inspectors you had told about the bodies?" Massu asked him walking up to him.

Porchon shook his head.

"No such luck, Mr Commissioner. My memory is still playing up."

"I'll make your memory behave itself. I'll tell you who they were. You told Bouygues and Doulet. Inspectors Boygues and Doulet."

Porchon snapped his fingers.

"*Voilà*! Now I remember! Oh, Mr Commissioner, do forgive me my memory loss. I was hallucinating a lot at that time."

He had been under medication, he told Massu.

"It made me hallucinate."

"Medication? Hallucinating?" asked Massu.

Porchon nodded.

The medication had been for a broken ankle.

Massu told Canitrot that he could take Porchon back down to his cell.

* * *

Despite the late hour - in fact, a new day had broken - Massu could not yet go home.

A couple with the surname of Marie - René and Marcelle - wanted to talk to him. They had been waiting since early evening.

"We wanted to flee France," said René Marie the moment the couple walked into Massu's office.

100

A friend had introduced them to a doctor who could help them do so. They had met the doctor at a barbershop that belonged to a certain Raoul Fourrier. The doctor had not introduced himself to them, but, having been told by the barber, they knew that his surname was Eugène. He wanted 90,000 francs from each of them. They had told him they would think it over. A day later they had heard rumours that he was involved with drugs. It had decided them not to take his escape route.

When they had read about the townhouse, René Marie continued, they had wanted to go to the police because they realised that Dr Eugène was none other than Dr Petiot.

However, the friend who had introduced them to Dr Eugène had begged them not to; the friend told them the police would hand all three of them over to the *Boches* and that they would be shot.

"What's your friend's name?" asked Massu.

"Porchon. Roland Albert Porchon," said René Marie.

* * *

Massu, driving home was certain that only one person was responsible for the townhouse's carnage: Dr Marcel Petiot.

He was also certain he could name three of the victims: Joachim Guschinov, Jean-Marc van Bever and Marthe Khaït. How they, and the others, had been killed, he still did not know. A report Dr Paul had sent in earlier in the day had not helped solve the riddle. The CME had reported that, the human remains having been sorted, he had 15 kilograms of badly burnt small bones; 11 kilograms of large bones; ten skulls; three garbage bins of tiny fragments of bones; three kilograms of hair; two full skeletons, and one half of a body at the mortuary.

One of the skeletons was that of a man who had been 1.80 metres tall. The second was that of a 1.3 metres tall woman.

As there were no bullet wounds in the bones, it excluded death by shooting, the killing method favoured by the Germans.

The advanced state of decomposition of the remains had so far made it impossible for him to determine the date of the deaths; so too, how the victims had been killed.

Asphyxiation, strangulation and poisoning were three possibilities.

-0-

CHAPTER EIGHT

Saturday, March 18, 1944

Early in the morning, Prefect Bussière, having kept the Germans informed of the Crim's investigation, received their authorisation to proceed to bring Dr Petiot to justice.

The prefect appointed the examining magistrate whose task it would be to compile a dossier that would be handed to the public prosecutor's office where the decision would be taken as to whether or not there was sufficient evidence to take the case to court.

The examining magistrate he appointed was Judge Jean-Georges Berry, previously from the Palais de Justice in Versailles, where seven years previously he had successfully investigated the German-born kidnapper and killer Eugène Weidmann, the last man to have been publicly guillotined in France.

Leading the Crim's investigation, Judge Berry was to interrogate all of those Massu had already interrogated as well as whoever would still come forward out of their own free will, or, who Massu would order to be brought in.

At the end of each day the judge would inform the Germans of the day's investigation.

He would have no choice in the matter.

Like the police, France's judges too had lost their independence because of the Occupation. In June 1940 at France's capitulation they had been ordered to swear allegiance to Hitler. Only one judge, a Judge Paul Didier, had refused to do so. His punishment was deportation to a German concentration camp where he still was at that time. He would survive the camp and after the war he would return to France.

-0-

PART TWO

CHILD, SOLDIER, DOCTOR AND MAYOR

CHAPTER ONE

Child

Félix Iréné Mustiole and Marthe Marie Constance, born Bourdon, both had a problem with names; he said that Iréné was a woman's name and Mustiole that of a bull, and she hated all of hers so much that she called herself Clémence. Therefore, when their first child - Marcel André Henri Félix - was born at 3A.M. on Sunday, January 17, 1897, at Number 100 Rue de Paris, then, as now, Auxerre's main street, they put little thought into naming him. The name Marcel was after Marcellus, saint of January 16, because the female Rosalina was that of January 17, and the names André and Henri were in honour of his grandfathers. The name Félix the couple added so as not to break with Petiot family tradition to name a firstborn son after his father.

Rue de Paris, the River Yonne flowing gently close by, runs south from a square in the heart of the town's business centre to a vineyard, where, since the seventh century, the Clos de la Chainette wines have been produced. Number 100, a two storey, partially timbered building where his parents rented a modest two-bedroom apartment on the top floor, is today an art school run by the town's council. Beside the building stands the Chapelle des Visitandines - the Chapel of the Order of the Visitation - constructed at the beginning of the seventeenth century for the Sisters of the Visitation of Mary whose convent was nearby at the time of Marcel's birth. Today, the town's history museum permanently displays the artwork of the late French artist, François Brochet, in the chapel; the collection includes the Massacre of the Innocents, a series of twenty carved human figures.

Félix and Clémence met at the local post office where they both worked; he was 29 and she was 21 years old. He was a technician installing telephone exchanges. She sorted the mail. It was a job she would give up when she fell pregnant.

When Marcel was two years old, Félix and Clémence put him in the care of one of his aunts, Henriette Bourdon, Clémence's older sister.

It happened that Félix was promoted to chief technician, which meant that he was to lay telephone lines across the Burgundian countryside, and Clémence, not wishing to be left at home, had decided to go on the road with him but that she would not take their little son with her. The boy would go to Henriette Bourdon.

Henriette, an illiterate spinster, shared her home with another spinster, Marie Gaston, also illiterate, whom she described as her maid.

The two women lived in an old brick house that stood behind a stone wall so high that all that could be seen from the house was the tip of the tower of the town's twelfth century Saint-Etienne cathedral. Devout Christians, the two were often seen dressed in black coats and veiled, walking down the road towards the cathedral to attend an early morning mass, their tiny charge walking unsteadily between them and holding on to the hem of the coat of one of them.

Later, married and the father of a son himself, Marcel, bitter at his parents' desertion of him - that was how he described it - said that he was either born out of wedlock or that he was conceived before the two were legally married. He also said that they had never loved him.

He was equally resentful towards the two spinster women.

He said that as they had never been mothers, they had had no idea how to rear a child. They beat him, he said, and they dragged him from his warm cot on cold and rainy winter mornings to take him to early mass. He said that when he grew too big for the cot they refused to buy him a bed so that he had to sleep with his legs pulled up almost to his neck; he said it gave him a pain in his back.

He also spoke of the high wall that was around the property and that they had kept a metal gate in the wall bolted because they did not welcome casual callers. At first, too short to reach the bolt, he had felt trapped. It had certainly also made him a lonely child because, although he could hear other children playing outside on the street, he could not join them.

* * *

Toddler Marcel was pretty.

On market mornings 'l'Henriette', as the old spinster was called, and Marie took him along when they went shopping and the fishmonger and the baker pinched his cheek and told him to admit that he was a girl and not a boy. However, when the fishmonger's wife gave him a shrimp and the baker's wife gave him a warm croissant, jam dripping from it onto his starched grey Knickerbocker suit, and he smiled at them, his black eyes sparkling, they said that he was, indeed, a boy.

Such sparkling black eyes, they said, would one day break the heart of many a girl.

What Henriette and Marie did not tell the stall keepers and their wives, but which they did report to Félix and Clémence in letters, which a scribe, their priest, had written on their behalf, was that the little boy was not settling down well. He cried often, he threw tantrums when he rolled on the floor or banged his head against a wall, he pulled up the plants in their garden or crushed their flowers, and he hit the two of them and kicked them, pulled their hair as well as bit them.

The two parents when they did reply to the letters always wrote that they were very sorry that their son was not behaving well, but they could not take him back immediately.

Only three years later, Marcel then five years old, did the two spinsters have something flattering to write about him to his parents.

They wrote that his uncle, Félix's brother, a local schoolmaster, had, a few months previously started to teach him to read and write and that he was already reading and writing like a child of ten. Knowing that they, being illiterate, were not best placed to judge reading and writing skills, they pointed out that this was the verdict of both his uncle and their priest. Both men, they wrote, thought that Marcel was a genius and that he would one day become someone really grand. Like a doctor.

As for the genius himself, when he would later so bitterly speak of his birth and childhood, he would say that having been able to read and write was a true blessing; it meant that the two old spinsters finally considered him sufficiently grown-up not to have to sleep in a toddler's cot. They bought him a bed.

In 1908, Félix and Clémence returned to Auxerre and to the apartment on the top floor at Number 100 Rue de Paris. Marcel joined them. He was eleven years old and a pupil at the local school; he had started school at the age of seven as French law required.

As the two parents learnt, their son was top of his class.

For a while Marcel could do not wrong in his parents' eyes, but then the two, having already witnessed their son's misbehaviour when on short visits to Auxerre in the past, became worried when one day they saw him stick a pin into a bird's eyes. When they asked Henriette and Marie if he had ever done such a bad thing before, they were told that he certainly had.

They would also learn from the two spinsters that their son liked to impale worms and insects on knitting needles and that he had killed his own cat. The story they heard was that one morning Henriette had found the cat's lifeless body under the bed in the boy's room. As his hands and arms were covered in scratches he had obviously either smothered or strangled the cat: the animal certainly had not died a natural death as it had not been ill. What was more he had before that tried to drown the cat: he had thrown the cat into a cauldron of hot water in which Henriette was soaking the week's washing. Fortunately, she had walked into the scullery just in time to save the cat's life.

Later, Marcel, reading about the dead cat in Paris newspapers, would vehemently deny that he had had anything to do with the cat's death; indeed, that he had ever taken the life of any living creature.

Still trying to digest such distasteful revelations about their son, Clémence, making Marcel's bed one morning, found that the sheets were soiled. Marcel had wet the bed.

As she and Félix knew several people who had young children who were wetting the bed, they thought that it was part of growing up.

Soon, they saw that his trousers were often wet: he had started to suffer from daytime incontinence.

Clémence took him to their family doctor, but reported back to her husband that the doctor had said that children often wet the bed and that all grew out of it.

This child, however, did not, and the daytime incontinence developed into incontinence of both the bladder and the bowel.

When he started coming home from school in tears because he had had an 'accident' in the classroom, Clémence took him back to the family doctor.

She also then discussed with the doctor her son's cruelty towards small animals, but she was again reassured by what the doctor told her; little boys were often cruel to their pet cats and dogs and it was nothing to become alarmed about. Of the double incontinence the doctor repeated what he had already told her about bedwetting; children grew out of such things.

Marcel continued to walk around with soiled clothes and his parents, trusting their doctor, ignored it.

They had something else on their minds anyway.

Clémence was pregnant. It was 1909, and she was 33 years old and Félix was 41, and 12 years had gone by since Marcel's birth.

Given no explanation as to his mother's expanding waistline, Marcel was sent back to Henriette and Marie's house to spend the final months of the pregnancy with the two spinsters.

On his return to the Rue de Paris apartment, he was again given no explanation for the presence of a baby. Neither did he want one because immediately he loved the little thing; a boy named Maurice. He would also later say that seeing his little brother for the first time, he had been unable to take his eyes off him. He would also say that until Maurice's birth, he had not loved anyone, and until he had met Georgette, his wife, the only other human being whom he had loved, was his brother.

Both loves would be reciprocated.

* * *

In 1910, the Post Office again promoted Félix. He became a site inspector, and he was to be transferred to the town of Joigny, 26 kilometres away. Maurice would be going along, but not Marcel. He, when he heard that he was to return to Henriette and Marie, refused to be separated from his little brother. He clung to Maurice and both children screamed at the top of their voices; Marcel in anger and Maurice, not understanding what was going on, in fear.

In Joigny, Félix's promotion allowed the Petiots to rent a comfortable house in the centre of the town. Marcel joined them during school holidays when Henriette and Marie would put him on a train. By then his double incontinence had stopped. It had stopped without treatment as the family doctor had said it would. He also no longer wet the bed. He still had bouts of aggressiveness when he would argue loudly with his classmates, but his teachers never intervened; they thought that a brilliant scholar - he was still top of the class - was intolerant of classmates who were not quick learners, and should not be reprimanded.

In 1911, the family said farewell to Joigny. Félix was transferred back to Auxerre. Marcel prepared to return home, but heard that he was to remain with Henriette and Marie. Again, he protested vigorously, but Clémence was not well - it was said that her 'nerves were bad' - and he was told that he should shut up because he was not to return home and that was final.

A year later Clémence passed away. She had been receiving treatment in a Paris hospital for her 'bad nerves' and had, as Marcel would claim in adult life, 'just faded away'. She was 36 years old and Félix was forty-four. He, unable to cope with his loss, sent Maurice to join Marcel at Henriette's house. Marcel was 15 years old and Maurice was three. The two spinsters, already having brought up Marcel, had little courage to raise yet another child, so Marcel announced that he would look after his little brother. In the morning, before he left for school, he bathed, clothed and fed Maurice. In the afternoon, after school, he played with him and, remembering how he had been taught to read and write by his uncle when he was little older than Maurice, tried to teach the toddler to read and write, albeit failing totally. The younger was perhaps too young still, or he might not have had the elder's intelligence.

Maurice would remain an academic failure.

* * *

Two years passed. The grieving Félix, having returned to Joigny, let Henriette and Marie know that he was to return to Auxerre and that he would not be setting off again. He thought that his two sons should return to live with him.

Once back home, Marcel's behaviour began to deteriorated yet again. He either incessantly argued with everyone or he would fall silent for days when he would even ignore Maurice. He also played truant from school when the headmaster would summon Félix to warn him that his son would be expelled should the truancy continue. Félix' response was to belt Marcel.

One day Félix was summoned to the school yet again. The headmaster told him that his son had fired a bullet into his classroom's ceiling. The noise of the shot had caused commotion throughout the school with frightened children and equally frightened teachers running out on to the playground. Would he know how the boy had got hold of a pistol the headmaster asked Félix. The latter knew. He was a firearms collector and Marcel had stolen a pistol from his collection. A few days later, having a drink with his friends in a bistro he admitted that he found his son firing off a pistol in the classroom rather funny. Marcel only wanted to brighten a boring lesson on colonial Africa, he said.

The headmaster, not finding the shooting incident amusing, informed Félix that he had no choice but to expel Marcel. On reflection, however, he decided to give Marcel a second chance: despite the boy's bad behaviour, he was a brilliant scholar and he should take that into consideration.

In February 1914, aged 17 and his mother dead for just under two years, Marcel collided with the law. The townspeople had been reporting to the post office's sorting office that letters they had posted had not arrived and the sorting clerks - once they had been Clémence's colleagues - had no recollection of having handled them. It was obvious that there was a thief in town. There was and he was caught red-handed; it was Marcel. He was on Rue de Paris pushing what looked like a short fishing rod into one of the post office's pillar boxes when a policeman walked up. The fishing rod was a stick with glue at one end. He was taken to the police station and Félix was sent for. The latter on hearing that his son was the town's letter thief dropped his head into his hands; he wondered what he was going to tell his late wife's colleagues from the sorting office. The police thought that Marcel had been looking for money or money orders to cash, or perhaps for embarrassing information with which he could blackmail the senders or the intended recipients.

As French law required - this is still so today - that a minor facing a criminal charge should be mentally assessed, a child psychologist was to speak to Marcel. Should the psychologist find him fit to stand trial, he would appear in front of a court for juveniles to face a charge of theft and damaging public property, and if found guilty he would be sent to borstal until he turned eighteen. Not waiting for the court's decision and finding no reason for clemency, the headmaster of his school immediately expelled him. The expulsion was not to be a problem; Félix's brother began tutoring his nephew at home.

On Thursday, March 26, Marcel, neatly dressed and his nails clean and his hair cut and oiled back from his face, and accompanied by Félix, who was equally dignified in dress and look, appeared before a judge for a preliminary hearing.

The child psychologist had already handed in his diagnosis; after having had a conversation with Marcel, he had come to the conclusion that the 17-year-old suffered from mental problems. He described those as hereditary. Félix, when he heard this, exploded. There was no insanity in the Petiot family and neither was there in that of the Bourdons he shouted at the psychologist and the judge. He demanded a second opinion.

Two months later, on Wednesday, May 6, father and son were back in court. A second psychologist had confirmed his colleague's diagnosis. Félix requested yet another assessment and again the judge capitulated.

In court, on Friday, August 14, six months after the commencement of the case, a third child psychologist confirmed his two colleagues' diagnosis. Before Félix could protest again, the judge gave his verdict. Marcel would not have to go to borstal, but he would have to receive treatment for his mental problems; he need not be institutionalised, but could receive his treatment as an outpatient. Félix was to choose the institution. He did no such thing. Secretly, while his brother had been tutoring Marcel at home, he had been looking for a school to send him to and he had found one in the town of Dijon. Marcel had only one year of study left before he could sit for his *baccalauréat* school-leaving examination. Usually, a *bachelier* was 19 years old. Such a feat had impressed the headmaster.

Father and son set off by train for Dijon. The town, at 150 kilometres from Auxerre, the school would be close enough for Félix to be able to keep an eye on his son while far enough not to have him under his feet all the time.

It is not known what reason Félix had given the Dijon headmaster for Marcel's expulsion from the Auxerre school, but, within two months, he was back at the Auxerre railway station and waiting for the Dijon train to steam in. Marcel had again been expelled. As the headmaster had told Félix in a phone conversation, his son had been caught passing pornographic sketches and postcards around his classroom and that he had also made 'indecent proposals' to the boys in his dormitory.

Back in Auxerre, Marcel returned to Henriette and Marie's house. His father had turned his back on him.

On Saturday, July 10, 1915, Marcel received his *baccalauréat* diploma with a mention of honours.

He had again studied at home, Félix's brother his tutor.

* * *

Marcel told his uncle that he wanted to become a doctor; in the autumn he would be enrolling at the medical faculty in Paris. Félix was told of that by his brother, and laughed. He believed that Marcel would never amount to anything in life. Or, if he did make his mark on the world, it would be for some no-good deed.

Marcel did not enroll at the Paris Faculty of Medicine. He decided that a medical career could wait. The Great War was raging and he was torn by an intense anger at the Germans for making war against his motherland. He was 18 years old and eligible for the draft. He wanted to go and kill the filthy *Boches*.

-0-

CHAPTER TWO

Soldier

Marcel waited impatiently to be mobilised. He spent the long summer days of that year of 1915 in Henriette and Marie's garden, his nose buried in a book. During the few months at boarding school in Dijon, he had become an avid reader and he had returned to Auxerre with a suitcase full of books. The suitcase he kept padlocked and under his bed; he had become interested in some very controversial people and he did not want the two spinsters to see the books' covers. He was especially interested in sexually uninhibited people. People like Don Juan; Casanova; the Marquis de Sade and the eighteenth century French nobleman, spy, fighter of duels and transvestite, Charles Genevieve Louis August André Thimothé also known as the Chevalier d'Eon to whom we owe the medical term for transvestism - eonism. He had also become interested in *Mademoiselle* de Maupin, the woman who had financed the Cusco Pavilion in Hotel Dieu Hospital where Commissioner Massu would one day take Georgette Petiot. Murderers fascinated him also. Two especially did so; Jack the Ripper and Joseph Vascher, Jack's French counterpart, guillotined in the last part of the nineteenth century for the slaughter of four teenage boys, six teenage girls and an old woman. Vascher had subjected his victims to the most depraved sexual assaults before suffocating them. After their deaths he had disembowelled them.

For six months Marcel read and waited for his call-up papers. Finally, tired of waiting, he enlisted. On Tuesday, January 11, 1916, six days short of his nineteenth birthday, he reported for duty at the army training camp in the town of Sens, 58 kilometres north of Auxerre and 116 kilometres south-east of Paris. In those later years when he spoke about his childhood, he would also make sure that everyone knew that he had volunteered and that he had not waited to be mobilised like some

117

coward. His enlistment number was '1097', he said. Believing it would advance his chances of getting into medical faculty later, he had requested to be inducted to a medical corps. Ten months later, on Tuesday, November 16, fully trained, he heard that he was to be an ordinary soldier of the trenches. He joined the 89th Infantry Regiment, also based in Sens.

In April 1917, on Monday 16, fifteen months in the army, Private Petiot saw his first great battle. He marched with his regiment to liberate the *Chemin des Dames* - the Ladies' Road - that was being held by the Germans. The road, twenty kilometres long and running along a rugged ridge between the rivers Aisne and Ailette, had been held by the Germans since the outbreak of war in 1914. He was one of a million *Poilus* - Bearded Ones - to go into battle under the command of General Charles Mangin. His regiment focussed on the Germans entrenched around the town of Craonne. On the first day of the offensive, the Nivelle Offensive, named after General Robert Nivelle, Commander of the French army, 40,000 Bearded Ones were killed or wounded. The final casualty figure stood at one hundred and eighty-seven thousand. Another 350 Allied soldiers were also listed as casualties. Craonne was destroyed.

Marcel was a casualty too.

The story that he would tell was that he had taken a direct hit in his left foot from a German shell. He said that wounded and in great pain he was carried by stretcher to a field hospital where his wound - it was ten centimetres in diameter - was dressed. He was given a strong sedative that plunged him into a deep sleep. When he awoke several hours later, he thought that he had died because all he could see were tombstones; the wounded had been evacuated to a nearby cemetery. At nightfall, still in great pain, he was moved to a church. He spent the night on its floor. The following morning he was transported to a hospital in the town of Orléans, 295 kilometres south.

He gave the date on which he was wounded: Sunday, May 20, 1917. The Nivelle Offensive had ended on Wednesday, May 9, 1917.

No one noticed the discrepancy.

* * *

In the hospital in Orléons, Marcel lay in a large ward lined with beds on which lay other war wounded. All were young men. Some were blind. Others had lost limbs or were covered in bandages from which seeped blood and pus. Compared to such suffering his wound seemed trivial to all, but him. It healed and he was told that he was to return to his regiment. He told the nurses that he could not wait to get back to the front. A few hours later he called a nurse to his bed. He told her that he had a fierce headache and violent pains in his chest. He was told he would not after all be able to rejoin his regiment. He seemed heartbroken at the news.

In the days that followed, nurses reported to the doctors that Private Petiot was not well. They said they had noticed that he jumped at sudden noise, fainted often, had violent and unprovoked outbursts and that he slipped easily from a state of euphoria into one of inertia when he lay on his bed, rubbing his hands together. The doctors diagnosed war neurosis - shell shock - and gas poisoning; the patient would have to be transferred to another medical institution.

Marcel, told what medical institution the doctors had in mind, flew into a rage. He was to be transferred to the town's mental asylum. He calmed down only when the doctors explained that no one thought he was mad, but that it was routine procedure to institutionalise shell shock victims.

* * *

Marcel settled down well in the asylum. He spoke politely to the doctors and the nurses. Soon, he helped the latter care for the other patients, all soldiers suffering from shell shock. Many a night he spent at the bedside of a soldier because he had heard him cry out in fear or pain; he would remain sitting there until daybreak.

Seemingly the fittest among the patients, he was given permission to venture out for walks in the town, the only patient allowed to do so.

One day he was told that there was no reason for him to remain at the asylum; he could return to his regiment. Yet, again, he spoke of how happy he was to return to active service. But, yet again, he had a relapse. His headaches and chest pains had returned. When told that his return to his regiment was delayed, he could hardly hide his disappointment; he lay on his bed staring up at the ceiling and ignored all the nurses' efforts to get him up and to eat.

At that time, one of the town's shopkeepers reported to the military police that a young man - he thought he was a soldier - had tried to sell him some army-issue blankets; the asylum used such blankets. The shopkeeper described the soldier: dark hair, dark eyes, very pale and very thin and obviously of a nervous nature because he was always rubbing his hands together. The military police asked the nurses to verify if they had lost blankets. Yes, there were blankets missing from their storeroom.

Next, patients began to report that someone was stealing from their bedside lockers. Not valuable items, but small personal things like letters and photographs.

Only one soldier was not reporting the theft of his possessions. This was Private Petiot, and, he was indifferent to the distress of the thief's victims. Could the thief possibly be him, the nurses wondered? After all, he was the only patient who ever went into town.

The asylum's administrators summoned the military police to investigate the thefts.

That night Marcel slept in the local military lock-up; the military police had no doubt that he was not only the locker thief, but also the blanket thief.

* * *

Again, Marcel settled down well. He was courteous to the guards and good company to his fellow inmates. Many of them were deserters who had wanted to get back home and he sympathised with their plight. He said he understood homesickness. He tried to cheer them up with a joke. Those were a little off-colour, but that made him even more popular.

Unbeknown to him his behaviour was being monitored and one day he was told that the army had decided that he would not be court-martialled. He would be committed to a mental asylum. He was told to pack his belongings as he was to be taken to the mental asylum in the town of Fleury-les-Aubrais, five kilometres north. Arriving at the asylum he shouted to the staff that he was not mad. The military psychiatrists who examined him did not agree; they reported to the army that he suffered from depression, melancholia, mental disequilibrium, obsessions, phobias and neurasthenia. Neurasthenia was described by Sigmund Freud

120

as a fundamental disorder in mental functioning with symptoms of excitability, hypochondria, lack of concentration and anxiety.

However, Marcel was treatable with tranquilisers, said the psychiatrists.

After a month of swallowing several pills daily he was on a train on his way to the spa town of Bagnères, 820 kilometres south-east in the Upper-Pyrenees region of France for a rest. He would have to stay for a month after which the army would decide what to do with him. An army orderly escorted him on the train journey and found him relaxed and charming. So did the staff at the sanatorium.

In Auxerre, Félix one day received a very friendly letter. It was from Marcel and it bore a Bagnères postmark. He read that his elder son was returning to Auxerre for a holiday after having successfully received treatment for shell shock. Considering shell shock an honourable ailment - it did after all mean that the young man had battled against the enemy - he told everyone that his son, the wounded hero, was returning home.

Marcel was to return to Auxerre by train. He was in the blue uniform of a Bearded One. He had eaten well at the sanatorium and had put on weight and having gone on almost daily walks in the hills at the foot of the Pyrenees, his face was tanned. At Dijon railway station, alighting to change trains, his legs gave way underneath him and he sank down to the ground. When the Auxerre-bound train steamed out, he was not on it. He was in an ambulance heading for the local military infirmary; the station master had summoned military paramedics. Regaining consciousness on his arrival at the infirmary he started to rant and rave about not being insane. Again, the staff thought otherwise. He remained at the infirmary until the army found an asylum that would accept him. It was in the town of Évreux in the Upper Normandy region.

It was June 1917 and he was 21 years old.

In the letter that he had written Félix, he had referred to the Rue de Paris apartment as home. Never before had he done so, and never again would he do so.

* * *

In the Évreux asylum the familiar scenario unfolded.

Marcel calmed down.

Soon, he was announced recovered.

He was told that he would be inducted into the military police while the army looked for a regiment that would accept him. His own wanted nothing more to do with him. He joined a military police unit in the town of Romainville, ten kilometres north of Paris. He stayed there for a few weeks until the 91st Infantry Regiment based in Charleville in the Ardennes Forest agreed to accept him; the second Battle of the Marne was raging and the Germans were almost at the gates of Paris. Every available man, even one with a history of mental illness, was needed.

He was to be a machine gunner.

Soon, he was feeling unwell yet again.

He complained to his commanding officers of headaches. He said the pain was so intense that he could not breathe and that he feared that he would have another convulsion because of the agony.

At first, Marcel was ignored, but, when he started to suffer mood swings, the army had another team of psychiatrists examine him. They diagnosed him as suffering from paranoia, amnesia, epilepsy and somnambulism. They also confirmed the diagnosis of neurasthenia that their colleagues who had examined him in the Fleury-les-Aubrais asylum had diagnosed.

He was declared insane.

It was March 1919, and the war had been over since the eleventh hour of the eleventh day of the eleventh month of the previous year, and Marcel, having been put on sick leave, could not be told that the army considered him a lunatic because he was nowhere to be found. He had disappeared into the ecstatic bustle of post-war Paris.

In Marcel's absence the *Commission de Réforme*, the military board that decided pensions and discharges, went ahead and assessed him as forty per cent mentally disabled.

He was to be discharged with a disability pension.

On Friday, July 4, 1919, his military career, which had begun 42 months earlier, officially ended. For most of those months, he had been either in hospital or in a mental asylum.

And, there had been the two weeks in a military jail.

* * *

Early in 1920, Marcel resurfaced.

He admitted himself to the asylum in Orléans where he had been a patient in 1917.

While there, the *Commission de Réforme* revised his case and increased his mental disability to one hundred per cent. He was described as depressive, hyper-emotive and melancholic with suicidal tendencies, which made him incapable of any physical or intellectual work. He needed permanent surveillance.

After a few days at the asylum he discharged himself despite the objections of the doctors.

Asked by them where he would be going, he replied that he was returning to Auxerre by train.

Reaching Paris, he descended and disappeared.

In order to have revised Marcel's case the *Commission de Réforme* had contacted Henriette Bourdin to ask her about his childhood. She had described him as having been a strange, though extremely intelligent, child. She said that he had told lies in order to make himself appear important, that he had been restless, that he had had a problem sleeping, and that he had suffered from a weak bladder and bowel until into his teens.

She had not mentioned the impaling of insects and worms and that he had killed his cat.

* * *

The year 1920 ended, and so did 1921.

Early in 1922, someone banged at Henriette and Marie's locked gate.

It was Marcel, a small suitcase on the ground beside him. He was, he said, back in Auxerre for good.

He had quite a story to tell.

He told the two spinsters that he had been studying medicine in Paris.

He was no longer just plain Marcel André Henri Félix Petiot, but Dr Marcel André Henri Félix Petiot.

He also told his uncle about his medical studies. He showed the man a letter dated December 15, 1921. It bore the emblem of Paris's *Faculté de Médecine*. The letter stated that he had passed his final medical thesis and that he had passed it with honours. The thesis was on Landry's Disease, also known as Guillain-Barre Syndrome, GBS, or polyneuritis, a nerve degenerating illness. He said that he had prepared and submitted the thesis while serving his internship in the Évreux mental asylum. It was in the Évreux mental asylum where he had been institutionalised - in French, *interné* - in 1918. Was he amusing himself by playing with the two nouns *interne* and *interné* – internee or house doctor - or the verb *interner* - to intern? Only he knew.

He also showed his uncle a copy of his forty-page thesis. He had dedicated it to *mes parents et mes amis* - my parents and my friends. Also to a Prof Rénon of the Paris Medical Faculty, the Doctors P. Daday and Bessières, and to 'all the doctors of Dijon Hospital and Évreux Mental Asylum'. Dr Daday he described as *directeur médicine chef* - director and head doctor. Dr Bessières - there was no initial for his first name, just as there also was not one for Prof Rénon - was described as *médecin adjoint* - assistant doctor. He did not stipulate at which hospital or hospitals the two practised or had practised. The thesis had been printed in Paris in 1921 at Number 26 Rue Monsieur-le-Prince in the sixth *arrondissement*. The printer was a man named Henry Ollier.

After the discovery of the human remains at the townhouse, Crim investigators wondered how Marcel could have studied medicine having been in mental asylums for most of the years from 1915 to 1921. In 1919, he was still in the army. In 1920, he was a patient in Orléans' mental asylum. Yet, in December 1921, he was a medical graduate. Even if he had benefited from the shortened and accelerated study programs made available to ex-servicemen, it would still have been hard, if not impossible, for him or anyone else to have obtained a medical degree in just two years.

The inspectors failed to solve the mystery, but, in 1944, Bessières, then a professor and head of Sainte-Anne Neurological Hospital in Paris, told the daily *Matin* that he remembered Marcel. He said that, in the early 1920s, when he was based at Évreux Mental Asylum, Marcel had come to work at the asylum. He said Marcel, who had told the staff that he was waiting to commence his medical studies, had worked at the asylum as an orderly. He described the work Marcel had done as of a *parfaite banalité* - a total banality. Marcel himself he described as *un fantasque, un exalté, très certainement déséquilibré mais par contre, un être extrêmement intelligent* - a weirdo, hot headed, very certainly unbalanced, but, on the other hand, extremely intelligent.

Marcel had not stayed in the job long.

* * *

Returning to Auxerre as Dr Marcel André Henri Félix Petiot there was one little thing Marcel decided that he had to do before he could start practising medicine. He appealed to the *Commission de Réforme* to reclassify his one hundred per cent mental disability status. He did not ask for it to be cancelled; only reduced. His argument was that he had faked his mental illness and that he had learnt to do so as a medical student. That his sojourns in mental asylums had preceded his so-called medical studies was another discrepancy. Again, no one had noticed.

On Friday, March 31, 1922, the commission complied; it reduced Marcel's mental disability to fifty per cent. It based its decision on a report a psychiatrist, Dr Jules Lévy-Valensin, had submitted. He had described Marcel as suffering from a pronounced depression with melancholy, inertia, hyper-emotionalism, memory loss and crying bouts and added that he suffered from epileptic seizures which had badly scarred his tongue because of biting it during seizures. Marcel was happy that his mental disability had been reduced, but he was not happy to learn that it meant that his pension would consequently be reduced as well.

On Wednesday, July 18, 1923, more than a year later, he underwent yet another mental assessment. That time, the psychiatrists, all appointed by the army, added *dementia praecox* - premature senility - fatigue, lack of interest in life, indifference to the future, inactivity, and coveting solitude to Dr Lévy-Valensin's diagnosis.

Marcel was already working as a doctor in a practice of his own, yet for the rest of his life he would remain fifty per cent mentally disabled and continue to draw his disability pension.

-0-

CHAPTER THREE

Doctor

Dr Marcel André Henri Félix Petiot, or, *Monsieur le docteur* as protocol demanded that he should be addressed, was welcomed back into the family fold. He was 26 years old and the incontinent boy who stole letters from pillar boxes and killed his cat had been transformed into a handsome young doctor with no antisocial behaviour. He did not drink and neither did he smoke.

He had been away for six years.

Félix wanted Marcel to live with him and Maurice. The latter was 13 years old and he loved his sibling as much as ever. Henriette and Marie also wanted Marcel to live with them and it was to their house that he returned. He moved back into his old room. The two spinsters had kept the room as he had left it. Even the padlocked suitcase filled with books was still under the bed.

Marcel planned to open a practice in town. He was penniless, but he planned to ask either Félix or Henriette for a loan. He approached Henriette first, but when the moment came for him to ask her he was too proud to do so. Instead, he telephoned Félix and he said he wanted to discuss something with him.

He was invited for dinner.

Félix Petiot's dinner began with compliments; father and returning son complimenting one another about everything. Marcel said that he liked the way Félix had laid the table and his upkeep of the apartment. Félix said that he liked Marcel's bow tie - the latter had started to wear bow ties - and that he liked his shoes and wanted to know whether he had bought them in Paris perhaps.

Marcel began a long monologue, speaking only about himself. He talked about his life as a Bearded One. He described trench warfare and soldiers' wounds and what shell shock was like. He told of how he had been wounded and he removed his shoe and sock to show off the scar. He said that once his wound had healed he had worked as an orderly in the hospital. The experience he had thus gained, he said, had made earning a degree a mere formality. He said that he wanted to practise in town and in the morning he would start looking for one he could join as partner.

Félix and Maurice listened.

Marcel saw that his brother's eyes were glistening with excitement and his father's with tears.

He thought that the moment was excellent to broach the subject of a loan, but a few minutes later, he was at the door letting himself out. The dinner had come to an end.

When he would later speak of his birth and childhood he would also speak of that night.

He would say that he had not asked his father for a loan after all. He would say that his father had made the words stick in his throat; Félix had told his son how proud he was of him and how proud his mother would have been and how he was hoping that she could be at the table with them because he would be able to tell her that they had brought a brilliant child into the world. "It was all about him, all about him," he would say.

The following morning, Marcel started to look for a village in which he could open a practice. During the night he had decided that he was not to remain in Auxerre. The village where he wanted to practise had to be in the vicinity because he did not want to be far from his brother. As for his father; he did not mind if he never set eyes on him again.

Marcel found the village he was looking for.

It was Villeneuve-sur-Yonne - Villeneuve on the Yonne River - 43 kilometres from Auxerre. It was home to two thousand souls, the Villeneuviennes and Villeneuviens, who lived in centuries-old stonehouses and still preferred the horse-drawn fiacre to the motorcar. There were two doctors - Dr Eugène Durand and Dr Robert Devoir - in the village, but they were elderly and the villagers needed a young doctor. Or so Marcel believed.

He was, as he also believed, that young doctor.

* * *

128

Marcel rented a small furnished cottage in the village. The cottage consisted of a living room and two small bedrooms, and its owners, a Monsieur and Madame Mongin, who had moved to another town, gave him a year's lease. Pleased to have a doctor as their tenant, they charged him a minimal rent.

On the day that Marcel moved in, all that he had to his name he carried over the threshold in three suitcases. One suitcase was the one of his childhood which was filled with books. Into the second suitcase, he had packed his clothes. In the third were a few medical instruments that he had bought second-hand in Paris.

He unpacked the clothes, the books and set the medical instruments out on a desk.

Dr Marcel Petiot was ready to start practising medicine.

But, oh no, not quite yet.

He was going to advertise his arrival.

He did so by distributing leaflets he had had printed in Auxerre. He had carefully chosen the wording: 'Dr Petiot is young, and only a young doctor can keep up with the latest methods born of a progress that marches with giant strides. This is why intelligent patients have confidence in him. Dr Petiot treats without exploiting his patients. His telephone number is 24'.

He delivered the leaflets himself on an old bike which he had brought along from Auxerre. He dropped a leaflet into each letter box and letter slot in the village, and he sped off across the countryside to leave leaflets at the farms.

The leaflet served its purpose.

On the day he opened his practice, his receptionist, an old woman who was also to clean and cook for him, ran between the front door to let patients in and the telephone on the wall in the kitchen to take appointments.

The Drs Durand and Devoir watched as their patients walked by and in the direction of the new doctor's cottage. The two were unable to do anything about it.

In 1923, the *Conseil National de l'Ordre des Médecins* - the Medical Council - which would discipline a doctor who advertised his skills today in France, did not yet exist. It would be founded only in 1944.

* * *

Monsieur le docteur Petiot was immediately successful.

The villagers when looking in at the village bistro after their consultations with Marcel, told of how he had known what was wrong with them even before they had opened their mouths to greet him.

They said that the moment they had sat down in front of him, he had said to them, "You were treated by stupid asses before, but you don't have to say another word, as I know exactly what is ailing you."

All would soon report that he had cured them.

They also spoke of what a generous doctor he was. The financially-needy ones said that he would not take their money and young mothers said that he did not charge for vaccinating their children. The elderly and old said that he prescribed them large amounts of medication to save them the inconvenience of having to call in every week or fortnight. And they said that they did not have to beg him for things like sleeping pills; he offered them without even having to be asked.

It was not only with money and medication that Marcel was generous. He was so too with his time. His practice was open seven days a week and he did home calls even if called out in the middle of the night. He also never rushed them through a consultation and would even prolong one by chatting away himself; he asked about their children, grandchildren, their siblings and about their problems, even their financial problems. He wanted to know whether they might have a large amount of money or perhaps some gold bullion hidden somewhere at home. If they told him that they did, he advised against such imprudence. "Put your money in the post office," he would say.

Petiot's landlords did not agree with his admiring patients.

The couple had the habit of calling in on their tenant unannounced and so, as they said, they got to know him well, in any case better than someone who would have spent only a few minutes in his company on a consultation.

They told friends that he was mean and demanding; he complained about the rent although they were charging him very little and he wanted them to replace the furniture.

They also complained that he was not looking after the property; the garden was untended, weeds having overrun the neat rows of rose bushes Mrs Mongin had spent so much time on, and dirty crockery, cutlery, pots and pans were piled up in the kitchen, and the sink was often blocked.

The two also described Marcel as argumentative and opinionated: whenever they tried to discuss anything with him, he would dismiss what they said as baloney.

After a while, others in the village, among them some of Petiot's patients, began to agree with the Mongins. Stopping for a drink at the bistro, they and its owner, a man named Léon Fiscot, but who was affectionately called Frascot - he, suffering from rheumatoid arthritis, had become one of Marcel's patients - discussed *Monsieur le docteur*.

They spoke of how they always offered him a drink, but that he never reciprocated. They agreed that he fortunately only ever wanted a *petit noir* - a small black coffee - the cheapest beverage in the bistro.

They spoke of how they disliked the way he would argue his viewpoint until not only they, but he too, had lost track of what he was saying and how he would then storm out from the bistro to return a few minutes later with a contemptuous smile on his lips, and to continue where he had left off.

They accused him of kleptomania. They said he stole from them when on house calls. Never something large, but small things like an ornament, ashtray or a book; books he found particularly difficult to ignore.

They said that he was unsociable. He never showed up at a meeting at the town hall to discuss village affairs; he never looked in when there was a party or a fête; he never attended mass. He was so unsociable, they said, that he seemed to wait until night had fallen before he would venture out. They saw him rush by their windows either on foot or on his bike late at night, a coat over his pyjamas and a fedora pulled low over his face. He always headed for the river and there he would sit in the dark. He never switched on the bike's headlight and when it rained he did not shelter under an umbrella.

After ten months the Mongins could bear Marcel no longer and sent him a letter to terminate their contract with him. He was to leave their property when his lease expired.

Furious, he fired back a reply. He was not going to move and he challenged the couple to try to make him, a Great War wounded hero, move.

The couple rose to the occasion.

On the day that the lease expired, they arrived at the cottage to see him off. The village bailiff, Henri Guttin, was with them.

Patiently, the three waited until the last patient had left and then they said that they wished to make an inventory of the furniture.

In stony silence, Marcel followed the three through the cottage.

The Mongins said that several items of furniture were missing. Guttin jotted the missing items down in an exercise book. Mrs Mongin was especially upset at the absence of a wood-burning kitchen stove, which she said was a valuable antique. They found Marcel's explanation of what had happened to the stove incomprehensible.

Mr Mongin, wishing to be rid of such a bizarre and unlikeable tenant, there and then instructed Bailiff Guttin to evict Marcel. Guttin said that he regretted but that he could not do that because in keeping with French law a tenant had to be given seven days to vacate the property before eviction could take place.

Marcel responded with a volley of verbal abuse that was not aimed just at the Mongins, but also at the bailiff.

The next morning, he moved. He turned up at Bailiff Guttin's office and threw the key to the cottage on the man's desk.

"*Voilà! La clef!*" he shouted.

Here it is! The key!

Not only had Marcel found another place to live, but he had bought it, and the transactions had been finalised soon after he had received the Mongins' original letter that they were terminating his lease. He had become the proprietor of a *maison de maître* - the house of a country squire.

The house at Number 56 Rue Carnot, the village's main street, was three storeys high. On the ground floor one stepped into a lobby from which led Marcel's waiting and consulting rooms. On the first floor, standing on a wrought iron balcony, one could see the twin medieval watchtowers, the towers of Joigny and Sens, that book-ended the street. One could also see the town hall, a two-storey, whitewashed corner building with numerous windows behind white shutters. So too could one see the village's Notre Dame de L'Assomption church, its façade blackened over the eight centuries of its existence. Being able to see the church would, later in life, have Marcel complain that wherever he had lived he had been inconvenienced by the sight of a holy place. In Auxerre it was the Order of the Visitation chapel and the Saint-Etienne Cathedral both near to his aunt's house; in Paris, the Saint-Louis d'Antin church, and in Villeneuve-sur-Yonne, that Notre Dame de L'Assomption church.

The house that he bought was not in all that good a condition. Some villagers would even have described it as shabby. It had belonged to a Brigadier-General Pierre Charles Robillard. The latter, deceased, had bequeathed it to the town with the understanding that his wife, Mathilde Françoise Marguerite Gabrielle Robillard, born Lucie, would be allowed to live in the property rent-free for the rest of her life after his death. Two years previously, she had passed away and the house had remained uninhabited while the town hall had decided what to do with it. The decision had been taken to sell it and Marcel had turned up just at that time. How much he had paid for the property is unknown. In 1944 the Crim failed to find a record of the sale transaction in the town hall's records and a title deed in the name of Georgette Petiot found with the Petiots' private papers in the family's Rue de Caumartin apartment also did not mention the price. She was to renounce all rights to it, and the house would stand abandoned for five years before the state seized it. It was put back on the market.

* * *

Marcel made a friend.

In search of furniture for his large four bedroom house - he had bought the property furnished, but he did not like what the Robillards had left behind - he had started to go to countryside auctions and, at one such auction he had struck up a conversation with the auctioneer's clerk, Gustave-Réne Nézondet.

In 1950, Nézondet, would, like Commissioner Massu, write a book about Marcel, 'Petiot: Le Possédé' - Petiot: The Possessed. He wrote about how they had met. 'Petiot and I were single, and that is all that chance needed for us to meet and become friends. Introspection is not my strong point, and I have never really tried to understand the attraction that this man exerted over me. Petiot seemed to charm the people who came close to him. I could never really figure out the reasons for this unspoken attraction that drew me towards him almost in spite of myself - and against all reason, which would have told me to keep out of his way. In the beginning there was perhaps a kind of curiosity. Very quickly and almost against my will, I started living in his wake. For a long time, I expected that he could and would do anything. When I met him, I did not know that he had had mental problems in the past. As he was different from other people anyway, it didn't seem strange that he had no close friends'.

At least two evenings a week Marcel would go to the bistro where Nézondet waited. The latter always drank wine; Marcel only black coffee. Nézondet invariably paid.

On a Saturday night the two would drive to nearby towns for a bite to eat.

Again Nézondet paid, but it was in Marcel's car that they drove. He had bought a yellow convertible Renault 40CV and on the day that he had driven down Rue Carnot for the first time to park the car on the pavement outside his house, all the neighbours had stepped out to watch.

Not only was the Renault the latest model on the market, but a car was a rare sight in that village of horse-drawn fiacres.

Nézondet was interested in village affairs and he encouraged his new friend to attend with him when the villagers organised a next meeting. Petiot agreed and soon he was telling all who would listen that the village sewage system was archaic and should be replaced; on warm days, an unpleasant odour arose from the drains. He disliked seeing children playing in the streets, which the children had to do because the village did not have a playground, so he said that one should be constructed. So too, he said, should an abattoir; the farmers had to drive far to have their animals slaughtered.

He also suggested a large wooden cross placed in the cemetery should be moved; it hindered vehicle access during funerals, he said. It was also an eyesore because the wood was rotting.

Also encouraged by Nézondet to do so, Marcel started to accept when a villager invited him for dinner in the evening, or for lunch on a Sunday. The widows had been inviting him from the time of his arrival in the village, but he had always turned their invitations down. He was an attentive guest, as the widows reported when they stood at the bistro's zinc-topped counter enjoying a mid-morning glass of *vin rouge* — red wine. They said that he complimented them on the elegance of their dress, on the flower arrangement in their dining room, on the quality of their dinner service and on their choice of wine although he pointed out that as a teetotaller his judgement was based on the vintner and the vintage. He also rose when a widow entered the room, helped her into her chair, offered to carve the roast for her and kissed her hand on bidding her goodnight.

Often Marcel would take Nézondet along when he went for dinner. He took him along to the home of a wealthy widow, Antoinette Fleury, one of his patients.

The old lady had a young maid and on the night that Marcel and Nézondet went for dinner, she showed them into her mistress's living room. She wore a tight-fitting black dress, an embroidered white apron tied around her slim waist, and a white, lace bonnet. On her small feet were very high-heeled shoes. She fixed large, brown eyes, first on the doctor, and then on the auctioneer's clerk. She smiled and revealed what Nézondet would remember until the end of his life as the whitest, shiniest teeth that he had ever seen.

Marcel had also noticed the maid's teeth. He had, in fact, noticed everything about her and liked all of it, and early the following morning, always a quiet time for the bistro, he walked in. He wanted to know about Mrs Fleury's maid and he knew that should anyone have information about her it would be Frascot because a bistro owner always knew everybody's business.

The maid's name was Louise Delaveau, but everyone called her Louisette.

Frascot did not know where she hailed from, but she was 26 years old and she did not have *un petit ami* - a boyfriend. She had not been working for Mrs Fleury all that long.

Louisette habitually called in at the bistro after the old lady had gone to bed and Frascot offered to put a word in for Marcel should he be interested. Marcel admitted that he was.

"But please be discreet," he asked.

The bistro owner said he would.

* * *

The following night as the clock on the wall behind Frascot struck ten, Marcel, his hair cut and shampooed that morning, stepped into the bistro. An icy rain was lashing the village and Frascot was alone. Almost immediately the door swung open again and in walked Louisette; earlier

135

that day she had admitted to Frascot that she had rather taken a fancy to the young doctor and would love to get to know him.

Marcel and Louisette shook hands.

No longer wearing her maid's white lace bonnet, long, dark-brown hair cascaded over the young woman's shoulders.

She wore a red coat, which she took off to sit. Marcel had steered her to a table in the bistro's darkest corner.

Frascot watched from behind the counter. He was pretending to be busy; he wiped spotless glasses and swiped at imaginary flies with a large red-chequered napkin. He kept it up for about half an hour and then he went to hang a 'closed' sign in the window and pulled the blinds down before he disappeared into the kitchen at the back. From there, he listened to Louisette quietly giggling; she seemed to find everything funny that the doctor was whispering to her.

After a while, the old bistro owner heard chairs scrape over the floor. He waited to hear his door bang and when it did he dashed from the kitchen to peep out. He was in time to see Marcel and Louisette walk away from the bistro. They were walking towards Marcel's house.

Dr Marcel Petiot and Louisette Delaveau were about to become lovers.

On some of those Saturday nights when Nézondet and Marcel had set off for dinner in one of the nearby towns, the auctioneer's clerk had hinted that they should pick up a couple of girls and book into an inn. Marcel had always refused. Such apparent disinterest in women, Nézondet had found puzzling. 'He always seemed distant and unfathomable on any subject to do with his personal life. He almost never talked of women with me. I got the impression that love was the least of his concerns', he would write in his book.

Yet, he did suspect that his friend was, indeed, interested in sex, because in his bedroom, in a jar and preserved in alcohol, was a specimen of the male and female genitalia. 'It was enough to have put any sensitive novice off physical love', he wrote.

* * *

Marcel made rules that Louisette had to obey.

She was never to reveal to anyone that they were lovers. She was to make sure that they were never seen together. Should they find themselves in the same place, she should ask to be excused and leave, but they were not to ignore one another because that would arouse suspicion; they were to shake hands and make small talk for a while and then she should leave. Should she be present when he called on Mrs Fleury in future, or on the next occasion that the old lady invited him for dinner, she should not even once look in his direction. The old lady, he said, should never witness any familiarity between them.

Louisette was also never ever to address him by his name in public. She was to call him *monsieur*.

He would obey his own rules too, he told her.

He would address her in public as Miss Delaveau; in private, he called her Louise because he considered the diminutive form 'Louisette' vulgar.

He would also never discuss her with anyone, he promised. It was a promise that he would keep; he did not even let Nézondet in on the affair.

'It happened a few times that I was at her mistress' house when the doctor arrived on a house call. Never did I witness any intimacy between him and the young woman', wrote Nézondet.

He did know which way the wind was blowing.

Everyone in the village knew because Frascot had not kept his promise to be discreet.

* * *

Several nights a week Louisette waited until Mrs Fleury had gone to bed, and then she set off for Marcel's house, to which she had a key. Each visit was planned beforehand, because Marcel, like Henriette and Marie, did not like visitors to turn up unexpectedly, not even if the visitor was a woman he would then take to his bed.

On those nights that Louisette did not visit Marcel, he would either walk over to the bistro for a chat with Nézondet or he would cycle down to the river and sit there in silence in the dark. Should it be the bistro that he had chosen, Frascot's patrons would wink and smile at each other. They knew that that was a night that the young doctor was going to sleep alone.

This way months passed and Nézondet became engaged and then he

137

got married, but Marcel continued to keep up the pretence that his life was one of celibacy. It did become so for several months as Louisette set off for Paris with Mrs Fleury. Alone, and obviously missing the young woman, he walked around the village almost every night, the collar of his jacket or overcoat pulled over his chin, or he sat reading at his bedroom window by the dim light of a lamp.

On Louisette and Mrs Fleury's return the affair recommenced. The villagers were somewhat surprised that it did because they had thought that the affair had ended. Before she had set off for Paris, Louisette had befriended another of the village's maids to whom she had admitted that she was having an affair with *Monsieur le docteur* Petiot and that she had missed a period and might be pregnant. The villagers had consequently thought that while in Paris she would have an abortion and that, as the doctor had not married her, she would not renew the relationship on her return.

The villagers did not know that Marcel had not only welcomed Louisette back with an open bedroom door, but that he had been wondering how it could be arranged so that she could move in with him.

It was of course inconceivable that lovers could live together, just as it was unthinkable that a doctor could marry a domestic maid, but soon Louisette moved in. It happened that Mrs Fleury had decided to return to Paris, but not to take her maid along again. Louisette had found herself unemployed and free to find another mistress or master. Just at that time, Marcel's maid, the same woman who had worked for him in the Mongins' cottage, had announced that she was to retire. Marcel was free to hire another housekeeper, and, as his house was large, she could live in.

The housekeeper was Miss Louise Delaveau.

Marcel and Louisette again fooled no one.

* * *

A year passed. It was New Year 1926. Marcel Petiot had been practising in the village for almost three years. He considered himself successful and he had good reason to do so because despite the gossip about him, the villagers still said that a more efficient doctor they could not wish for. Patients from all over the area had also started to consult him.

That spring Louisette started to put on weight. The villagers noticed and they said that she was obviously pregnant again - many still believed that when she had gone to Paris with Mrs Fleury, she had had an abortion - and they wondered whether *Monsieur le docteur* Petiot would be making an honest woman of her that time.

Nézondet also wondered whether his friend would finally tie the knot. He was still not in Marcel's confidence. He had actually seen very little of Marcel since Louisette had moved into the Rue Carnot house and he was greatly surprised when his friend rushed up to him on the street.

'He started to talk, but nothing that he said made sense. I turned to look at him while we were walking and I saw that tears glistened on his eyelashes. Suddenly, he grabbed my hand. She's gone, he said. He was in a pitiful state. He looked like an animal unable to bear his suffering. He said he also wanted to leave. I took him for lunch. For a very long time, he sat in silence. He kept his eyes on one spot, his movements were jerky, and his hands trembled slightly. All of a sudden, he seemed to have found the solution to whatever his problem was. He seemed relieved and he started to eat', he would write.

Louisette had left Marcel and the village.

Later that day, Marcel burst into the bistro. He wanted to know if anyone could recommend a housekeeper. He needed one as his had left. He ranted on about how well he had treated Miss Delaveau yet she had still walked out without having given him notice. Frascot's patrons looked at one another and smiled. They were certain they knew where Miss Delaveau had gone; to Paris for another abortion and she would soon be back, her waist slim.

Louisette did not return.

The month of May came. The days were warm. On Sunday afternoons the village children played hopscotch under the horse chestnut trees that grew alongside the river. Their fathers sat nearby fishing.

One Sunday a bad odour rose from the water.

The following morning a villager went to see if a hare or rabbit might not be lying dead in undergrowth on one of the banks. He saw that a wicker trunk was trapped between two large stones. He waded into the water to see what was inside. He found a badly decomposed, headless body of a woman.

As Villeneuve-sur-Yonne was too small to have a police force, the local gendarmerie had to decide whether to open a murder investigation. At the head of the gendarmerie was Captain Urbain Coureau. He was friendly with Bailiff Guttin. The latter told him that he thought that the headless body was that of Louisette and that *Monsieur le docteur* Petiot had murdered her. The captain sent his men down to the river to look for a head; he wanted a head before he was to open a murder file. None was found. Still believing that he had no evidence of foul play and as no one had officially reported the woman missing, he declared that he was not to pursue the matter. He sent the headless body to his headquarters in Dijon for disposal.

The villagers said that they agreed with the bailiff.

One of them said that he had seen the doctor cement the floor of his gardening shed and that it was around the time that Louisette had disappeared. Another said that he had seen the doctor and another man push a wheelbarrow towards the river. It had been late at night. On the wheelbarrow was a sack; it held something with the shape of a human body in a foetal position. He said that the second man was Nézondet. In his book, Nézondet would deny that he had anything to do with Louisette's disappearance. 'Someone claimed to have seen us, the doctor and me, at nightfall, pushing a wheelbarrow with something in the form of a body on it towards the river. I had a van, and the doctor had a car and, what was more, his garden bordered the river, which appears to me to have made it unnecessary to use a wheelbarrow', he wrote.

Marcel's garden did not border the river.

* * *

Marcel hired another maid. He told her that should Louisette return, she should throw her and her belongings out. Louisette had taken nothing with her when she left.

Mrs Fleury's house was burgled and set alight. It almost burnt to the ground. Captain Coureau decided it wasn't worth looking for the burglar and arsonist.

Neither Louisette nor Mrs Fleury ever returned to the village. Neither were they ever heard of again.

In 1944, the Quay could find no documents in the archives of either the Villeneuve-sur-Yonne or Dijon gendarmeries relating to the discovery of a headless body of a woman in the Yonne in 1926. France being occupied, they thought that the Germans had probably destroyed some files. Or they were destroyed before the war on the orders of someone locally with authority.

* * *

It was July. France began to prepare for municipal council and mayoral elections.

Marcel walked into Frascot's bistro; Nézondet stood at the bar. The two shook hands. They appeared happy to see one another. As always it was Nézondet who paid for Marcel's small black coffee.

Marcel Petiot had news. Not wanting the other patrons to overhear, he stepped closer to Nézondet.

"I'm going into politics," he whispered.

He had decided that he was going to run for the position of Mayor of Villeneuve-sur-Yonne.

In his book, Nézondet would claim that he could not believe his ears.

"To succeed in life, one must either be rich or hold a high position. And one must have it in you to be able to control people. To impose your will on them. On those who can make it tough for you," Petiot had told him.

-0-

CHAPTER FOUR

Mayor

No sooner had Marcel told Nézondet that he wanted to be Mayor of Villeneuve-sur-Yonne, than he started campaigning. He supported the Radical-Socialist coalition government of President Gaston Doumergue.

In 1926, France was still struggling to recover from the devastating losses of the Great War. More than 8.5 million Bearded Ones had gone into battle. Of them, 1.4 million had lost their lives, and another 4.4 million had been wounded. More than half a million had suffered the humiliation of being taken prisoner by the Germans. There had also been the loss of 55,000 kilometres of roads, thousands of bridges, hundreds of railway lines, 812,000 buildings and 54,390 square kilometres of farmland. All those roads, bridges, railway lines, buildings and farmland had to be reconstructed. France also had to repay millions of dollars borrowed from the United States, a task so gargantuan that the franc collapsed.

Post-war Villeneuve-sur-Yonne was also in need of reconstruction. Candidate Petiot promised he would do it.

He began his campaign by having leaflets printed.

Remembering how lucrative his advertising leaflet had been on his arrival in the village, he was certain that his campaign leaflet would be as rewarding. Not only did he again deliver the leaflets himself, but he left some with the magazines in his waiting room and clipped one to each prescription he issued.

One evening, he held a meeting in the school hall; the principal was both a patient and supporter. He wore a dark pinstripe suit, new white shirt with starched cuffs and collar, a new colourful bow tie and uncharacteristically gleaming shoes - another complaint of the villagers had been that he never polished his shoes - and looked every bit the successful Parisian politician.

143

He began the meeting by introducing himself despite the fact that every soul in the hall knew him. He said he was an *ancien combattant* - an ex-serviceman. He spoke of having been wounded during the Great War. He spoke of the horror of warfare and said that he had become a doctor because that horror had taught him to love life and all living creatures.

He asked the audience if they knew why he had chosen to practise in a small village and not a large city like Paris.

Before anyone could reply, he did so himself.

"I could have been rich had I chosen to practise medicine in Paris rather than here in Villeneuve-sur-Yonne, but I prefer to treat honest folk and not those shirkers in Paris," he said.

At the end of the meeting, the people lined up to shake his hand.

Judging the meeting a great success, Marcel called several more. Those soon became rowdy events. Delivering his speech, he stamped his feet, waved his arms, gesticulated with his hands, shouted and laughed. He also burst into tears recalling his days as a Bearded One. Those in the school hall who had already decided that they would be voting for him, cried with him. The others slow handclapped and whistled.

The ballot days were Sunday, July 18 and Sunday, July 25; the final round would be a head to head between the two front runners. Voters - only men over 21 years of age - would be presented with a list representing the various political parties and the name at the top of the winning party's list would be the village's new mayor.

Marcel's name headed the Radical-Socialist coalition list.

On the first Sunday, the coalition was the front runner, and, on the second, it swept to victory with an eighty per cent landslide. An internal party vote confirmed Marcel as its leader; he was the village's new mayor. His supporters went wild. They strung lights up along the river and made accordion music to which they danced all through the night. Wine flowed freely. Those who had not voted for him - he had started to call them his enemies - watched from a distance. They predicted an unhappy future for the village.

Two such enemies in particular found Marcel's victory difficult to accept: Bailiff Guttin and Captain Coureau.

The captain had, in the time since Louisette's disappearance, come to the conclusion that the headless body which had been found in the river had, indeed, been hers, and that Marcel had murdered her. He just could not prove it.

He had similarly decided not to investigate an incident that had occurred during the campaign. One night, just as Marcel had finished another of his long and boisterous speeches and one of his 'enemies' was to step onto the podium, the village had fallen dark. In the resulting chaos the meeting had to be called off. The next morning the captain had found that an electrical junction on Rue Carnot had been sabotaged. He was certain that Marcel was the culprit, but the latter, when challenged, had angrily protested that he knew nothing about electricity. Maurice was already working as an electrician in Auxerre.

* * *

Today, in France, a mayor's duties are numerous.

In 1926, in Villeneuve-sur-Yonne, it was no different.

Marcel had to keep the village and its vicinity neat, secure and peaceful. He had to maintain its civil register of births, deaths, marriages and divorces, establish the electoral and draft rolls, take care of the old and the poor, create jobs, plan and oversee the construction and maintenance of public buildings, and officiate at marriages. French law, however, decreed, as it still does today, that a mayor should never act independently. He had to consult with a *conseil municipal* - a municipal council - made up of *conseillers délégués* - councillors, the men who had been on the list that the ruling party had presented to the voters. Those councillors were, in turn, assisted by a team of *conseillers municipaux* - municipal advisors. All fell under the jurisdiction of a *conseil régional* - a regional council - headed by a president elected for six years, but who could himself not act independently as he fell under the jurisdiction of the politically-appointed prefect of the relevant prefectural subdivision.

Petiot consulted with no one.

In his first week as mayor he told the town hall staff that only he would be signing letters and issuing communiqués and orders and negotiate and sign contracts. To put action to his words, he locked all the filing cabinets and said that anyone who needed to retrieve a file or document from a cabinet should call him to unlock it. Before long he signed contracts with companies to build the village an abattoir, to replace its sewage system and to construct a playground for the children.

145

When the councillors criticised him at a meeting for having acted unilaterally he told them that he had only honoured his campaign promises; he had promised the villagers an abattoir, a new sewage system and he said that the first thing that he would do if elected would be to give the children a playground. So why were they criticizing him, he wanted to know. Their reply was that they had only mentioned the contracts because they wondered how he intended to honour them on an annual budget of 700,000 francs, or 350 francs annually per inhabitant.

"I can and I will," he replied.

* * *

Considering himself not only a great success as a medical man, but also as a mayor, Marcel decided that there was still something missing in his life. It was a happy home. To have one he needed a wife, but not just any wife. She would have to be someone special, very special. She would have to be beautiful, elegant and intelligent, and she had to be a member of the *bourgeoisie*. Yet, crucially, he had to be in love with her.

He found the girl he was looking for; the 23-year-old Georgette Valentine Lablais from Paris. He met her as he had met Louisette - at a dinner. Unlike Louisette, the future Mrs Petiot did not serve at the table; she was a guest. She was spending a few days with an aunt in Seignelay, her birthplace, and that night at dinner her fellow guest was her aunt's doctor.

Held by the Gestapo in Fresnes, Marcel would send Georgette a message. He told her that he loved her more than anyone else in the world.

* * *

Marcel and Georgette were married in Seignelay. It was on Saturday, June 4, 1927, a warm and sunny day and, as the couple said, it was a perfect day for a wedding.

Long Arm, Georgette's father, brought his chef from Paris to cook the bridal couple and their guests a sumptuous dinner. Félix, Henriette and Marie attended. Maurice, too. He was 18 years old. He stood a head taller than his brother and everyone wanted to know from the groom

146

who the handsome young man was.

After the reception, the newly weds drove back to Villeneuve-sur-Yonne. There would be no honeymoon. Marcel felt that he could not absent himself from the town hall or from his practice. French law had allowed him to continue working as a doctor after his election as Mayor.

On Thursday, April 19, 1928, ten months and thirteen days after the wedding, Georgette gave birth to their son, Gerhardt Claude Georges Félix. Why the couple had chosen the German version of the French name 'Gerard' they never explained. Neither did they explain why they had chosen to honour the hated Félix but did not respect the Petiot family's tradition of naming a son after his father.

However, Petiot did say that his son would want for nothing in life.

The boy would be cherished.

* * *

Six months after Gerhard's birth the Villeneuve-sur-Yonne station master called in at the town hall. He wanted to speak to *Monsieur le Maire*. As he would say later on that day, standing with his elbows resting on the zinc-topped bar in the bistro, their mayor was a thief.

The station master story was that, on the previous night, a little before midnight, one of his signalmen, the only person on duty at that time, had seen a yellow car pull away fast from one of the warehouses and, checking to see if there had been a break in, he had found that six canisters of petrol which were awaiting collection were missing. A nearby fuel depot had dispatched the petrol to their mayor, but he had not yet picked it up; he was arguing about payment, wanting to settle the bill later whereas the depot wanted payment on collection. Only one villager apart from the station staff knew that there were canisters of petrol in that warehouse and only one villager had a yellow car - their mayor.

Marcel was outraged that he should be accused of theft. He said that, as Mayor, he was entitled to free petrol, yet it was an expense that he had never claimed. The villagers should applaud him for his generosity instead of allowing the station master to accuse him of theft. The state-owned railway company decided to charge him with theft all the same.

The Petrol Theft Case, as it was to become known, was to be heard at the *Tribunal de Première Instance*, the court dealing with minor offences, in the town of Sens. It was in the town of Sens where Marcel had served with the 89th Infantry Regiment.

On the day of the hearing Georgette went along.

Neighbours peeped from behind curtains and reported that when she got into the yellow car she was laughing. She had already told them that her husband was innocent.

In Sens a Paris lawyer hired by Long Arm waited. The latter agreed with his daughter that her husband was innocent. If father and daughter were aware that it was not the first time that Petiot was facing an accusation of theft, they kept the knowledge to themselves.

At the end of the day, the neighbours, again at their windows, witnessed Marcel and Georgette's return. She was again laughing. By morning, the news had spread throughout the village that *Monsieur le maire* was home. He must have been found not guilty. Bunches of flowers sent by patients and villagers, who still supported their Mayor, began to arrive at the town hall and at the Petiots' house.

What no one knew was that Marcel still faced the theft charge. In court, having been asked to explain the fate of the canisters of petrol, he had given such an incoherent explanation that the presiding judge had requested that a court-appointed psychiatrist should assess his mental state. Only after that had been done, said the judge, could he pronounce a verdict.

* * *

As the case would take months to return to court, the Petiots got on with their life and the villagers with theirs and no one mentioned the stolen petrol canisters anymore.

Two months went by and Christmas time came.

In the afternoon on Christmas Eve, Marcel, Georgette and the eight-month-old Gerhardt set off in the yellow car to join Félix and Maurice in Auxerre for that night's traditional midnight *reveillon* feast.

On the day after Christmas the three Petiots returned to Villeneuve-sur-Yonne. It was a Wednesday and as the day would not be a bank holiday, Marcel wanted to open his practice as he expected many of his patients would come in for medication for a *crise de foie* - a bilious attack - from having eaten too much *foie gras*.

He was right.

On arrival his waiting room was already packed and to his surprise even someone who was not one of his patients was waiting for him. It was Captain Coureau. He had come, as he would tell Marcel, not to consult *Monsieur le docteur*, but to tell *Monsieur le maire* about a theft in the village; the large wooden cross in the cemetery had been stolen.

The captain said that on Christmas morning villagers, arriving at the cemetery to put flowers on the graves of their loved ones, had to their consternation seen that where the cross had stood for as long as they could remember, there was just a hole in the ground.

"Have you removed it?" asked the captain. "If so, return it immediately, please."

As those in the waiting room would tell Frascot's patrons later, their doctor had flown into a rage at the question.

Splattering saliva over the captain, he shouted, "Go on, search me! I don't think I've got it on me, but perhaps you think that I do!"

He spread his arms and legs to facilitate the gendarme's search.

The latter, in fear of the furious man in front of him, fled.

Georgette, as before, believed in her husband's innocence.

Again too, did Long Arm. He had already decided that the villagers were jealous of the brilliant young doctor.

As for Marcel, he sought solace by adopting a stance of great sorrow. He told anyone who would listen that the cross must be more than three metres high and that it must weigh at least two hundred kilograms and it would have been impossible for him to have carried it off. He would have needed digging equipment to have dug it out and a truck to have carted it away, but first he would have had to lift it onto the truck and for that he would have needed a forklift.

A week later a farmer turned up at Captain Coureau's office and reported that another farmer had told him that he had helped Marcel to remove the cross and that the doctor had paid him handsomely.

The cross, the farmer told the captain, lay at the bottom of the river.

"Oh, forget it!" yelled Coureau.

He said that the whole business was too ridiculous to waste his time on.

The cross was never found.

* * *

149

On Wednesday, January 29, 1930, the Petrol Theft Case was to be heard. Marcel felt confident that it would go in his favour. He had undergone the mental assessment and he had been given the result. The court-appointed psychiatrist had not only found him sane, but a man of integrity.

Georgette, for a change, did not share her husband's confidence. Certain that he was going to be locked up, she preferred to await the news at home rather than to accompany him to Sens. She had his promise that he would telephone her the moment the verdict had been delivered.

In Sens, Marcel's Paris lawyer was again waiting. He, too, believed that the case would be thrown out, yet, taking no chances, he briefed his client on what and what not to say. He particularly did not want Marcel to deliver another protracted explanation as to what might or might not have happened to the canisters of petrol.

At the end of that day the telephone rang in the Petiots' house. Georgette had been standing beside the phone for at least an hour and she picked up instantly.

"Marcel? Marcel, is that you?"

There was no reply.

Such silence meant only one thing.

"How long did they give you?" she asked.

"Three-month suspended and a fine of two hundred."

He said that his lawyer had lodged an appeal.

Later that night, back home, he raved at the judge's cheek of having found him, a Bearded One, a doctor and a mayor, guilty of theft.

Captain Coureau was angry too, angry because Marcel had received only a suspended sentence and such a small fine. Yet, he could not stop smiling. He knew something that Marcel did not.

On Thursday, February 6, eight days later, Marcel received a visitor at the town hall. It was the prefect. He brought the news that the Regional Council had discussed Marcel's behaviour, and its councillors and president had voted to suspend him for a month. The suspension was effective immediately.

The prefect made it clear that he would have preferred to have dismissed Marcel outright, but that the law compelled him to apply a month's suspension as a first warning. He had, he pointed out, sent a request to Minister of the Interior Pierre Laval in Paris to be allowed to extend the suspension to three months. He was still awaiting the minister's reply.

As his secretary, a man who was long past retirement age, but to whom Marcel had taken a liking and had not wanted him to leave, would tell the rest of the town hall staff that their mayor had not said a word throughout the prefect's visit.

It is not known what Marcel told Georgette when he arrived home at an hour when he should have been at the town hall, but early the following day she stood out on the pavement chatting cheerfully to passersby.

All through the suspension Marcel continued to treat his patients as if nothing had happened.

On the day that the month's suspension ended the prefect waited at the town hall. Interior Minister Pierre Laval had sent his reply. The suspension had been extended to three months.

That time Marcel did not remain silent; he was heard throughout the building shouting insults at Laval.

In April, the appeal in the Petrol Theft Case was heard.

Marcel was again confident that the hearing would go in his favour. Georgette agreed.

The two were right.

The judge, having decided that Marcel's shell shock experience had impaired his sense of responsibility, and deeming it such a noble reason, had withdrawn the theft accusation.

Marcel, delighted, immediately wrote to the prefect. He demanded that his suspension should be lifted. It was.

"The man is a criminal," fumed a furious Captain Coureau. "Give him time and he will step out of line again."

His prediction would come true.

* * *

Two months passed. It was a Tuesday evening in June. A sliver of smoke rose in the sky north of the village. There was a dairy in that direction. Armand Debauve, the dairy owner, was in the bistro; he never missed his Tuesday night drink. The home he shared with his wife, Henriette, was in the dairy grounds. She was at home.

No one in the village was alarmed at seeing the smoke; smoke always poured from the dairy's chimneys. Soon flames accompanied the smoke. Someone ran to the bistro to tell Debauve that his dairy was on fire. He said that it could not be because Henriette was at home and cooking their dinner and she would have summoned the fire service. He stepped outside all the same to have a look and the next minute he was running towards the smoke and flames, all those who had been in the bistro with him, following. Halfway to the dairy, the village fire engine roared by. Captain Coureau, only partially dressed, was clinging to its side. It was not the dairy that was burning. It was the Debauves' two storey home. Part of the roof had already collapsed.

The firefighters found Henriette in the kitchen near to a door that led down to a scullery. She lay with her face down and her legs were trapped under a beam that had crashed down from the ceiling. The firefighters, the captain assisting them, lifted her onto a stretcher and carried her outside. A stunned Armand Debauve looked on. He was not told that his wife was not breathing, but, because of her staring eyes, he guessed as much. Gently, the captain broke the terrible news to him: his wife was dead, but she would not have suffered, as asphyxiation would have killed her within minutes, he said. All that the dairy owner was capable of doing was to sink to his knees beside his wife's lifeless body. Neither Coureau nor the firefighters dared tell him that one side of his wife's head was caved in.

The firefighters extinguished the blaze.

Captain Coureau's men arrived. So did Marcel and Georgette. They rode up in the yellow car. They were on their way to Sens to see a film. Told that Henriette Debauve was dead, they offered their condolences to the newly created widower. Marcel fetched his medical case from his car and rapidly checked for a heartbeat; one never knew, he said. But no, Henriette Debauve was dead all right. A few minutes later, the couple drove off. They did not want to miss the film.

Marcel had not looked at the dead woman's head.

Once the firefighters had announced that what was left of the Debauves' house was safe to enter, Captain Coureau's men went inside and discovered that cupboards and drawers had been rifled and their contents scattered over the floors. On the Debauves' double bed in a first storey bedroom lay a flat iron bar, which they thought had been used to pry open a safe in one of the bedroom's walls. On the bar were three bloody fingerprints. They called Armand Debauve and he said that a tin which contained 20,000 francs was missing from the safe. He knew the amount, he said, as his wife always kept that much cash in the house in case of an emergency. Handed the iron bar, he said that he recognised it as one that he kept in his gardening shed. He went with the captain to have a look whether the iron bar was still there; it was not. He also found that a large hammer was missing from the shed.

Captain Coureau theorised that Henriette Debauve had obviously been murdered and that a villager must have murdered her with theft as motive. He quite harshly told the grieving widower that he and his late wife had not exactly hidden the fact that they kept a stash of emergency cash in their house. Just as they had also not hidden the fact that every second Tuesday of a month they had even more cash in their house because on every second Wednesday they paid the farmers who supplied them with milk. He said that the murderer must have thought that Henriette had also gone to the bistro, but having found her at home, had to kill her to silence her. The setting alight of the house was to cover up the crime.

Armand Debauve agreed with the captain. He said that, when he had set off for the bistro, there were altogether 235,000 francs in the house, which included the emergency cash, the farmers' payment and the dairy's petty cash. The murderer had had a lucrative evening.

The following morning, Marcel, as Henriette Debauve's doctor, issued a death certificate. He noted the time of the woman's death as 7:30 P.M. As was, and still is, the custom in France, he did not stipulate the cause of death. Later in the day, gendarmes found the missing hammer. It lay trapped between two stones in a stream behind the Debauve's dairy complex. A footpath led from the dairy to the stream and from there to the village. There was not a villager who did not know about that footpath; all used it as a shortcut when they had been to the dairy to buy milk.

* * *

The gendarmes were also to find a clock in the burnt debris. The clock

153

used to hang in the Debauves' kitchen.

The clock had stopped at 7:30 P.M.

The date of the fire was March 11.

Fourteen years later, and at just about that time, Corporal Boudringhim and his men would discover human remains in the basement of Dr Marcel Petiot's Rue le Sueur townhouse.

* * *

Soon, Frascot said that he knew who had murdered Henriette Debauve. He said that earlier on that evening he had driven past the dairy complex and he had seen a man hurry across its yard towards the Debauve's house. He said that it had not been the first time that he had seen that man near the dairy; the man, he said, was having an affair with Henriette Debauve.

The man was Dr Marcel Petiot.

Captain Coureau passed Frascot's information on to his headquarters in Dijon.

On Tuesday, March 25, Dijon Police sent two detectives to the village. The two spent a day going through what was left of the Debauve's house and fingerprinting the dairy's 22 employees in order to find a match to the fingerprints which had been found on the flat iron bar.

They did not fingerprint the villagers. They did not even question them.

Back in Dijon they handed their report over to their superiors. 'As there is a lack of evidence, we do not recommend an investigation', they had concluded.

Undeterred, Captain Coureau tried to take Marcel's fingerprints at a municipal council meeting. In 1980, Robert Seguin, the man who had succeeded Marcel as Mayor of Villeneuve-sur-Yonne, described to the writer Jean-François Dominique for the latter's book 'L'Affaire Petiot' - The Petiot Affair - what had happened at the meeting. Dominique wrote, quoting Seguin: 'Petiot, beside himself with rage, repeated his refusal to be fingerprinted. Losing total control of himself, he tore a page from the notes being taken of our meeting. He stuck his fingers into an inkpot and pressed them down onto the page. He then hurled the sheet of paper towards us and shouted: do with it what you want! You will see that it

154

will get you nowhere. He left, slamming the door behind him'.

Seguin dutifully put the sheet of paper into an envelope and mailed it to Dijon Police. They did not acknowledge its receipt.

Henriette Debauve's death remains a mystery. Just as with Louisette Delaveau's disappearance, in 1944, the Quay could not find a file for the case. Later, after the law had dealt with Dr Marcel Petiot, a file did turn up at the Quay. All that was in it was Captain Coureau's report and that of the two Dijon detectives. Neither Coureau nor the two detectives had speculated on who might have murdered Henriette Debauve.

* * *

Marcel dismissed Frascot's story as silly and provoked by jealousy. He said that the bistro owner was jealous of his success and prosperity.

Frascot stopped repeating the story. His rheumatoid arthritis had flared up and he was in too much pain to stand about in the bistro gossiping. In the past, Marcel's medication had relieved his pain, but he had been refusing to consult him after the fire, but, humbly, he had no choice but to return.

Marcel was happy to have Frascot back as a patient. He told him that there was a wonderful new treatment on the market for his ailment.

"The treatment, an injection, is so new that it's not even in the pharmacies yet. If you want, I will inject you," offered Marcel.

Frascot agreed.

A while later, back in his bistro, Frascot started to feel unwell. He told his patrons that he found it difficult to breathe. They helped him into a chair and one went to fetch Marcel. He arrived at the bistro just in time to witness Frascot's final breath. The bistro owner, he said, had suffered a fatal aneurysm.

Despite that not one in the village accused Marcel of having caused Frascot's death with his new medication, the village's pharmacist, a man named Paul Maynaud, began to say that the dosages the doctor was prescribing to his patients were too high. Some dosages, he said, were so high that they could be lethal. He told of how he had refused to fill one of the doctor's prescriptions for a small boy. A very irate Marcel had then walked into his pharmacy to insist that the medication be handed over to the child's mother. He said that Marcel had told him that if the medication killed the child then the mother would be freed from the ordeal of having to care for him, but that the medication might well cure him. So what was the problem the doctor had wanted to know.

The Drs Durand and Devoir also spoke out. They accused their young colleague of being incapable of making a correct diagnosis. Furthermore, his treatments were downright dangerous, they said.

Encouraged to hear what those who were, by their reckoning medical experts, were saying, the villagers also voiced their suspicions. They said that Dr Petiot was so successful and prosperous because he was performing abortions for women and girls from the neighbouring villages.

Just as Marcel had dismissed Frascot's claims that he had murdered Henriette Debauve, he again dismissed what was being said about him. He said that he knew for a fact that the pharmacist hated him; Paul Maynaud had been his predecessor at the town hall.

The Petiots got on with their life.

Almost every Saturday night, Marcel took Georgette dancing; Nézondet had by then opened his small leisure complex. The couple always turned up before opening time.

Nézondet would write in his book that he thought that the two always arrived early so that they could eat with him for free before the dancing started. He would complain that neither liked to spend money.

On those Saturdays that the couple did not go dancing, they took the train to Paris. Gerhardt, two years old and perfectly behaved, went along. It was at that time that the couple discovered Hotel Alicot.

In Paris, Georgette shopped for clothes and Marcel shopped for books. The bookshops of the capital's Latin Quarter were his favourites.

In the evenings they either went to the cinema or they dined at Chez Marius, Long Arm's restaurant. Gerhardt went along to the restaurant. Having become a widower, Bras Long was always delighted to see the three walk in. He dearly loved his only child and he adored his little grandson and his son-in-law. He was certain a brilliant political career awaited the latter if he should move to Paris.

Marcel did not tell Long Arm that moving to Paris was something he was thinking about.

* * *

In July 1931, fourteen months after Henriette Debauve's murder, Marcel was yet again in trouble. The town hall staff said that he was stealing from its coffers. He would not allow them any access to the accounts and that meant only one thing: he was embezzling the village's money. Captain Coureau heard about it and he asked the prefect to send an auditor over to verify the accounts.

On the day that the auditor arrived, Marcel first refused to hand over the books, next he hurled them at the man.

"I dare you to find discrepancies in my books!" he shouted.

The auditor found discrepancies.

In the report that he handed over to the prefect, he accused *Monsieur le maire* of having signed building contracts with builders no one had ever heard of and of having paid bogus contractors for doing nothing. He added that the mayor had also bought large quantities of material for the village school, which the school had never requested or received, yet the town hall's books showed that payment had been made to the suppliers, who were also completely unknown. He further reported that he had found that money that had been paid by 138 foreigners for resident permits was missing, and that an inventory of the town hall's furniture had showed that some items were missing.

In a letter to the prefect, Marcel blamed his staff, especially his secretary, the man he had asked previously not to retire, for the discrepancies. Gallantly, he begged the prefect to be lenient; he wrote that because of his secretary's advanced age, the man was no longer so alert.

On Tuesday, August 26, a letter from the prefect arrived at the town hall in reply to Marcel's reply. The latter read that he had yet again been suspended. He called his secretary to his office and said that he was going home; he did not say why. The first thing he did at home was to write a letter of resignation to the Municipal Council. He pointed out that he was resigning because he found the pleasure it was giving him to do so irresistible. The prefect, he ignored.

As French law demanded - it still does today - that a municipal council should, after a mayor's second suspension, step down, a new two-round municipal council and mayoral election had to be held. Until such time a three-man team was to run the town hall. Bailiff Guttin was one of the three.

The election's first round was scheduled for Sunday, November 15; the second and final for the following Sunday, November 22. Marcel's name headed the Radical-Socialist Party's electoral list. The Bailiff's headed a second list, Dr Durand a third, and Councillor Seguin, the man who would later speak of how Dr Marcel Petiot had reacted at a council meeting when an effort had been made to fingerprint him as a suspect in Henriette Debauve's murder, headed a fourth.

Marcel's second campaign for the mayorship of Villeneuve-sur-Yonne differed from his first in that he focussed on his achievements rather than making new promises, and that he was in tears most of the time but never shouted.

His supporters, by then there were few, again wept with him.

Sunday, November 15, Bailiff Guttin and Dr Durand were defeated. The second and final round would be between Marcel and Councillor Seguin.

The closing minutes of Marcel's very last meeting before that Sunday would be remembered in the village for a very long time. He cupped his hands over the microphone, started to say something, but suddenly dropped his head and started to cry. He cried for several long minutes, then he lifted his tear-stained face to the anguised villagers who were staring at him in silence and whispered into the microphone, "Oh, I am guilty! I confess that I am guilty of a serious crime... I stand accused of loving the people too much. I confess that this is true."

His few supporters stood to cheer him.

Councillor Seguin's supporters groaned, got up and walked out, but their man became Villeneuve-sur-Yonne's new Mayor.

Marcel told his last few loyal patients that he did not mind that he was no longer the village mayor. They knew the reason why he did not mind. That October, while the campaign was at its most fervent, he had been elected to sit, as general councillor, on the Regional Council of the prefectural subdivision of Yonne, under which Villeneuve-sur-Yonne fell.

That meant that Mayor Seguin could take no decision in the village without first having to consult him and the other general councillors.

* * *

Once more, the Petiots got on with their life.

Marcel began investing in real estate.

His first purchase was Number 58 Rue Carnot, the house next door to the family home. He bought another house in the village as well; Long Arm came in with him on the deal. Maurice, aged 22 and newly married, and as devoted to his older brother as ever, became the rent collector and handyman for the two landowners.

With many of his patients having returned to the other two doctors because of all the trouble Marcel had been causing, the latter confessed to his family that he was rather bored. The boredom he manifested by spending afternoons repairing his yellow car out on the pavement and to test drive it at a great speed up and down the street afterwards.

* * *

On Saturday, August 20, 1932, nine months after having lost the election, Marcel was again accused of theft.

As Mayor, he had been allowed free electricity, but, on his dismissal his meter, according to French law, had been reactivated. He had protested strongly to the electricity company's director, a man named Antoine Mouret that out of courtesy, the company should have offered him free electricity for the duration of his stay in the village. Not having waited for a reply from the electricity company, he had deactivated his meter himself, which was not discovered until a reading when the meter had stood at zero. Again as he had done during the mayoral campaign when the village had suddenly gone dark, he had claimed that, as he knew naught about electricity, he could not have deactivated the meter himself. He said that the meter must be out of order. A technician had checked the meter and had announced it in prefect working order. Furious, Marcel had told Mouret that the company could stuff its electricity up its arse because he and his family could cope perfectly well without electricity: the company was not to reactive their meter. However, when his neighbours had begun to report that at night they could see thin fingers of light penetrate through the slats of the shutters in front of the Petiots' windows, Mouret, with Captain Coureau's connivance, had programmed an evening power cut to Rue Carnot's houses to see if there would still be light behind the Petiots' shutters. There was indeed and on verifying it was found that the Petiots' house was connected directly to an electricity grid which stood a short distance away, thus bypassing that of the street. Marcel was immediately charged with stealing electricity: a charge he dismissed vehemently as ridiculous, yet again claiming that he knew nothing about electricity.

The case was again heard in Sens and Marcel was again certain that he would be acquitted.

He was found guilty.

He stood motionless and, for a change, speeceless, listening to the verdict.

He was to go to jail for 15 days, and he had to pay a fine of 300 francs. Police already stood at the back of the courtroom waiting to lock him up.

Quickly, his lawyer, the same one he had hired for the Petrol Theft Case, lodged an appeal and he was allowed to leave.

* * *

Back home, night having fallen, Marcel took crying Georgette in his arms and told her that he had been thinking for some time of them leaving the village. Life in such a backwater was not for them, he said. It was for people with small minds. Or, no minds whatsoever.

They were going to move to Paris.

Immediately, Marcel started to look for a medical practice in the capital that he could buy. The practice had to be in a smart area of the city because he wanted a better class of patient than Burgundian country bumpkins, as he told Long Arm.

To his surprise Paris practices were expensive - his court cases had depleted his cash flow - and he had to set his sights lower and buy the practice at Number 66 Rue de Caumartin. He was pleased though to know that because Printemps and Galaries Lafayette department stores were nearby, a good class of person would visit the neighbourhood. He would not be descending the Parisian social ladder by too far.

He bought the practice from two doctors, the Dr Michel Garnier and his partner the Dr Charles Valéry. In 1944, the Quay could not establish what he had paid the two; they could not be found. Some of the street's residents told the police that they had heard that Dr Valéry had fled to

Argentina in 1942 and that, coincidentally, Dr Garnier had also set off that year, but in which direction, they said, they did not know.

-0-

Dr Petiot as the 25-year-old doctor in Villeneuve-sur-Yonne. (Copyright LAPI / Roger-Viollet, Paris, France.)

Dr Petiot as the Paris doctor. (Copyright LAPI / Roger-Viollet, Paris, France.)

Georgette Petiot. (Copyright LAPI / Roger-Viollet, Paris, France)

Dr Petiot (second from right) in the Paris court. In front of him sits his solicitor, René Floriot. Behind him can be seen the suitcases left behind by his victims. (Copyright LAPI / Roger-Viollet, Paris, France)

The basement burner in which Petiot burnt the remains of some of his victims. (Copyright LAPI / Roger-Viollet, Paris, France)

Rue Le Sueur (Copyright author)

DIE IN PARIS

PART THREE

MURDER

CHAPTER ONE

Paris

Marcel, Georgette and five-year-old Gerhardt arrived in Paris on a cold day in January 1933.

While Georgette unpacked, Marcel removed his predecessors' shingle from the front of the building and replaced it with his own, one of black marble. He had decided he would receive patients in the afternoons only to leave mornings free for house calls.

The shingle in place, he set off on foot - he had left both his bike and car with Maurice in Auxerre - to distribute leaflets advertising his arrival and his skills. He was certain that just as in Villeneuve-sur-Yonne, the leaflets would pull in patients. He planned to walk as far as he could possibly go, because he wanted patients not only from his own neighbourhood, but from all over Paris.

He left his leaflet at shops, bistros, restaurants, hairdressing salons, barbershops, with *concierges* of apartment buildings, doormen of music halls and nightclubs. Also at pharmacies, medical laboratories and dental practices. He even left some at brothels: of those there were many in his neighbourhood. In the north, the ninth *arrondissement* ran into the red-light and strip club district of Pigalle, and, in the east, into the wholesale market district of Les Halles, another haunt of prostitutes.

Marcel had put much thought into the wording of the leaflet.

Finally he decided on the wording.

It read:

'Please note that the medical clinic on the first floor of Number 66 Rue de Caumartin, previously run by Dr Garnier and the well-known Dr Valéry, university prize winner, is now run by:

'Doctor Marcel PETIOT. Graduate of the Paris Medical Faculty in 1921. Regional councillor for the Yonne. Ex-intern of hospitals and

171

asylums, and hospital and hospice doctor. Clinic director. Doctor in charge of the permanent medical office of the Seine Prefectural Subdivision.

'The clinic is right in the centre of Paris and is close to all transport - bus and Métro; Saint-Lazare and Caumartin stations. It has the most modern and sophisticated equipment, including X-ray, UV, UR, superficial and deep radiotherapy, radio-active substances, laboratory, galvanisation and faradisation, ionisation, cryotherapy, diathermia - all frequencies, high-power shortwaves, induced fever, electric scalpel, surgical instruments, ozonotherapy, aerotherapy, etcetera.

'This advanced equipment allows DR MARCEL PETIOT to practise general medicine and gynaecology in the best possible conditions, and with all the resources of the best specialist instruments.

'In 1921, DR MARCEL PETIOT developed a technique allowing the complete suppression of pain in childbirth without general or local anaesthetic and without potentially dangerous surgical intervention.

'The method permits pain suppression in even the most painful complaints (sciatica, rheumatism, neuralgia, zona, neuritis, ulceration and cancer).

'He is the AUTHOR of papers on nervous diseases and their modern treatment (particularly in the treatment of recurring complaints and drug/alcohol addiction).

'He is the ORIGINATOR (in cooperation with a well-known physiologist) of a technique and material permitting the cure of any non-generalised tumour, not affecting the vital organs. This includes not only external or internal ganglions, cysts, lipoma, polyps, vegetations, warts, strawberry marks, goitres, deformities, tattoos, scars as well as fibromas and malignant tumours and even deep cancer before its terminal stage.

'The application to ulcers, varicose veins and haemorrhoids leads to very rapid and definitive results.

'Analogous principles permit the regulation of the endocrine glands and the treatment of states of general deficiency - arteriosclerosis, anaemia, obesity, change of life, diabetes, cardiac or renal insufficiency, arthritis, nervous breakdowns and senility.

'Personalised methods allow a maximum and rapid absorption of the active medical substances, thanks to the appropriate catalysts - chemical, microbial and physical. The control of nervous and circulatory nervules, oxozone (very concentrated ozone, supplied by special apparatus), electrotherapy, ionisation, radioactivity...

'The application of this information increases the effect without increasing the medicinal dose and gives convincing results in the most obstinate illnesses and in the most hopeless cases, notably: In acute and chronic respiratory conditions, influenza, pneumonia, emphysema, asthma and especially tuberculosis.

'In infectious diseases of the blood, gastritis, enteritis, appendicitis, nephritis, furunculosis, salpingitis, gonorrhea, syphilis (with addition of sero and autoserotherapy).

'In organic diseases relating to the bones, generalised neoplasm, cardiac lesion, the liver and stomach, fatigue etc

'Thanks to rapid means of transport, he can respond very promptly to calls to his telephone: PIGalle 77-11.

'He is very willing to work with a patient's regular doctor when the means at his disposal or his personal methods are required.

'The fees are quite affordable, even for those with the most modest incomes. The Social Security and Word-Accident formalities are of course accepted.

'DR MARCEL PETIOT, a veteran invalided out of the army, is honoured by the confidence shown to him by veterans and retired personnel. He accepts vouchers for free treatment.

'Director of two clinics, with assistants chosen from various sectors of Paris and the suburbs, disposing of ambulances and appropriate portable equipment, he is also doctor in charge of the permanent medical office.

'The organisation provides day and night urgent medical assistance for his clientele - trades people, hoteliers, landlords, restaurateurs, theatre directors - without obligation. They are thus guaranteed against ALL expenses, indiscretion, trouble and responsibility.

'Simply Call PIGalle 77-11.

'Private individuals are at liberty to accept this service when their regular doctor is absent.

'When necessary, the patient is quickly taken to the private or public hospital of his choice.

'DR MARCEL PETIOT requests that you excuse his use of this vulgar form of publicity in order to inform the public that he has set up practice in the centre of Paris for all consultations and home treatment requested through the family doctor.

'And, for the special medical care briefly indicated above.

'DR MARCEL PETIOT would be most grateful if you would make a note of his address: 66 Rue de Caumartin, PARIS-IX, and of his telephone number: PIGalle 77-11'.

Marcel was right. The leaflet drew patients but still not satisfied, he asked Long Arm to tell the parliamentarians who lunched and dined at Chez Marius about him. He also asked two of Georgette's cousins living in Paris to spread the word that he had arrived. One, Andrée Lablais, was a secretary with the Dutch electrical company, Philips; she promised she would tell her colleagues of the new brilliant doctor. The other, Paulette Vallée and her husband, Raymond, an insurance policy salesman, promised they would send all clients in need of the medical certificates required for policies, to Cousin Petiot.

Nézondet was also asked to spread the word that a new doctor was in town. Without a woman in his life, and jobless, he spent a large part of his nights in the capital's bars and nightclubs. Before he had left Villeneuve-sur-Yonne to follow the Petiots to Paris there had been rumours in the village that he had his eye on Georgette, but Marcel having laughed it off, it had not affected the two's friendship. It was on those nocturnal excursions of his that he was to look for patients. That most, if not all, of the patients that he would recruit thus would be either in prostitution or drugs, was not something that bothered either him or his friend.

It was not only patients that the leaflet sent Marcel's way, but also trouble. Two doctors, a Dr Raymond Tournay and a Dr Pierre Millet, decided they could not allow a colleague to get away with such outrageous self-promotion and, what was more, such bogus claims. They complained to the only organisation they thought could do anything about it, *le Syndicat des Médecins de la Seine* - the capital's medical trade union. The two wanted Marcel's licence to practise medicine in Paris withdrawn. The SMS said there was nothing it could do; it was not illegal for a medical man to advertise his skills, only unethical, and being unethical was not against the law.

What the SMS did not know was that Marcel was, indeed, doing something illegal. He had not registered his practice with the Paris police. He was therefore practising medicine without a licence, and that was, indeed, against the law. He would let more than a year pass before he called on the police of his *arrondissement* on Monday, July 2, 1934, to do so. The proof he gave the police that he was a medical doctor was the letter from the Paris Medical Faculty he had already shown around Auxerre in 1923. The police did not question the letter's authenticity; neither did they demand to see his medical diploma. They licensed his practice.

Marcel had a reason why he wanted to be legitimate.

The case of the stolen electricity - the Electricity Theft Case - appeal was to be heard in Paris on Thursday, July 26.

That was three weeks away.

* * *

On that July morning, Marcel and Georgette took the Métro to the Palais de Justice. She was deathly pale and silent. He did not stop talking: earlier he had told her that he was confident he would win the appeal. She was not: she was sure that the Sens verdict would be upheld and he was going to be sent to jail.

Marcel was polite in court. Smartly dressed in a dark suit and black bow tie, he spoke only to reply to a question. That was how his lawyer had briefed him.

A few hours later the two were back on the Métro. Georgette was again silent. That time, so was Marcel. He sat with one hand on Georgette's knee and she tapped her feet nervously to the rhythm of the train. His 15-day jail sentence had been squashed, and the fine of 300 francs had been reduced to a hundred francs but he had been told the conviction would be recorded. Thus, he had become a convicted criminal.

"I've been convicted, yes, but that doesn't prove that I'm guilty," he murmured to Georgette.

The law forbade a convicted criminal to hold an elected post. As Marcel was still a property owner in the Yonne, he had remained a member of its regional council, but he was obliged to resign. He did not do so. The council asked him to or he would be dismissed. He still did not. He dared the council to dismiss him, the ex-serviceman, and one who had taken shrapnel in the foot for France.

The council rose to his challenge.

Wednesday, October 10, it dismissed Marcel. It was the third anniversary of his election to the council.

"Speak of an insult upon an insult!" he thundered to Georgette.

Not one to leave the last word to someone else, he sent a letter off to the council. He wrote: 'I have the regret to inform you that my current professional obligations and my absence from the region no longer permit me to fulfil my duties as general councillor. Consequently, I would ask you to accept my resignation as of this day'.

The council did not reply.

* * *

November came.

Two detectives arrived at the Petiots' apartment. They explained they had come because of the inexplicable death of a young woman. The *mademoiselle* had died the previous night.

Marcel asked the dead girl's name.

It was Raymonde Hanss.

Georgette, present, grasped her throat. Raymonde Hanss, an unmarried 33-year-old was her dressmaker.

According to the two detectives, a Mrs Coquille, Raymonde Hanss's mother, had told the police that Marcel had been supplying her daughter with the painkiller 'Optalidon'. She had explained that Hanss had needed a painkiller for chronic toothache because of bad teeth: frightened of dentists, she had refused to consult one. The doctor had told the young woman that she could take an 'Optalidon' whenever she needed to.

Coquille had furthermore explained to the police that her telephone had rung late the previous afternoon. Dr Petiot was on the phone. Her daughter, he had told her, was at his practice, and she was not feeling well. She was to come and collect her.

Having rushed to Rue de Caumartin, Coquille had found her daughter, not in the consulting room, as she had expected she would, but lying asleep on a bed in one of the Petiots' bedrooms. Hanss's clothes had been disturbed.

The doctor had called a taxi and had helped the driver carry her sleeping daughter to the car. At the car he had handed her a bottle of 'Coramine' pills. Her daughter was to start taking the pills on waking up: she had to take two pills initially and to repeat the dose whenever necessary.

She had thought 'Coramine', an analeptic drug, was another painkiller.

Dr Petiot had promised to look in on her daughter in the morning, but during the night it had been necessary to summon him; Hanss's breathing had become irregular. He had arrived very quickly and had felt her daughter's pulse, had looked into her eyes by the light of a small flashlight, and had announced that she was fine and sleeping soundly.

In the morning, she had found her daughter dead.

Marcel dismissed the story repeated to him by the two detectives with a wave of a hand. Hanss had been a drug addict, he said. Both he and his wife had warned her about the drugs, but she would not listen. She had been on heroin. On numerous occasions she had asked him to give her some; he had refused. He had instead prescribed the non-steroidal and anti-inflammatory analgesic 'Optalidon'. He had warned her that too large a dose could cause insomnia, asthma, kidney failure and a glucose deficiency in the blood. Again, she had refused to listen to him and had taken one, even several, whenever in pain. He had given her the 'Optalidon' only because he had pitied her and wanted to help her. She had then developed an abscess in her mouth, which she had wanted him to treat by extracting some of her teeth. He had also refused to do that. He had instead given her a morphine injection for the pain; one only. Again, only because he had wanted to help her. He had given Coquille the bottle of 'Coramine' because he had feared that Hanss had taken too large a dose of 'Optalidon', which would have affected the sugar level in her blood: the 'Coramine' would have corrected it. The previous night when he had examined Hanss, there had been no indication she was in danger of death. The only danger she had been in was being asphyxiated by all the curious neighbours who crowded around her bed. He had asked them to go. She had been sleeping soundly when he had left her. He presumed, he added, that on waking up she had taken a strong dose of heroin. It would undoubtedly have killed her.

The two detectives told Marcel that he should not leave Paris.

"I don't see why I shouldn't if I want to! I didn't have anything to do with this stupid girl's death!" he protested.

Georgette walked the two detectives to the door. She asked them to tell Coquille she was deeply sorry for what had happened to her daughter.

"Please tell her that, if my husband and I can do anything for her, she need only pick up the telephone and call us," she said.

Neither of the two indicated they had heard her.

Raymonde Hanss' body lay at the Médico-Légal Institute for several weeks while the police pondered whether to charge Marcel with professional misconduct, perhaps even with involuntary manslaughter. Deciding they had insufficient evidence to make either of the charges stick, they released the body for burial.

In 1944, Coquille asked the Quay for her daughter's case to be reopened. The Quay refused. An inspector explained to the woman that the main piece of evidence against Dr Marcel Petiot - the report of the post-mortem undertaken on her daughter's body - was missing.

The inspector could not explain how the post-mortem report had been mislaid.

* * *

For the following five months Marcel lived, to all appearances, a quiet, law-abiding existence. He took Georgette and Gerhardt to the cinema and the theatre, he took them to Chez Marius for dinner, and he took them on holiday to Auxerre.

April came. It was Saturday, late afternoon. Easter was eight days away. It was raining heavily. Marcel was alone at the apartment; Georgette and Gerhardt had gone to visit Long Arm who was in the process of selling his restaurant to retire to Seignelay.

The Petiots' telephone rang. Marcel picked up. The caller identified himself as a police inspector. He wanted to speak to Dr Petiot. Marcel said the doctor was not in and wouldn't be back until after Easter. He offered to take a message. The police inspector said it would not be necessary.

Half an hour later, the Petiots' doorbell rang.

Two detectives stood on the landing. They asked for Dr Petiot. Marcel said they were talking to him. The two asked whether they could step in for a moment; they needed to ask a few questions.

A Mr Cotteret, shop assistant at Librairie Gibert Joseph, a bookshop on Boul'Miche, had reported that he had seen a man slip a book into the inside pocket of his raincoat. The man had left without having paid for the book. Cotteret had rushed after him, but had only been able to catch up with him some distance away. The shoplifter had explained that he was a doctor and in a great hurry to get back to his practice; he had shown Cotteret his identity card and offered to pay for the book. Since it was the shop's policy to charge shoplifters, Cotteret had refused to accept the 25 francs the shoplifter had tried to push into his hands. The shoplifter had next become aggressive; he threatened to bash Cotteret's face in and shoved him aside so forcefully that the shop assistant had fallen to the ground. The shoplifter had then run off at full pelt. The name on the identity card was Marcel André Henri Félix Petiot.

Marcel admitted to the two inspectors that he had been in the bookshop that morning, but he certainly had not stolen a book. He explained he was a scientist and working on an extremely complicated project and he had been very deep in thought in the shop. He had not run away and he had not threatened the shop assistant. He certainly never shoved the man out of the way. And he had offered to pay for the book. Again, he offered to pay for the book.

Georgette and Gerhardt chose that moment to walk in. She looked into the living room, told Gerhardt to go to his room and went into the kitchen and closed the door.

Gerhardt went to his room.

The inspectors prepared to leave. They asked Marcel to call in at their police station, the local one in the ninth *arrondissement*, on the Monday. He was to be there at 3 P.M. sharp.

At the door, Marcel asked the two not to call Georgette in for questioning.

"She would only worry, and there is nothing to worry about," he said.

Monday afternoon, Marcel arrived at the police station an hour late. He was escorted to the office of the inspector assigned to the case. No sooner had he entered the inspector's office than he began to cry. Sobbing, he pushed a letter across the inspector's desk: he wanted him to read it. The inspector, embarrassed at a grown man's tears, did not at first know what to do, but, after a few moments of silence, he read the letter. Afterwards, he told Marcel that he could go home, but that he should not leave Paris. He saw Marcel, who was still crying, out; on his way back to his office he halted at the duty officer's desk. He had, he said, just had a madman in his office.

Marcel's letter was an explanation of what had happened in the bookshop.

He wrote that he was a scientist and inventor and that he had left the bookshop without having paid for the book because his mind had been on his latest invention, a machine to relieve chronic constipation. He was encountering a difficulty with the machine's power supply and the book he had walked off with was a manual on electricity; in it he had found a solution to the problem. He explained that he had been suffering from chronic depression since a Great War injury and as he had already spent time in a mental institution because of the shock of the injury, he feared that should the bookshop charge him, he would have to return yet again to an asylum. He would rather kill himself than do so.

He also wrote that he had invented a perpetual motion machine that would 'run until the end of time'.

He had clipped several bills and receipts for equipment he had bought to perfect his inventions to the letter. Most of those were from hardware stores and were for tools like hammers and spanners. The rest were from pharmaceutical companies and were for banal medical instruments.

The examining magistrate assigned to the case sent Marcel to a psychiatrist, Dr Marcel Cuiller. The latter had already come across Marcel: he was the psychiatrist who had examined him in Sens during the Petrol Theft Case.

Two months later Dr Cuiller handed over his report. He described Dr Marcel Petiot as a man who had given him the impression of 'being depressive, unbalanced and of suffering from inventive delirium. He claims to have discovered perpetual motion and a pump for faeces, and was in a state of lunacy at the time of the action. He can not be held responsible for any of his actions'.

Marcel should enter a mental asylum immediately as he was not only a danger to himself, but also to society, the psychiatrist stated.

Accordingly, Librairie Gibert Joseph withdrew its complaint.

Marcel was elated despite that he was yet again heading for an asylum.

The examining magistrate informed Marcel that he was allowing him to find an asylum himself, but he had only a few days to do so or the court would admit him forcibly into an asylum of its choosing.

Georgette began looking for a private clinic that would accept her husband. She believed it was best for him to go and have a rest. Not for a moment did she believe he was mentally unstable. He was tired. No he was exhausted: the move to Paris and building up a practice from scratch had taken a lot out of him. She was certain he would be fine after a rest in some quiet place.

Marcel decided what that quiet place would be.

Saturday, August 1, accompanied by Georgette, he took a taxi to Ivry, a commune on the southern perimeter of Paris. The commune was known for its cemetery because there lay those who had been guillotined.

Marcel entered the clinic of Dr François Achille-Delmas, considered the world's best psychiatrist and psychoanalyst. His name would be mentioned often in the years to come as the psychiatrist who had treated Lucia Anna Joyce, daughter of James Joyce. Lucia had entered the clinic for the first time while Marcel was there. Dr Achille-Delmas would also go down in history as the man who dared analyse Adolf Hitler in his 1946 book, 'Hitler: Essai de Biographie Psychopathologique' - Hitler: a Psycho-pathological Study.

Marcel was calm and charming on arrival. He carried one small and one large suitcase. In the small one were clothes and toilet articles. The large one was filled with books. Dr Achille-Delmas and his staff were impressed by their new patient's choice of reading matter: scientific manuals.

Two weeks at the clinic and Marcel spoke of leaving.

Georgette must get him out, he said.

She appealed to the *juge de l'application des peines* - the judge responsible for overseeing the terms and conditions of sentences - to allow her husband to be discharged. She based her request on an assessment of his mental state which Dr Achille-Delmas had made. He was suffering from a mild form of manic depression, a perfectly controllable condition, as she wrote in her letter.

The judge wanted another psychiatrist to examine Marcel.

The task was handed to Dr Joseph Rogues de Fursac, pioneer in psycho-analysis and renowned for books like 'What Makes Men Misers', published in 1911.

Dr Roges de Fursac did not like to disagree with Dr Achille-Delmas, but he pointed out all the same that he thought that Marcel was chronically unbalanced, although calm.

Marcel was to remain institutionalised.

Georgette approached the appeal court.

Another psychiatric evaluation was needed, but Marcel refused to have any more 'cranks' examine him. He told Georgette to write to French President Albert Lebrun to plead for his discharge. She did. She did not receive a reply.

Reluctantly, Marcel agreed to undergo the psychiatric evaluation.

Three psychiatrists, the Professors Georges Paul Génil-Perrin, Paul-Marie Maxime Laignel-Lavastine and Henri Claude, arrived at the clinic. Indiscreet staff called them over and told them what Marcel had been saying about them; he had called them nonentities not worthy of examining him. All three were legendary worldwide for their research of the human mind and neurological disorders. Génil-Perrin and Claude were also famous for their psychological analysis of Eugéne Weidmann.

Hearing what Marcel had called them, the three psychiatrists fled in fear from the clinic.

In December, four months later, the three, ordered to do so by the court, bravely returned.

Marcel was waiting and received them with a broad smile.

In the report they handed in, they declared: 'Petiot displays no mental disorders and all his psychiatric history is thoroughly suspect, as his contacts with military and civilian psychiatrists always coincided with his difficulties with the law. The psychological anomalies that he displays - amorality and instinctive perversion - are not of a nature to diminish his criminal responsibility'.

Marcel could return home. He had been at the clinic for six months.

Back home, Gerhardt was waiting. He threw his arms around his father; he was so very happy to see him. Although Georgette and Long Arm had visited Marcel at the clinic - Georgette had done so almost every day - Gerhardt had not. Marcel had not wanted his son to see him locked up in a mental asylum.

The next afternoon, Marcel was at his desk. His waiting room was packed; the patients were thrilled to have their doctor back. Georgette had told them, and the neighbours, that her husband was taking a sabbatical to study abroad.

As soon as there were no further patients in his waiting room, Marcel set off to tell three men he had befriended - Fourrier, Pintard and Porchon - the same tale. He knew Georgette would not have told them; she was unaware of the friendship.

Nézondet had been told the truth.

* * *

Early in 1936, two years after Hanss's death, but only a few months after his discharge from Dr Achille-Delmas' clinic, Marcel was appointed district surgeon of the ninth *arrondissement*. He won the appointment on the merit of a *curriculum vitae* in which he repeated the claims he had made in his advertising leaflet. He also still claimed he was a member of the Regional Council of the Yonne, despite having been dismissed, and also that he was in charge of the Permanent Medical Office of the County of the Seine. There was no such office. The police did not check the authenticity of his claims. Neither did they verify whether he had a criminal record or a history of mental illness.

As district surgeon, he had the right to attend post-mortems, and issue and sign death certificates. He also had access to Paris's post-mortem archives. He could look up Hanss' post-mortem report and remove whatever he wished from it. Even tear it up and chuck it into the wastepaper basket.

* * *

For two years Marcel, to all appearances, did not step out of line.

Apparently, he had decided to make some money as he began to speculate on the property market. One property he bought was the apartment building at Number 52 Rue de Reuilly in the twelfth *arrondissement* where Georgette would spend the night after the discovery of human remains at the townhouse.

183

However, at the end of 1938, he was back in court. He faced a tax fraud accusation. He had declared an income of 29,700 francs for 1937, yet a Paris doctor's annual income would have been closer to half a million francs. He had also not declared the income he had made from rent from his various properties.

In the dock, he insisted he was a very poor man despite the fact that he was doing his best to find more patients. He claimed that he did house calls on foot because he could not afford to buy or run a car, and that he and Georgette had not eaten in a restaurant nor stepped into a bistro for years because they just did not have the money to have done so. They also had not taken a holiday for years. He said that they did not even have a bedroom to sleep in. They slept on a mattress on the floor.

He was fined 25,000 francs and he paid it reluctantly.

"Only idiots don't cheat with their tax declarations," he told Long Arm.

* * *

September 3, 1939, the Second World War began.

Marcel was exuberant.

He hung the French *Tricolore* banner over his desk and told his patients he was ready to battle the *Boches*. He showed them his Great War wound and said he was prepared to give his life for France. He told his family that because of his Great War injury he would not be mobilised; he could continue to practise medicine *paisiblement* - peacefully. He even told Félix, and Long Arm, back in Seignelay and Léone Arnoux already living with him, that they need not fear that the war would cause them hardship. He would provide for them. Long Arm and even the hated Félix were financially comfortable, mainly because of real estate deals they had gone into with him, but all the same, he promised to look out for them.

For the first months of war Marcel listened to the radio every morning. There was not much going on. A few artillery exchanges with the enemy and the sightings of their reconnaissance incursions into French airspace were being reported. He said that it was not war as he remembered. War was trenches. War was horrible wounds and spilling one's blood and guts. War was destruction and death.

The winter of 1939 to 1940 was exceptionally cold. In Eastern France, the temperatures fell to minus four degrees Celcius. Wine growers reported wine in their cellars was turning into blocks of ice. Marcel, Georgette and Gerhardt still regularly went to the cinema. They saw newsreels of French soldiers on the front chopping up and boiling frozen blocks of wine to have something to drink.

It was also cold in Paris. It snowed frequently and shards of ice hung from the tarpaulin over La Chope du Printemps. Mr Bézayrie's waiters also boiled red wine; the patrons drank the mulled wine with their *plat du jour: steak frites* or *pot au feu*. Shortages and rationing were still only a bad memory of the Great War.

In the spring of 1940, the war began in earnest with the *Blitzkrieg*. The Germans attacked and conquered Denmark and Norway, Holland, Belgium and Luxembourg. The latest radio reports urged the French to defend France. Announcers shouted the refrain from *La Marseillaise: Aux armes citoyens!*

One mid-June morning, another voice came on the radio; a trembling, old man's voice. "*Il faut cesser le combat*," said Marshal Philippe Pétain, hero of the previous war. The fighting must stop.

Marcel could not believe his ears. He could not believe he had heard the *Maréchal* say such a thing; he knew him as a great patriot who had fought the *Boches* with all his might in the Great War.

The north and east regions of France fell to the Germans. Fearful that German Stukas would start bombing Paris, Parisians began to flee. Petiot watched the 'cowards' snarl up the street below with cars, trucks and anything with wheels; baby carriages, bathtubs, beds, wheelchairs. He swore he would never flee.

Saturday, June 22, France officially admitted defeat at the hands of the Germans. A Franco-German armistice was signed. Hitler annexed that part of France bordering Germany and he handed the area bordering Italy over to Benito Mussolini, his Fascist ally in Rome. What was left of the country was divided into the northern occupied zone, which included Paris, and the southern free zone. Mined and marked with barbed wire, a demarcation line separated the two.

With France cut up, the Germans disbanded the defeated French army while maintaining a force of 100,000 men under their command: the soldiers were to keep domestic order. The police were to assist them.

185

The Germans took down all the *Tricolore* banners flying in both zones and hoisted a revamped *Tricolore* to which the double-headed Frankish Axe or 'Francisca', Attila the Hun's favourite weapon, had been added. One of the old *Tricolore* banners was put in a glass display case in Les Invalides Army Museum; the remains of Napoleon rested nearby. Meanwhile, in his headquarters in the spa-town of Vichy, Pétain, the man who would help govern the two Frances, replaced the French motto - *Liberté, Égalité, Fraternité* - Freedom, Equality, Brotherhood - with the more nationalistic, *Travail, Famille, Patrie* - Work, Family, Motherland. *Les années noires* - the dark years - began.

Marcel was determined that not one night would Georgette and Gerhardt go to bed on an empty stomach. He loved them too much and wouldn't allow them to suffer. And he would make sure they survived the war.

He bought a bike and a cart. He painted the bike green and registered it with the licence number 3866-RD7 at the ninth *arrondissement* town hall. The cart was an ordinary barrow boy's cart; not large and heavy, he could attach it to his green-painted bike should he have something to transport.

He also bought a large townhouse; Number 21 Rue le Sueur. The price of real estate plunged because of the war, so he thought paying 495,000 francs for the property was getting it at a bargain price.

A cool September morning, he took possession of his new property.

It was 1941.

He rode the Métro to the townhouse. Obligado was the nearest underground station, but the Germans had closed most stations to economise on electricity and Obligado was closed. He descended at the next nearest station; l'Étoile beside the Arc de Triomphe monument. From the station he walked down Avenue de la Grande Armée to the townhouse; an eight-minute walk. Rue le Sueur was named after Eustache le Sueur, the painter. Many of the neighbouring streets were also named after artists: Pergolèse, Puccini, Berlioz and Victor Hugo.

Marcel walked through the townhouse's large empty rooms. They were cold; cold like a mortuary. Once his clinic had opened, the rooms would be cosily warm, that he knew. In the basement stood two coal and wood burners and these would heat the house.

Indeed, those burners would be put to good use: excellent use.

The townhouse would be put to good use too.
He planned to convert the property into a mental clinic.
He was going to make some money.
First, he would have some renovation work done to the house.

-0-

CHAPTER TWO

Good Neighbour

Two months after the masons had finished their work at the townhouse, preparing its conversion into a mental clinic, the doorbell of the Petiots' apartment at Number 66 Rue du Caumartin rang.

It was 11 A.M. on Christmas Day.

Marcel was the only one at home. Georgette and Gerhardt had gone to spend that third Christmas of war, and the second of the occupation with Long Arm and Léone Arnoux in Seignelay. They would be away for a fortnight.

Joachim Guschinov, the furrier from Number 69, stood on the landing. He was expected. He wore his best suit and he clutched a fedora in hands that trembled slightly. He had been to the Petiots' apartment often, but it had always been as a patient. On that Christmas day, he had come to talk business.

Marcel took Guschinov into the living room and offered him an aperitif; he would be drinking coffee himself and from the rich aroma that drifted from the coffe pot it was clear that it would not be ersatz that he would be drinking but the real thing.

Guschinov accepted the offered aperitif and Marcel began to pour some *Bhyrr* into a glass.

"Tell me when to stop, Mr Guschinov," said he before he had even poured a finger's depth into the glass.

"Stop, please, *Monsieur*," said Guschinov immediately because he had heard that the doctor was a frugal man.

Handed the glass, he raised it to his lips and proposed a toast.

"To peace," he said.

"To peace, and, Mr Guschinov, may this be our last Christmas under German Occupation," replied Marcel.

189

Guschinov had always had an eye for the finer things in life and he did not fail to notice the aperitif glass was made of crystal and the cup from which his host was drinking the coffee was porcelain.

"You are a lucky man, Mr Guschinov, because without doubt, this *will* be your last Christmas under the Germans. But I will not be so lucky," said Marcel.

An hour later, his business with Marcel done, the furrier ambled across the street, back home. He had a lump in his throat and his eyes were filled with tears. He certainly did not feel lucky. He was 42 years of age; his hair had been black only months before, but worry had turned it grey. He had lost weight; the corpulent frame, of which he had been proud because for him it meant he had made it in life, had shrunk. In the home into which he had poured much thought and money to make it beautiful and comfortable for a wife and children, there was only his wife, Renée.

Joachim Guschinov was going to flee France.

And Marcel was going to help him do so.

* * *

For some time Guschinov had known that because of the Nazis, both the German ones and their French counterparts like Pétain, he would have to flee.

He had first discussed such a flight with Renée in 1940 when, acting on behalf of the Germans, the Vichy government had started to introduce the Jewish Statutes: a series of laws that excluded Jews from French public life.

The first statute, issued on September 27, within two months of the 1940 fall of France, had ordered Jews to register in a census, and all Jewish shop owners, therefore him too, to display the words *Judische Geschaft* in their windows.

The second, on October 3, had compelled Jews to have their identity cards stamped with the word *Juif.* That statute had also defined who was a Jew, and forbade Jews to hold elected posts, work in the civil service, the armed forces and police, or as journalists. Neither could they teach.

The third, dated October 4, had made it possible for Jews to be interned in special camps, and for foreign-born Jews to be forcibly removed to special living areas.

Each statute had been signed by Pétain in his capacity of Head of the French state, and had been co-signed by various Vichy government ministers.

The only reason Guschinov had not yet fled was Renée. Not feeling threatened because she was not Jewish, she had refused to go. But, finally, the furrier had made his decision; he would go and she would stay.

He was going to Argentina.

He was going to Argentina with Marcel's help.

* * *

Joachim Guschinov's life story was known in the neighbourhood. Proud of what he had made of himself, he had told it often enough.

He had arrived in Paris from his native Poland as a penniless twenty-year-old Jewish refugee. The Great War had only just ended and thousands of Jews, most of them Polish or Russian, had fled to what was considered Europe's most non-racist, religion-tolerant and welcoming country: France. For his first years in Paris, he, an emaciated young man speaking French haltingly with a pronounced Yiddish accent, had lived in a hostel without heating or hot water. He had done odd jobs; he scrubbed pots and pans in restaurants, worked as a gardener and as a railway porter. He had become a Jewish tailor's assistant, then, with money borrowed from the tailor at the high interest of 25 per cent because he was unable to provide collateral, he had opened his own furrier shop. In 1933, when the Petiots settled on the street, the shop had already become successful enough to afford the wages of two assistants, Jean Gouedo and a Miss Riquet, a spinster in her forties whom everyone called La Riquette. He had by then left the hostel to live in a room at the back of his shop. And he had married Renée Legendre from the very Catholic region of Sarthe, south-west of Paris.

What the neighbours also knew about Joachim, but which he had obviously not told them, was that his marriage was not all that happy. One rumour was he had a roving eye; another, that it was Renée's eye that wandered. He was supposed to be in a relationship with a waitress from La Chope du Printemps, a woman named Bernadette Fraysse whose husband worked for a gold bullion dealer. Renée was apparently having an affair with Jean Gouedo.

Another rumour was that Joachim suffered from venereal disease. He was one of Marcel's patients and the doctor did regularly go to the shop to give him an injection.

* * *

Guschinov sat down with Renée. He wanted to tell her what Marcel had told him.

An Argentinian diplomat, a friend of the kind doctor across the street, would help him to get away from the Nazis. The diplomat wanted 25,000 francs for the passport on which he would be travelling. It would not be a fake, but a genuine Argentinian passport issued in Buenos Aires. The diplomat wanted another 500,000 francs to cover the fee of the people smuggler who would take him from Occupied France to Vichy-France and then across the border to Spain. A people smuggler's fee was 10,000 francs but the diplomat was including the passage on a neutral freight ship from Spain to an African port, the passage from there to Buenos Aires, and the bill for the hotel accommodation on arriving in Buenos Aires.

"The doctor said that it might sound a lot of money, but considering what is at stake - my life - it is a very reasonable fee. His friend certainly wasn't out to make money from the heartbreak of others," said Guschinov.

He also had to have one thousand United States dollars in notes sewn into the lining of the jacket he would be wearing on his journey; it was just in case he had to make emergency purchases during his flight. And he would have to have enough cash on him to pay the daily rate of 400 francs his board and lodging were to cost at the safe house where he would have to await departure.

That was not all.

He was to take whatever gold bullion and jewellery he had, and he should take no fewer than three pelts, preferably mink, with him if he planned to start a furrier business in Buenos Aires. The pelts would be to kick-start his new business.

"I've been sworn to secrecy. I can tell you, but no one else," said

Guschinov to his wife.

In the morning, he told Gouedo. He had to tell him, he reckoned. He wanted him to buy the shop to rescue it from German hands. The asking price was 75,000 francs far below the shop's value, but the understanding would be that after the war he would be allowed to buy it back at the same price.

La Riquette, having overheard part of the conversation, was also told. Fraysse was also told; her husband was going to be approached to exchange gold bullion into cash on the black market.

The Argentinian diplomat insisted on being paid in cash.

* * *

New Year's Day 1942, the furrier shop remained closed.

Upstairs, Guschinov and Renée packed two suitcases for his flight scheduled for the next evening. Marcel had warned Guschinov he could only take two suitcases because walking around the Paris streets with more would draw attention. The mink pelts filled one case.

Early evening, Gouedo and La Riquette arrived. They helped remove all labels and JG monograms from the clothes Joachim was to take. That was another of the doctor's instruction; all labels and monograms had to be removed. They also helped sew the dollars into the lining of the jacket he planned to wear.

In the morning, Friday, the Jewish Sabbath, the shop still closed, Gouedo and La Riquette returned.

They said a tearful goodbye to Guschinov.

Late afternoon, Guschinov walked around the apartment and drew the blackout curtains. He lit the Sabbath candles and called Renée to come and sit down for the Sabbath meal. The two ate in silence. Guschinov was to meet someone - who the doctor had not said - in the sixteenth *arrondissement* on the corner of Avenue de la Grande Armée and Rue Pergolèse to be escorted to the safe house; it was in the sixteenth *arrondissement*, too. He would have to be vaccinated for his trip while at the safe house. The doctor himself would give him the vaccination shot.

Guschinov and Renée set off by Métro. She was going to go as far as l'Étoile station. Each carried a suitcase. On the train the furrier's lower lip started to tremble.

"I'll tell you what," said Renée. "I'll walk with you to Rue Pergolèse."

On Place de l'Étoile beside a blue, green and white sentry box, a black and white wooden board signposted the direction to various German military headquarters: Ortslazarett in Le Vésinet, LN-Werkstatt in Suresnes, Kfz. - Inst Park 503 in Neuilly, Kriegslazare in Garches. A young, handsome German soldier in a smart new *feld-grau* uniform stood in the sentry box. He smiled at Rénee. Her husband grabbed her by the arm and urged her to walk faster.

The restaurants, bistros and shops the two passed were dark.

They passed a *vespasienne*, the circular Paris street urinal. It was covered in anti-Jewish slogans and torn posters for the anti-Semitic 'Le Juif et la France: La France aux Francais: Le Péril Métèque' - The Jew and France: Return France to the French: The Yid Peril - exhibition, held in Paris a few weeks previously.

They reached Rue le Sueur, the Eiffel Tower at the end of it. Le Crocodile was dark too.

They walked on towards Rue Pergolèse.

Reaching it, Renée put down the suitcase she was carrying.

"I'll wait with you, Joachim," she said.

"No! Dr Petiot said I must be on my own."

His voice was thick with emotion.

He started to cry. Renée, too, started to cry.

Tenderly, they bid each other goodbye.

It was not going to be a long goodbye. They were to see each other again, and soon; the *Boches* were going to lose the war and Guschinov would return to a liberated Paris.

Renée walked back to l'Étoile station. Halfway there, she turned to wave to her husband. He was already gone.

The following morning, Gouedo and La Riquette arrived early at the shop. They asked Renée whether her husband had got away safely.

"Oh, yes, he got away safely," she told them.

She added that Dr Petiot was a good man; a good neighbour.

"So he is," they agreed.

Renée's eyes were red.

She had spent most of the night crying.

* * *

In the afternoon, Georgette and Gerhardt returned from Seignelay. They had enjoyed a wonderful holiday and Christmas with Long Arm and Léone.

Marcel told them he had also enjoyed Christmas.

* * *

Tuesday, January 20, eighteen days later, the Wannsee Conference on Wannsee Lake in south-west Berlin was convened by *SS-Obergruppenführer* - Lieutenant General - Reinard Heydrich, Head of the RSHA. In ninety minutes, the Final Solution, the Nazi policy to murder eleven million Jews, was drafted. According to the formal minutes of the conference - the Wannsee Protocol - there were some 865,000 Jews in France, of whom 165,000 lived in Occupied France. Friday, January 30, ten days later, Adolf Hitler confirmed the Final Solution speaking at the Berlin Sports Palace.

"The old Jewish law of an eye for an eye and a tooth for a tooth will be applied," he said.

It would mean the complete annihilation of the Jews.

In Paris, the Nazi propaganda film about Polish Jews, 'Der ewige Jude' - The Eternal Jew - directed by Nazi filmmaker, Fritz Hippler, under the supervision of Joseph Goebbels, German Minister of Propaganda, was being shown. Polish Jews, of whom Joachim was one, were portrayed as filthy, corrupt, lazy, physically-ugly and sexually-perverted sub-humans. Thousands of Parisians fell in line to see the film.

Renée, discussing a scene from the film in which a rabbi was seen slaughtering a cow in a supposedly bloody ritual, told Gouedo and La Riquette she thanked God for having sent Dr Petiot to Rue de Caumartin.

"He's saved Joachim's life. The Nazis won't be able to kill him now."

She waited patiently to receive news via Marcel that her husband had arrived safely in Argentina. End February, no longer able to stand the tension, she went to ask him.

"I am just about to call in at the shop," said Marcel.

He had received a postcard from Guschinov.

"Here."

He pushed a postcard, the kind without a picture, across his desk.

"Read it. I am afraid that you would not be able to keep it. Security, you know. There are still so many waiting to go, and we cannot endanger their lives."

The postcard was not addressed to anyone, it was unsigned, and there was no date or stamp on it.

Renée read the words written across it.

'Have arrived. Was ill during crossing. Perfectly recovered. You can come'.

She thought she recognised the writing as her husband's. Yet, she felt he must have been either standing when writing the card or he was in great haste; his usual tiny, sophisticated script contained letters of unequal size, and the words were jumbled.

Marcel told Renée that her husband had sailed from Spain to Senegal and from there to Buenos Aires.

"He was a little nervous during the Atlantic crossing. The weather was stormy," he said.

He wanted to know how Renée felt about joining her husband. She replied she was still thinking about it.

"When you've made up your mind, I will arrange it all."

"Thank you," she said. "You are most kind, *Monsieur*."

A few days later, Marcel went to the shop and asked Gouedo to tell Renée she should come to his practice; he wanted to tell her something. She rushed across the street.

"I've received word from Mr Guschinov again. A note this time," said Marcel.

Renée grabbed the piece of paper from her neighbour's hands.

She read it.

'Business going well. I doubled in two months. Come immediately'.

The words were scrawled on the letterhead paper of Buenos Aires's Alvear Palace Hotel. There was neither signature nor date.

Renée was again not allowed to keep the note.

* * *

In the following months, Marcel fought the accusation that he had supplied the missing Van Bever and the missing Marthe Khaît's daughter, Raymonde Baudet, with drugs.

-0-

CHAPTER THREE

Angel Maker

Friday, June 5, a young woman named Denise - Lili to her family and friends - Hotin climbed the stairs to the Petiots' apartment. Marcel opened to her knock. Seeing her, he looked startled, but only for a moment. He asked her to step inside. Several patients were in the waiting room, but she was taken straight through to his consulting room.

Lili Hotin explained the reason for her visit and Marcel said that he saw no reason why he would not be able to help her, but, as she had probably seen, he had several patients waiting and, on Fridays, he received only until 3 P.M.

"It's already after two. Could you come back?" he asked.

She said she could.

"But I will have to ask you to come to my other practice," he warned.

Ninety minutes later, Lili was back at the apartment she had earlier set off from. The occupants, Mrs Mallard, a retired midwife, and her divorced daughter, Gilberte Mouron, fifty years old, were surprised to see her so soon again. She had told them she was going to see Dr Petiot to ask him for a little favour and that she would be going home afterwards; home was a farm outside the village of La Neuville-Garnier, forty kilometres north of Paris. What the little favour was she had not told them.

"The doctor couldn't see me, but I'm to go to his other practice later," she told the two.

The second practice was in the sixteenth *arrondissement* and she was to wait for him on Avenue de la Grande Armée. He would pick her up there.

Lili did not return home to the farm.

* * *

197

Lili Hotin's story began during the Christmas season of 1940.

Mademoiselle Nelly Denise Bartholomeus, known by her childhood nickname Lili, was a salesgirl at Lancel, the luxury leather goods shop. With shapely legs, a tiny waist, round face and a turned-up nose, she was easily the prettiest of the Lancel 'girls'. It was, therefore, not surprising when a young farmer, a Jean Hotin, in Paris for a few naughty days, made straight for her counter on walking into the shop. Jean was a daddy's boy. Daddy was Jean Hotin Sr. a wealthy, widowed farmer and the Mayor of La Neuville-Garnier. Jean Jr., 27 years old, was good-looking, but weak, and consequently under Daddy Hotin's thumb. The only time he was able to do as he wished was when in Paris. What he wished to do was to fall madly in love. He did, with Lili. She was 26 years old.

On June 5, 1941, six month later, Lili and Jean were married. In his capacity as Mayor, Daddy Hotin officiated at the marriage. It had been hard for Jean to persuade his father that, with her Parisian ways, Lili would make an ideal farmer's wife. She loved to dance, have a drink, and buy pretty clothes. She also smoked and she was not a virgin, though Daddy Hotin would not have known. Jean, of course, did. On their wedding day he also knew she was three months pregnant.

La Neuville-Garnier's two hundred inhabitants loved to gossip. They also gossiped about Lili's expanding waist. The gossip reached Daddy Hotin's ears. He called Jean and Lili into the kitchen to explain to him what was going on. Two weeks later the couple set off for Paris. One of Lili's girlfriends had told her of a *faiseuse d'ange* - an angel maker or backstreet abortionist - who could restore her former tiny waist.

The angel maker was Mallard. She was 84 years old and lived in the red-light district of Pigalle. She denied to the couple that she performed abortions but said that she could recommend a doctor who did. She telephoned him. He agreed to do the abortion, but would not be able to do so immediately. His fee was 5,000 francs. A few days later, the small procedure was done in Mallard's apartment; Jean had stayed at the farm. Working away, the doctor had tried to convince Lili that he was not an angel maker. He said he was a champion of women's rights. A woman had the right to choose when she wanted to become a mother. Her body did not make that possible. Fortunately, science did. Lili paid with money Daddy Hotin had given her.

After having spent two nights with Mallard and Mourin to recuperate,

198

Lili returned home.

Soon, Lili and Jean's marriage started to break up. The villagers said it was because Daddy Hotin, a mean man, was forcing Lili to work with Jean in the fields. They also said the baby Lili had got rid off had not been Jean's. Daddy Hotin called another kitchen conference and told Lili to return to Paris to ask the doctor for a letter stating that he had not performed an abortion on her; he had treated her for pneumonia. Daddy Hotin even wanted the doctor to state he had applied cupping glasses and mustard plasters to her body as treatment.

Lili, obedient, returned to Paris on June 5. It was her first wedding anniversary. She was expected back on the farm for dinner although it was not going to be anything special. Anniversaries, even birthdays, were by rule ignored in Daddy Hotin's house.

The young woman did not return.

In the morning, Jean was out in the fields as usual. He was not particularly worried about his wife's absence. She had probably met up with a girlfriend and decided to stay overnight in Paris, he told Daddy Hotin.

The day ended. Lili was still not back. Jean still did not worry. Lili was probably spending another night in Paris.

Two days passed.

Lili's mother telephoned Jean. She had received an incomprehensible letter from her daughter mailed in Paris. She wanted to know from her son-in-law what was going on. Lili had written that she was in Paris, but ill with pneumonia. She emphasised she was not in Paris for an abortion as she knew was being said in the village. She had accordingly decided not to return to the farm, but to set of for the city of Bordeaux, 580 kilometres south-west of Paris. She would be joining friends. She asked her parents not to worry about her; she would be in touch shortly.

The woman wanted to know what this was about an abortion and Jean said that he had no idea what Lili was talking about.

Three weeks passed.

It was Jean's turn to receive a letter from Lili. The letter also bore a Paris postmark. Lili wrote that she was very sad to have to be away, but something was preventing her from returning to the farm. She did hope nonetheless that she would be able to return soon. She addressed Jean as, *mon cher petit Jean* - my dear little Jean. She signed off with tender love.

199

The dates on the Paris postmarks were illegible.
Jean got on with his life.
There were cows to milk; there were fields to plough.

-0-

CHAPTER FOUR

Killing Jews

A day after Lili's disappearance, Marcel and Georgette set off to dine with Georgette's cousin, Paulette, and her insurance salesman husband, Raymond Vallée.

The dinner was scheduled for 6 P.M.; it would give the Petiots and the other two guests, a Dr Paul-Léon Braunberger and Marguerite, his wife, both 66 years old, a chance to get home before the curfew sounded at ten o'clock.

Marcel talked a lot at the table.

He said he wondered who could afford to buy poultry on the black market; he certainly could not pay the current asking price of 1,800 francs for a goose or duck. He could not even afford to buy butter at 107 francs per portion on the black market. The Vallées were in a similar situation obviously; dinner was potato soup and the 190 grams of meat allowed per person per week.

He also spoke of the increasingly vulnerable situation in which Jews found themselves. As if only he were aware of it, he pointed out that because of a census held in January, Jews were no longer allowed to move house and they were forbidden to be out between 8 P.M. and 6 A.M. Jewish, the Braunbergers were breaking that Nazi law.

He also vented his disgust at the first deportation of Jews from France which had taken place three months previously, on March 28. Over a thousand Jewish men, all prominent and respected members of French society, had been taken by train from the French-administered internment camp of Drancy on the northern outskirts of Paris, and from the *Wehrmacht*-administered camp of Compiègne, 81 kilometres from Paris, to whence no one knew.

Dr Braunberger did not participate in the conversation.

201

From the cost of food to the plight of the Jews, Marcel steered the conversation to medical matters. He spoke of cancer and the available treatments, but that none was really effective. If only people would listen to him, he said; he was able to cure cancer. He *had* cured cancer.

Dr Braunberger again said not a word, but on leaving he whispered to Pauline and Raymond, "Tonight, I was in the company of a genius, or, perhaps, in the company of a madman."

A few days later, the Braunbergers' telephone rang. Marcel was on the line. He invited Dr Braunberger for a drink in a bistro. Dr Braunberger accepted; he was curious to hear why Dr Petiot wanted to see him. Back home after the meeting, he told his wife that the doctor had offered to help the two of them flee France. He assured her he had not breathed a word to the doctor that they already had plans to flee. Neither had he told him that in preparation for their flight, they had been sending money and valuables to a relative in the Mediterranean port city of Nice.

Saturday, June 20, a few days later, at exactly 8:30 A.M., the Braunbergers' telephone rang again. Both were a little startled; normally on the Sabbath their telephone remained silent.

"Duret? Rue Duret? Sixteenth *arrondissement*? L'Étoile? L'Étoile Métro station? Certainly, I will come. At 10 A.M., you said? Right then. I will be there at ten sharp," Mrs Braunberger heard her husband say.

Dr Braunberger was still in pyjamas. Quickly he dressed; he put on a grey suit and a light-blue shirt and white bow tie. A dandy with a grey goatee and neatly-trimmed grey moustache, he had his shirts with their size forty collars handmade by the shirt maker, David of Number 32 Avenue de l'Opéra. That morning's shirt had a dark blue bodice with a white pinstripe. He also put on a handmade fedora; the milliner was Gelot, also from the Opéra district, and one of Paris's finest. The caller, who had not identified himself, was waiting on Rue Duret for him. Someone had been taken ill in an apartment on the street; the caller would take him there.

Mrs Braunberger walked her husband to the door. She checked that the obligatory yellow Star of David on his jacket was visible, but not too obvious. Since May 29, like all French Jews over the age of six, the Braunbergers had been wearing the star with the word *Juif* on it, on the left side of their chests. They had gone to their town hall with their identity cards, which already bore the word *Juif*, to be issued with the stars. They had to take their ration books along so that the few square centimetres of cloth which had been used to make the stars could be deducted from the ration for textiles they were allowed each month.

Dr Braunberger promised he would be back as soon as possible.

"I'll worry if you don't," said his wife.

He picked up his medical case. In it was his wallet. In the wallet were his identity and ration cards and some small change.

He did not return home.

In the afternoon, the Braunbergers' doorbell rang. Mrs Braunberger, worried, had gone to lie down. The couple's maid, a Mrs Callède, opened the door. Because she was also the doctor's receptionist she recognised the man on the landing. He was a former patient; Raymond Vallée. She knew Vallée no longer consulted the doctor. She also knew that Vallée had started to consult his wife's cousin, a Dr Petiot. She was surprised to see him.

Vallée asked whether Dr Braunberger was in. She said he wasn't.

"And Mrs Braunberger?"

Callède said Mrs Braunberger was lying down because she was not feeling well.

"I have a message for Mrs Braunberger," said Vallée. "Can you please call her?"

Mrs Braunberger was also surprised to see Vallée. Although she and her husband had dined with him and his wife two weeks previously, they were not friends. They even addressed each other by the polite *vous* and not the familiar *tu*.

Vallée handed Mrs Braunberger a letter. The postmark showed the letter had been handed in at 11A.M. that day at a post office on Rue la Boétie in the eighth *arrondissement*. It had been sent by *pneumatique* to the Vallées's apartment where it had arrived just before noon, delivered like a telegram by a postman on a bike. Written on Dr Braunberger's letterhead, the letter bore no date, and was addressed to Raymond Vallée. It read: 'I was almost arrested, but just got away. Tell my wife that I won't be coming home, that she should prepare two suitcases for her most valuable things to be ready to leave for the free zone before going abroad. I will send word when she can come and join me. She mustn't talk to anyone about all this; she should tell the clients that I fell ill in the suburbs and can't travel back yet'.

The handwriting looked like her husband's, but he must have written the letter in great haste because the writing was uneven, thought Mrs Braunberger.

She explained to Vallée that her husband had gone to keep a 10 A.M. appointment with a patient, but had not returned. Thinking that the Germans had arrested him because they had seen his Yellow Star of David had made her sick with worry. Knowing he was safe, she was much relieved. She asked the bearer of the good news not to speak of what had happened and he promised that he would not. As he said, he could not figure out why the doctor would have written to him to ask him to give her such a personal and sensitive message.

Monday, June 22, two days later, another letter, also written on Dr Braunberger's letterhead, undated and again sent by *pneumatique* from Rue de la Boétie's post office, arrived at the Braunbergers' apartment. It was addressed to Mrs Braunberger, and it was again from her husband. '*Ma chère amie*, I almost got arrested. I managed to escape arrest and all the consequences. It is too dangerous to see each other again. I'm sure you're being watched, so take care. Be suspicious of everything. Don't talk to anyone. I'll tell you what to do when the time comes, we'll have to save all we can. Write some letters to tell people we're going, so that they can be delivered after our departure. With love, Dr Paul Braunberger'.

She failed to understand why her husband would address her as *ma chère amie*— my dear friend. Not only was it an outmoded seventeenth century form of address between spouses, but whenever they had been apart in the past, he had always begun his letters to her with, *ma chère* Maguy- my dear Maguy. She also found it strange that he had signed the letter 'Dr Paul Braunberger'.

Rue de la Boétie was a 15-minute walk from Rue de Caumartin.

Later in the day, Mrs Braunberger heard that Jews had been forbidden to practise liberal professions. Her husband's career had come to an end. He had graduated from the Sorbonne in 1902 and had fought for France in the Great War with the rank of captain. After his demobilisation he had set up his Paris practice. He also worked for the *Assistance Publique*, the French state medical service.

The next day, June 23, Mrs Braunberger received yet another letter from her husband. Again it was written on his letterhead, was not dated, and had been handed in at the Rue de la Boétie post office. 'My darling, I hardly dare to write to you. I'm afraid my letters will be intercepted; be brave. I've written to tell my friend Vallée what to do. He'll take you, so get ready to leave next Saturday. Don't say anything to my brother or anyone. Do this for the best. I'll see you soon. With lots of love. P.S. Burn all my letters'. It was again signed 'Dr Paul Braunberger'.

The following morning it was Vallée's turn to receive yet another letter from Dr Braunberger. It was written on plain paper and was mailed at a post office on Rue Bayen in the seventeenth *arrondissement*, a ten-minute walk from Rue le Sueur. The doctor wrote: 'My dear friend, I know that your doctor cousin has bought a house near the Avenue de Bois and that he won't move in until after the war; do you think you could arrange with him to have all my furniture and other stuff in my house transported to his house? I would really be obliged if it could all be done within 48 hours, and I thank you sincerely'.

The Avenue de Bois mentioned in the letter was the previous name of Avenue Foch. The street's name was changed in 1929, but, in the 1940s many Parisians continued to call it Avenue de Bois.

Vallée took the letter to Mrs Braunberger. He had not, he assured her, told her husband that his wife's cousin - Dr Petiot - had bought a house near Avenue Foch.

"I could not have, because I didn't know it myself," he said.

Tuesday, June 30, 1 P.M., Callède answered the telephone in the Braunbergers' apartment. On the line was a very angry man; he did not identify himself. He said he wanted to tell her something about Dr Braunberger. He had managed to get the doctor to the free zone, but the two of them had almost been caught. "He was a bit crazy on the Métro already. When we got to the checkpoint, he did some stupid things, so we were almost taken."

He had decided he would not help Mrs Braunberger to escape.

"She will have to look after herself, because I have been too badly awarded!" he shouted.

Callède, fearing the man was going to hang up, quickly offered him money. "Come to the apartment, and we will make up for any inconvenience you have suffered."

He refused.

"What's more, I've got a letter that I'm supposed to bring her, but I won't do so now. I'll put it in the post instead," he said.

"How is the doctor?" Callède dared ask.

"I left him to make his own way to Spain or Portugal," snapped the man.

Wednesday, July 1, the letter, on plain paper and undated, arrived. Dr Braunberger had written: 'My darling, follow the person who gives you this letter. He will give you instructions for coming to join me. I will see you very soon. With love. Dr Paul Braunberger'.

The letter was mailed at a post office on Quay de Valmy on the Canal Saint-Martin in the north of Paris. The canal flowed into the River Seine. Parisians dumped things they no longer wanted - old broken settees, bicycles, prams, wheelchairs, dead domestic pets and foetuses that had been aborted - into the canal. It had also happened in the past that a murderer or two had thrown a body into the canal.

Soon after Dr Braunberger's strange departure, Paulette Vallée told Georgette the doctor had fled France, but she was not to talk about it; it was a big secret. Georgette asked Paulette to let her know should there be news of the old doctor in future. Paulette promised she would.

Marcel too enquired as to Dr Braunberger's wellbeing; he asked Vallée.

"No news from him yet," replied Vallée.

"Tell me when there is news from the old man," said Marcel. "I'm interested."

In 1944, Mrs Braunberger would tell the Quay she had believed her husband had, through God's Mercy, escaped Gestapo arrest, and had reached England safely. It was something she *had* to believe.

"I could not have continued living otherwise," she said.

* * *

Thursday, July 16, three weeks later, Margaret – Greta - Kneller, Jewish, heard car doors slamming on the street below the small, second storey apartment on Avenue du General Balfourier in the sixteenth *arrondissement,* she shared with Kurt, her husband, and René, their seven-year-old son. She ran to the window, but before she reached it, she halted. She had heard voices; they were speaking in French and German. René sat on the floor, playing with cars. As if in a play often rehearsed, she swept him up in her arms and ran from the apartment. She mounted the stairs three at a time and prayed that the woman who lived in the apartment on the floor above, *Mademoiselle* Roart, was home.

Christiane Roart, a middle-aged spinster, lived alone. She was home. She was already standing at the door.

The two women, firm friends, had decided long before that should the Germans or their French lackies ever turn up, the Knellers would flee to Christiane's apartment to hide.

Such a moment had come.

Greta, Christiane and René listened at the apartment door. They heard heavy footsteps ascend the stairs. They heard knocking at the Kneller's door. It soon turned to hammering. René started to whimper. Greta picked him up and put a hand over his mouth. The hammering stopped and footsteps descended the stairs. Next, they heard the voice of the building's *concierge*. The woman was saying she had not seen Greta Kneller for some months. The footsteps started coming up the stairs again. The *concierge* had a key to each apartment, and the French- and German-speaking men were telling her to shut up and unlock the Knellers' door.

A key turned in the lock.

Ten very long minutes passed.

The Knellers' door slammed.

The footsteps started to descend the stairs again; a car revved up and drove off.

Greta and Christiane waited a few minutes.

"I must phone Kurt," said Greta.

He was at work. He promised to return home immediately.

Kurt and Greta had been thinking of fleeing France for more than a year, but they had kept on hoping that there would be a miracle; one morning they would wake up to hear the Germans had gone in the night. That the war was over.

Greta told Christiane there would be no miracle. The time had come to flee.

Kurt agreed.

He knew something the two women did not. At that very moment, all over Paris, Jews were being rounded up *en masse*. The roundup had begun at 4 A.M. Thousands of Jewish men, women and children were being grabbed from their homes, even grabbed off the streets, in the ninth, tenth, eleventh, eighteenth, nineteenth and twentieth *arrondissements*. It was not the Germans doing it, but French police and gendarmes. The Jews were being taken to schools, cinemas, theatres and police stations. From there, in buses, packed in like farm animals, to an indoor bicycle racing stadium; the *Vélodrome d'Hiver*.

The Cycling Track of Winter.

* * *

Too frightened to return to their apartment or even remain in the building, Kurt and Greta left René with Christiane and went to the apartment of another friend, a Clara Noé.

Clara lived in an apartment on the neighbouring Rue Erlanger. She wasn't surprised to see Greta and Kurt. She was aware of the roundup and had hoped her friends would have the wisdom to come to her apartment to hide. They told her a doctor, a saint of a man, had offered them help to flee France. They were going to take up his offer.

In the morning, Kurt returned to Christaine's apartment. He wanted her to keep René for another day. He also wanted her to go down to their apartment and to pack clothes for him, Greta and René: a man would fetch those the following day.

"Pack enough for a long stay away from home. I've been to see the doctor who's going to help us get out of here. And now we are off, Christiane," he said.

Kurt Kneller was born 45 years previously in Breslau, Germany. He came from a modest Jewish family whose menfolk had been watch and clock repairers for two generations. He was to have been a watch repairer too, but short-sightedness had made it impossible. Instead, he repaired radios. He had come to Paris in 1933; he had seen no future for a Jew in Hitler's Germany. He had arrived with a small nest egg of watches and jewellery; those he had kept should it ever have become necessary to flee Hitler again.

Kurt had met Greta Lent in Paris. She was 33 years of age. A German Jew like him, she hailed from Berlin. Wearing thick lensed, black rimmed glasses and already going bald, Kurt had married the pretty dark-haired Greta with the high cheekbones on Thursday, December 6, 1934. She was four months pregnant. René was born on Wednesday, May 8, 1935.

In 1937, Kurt had applied for French nationality, but war had arrived first. Determined to fight the Nazis, he had joined the French Foreign Legion. Demobilised at the fall of France, he had returned to the Avenue du General Balfourier apartment. Forbidden to work with radios because he was a Jew, he had taken a job in a small electrical appliance factory on Rue Saint-Lazare; nearby was Rue de Caumartin. The factory's owner, a Swiss, named Ernest Jorin, had known he was Jewish, but had not minded. He had introduced Jorin to Greta and when René had fallen ill with bronchitis, he had asked Jorin if he knew of a doctor who would risk treating a Jewish child: it was against the law for doctors to treat Jews. Jorin had told him that he would ask his doctor whether he would. The doctor had immediately agreed. Nazi law be damned, the doctor had said.

The doctor was Marcel Petiot.

* * *

On Saturday, July 18, at 6 P.M., Christiane, as asked, took René to Clara's apartment. The boy, his light brown hair hidden under a cloth cap, and wearing brown shorts, white shirt and a red hand-knitted pullover, was visibly perturbed. He threw himself into his mother's arms and shouted loudly that she should never leave him again.

Earlier in the day, a man had called at Christiane's apartment with a cart to collect the suitcases, two large and five small ones, she had packed for the Knellers. She had slipped some family photographs and a few things she knew were of sentimental value into the suitcases with the clothes. The man was in his late thirties and had dark hair and eyes. He had lifted René on to his lap. René had acted as if he knew the man and did not like him; he had scrambled off his lap as fast as he could.

Kurt and Greta told Christiane they had been to a photographer to have identity photographs taken for their new passports. The doctor who was helping them to flee had recommended the photographer. Kurt was going to be given a Belgian passport and Greta, a French one. Her birthplace would be given as Alsace, the region on the French-German border the Germans had annexed. Having been born an Alsatian would mean that she was friendly towards Germany; it would be a great benefit should her path cross that of a German.

They were, at that very moment, waiting to commence their flight, they also told Christiane. The doctor was going to come and pick up

Kurt. The following afternoon he would pick up Greta and René. Kurt would wait for them at a safe house somewhere in the sixteenth *arrondissement*. They were to be vaccinated. They would be going to Spain to sail from there to an African port and then on to Argentina.

Christiane bid the Knellers goodbye. She cried; so did Greta. Christiane was René's godmother. On her recommendation, he had been baptised just a month previously, and she had been telling him Bible stories so if he should fall into the hands of the Germans, his conversion to Christianity would appear genuine despite that he was circumcised.

At 7 P.M. a man arrived at Clara's apartment. He came to fetch Kurt. He did not introduce himself, but asked Clara to follow him and Kurt at a short distance; he feared they would be tailed and she should rush over to tell him if that was so.

Clara slipped into comfortable shoes; the Métro station they were going to walk to was at least eight blocks away. She also went to the bathroom. She was away for no more than five minutes. Returning to the living room, there was no one there. Kurt and the man had already set off; Greta and Réne were in their bedroom. René was crying and Greta was trying to calm him.

Clara rushed after Kurt and the man. She followed them for three blocks, then she decided what she was doing was ridiculous.

She went home.

On Sunday at 7 P.M. Christiane returned to Clara's apartment. She wanted to see Greta and René once more before they set off. A weepy Clara told her she had arrived too late. The man, the same one who had come for Kurt, had come for them. René had been terribly frightened; he had not wanted to go.

Clara asked Christiane whether she knew the Knellers had paid the doctor, the one who was helping them flee, the sum of 150,000 francs: 50,000 francs for each of them. He had told the couple it was his special price for families.

A few days later, the man who had fetched the Knellers' luggage, returned to their apartment. He had his cart with him. Finding the door locked, he wanted the *concierge* to unlock for him.

"I need to pick up some furniture," he said.

The *concierge* called Christiane and asked her what she was to do. Christiane told her to tell the man to push off. He left. The next morning, he was back. Again, the *concierge* refused to let him into the apartment.

"I am warning you! If I can't get the Knellers' furniture, I won't help them to flee!" he shouted. He was enraged.

Frightened, the *concierge* let him in but she allowed him to take only some linen.

"I told them not to write to you, but I suppose they will do so anyway!" said the man menacingly over his shoulder.

Tuesday, August 4, seventeen days after the Knellers' departure, Christiane received a letter, mailed in Paris, from Greta. She wrote that Kurt had been taken ill and she was very tired, but they hoped to be leaving Paris shortly. She signed the letter 'Margaret'.

Christiane found it strange; never had she called her friend anything but Greta.

She could tell Greta was tired; her usually neat handwriting was almost illegible. That was probably why she had called herself Margaret.

Afraid that the Germans might raid the building in search of the Knellers, Christiane burnt the letter.

She received another three postcards from Greta: one, mailed in Paris, the other two in the town of Castres, near Toulouse, seven hundred kilometres from the capital. The cards were signed 'Marguerite'. In the one mailed in Paris, she had written that Kurt's mental health was deteriorating alarmingly every day, and she might have to have him institutionalised. The second of those mailed in Castres, gave the impression that the Knellers had already reached Spain. Greta had written that René - she called him 'the child' - had given her and Kurt much trouble during the French-Spanish border crossing. She did not explain what kind of trouble she was referring to.

Christiane burnt the cards as well.

Clara and Ernest Jorin also received a card each from Greta. The cards had also been mailed in Castres and signed Marguerite.

Clara burnt hers.

Jorin kept his. It was an incomprehensible string of words. "*Monsieur*, we left in a hurry, but it was necessary because my husband fell ill. I do not know what will become of us. You keep... business... My husband always speaks of you... My good... health, but..."

Greta had always called Jorin by his first name Ernest.

Saturday, August 8, a bargeman saw that some bags had been caught in bushes on the bank of the River Seine at Asnières, ten kilometres north-west of Paris. He poked a stick into one of them. It contained body parts. He lifted the bags onto the deck of his barge. His mate helped him.

The two summoned the police.

The bags contained the legs, feet, arms, and upper part of the torso of a child, and the head, one arm and the lower part of the torso of a woman.

The police took the remains to the Médico-Légal Institute.

The institute's chief, Dr Albert Paul, examined them. He informed the police that the child was male and about seven years old. The woman was middle-aged. Because of the advanced state of decomposition, it would be impossible for him and his team to determine the date or method of death.

A few days later another bargeman found the head of a man at the same spot.

Dr Paul said he was not even going to attempt to guess the man's age.

* * *

On a morning towards the end of August a woman with hair dyed the colour of champagne walked into a Paris bar. She sat down at a window table. Bar Jobert was a favourite hang-out for the criminal underworld; both the red-light districts of Pigalle and Les Halles were close by. Elegantly dressed in a skirt, blouse and jacket and with large sunglasses perched on her nose, she looked out of place. At adjoining tables sat scantily dressed prostitutes freshening up with an ersatz coffee after a night on the streets or in the district's small *baisodromes* - brothel hotels. At the zinc-topped bar stood their pimps waiting for the night's takings to be handed over.

The woman at the window table, Rudolphina - Eryane - Kahan, gave a sigh of relief on seeing three men cross the street. She had an appointment with one of them. Fearing he might not see her, she tapped a long, red fingernail against the window. Dr Louis Théophile Saint-Pierre introduced her to his two companions. She had heard of one of them: Henri Guintrand, a.k.a. Henri le Marseillais, a swindler, card sharp, smuggler and pimp with eight convictions.

The other, Edmond Pintard, held a hand out to her.

212

"Francinet, call me Francinet," he said.

Saint-Pierre practised from a room in a nearby rundown hotel. He had four convictions for abortion, assault, and breaking and entering. A few months back, Eryane, not only his friend, but also a patient, had revealed that she was thinking of fleeing France. He had told her he might be able to help her. He said that another of his patients had successfully fled with the help of yet another patient. The latter had a friend, who had a friend who ran an escape network. Pintard was the friend with the friend who ran an escape network. Henri Guintard had come along to vouch for Pintard's integrity.

Eryane and Pintard set off, and the latter gave Eryane more information as they walked. The man with the escape network was waiting at a barbershop. The barber, one Raoul Fourrier, was also in the escape chain. It was there at the barbershop that the escapees gathered before they set off. It was also there that the man with the escape network interviewed them. He was a Dr Eugène. He was in the Resistance. He was a very brave man; a great hero. Eugène was of course his undercover name.

"I can't reveal his real name. Secret, you know!" said Pintard and winked.

Eryane Kahan was 48 years old. She was born in Cernauti, Romania, but had grown up in Vienna. She was a childless spinster and had no relatives in Paris, even in France. She was a trained nurse, but, without a job despite that she was not only fluent in French, but also in German and Italian, and, of course, she spoke Romanian, too. Her French was heavily accented, made more so by a husky voice. She was Jewish, but that she kept to herself; defiantly she refused to wear the yellow Star of David.

Fourrier's barbershop comprised a waiting and reception area, and six small cubicles; those were behind bamboo curtains. Over all pervaded a smell of peroxide, henna, perm lotion, talcum powder, and stale cigarette smoke, ersatz coffee and pre-war dinners.

Dr Eugène - Marcel - was waiting at the barbershop.

After having shaken hands with the attractive visitor - Marcel would afterwards tell Fourrier and Pintard that Eryane did not look a day older than 28 and they would tell him that they agreed - steered her towards one of the cubicles. He drew the bamboo curtain and they sat down: he,

213

on the barber's stool, and she, in the barber's chair.

He explained he was the head of a Resistance cell code-named Fly-Tox. It specialised in helping people to flee France. There was a fee for the escape route. The fee was so small that it was hardly worth mentioning. Included in the fee were the costs of a passport, the cost of all the necessary travelling documents, the people smuggler's fee, as well as the passage from Spain to Africa and from there to Argentina.

"How much?" asked Eryane.

"Twenty-five thousand," Marcel replied.

She paled.

"I don't have that kind of money," she said.

Marcel didn't flinch.

They could come to an agreement he said. He, or rather Fly-Tox, needed an interpreter. She could become its interpreter and she could work her way to Argentina. She could also introduce potential escapees to him. Fly-Tox would give her a percentage of its fee.

"In fact," he said, "our fee is not fixed at 25,000 francs. It can rise to 50,000 or even 100,000 francs. It depends on the risk involved. But rest assured, you will be generously remunerated."

Eryane said she would think over the offer.

Fourrier and Pintard had listened to the conversation. For a year and half they had already known of their friend's Resistance involvement and that he headed a cell. They greatly admired him yet the code names Fly-Tox and Dr Eugène always gave them a giggle. Eugène was the name of the range of hair products Fourrier used and Fly-Tox was the name of the insect repellent he killed cockroaches with. There were dozens of flacons of Eugène products arranged on the shelves, and a canister of Fly-Tox stood on the floor.

* * *

August ended.

Georgette, looking back, thought the month had been a busy one for her husband. Every morning he had gone off on his bike. Often, he had also set off at night, taking the cart. As a doctor, he had an *ausweis*. She had presumed he had gone out to make house calls. She had not asked herself why he would need a cart when visiting his patients. Despite his heavy workload he had taken her to see the film, directed by Henri-Georges Clouzot with Pierre Fresnay and Suzy Delair, all Parisians were talking about. The film was about a murderer who left a visiting card in the name of *Monsieur* Durand, Number 21 Avenue Junot, on the bodies of his victims. The title was '*L'assassin habite au 21*' - The Murderer Lives at 21.

He had also taken her dancing.

The song everyone danced to was '*Mon amant de Saint-Jean*' - 'My lover from Saint-Jean' - sung by Lucienne Delyle.

He had held her very close and she had looked deep into his dark eyes.

Rhythmically, they had moved to the words:

When he held me tight,
I lost my head, I couldn't help it.
Don't we always believe
sweet words of love.
When his eyes cast their spell
I didn't think twice, just gave him
the best of myself.
Fine talker, every time he lied,
I knew it and I loved him.

-0-

CHAPTER FIVE

Killing Gangsters

A few days after Pintard had collected Eryane at Bar Jobert he was back there. Two glasses of red wine stood on the table in front of him. He had already ordered for the man he was waiting for. He saw him walk up; it was impossible not to notice Joseph - Jo the Boxer - Réocreux, Number Two in one of Paris's most dangerous and, therefore, respected criminal gangs. That morning, as usual, the 34-year-old with a broken nose, and five and a half years behind bars for assault, wore a white, v-necked tennis sweater, white flannels and a pair of black, crocodile-skin shoes. Pintard thought the whores in the bar could touch up their make-up in the shine of those shoes.

Réocreux was desperate to flee France. Life in Occupied Paris had become too hot for him; he had been augmenting his pimping income by snitching on rival gangs to the French Gestapo's chief, forty-year-old Frenchman, Henri Lafont - Mr Henri - as he was known, but who was born Henri Chamberlin. The gangster, having heard of Dr Eugène from Pintard, wanted to meet the doctor.

It was a forty-minute walk and the Paris pavements were potholed and he had paid a lot of money for his 'crocs' so Réocreux complained all the way to Fourrier's barbershop. He was even more upset on stepping into the barbershop. The walls were dirty and cracked, and with a nose accustomed to the sweet fragrance of his prostitute girlfriend's perfume, he thought the place stank like a sewer.

He also did not like the look of Marcel. His gangster's 'third eye' saw untrustworthiness written all over his face.

"*Il me fiche le trac*," he whispered to Pintard.

He puts the wind up me.

Pintard told Réocreux to relax.

"Dr Eugène's a saint," he said.

Marcel explained to Réocreux what taking the escape route entailed.

Escapees waited for a few days at a safe house where they were to be vaccinated. There should be no labels and monograms on their clothing. They could take as much gold bullion, jewellery and cash with them as they wished.

"In fact," he said, "I highly recommend that you do because you wouldn't want to leave anything behind for the Germans, now would you."

His fee was 100,000 francs.

It was non-negotiable.

In the morning, having developed a cold during the night - or so he told Pintard – he asked the latter to go to the barbershop to take a message to Dr Eugène. Pintard was to tell the doctor that he would not be able to flee right away because he was too sick. He was going to allow another member of the gang, François - the Corsican - Albertini, 34 years old, to set off before him.

Marcel did not appear to mind.

"I don't like a man who carries hand grenades in his trouser pockets," he told Pintard.

Réocreux's trouser pockets always bulged, but not because he carried hand grenades. Flashy, he liked to walk around with lots of money on him.

Albertini was a *deuxième couteau* - a second knife. In the criminal underworld, it meant he was not made of the right stuff needed to walk up to a man and shoot him between the eyes. He could only be trusted with menial jobs; staking out houses targeted for burglary, hanging around brothels to keep an eye on girls suspected of cheating with their earnings, driving getaway cars and looking after gangsters who had gone into hiding. Always a trustworthy second knife, he did what he was ordered to do. Ordered to get ready to leave France, he didn't argue.

Pintard made the introduction between the physically unattractive Albertini - he had a crop of unruly, oily black hair and a mouth too small for his face - and Marcel.

The meeting took place in a bistro rather than the barbershop.

If Albertini shared Réocreux's doubts about Marcel, he did not let on, but he did have a request to make; to be allowed to take his girlfriend along. His girlfriend, Annette - the *Pute* - Basset a.k.a. Annette Petit was, as her sobriquet indicated a *putain* - a prostitute. She worked under Albertini's protection. She hailed from Lyon where her family lived in blissful ignorance of what she was up to in Paris. Despite a luxurious mane of black hair, a marked squint in her left eye made it impossible to call her beautiful.

Petiot told Albertini that taking Basset with him wouldn't be a problem, but he could not bring anyone else.

"We can get only two people at a time to South America."

It would cost Albertini an extra 50,000 francs for taking Basset along.

Late September, Albertini arrived at the barbershop. Petiot was waiting. The woman with Albertini was not Basset, but Claudia — Lulu - Chamoux. The obeying *deuxième couteau* had been ordered to take Chamoux with him instead of Basset. Chamoux, forty-five, was also a prostitute; Réocreux was her pimp, and her lover. He wanted her to keep an eye on Albertini; he was sending several million francs out of the country with him and he was not going to take the chance that Albertini would make a runner with the money. Later, when he too set out, he would take Basset with him.

Two weeks after Albertini and Chamoux's departure Petiot gave Fourrier a letter written on a small sheet of blue paper. Fourrier and Pintard were to show the letter around Bar Jobert. They were to make sure Réocreux read the letter, but, for security reasons, he was not to keep it; Petiot wanted it back.

The letter was from Albertini and it was addressed to Réocreux.

Albertini reported that he and Chamoux had arrived safely in Buenos Aires. He wanted Réocreux to join them, and not to forget to bring Basset.

The letter was undated and written in a childish scrawl.

There was no envelope.

A few days later two human thighs were found floating on the River Seine. Those were taken to the Médico-Légal Institute.

They were too decomposed for Dr Paul to be able to even establish the gender of their owners.

* * *

219

At this time Mrs Braunberger, desperate because she had no further word from her husband, reported him missing. The police asked her whether she really thought that they were going to look for a missing Jew.

* * *

On a cold November day, Réocreux, Basset and another prostitute - she would be identified by the police only as Miss X - climbed the stairs to the barbershop. They were setting off for Argentina. Marcel had not wanted to take the three of them together, but, because Réocreux had told him it was three or none, he had capitulated. The three wore fur coats and hats and were covered in gold and diamond jewellery.

Réocreux also wore his crocodile-skin shoes; there was no way he was going to leave those behind. On Marcel's recommendation, he had had the heels hollowed to be filled with precious stones. He had bragged in Bar Jobert that he was furthermore taking 1.5 million francs with him in cash.

Soon, Pintard showed more letters around the bar. They had been written by Réocreux; he and the two women had arrived safely in Buenos Aires. He urged anyone who could no longer live under the Nazi boot, to take the Fly-Tox escape route.

The patrons noticed many of the words were incorrectly spelt.

"So what do you expect, hey?" asked Pintard.

Gangsters were not the most educated men on earth.

Pintard and Fourrier also noticed something. Marcel was wearing a gold Swiss watch. It was Réocreux's; it had been on his left arm the day he, Basset and Miss X had set off.

"Did he leave the watch with you?" asked Pintard.

"He gave it to me in gratitude for saving his life," replied Marcel.

Albertini and Réocreux's boss, 'godfather' Adrien - the Basque - Estébétéguy a.k.a. Cold Hand Adrien, 45 years old, also wanted to take the escape route.

Estébétéguy's face bore witness of a life of fraud and violence and six years in prison for assault on a policeman; his mouth was twisted into a lopsided grin, he had permanent bags under his eyes, eyes that rival 'godfathers' said reminded them of those of a snake. He was not only a gangster, but like Réocreux, an informer for the French Gestapo. Getting to the end of his six-year prison sentence at the start of the Occupation, the Germans had released him so that Henri Lafont could make use of his holdup and robbery expertise. On the payroll of the Service for the Recuperation of Jewish Property, he had been robbing Jews by bursting into their homes and shouting *police allemande! -* German Police! - at the petrified Jews. He wanted to flee France because he had been helping himself to some of the stolen goods despite that the Germans allowed Lafont and his men to keep twenty per cent of the stolen goods as payment.

It was again Pintard who escorted Estébétéguy to the barbershop to meet Dr Eugéne.

Estébétéguy wore his most expensive suit and a shirt he had bought from Sulka, the expensive men's boutique on Rue de Rivoli; a Sulka shirt was second in elegance only to a David shirt.

Estébétéguy told Marcel that another of his men, Joseph Didoni Sidesse – Zé - Piereschi, also wanted to leave. Piereschi, a 49-year-old pimp with a toothbrush moustache and a fondness for silver-coloured ties, wanted to take his 24-year-old girlfriend, Josephine Aimée Grippay, known as 'Paulette, the Chinese Woman' because of dark, slanted eyes inherited from her Vietnamese mother, with him. Estébétéguy also wanted to take his girl, Gisèle Rossmy, 34, along. Despite looking ten years older, she had aspirations of becoming a film star; while waiting for her lover to launch her career, she tap-danced in a music hall under the stage name Gine Volma.

Estébétéguy and Piereschi were to swap girlfriends too for the journey to make sure there would be no double-crossing; Grippay going with Estébétéguy, and Rossmy going with Piereschi.

Grippay, before her departure, told a prostitute friend that she and Piereschi were leaving for Argentina, but separately. They were each taking 800,000 francs. The money would finance a brothel they planned to open in Buenos Aires. Rossmy also told a friend she was leaving for Buenos Aires; Estébétéguy was going to manage her career there.

The two women were in tears saying goodbye to their friends.

Piereschi and Rossmy set off first; a few days later Estébétéguy and Grippay left.

Pintard and Fourrier witnessed each departure. They leant out of a window of the barbershop. Not that they were curious to know in which direction Marcel was walking with the escapees. No, they wanted to watch the women's bottoms wiggle as they strutted off in high-heeled, ankle-strapped shoes.

Proof that the four had arrived safely in Argentina was a halved Argentinean banknote.

"One of the women sent it," explained Marcel.

-0-

CHAPTER SIX

Killing Jews Again

The news of the gangsters' successful departure reached Eryane Kahan through her friend Saint-Pierre. Immediately, she asked Pintard to ask Dr Eugène whether she could see him. She knew a family, Maurice Wolff, his wife, Lina, and Rachel, his mother, who wished to flee either to Switzerland or the United States. They were German Jews. She wanted to introduce them to the doctor.

Eryane lived in a boarding house at Number 10 Rue Pasquier in another of Paris's elegant *arrondissements*, the eighth, but the street was shabby and noisy; two buildings from the boarding house, a brothel reserved for Germans had opened, and night and day rowdy, drunken soldiers came to enjoy what was on offer.

A German soldier also visited the boarding house, a dashing Luftwaffe sergeant named Wesling; he was Eryane's lover. Adrienne Ginas, the boarding house's manager, smiled every time she saw him pass her ground floor quarters. She knew Eryane was Jewish. She also knew, at least she suspected, Eryane was in the Resistance; many Frenchmen also visited her and they always tried to hide their faces in their fedoras which could only mean one thing: they were resisters collecting information about German troop positions Wesling had revealed to Eryane.

Eryane had met the Wolffs through one of her friends, a Rachel Gingold, also Romanian and Jewish. Gingold, real name Rachel Sobelman, and pretending that she was Catholic, was a dentist and practised openly although it was against the Nazis' law for Jews to work in any medical field. The Wolffs had approached Gingold after another friend, an Ilse Gang, also Jewish, had told them that Gingold has a friend, one Eryane Kahan, who knew a French doctor who helped people to flee France. Eryane, Gang had said, lived in a 'Jewish friendly' boarding house. She meant that Jews were given refuge at the boarding house.

The Wolffs, having met Eryane at Gingold's apartment, and having been told that the doctor certainly would be able to help them flee, had immediately moved into the boarding house. The obliging Ginas had given them a comfortable family room on the first floor.

The family had been fleeing the Nazis since Hitler's rise to power in 1933.

First to have left their hometown of Koningsberg had been Moses Israel, 27 years old and having only recently married Lina Braun from Breslau, ten years his senior. They had settled in Paris where Moses Israel started to call himself Maurice and set up a branch of his wealthy father's lumber business, the Incona Lumber Company.

In 1936, Wolff Snr., named Salomon, but known as Sally, and Rachel, his wife, and Heinrich, their younger son, had also left Germany.

The three had settled in the Netherlands, in the city of Amsterdam.

Maurice and Lina, not having felt secure in France because of French diplomats' conciliation with the rising tide of Nazism in neighbouring Germany, had joined them.

Finding the Dutch much more welcoming than the French, Sally, Maurice and Heinrich had successfully run the lumber company from Amsterdam.

In 1940, Sally had passed away and the two brothers had continued to run the company despite that the Germans had occupied the Netherlands, as they would France.

In 1942, the Germans having seized all Jewish-owned businesses, Maurice and Heinrich had decided that the time had come for them to find another country that would have them.

Heinrich had set off first and when there had been no news from him for months, Maurice, believing that the Germans had arrested his brother, made plans for him and Lina to return to France. Rachel, already in her late sixties, would be going with them.

The three had crossed the Belgian border with documents identifying them as Dutch nationals, and on reaching Antwerp, Maurice had continued to the French border without Lina and Rachel. The plan was that he would see how it went in France and should he have felt secure, he would have arranged with a people smuggler to fetch the two women. Gendarmes, patrolling the Belgian-French border had however spotted him and he was arrested and locked up. He had almost a million francs in cash and jewellery on him. The warders had quickly found those and one of them who was vehemently against the Germans, had offered to safeguard the money and jewellery for him and to help Lina and Rachel to get from Antwerp to Paris. Maurice had not been held for long - he was after all travelling on what the gendarmes thought were genuine Dutch documents - and joined the two women in the Hotel Helvetia on Rue Tourneaux in Paris's twelfth *arrondissement*, another 'Jewish friendly' hotel. However, the Helvetia had started to draw the attention of the Germans and the three had to move on. A frantic race, from backstreet hotel to backstreet hotel to stay ahead of the Germans, had then begun. Finally, they had met Eryane.

Marcel changed his *modus operandi* for the Wolffs.

He would go to the boarding house to meet them, instead of them going to the barbershop.

Ginas was present for the first few minutes of the meeting.

As she would recount later, the doctor whom she was told was a Dr Eugène, talked art and literature to the Wolffs. It impressed her.

Eryane witnessed the rest of the meeting.

She would recount that the doctor - she still at that stage thought he was named Eugène - asked for 50,000 francs from each of the Wolffs and he told them that he would make an exception in their case: he was allowing them to set off together.

The three went to Ilsa Gang to say goodbye. They were full of praise for the kind doctor who was helping them to flee France and the Nazis.

A few days later, 1942 close to its end, Dr Eugène was back at the boarding house. The Wolffs were waiting.

They said their goodbyes to Eryane and Ginas and left with the doctor.

The next day, the moment night fell, Marcel was back at the boarding house. He was on his bike and he had brought his cart. He had come to pick up what the Wolffs had left behind. On his way out Eryane stopped him.

"I think I've earned my passage now, don't you?" she asked.

"You're far too valuable to Fly-Tox; we can't let you go yet," he replied.

Eryane called on Ilse Gang. Did Gang not know of more Jews who wanted to flee, she asked. Gang did. She knew of six; three couples. She had already given one of the couples the boarding house's address.

"Might you not want to leave, too?" asked Eryane.

"Thank you very much, but no," replied Gang.

She and her husband would risk remaining in France.

Back at the boarding house, Eryane found that the couple, Gilbert and Marie-Anne Basch, had already moved in. Ginas had given them the room the Wolffs had had.

Marcel met the couple.

He had them go to the barbershop for the meeting.

He gave them the same instructions he had given the Wollfs, the Knellers, the gangsters and Joachim Guschinov about monograms and labels and not taking more than two suitcases and having to wait at a safe house where they would have to be vaccinated. They asked him only one question. There were six of them, could he help them all, and could they leave together? It would be great if they could set off together, they told him. He replied it would unfortunately not be possible for them to leave at the same time. They would not even be able to leave on the same day. It would be safer to allow a day or two between departures.

His fee for six people would be 300,000 francs.

Gilbert and Marie-Anne Basch's story was similar to that of the Wolffs.

Born in Germany, they had considered themselves German, but on Hitler's rise they had decided it would be wiser to leave. They had fled to Paris; Gilbert spoke French fluently. Feeling the French didn't really want them, they had left for Amsterdam. There, Gilbert had become the representative of a French cosmetic company. He had told his employers his surname was Baston and that he was from Belgium. Marie-Anne had begun using her maiden name Schonker along with Basch and Baston. She had even used a fourth surname, Hollander.

Marie-Anne's parents, Chaima and Franziska Schonker, had joined them in Amsterdam.

So had Marie-Anne's sister, Ludwika, and her husband Ludwik Arnsberg.

All had pretended to be Belgian.

Chaima had taken a job as representative with Jean Patou, the French *haute couture* house, as well as with a German company, Junge und

Gebbhardt. He and Franziska had started to use the surname Stevens. The Russian-born Franziska had also begun to use her maiden name of Ehrenreich, and yet still another surname, Eemans, which she thought sounded Dutch.

Ludwika and Ludwig Arnsberg had also started using other surnames. Ludwig had chosen Anspach. Ludwika had chosen Hollander, the surname Marie-Anne was already using.

For such playing of surname musical chairs, they had used nine surnames between them: Basch, Baston, Schonker, Stevens, Ehrenberg, Eemans, Arnsberg, Anspach and Hollander.

And they had been able to get along in four languages: German, Dutch, French and Russian.

The three couples had left Amsterdam at the same time, but the Schonkers and Arensburgs had headed for the French city of Nice. The Mediterranean city fell in the Italian-administered Riviera and Chaima had decided Jews would be safer there than in German-occupied Paris; Mussolini's men treated Jews more kindly than Hitler's, he said.

In Nice, the two couples had lived openly in a luxurious hotel, the Continental, on Rue Rossini, close to the Promenade des Anglais. Feeling comfortable and secure, Chaima had tried to convince Gilbert and Marie-Anne to join them, but Italian Gestapo agents had taken up residence at the hotel which had decided him that Paris might be a safer place after all for Jews than Nice. Having already paid a Dutch people smuggler a million francs for the Amsterdam to Nice escape route, he had paid another people smuggler, a Frenchman named Robert Malfet, the equivalent to get him, Franziska and the two Arnsbergs up to Paris. Before the Occupation Malfet had worked as a *chauffeur* for wealthy businessmen and he was using the geographical knowledge of France he had thus gained for his people smuggling activities.

Departure on the trek of 1,001 kilometres across France was scheduled for Friday, New Year's Day, 1943.

The journey promised to be risky - the Germans would be everywhere because a month previously they had moved troops into Vichy-France and had occupied it too although they had allowed Pétain's government to remain in office - but the experienced Malfet had explained to the four that he would be breaking the journey up into stages.

They were to board a train in Nice for Lyon, 470 kilometres north. In

Lyon, they were to take a Post Office coach for the next stage, the 73 kilometres to the town of Macon. From Macon they would have to walk the sixty kilometres that separated it from the town of Buxy. In Buxy, they were to continue, still on foot, to Chalon-sur-Saône, twenty kilometres away. The fifth stage of the journey from Chalon-sur-Saône to Dijon, some 68 kilometres, they would again do by Post Office coach. In Dijon, they would board a train for the final 310 kilometres to Paris.

As Gilbert and Marie-Anne told Marcel, their relatives had set off from Nice as planned, but they had no idea how far they had got.

Tuesday, January 12, twelve days on the road, the two couples, totally exhausted and their nerves stretched to the limit, arrived at the boarding house.

Ginas had rooms waiting.

Two weeks later, Marcel fetched the Arnsbergs.

The next evening, he picked up the Schonkers.

The day after, Gilbert and Marie-Anne.

Not discreet about their personal affairs, they had told Eryane and Ginas they had brought all their cash, gold bullion, jewellery and furs from Amsterdam and they were going to take all along again when they embarked on Dr Eugène's escape route. They did; after their departure the cupboards in their rooms were empty.

Before people smuggler Malfet returned to Nice, Eryane took him out for drinks and a chat. After quite a few glasses of wine, she told him that she was the secretary of the doctor who ran the escape network. She would pay him well if he could find escapees for it. He did not hesitate. He would certainly find escapees. He already knew of a couple who wanted to leave, he told her.

* * *

At that time, Jean Hotin, husband of the missing Lili, arrived in Paris. It was urgent he obtained a divorce; he wanted to get married again.

Jean's first stop was Mallard's apartment. She told him that she had no idea Lili had not returned home after she had seen Dr Petiot.

"Ah," exclaimed Jean. "That's the name I am after!"

She gave him Marcel's address.

"He's a charming man," she said.

It was 12:30 P.M.

Jean found the practice closed.

He checked the opening hours on the shingle.

The practice was not to open until 1 P.M.

He had half an hour to wait.

He waited for ten minutes and walked away.

He was not going to hang around longer.

He took the train back to his father's farm.

* * *

If Marcel had done a calculation he would have learnt that since Guschinov's departure in January 1942 he had raked in 1.775 million francs. In cash alone. He could have bought himself another three Paris townhouses, each as large as Number 21 Rue le Sueur.

He had suffered one setback, though. It had been minor, but he had gone on about it for weeks.

Two potential escapees, Michel and Marie Cadoret de l'Épinguen, he was an interior decorator and she a psychiatrist, and Jewish, sent by Malfat via Eryane, had made a reservation to set off, but had cancelled.

In 1944, Michel Cadoret de l'Épinguen would tell Massu, "My wife and I had the impression of considerable confusion. We were told lots of things, but we sensed that there was nothing behind the words. We would have to use false papers identifying us as diplomats. We were to hide in a house belonging to Dr Petiot and to have the injections necessary for going to Argentina. Petiot - we were told he was a Dr Eugène - said that these injections would let us 'disappear'. It all seemed suspicious, and we did not go any further with the plan."

Marcel had been unable to tell them at which Argentinian port their ship would dock; Michel had lived in Argentina as a bachelor and he knew the country.

They also had not liked Marcel's grubby hands and dirty fingernails.

What had finally convinced them to have nothing more to do with him was when, in a discussion about the difficulty in obtaining medications because of the Occupation, he had told Marie that she should put her patients on 'Peyote', also known as 'Mescaline', the hallucinogenic drug made from the cactus plant. 'Peyote' was popular with the patrons of Paris bars and nightclubs; easy to make, any family doctor, pharmacist or hospital nurse with a sink, table, a bucket and a couple of test tubes could have done so.

At Marcel's request the couple had left a deposit with him of 55,000 francs against a total payment of 150,000 francs. Their teenage son was going to flee too. Having cancelled, they had asked for their money back, but he had gone into a rage. Fly-Tox did not return deposits, he shouted. Eventually, he had paid up. The couple had threatened Eryane and Malfat with legal action, and Eryane, in a panic, had rushed to the barbershop to leave a message for Dr Eugène that he had to pay up or he - they all - would have the Gestapo on their doorsteps.

-0-

CHAPTER SEVEN

Looking for Dr Eugène

It was spring: May.

In Paris the days were longer and warmer and the horse chestnut trees were in bloom.

A young, attractive, dark-haired Jewish woman, Pauline Dreyfus, descended from a train at Gare de Lyon railway station. She had left the city of Lyon earlier in the morning. Nervous - she did not have the required documents for travelling and neither did she wear the yellow Star of David - she started to walk to an apartment building on the elegant Avenue George V off Avenue des Champs-Elysées. She climbed the stairs to a third storey apartment. Not wishing to be heard, she had removed her shoes. She let herself in. Someone in Lyon had given her a key. The apartment belonged to a Jewish couple who had fled France at the outbreak of war. They had left the key with a relative. He was allowing Jews to hide in the apartment.

The apartment was dark and cold, but Pauline knew that it would be dangerous to switch on the lights and make a fire. She lit candles that had been prophetically left on a table, but ignored the logs piled invitingly in front of a fireplace; a smoking chimney would draw the neighbours' attention. Fortunately, she had brought a thick sweater with her.

She had come to Paris to try to buy the release of Yvan, her husband. The Germans had arrested him the previous November and were holding him at the transit camp in Compiègne, eighty kilometres north of Paris. He was being held in the sector reserved for political militants until his deportation to either, Buchenwald, Mauthausen, Ravensbruck, Auschwitz or Dachau concentration camp.

It was Pauline's third trip to Paris to buy Yvan's release and she hoped that she was going to be successful. She knew that she had to be

231

successful because Yvan was bound to be in an upcoming transport. That was something that she could not allow to happen and on leaving Lyon she had told herself that she would not return without her husband. She had told their six-year-old daughter 'Pomme' - Apple - her father's nickname for her, she was going to bring her daddy back. She had made the child a promise, a promise she was hell bent on keeping. Therefore, apart from a warm sweater, she had also brought a large sum of money with her to Paris. She knew, everyone knew, that there were German officers who were open to bribery. She was prepared to pay whatever it took to buy such an officer's goodwill.

Pauline unpacked her suitcase; next, she set off again.

She had an appointment with a man who would help her find such a corrupt German officer. She was to meet the man in a bistro. His name was Marcel Dequeker. A short, well-set, grey-haired man in his fifties, he was the manager of the *Théâtre des Nouveautés* near Fourrier's barbershop. He was also a scrap iron dealer, and a Gestapo informer. As the latter, he allowed the Gestapo to use his scrap iron business to move goods confiscated from arrested Jews.

In the bistro, Pauline came straight to the point.

"That which we have discussed over the phone, can it be done?" she asked.

"It can be done," confirmed Dequeker.

He had a friend, he explained, who knew someone high up in the Gestapo who could get Yvan released.

"How much?" asked Pauline.

Dequeker explained that buying a detainee's freedom was costly.

"The Germans are greedy bastards," he said.

"How much?" she repeated.

"They won't turn down one hundred thousand," replied Dequeker.

She immediately agreed to the sum. She had 100,000 francs in cash and gold bullion in the apartment. She was willing to hand it all over. She would go and get the money.

A few hours later, Pauline and Dequeker met again, but on a pavement near to the apartment; gold bars were heavy. Dequeker was not alone. He had brought the friend he had mentioned, Jean Aimée Guélin, also in his fifties, along. The latter, an unsuccessful lawyer, was moonlighting as co-manager of the *Théâtre des Nouveautés*. Fluent in

German, he was, like Dequeker, informing for the Gestapo. He had come to tell Pauline that the Gestapo officer they were going to make a deal with did not think 100,000 francs was enough.

"So how much does he want?" she asked.

"Another seven hundred thousand."

Pauline blanched, but the thought of Yvan drove her on.

"Fine," she said "I'll give you the money."

She hoped she would be able to raise the extra seven hundred thousand. Quickly, the men in the Dreyfus family came to her assistance. They told her where in Paris she had to go to fetch the money.

The following morning, Pauline waited for Dequeker and Guélin on a bench in front of Fouquet's, the Avenue des Champs-Elysées restaurant. She had the money in a suitcase. Dequeker and Guélin told her there was a hitch. She would have to give the Gestapo officer another four million francs to secure Yvan's release.

"I do not have that kind of money," she said, her heart pounding.

"Then there's no deal," replied Guélin.

He also told her that the money she had already paid would not be returned to her.

"Expenses," he said.

"Two and a half million," she offered. "I can give you another two and a half million."

Guélin shook his head.

"Three seventy-five."

"Three million."

Guélin again shook his head.

"Three and a half million," he said, "but not a franc less, I'm afraid."

Pauline agreed, but on one condition.

"I will give you the money only when Yvan stands in front of me, a free man."

Guélin thought about it for a moment.

"D'ac," he said. D'accord. OK.

Pauline felt faint.

Again, she asked the Dreyfus men to help her out; again they did.

Meanwhile, Dequeker and Guélin took the 700,000 francs to the Gestapo officer. He was Yodkum from IVB, the Jewish Affairs Department, the man who would send Massu a report in 1944. Having

heard from his informers that a Dr Eugène was running an escape
network, he had ordered his informers to find a *mouton* - a stool pigeon -
to infiltrate the network. Yvan Dreyfus was going to be the stool pigeon.
Delighted with his breakthrough, Yodkum sent a report, dated, May 8,
1943, to his Paris superior, *SS-Obersturmbahnführer* Heinz Röttke.

'I had given instructions to one of our informers to gather
information on an escape network, which has South America as
destination. I have consequently learnt that, every three weeks, a group of
people leaves for Spain.

'The travellers must pay an initial amount of 50,000 francs. They must
also supply ten passport photographs. They must also give their names
and full addresses, which the network then thoroughly verifies. This is
done by a French police inspector.

'The departure date is announced only three or four days in advance
while the exact place of departure is revealed only a few hours in
advance. A member of the escape network then takes the travellers to a
safe house, which is a hotel or a doctor's apartment. The daily rate for
staying at this safe house is 400 francs.

'From this moment on, the travellers are not allowed to write to or try
to contact anyone. After several days at the secret safe house, the
travellers are taken to a train station and handed over to two or three
other members of the escape network. The travellers now have to hand
over another 50,000 francs each. On receipt of the money, they are given
false passports.

'All money and jewellery the travellers have with them, they must then
also hand over to the escape network's men. But those will be returned
on reaching the Spanish border. Each traveller is free to take as much
money as he wishes with him. It is assumed that this escape network is
run by high French officials or the upper classes.

'According to my informers, the doctor deals not only with Jews, but
anybody presented to him, terrorists and notably deserters from our army
or services, who desire to escape as several sources have confirmed...

'Based on my long investigation, it appears to me that this
organisation is remarkably efficient.

'I recommend that surveillance is set up all along this underground
railway to enable us to study the methods employed to cross the line of
demarcation and the various frontiers'.

Yodkum had a problem, though. How to divide the money he was going to get out of Pauline Dreyfus. Dequeker and Guélin would have to be paid. So also another two informers, Pierre Paul Péhu and Marcel Chantin, involved in the scheme. Dr Eugène's fee would also have to be paid, but it would be taken back on the latter's arrest. And, of course, he, himself, would have to benefit financially too; in fact, his share had to be biggest of all.

Wednesday, May 12, Péhu, 52, a dismissed police commissioner and an enthusiastic Gestapo torturer, set off for Compiègne to fetch Yvan. Physically strong, he was sure that he would be able to restrain Yvan should he try to make a dash for it. And a glib talker he also knew that he would be able to persuade Compiègne's *Wehrmacht* administrators to accept Yodkum's written demand to let Yvan go.

That same day Péhu returned to Paris. He was alone. Yvan had refused to leave the camp.

Pauline asked why.

Guélin explained that the Gestapo officer they were dealing with had drawn up two pledges for Yvan to sign, but he had refused to do so. The pledges - Yvan was to give his word he would never again participate in any anti-German action and that he agreed to infiltrate a Paris-based escape network run by the Resistance, and denounce it to the Gestapo - were bogus, he assured Pauline.

"Can you not give us an object or a word to give your husband so that he could know you want him to sign?" he asked.

She gave him the word Pomme.

He returned to Compiègne. He took Marcel Chantin, forty, a director of the Banque Régionale Parisienne along. Taking Chantin along was to thank him for his role in setting Yvan up; he had been the first to learn that a Dr Eugène was running an escape network and to tip off the Gestapo. Chantin loved spending his nights in bars and it was in his favourite, Bar Jobert, drinking with a pal – Pintard - he had learnt about Dr Eugène.

Yvan signed the pledge.

Friday, May 14, he, Chantin and Péhu arrived in Paris.

The very pleased Chantin and Péhu took Yvan straight to Yodkum's office. Leaving him there, the two went to get the money from Pauline. Hearing Yvan was at Gestapo headquarters, she refused to hand over the money.

"I will do so only when Yvan stands right in front of me," she said.

Chantin and Pèhu went to fetch him.

Gallantly, the two gave the couple a few precious minutes alone in the living room; they went to the kitchen on the pretext of wanting to drink water.

In the evening, a relieved Pauline and a happy Yvan dined with a very cheerful Guélin in a restaurant; the latter had chosen the restaurant. He told them he would pay the bill and they were not going to order from the miserable wartime fixed menu, but from the chef's special menu. The two knew that a chef's special menu was reserved for German officers and patrons like Guélin - *collabos*.

Over dinner, Guélin told Yvan he would take him to a barbershop in the morning. "Not for a short back and sides," he joked.

It was to meet Dr Eugène, head of the escape network he was to infiltrate.

"You will ask him to help you get away from the horrible Nazis," he said.

He winked.

Yvan also winked; at Pauline.

He had already decided that he was going to tell Dr Eugène that he had been sent to infiltrate his escape network.

He was also going to ask him to whisk him off to London.

He had no doubt the doctor would do so.

* * *

Yvan, 38, had been born into a wealthy Jewish family from the region of Alsace.

The men in the family had been silk traders for generations, but Yvan had gone to the USA to study electrical engineering. On his return to France he had settled in Lyon and there he had married Pauline Rein. In 1939, aged 32 and back in the States on business, he had heard that France was at war with Germany. His American business associates had tried to persuade him not to return home and to bring his wife and daughter to the safety of the States, but he had rushed back to France to enlist. "I'm a Frenchman. My wife and my child were born in France. My home is in France. My business is in France. Now that France is in trouble, I cannot desert her," he had said.

He had become a non-commissioned officer in the French artillery and on France's capitulation and back in Lyon he had started to repair radio transmitters for the Resistance. He had a perfect cover, or so he had thought; he had opened an electrical appliances and radio shop. One day he had met another radio shop owner, Maurice Petiot from Auxerre. They had got on well.

His cover had not been as sound as he had thought and soon he and eight men, three of them his cousins, all in the Resistance, were on the run from the Germans. They wanted to join General de Gaulle and the Free French in London. They had reached the town of Montpellier, 756 kilometres south from Paris and close to the Spanish border, but there gendarmes had apprehended them. Yvan had been held in an internment camp in the town of Nîmes, 51 kilometres from Montpellier, but from there he had been brought back to Paris and was then interned in Compiègne to await transportation to one of the Germans' concentration camps.

* * *

Pauline and Yvan spent the following three days and nights in the apartment. They didn't venture out. Not only had Pauline gone to Paris without the obligatory permit to travel, but Yvan, his identity card having been confiscated on his arrest, was without any identification documents. And neither had a yellow Star of David to sew onto their overcoats.

Remaining indoors wasn't a problem. They had much to talk about and many plans to make for their future with Pomme once the war was over.

On the fourth day day after Yvan's arrival in Paris - Wednesday, May 14 - Guélin arrived at the apartment. He had gone to collect Yvan. He was going to take him to have some photographs taken because Dr Eugène needed ten photographs - five full face and five in profile. Afterwards he was going to take him to a barbershop to meet the doctor.

Guélin carried two heavy suitcases and Pauline and Yvan wondered why but did not ask him.

Yvan put on his overcoat.

At the door of the apartment, he turned to Pauline.

"I won't be long," he told her.

She wanted to know for how long exactly he would be out.

"I should be back in a couple of hours," he replied.

Guélin nodded in confirmation.

"*Bon*," said Pauline. Good.

Almost all of the previous night she had tried to persuade Yvan to return to Lyon with her. She had told him her intuition warned her that the people they were dealing with, Yodkum included - Yodkum especially - could not be trusted.

Yvan kissed Pauline on her forehead. Next, on her lips. Only lightly. They weren't saying farewell, only goodbye. He left with Guélin. Pauline locked the door and listened to their footsteps descending the stairs. She listened until she heard the click of the street door closing.

Guélin took Yvan to the barbershop. Fourrier waited on the landing. He told Guélin that 'the doctor' wouldn't be coming. He was going to take Yvan to where the doctor was waiting. Guélin wanted to go along, but Fourrier refused.

"Wait here," he said. "Doctor's orders!"

Guélin felt that he could not refuse; Fourrier had promised him a percentage of the commission that the doctor was going to pay him for having sent him an escapee.

Yvan followed Fourrier from the building. Guélin had given him the two suitcases to carry. He was told they were filled with old newspapers and a few stones. "It's to bluff the doctor, because as we know you aren't going anywhere," Guélin had told him with a wink and a smile.

Within half an hour of setting off with Yvan, Fourrier was back at his barbershop. He told the waiting Guélin that he had handed Yvan over to the doctor - Dr Eugène - but the latter had not paid the commission. Guélin would have to return later to the barbershop to pick up his share.

Fourrier was unaware that two IVB4 agents, sent by Yodkum to discover the address where Dr Eugène was hiding escapees, had been tailing him and Yvan.

Those two agents would return to Rue de Saussaies to report to Yodkum that the doctor had given them the slip. They said that when Fourrier and Yvan left the barbershop, they had walked west to Place de la Concorde where another man had joined them. That man was about

1.70 metres in height and very thin and he was clean-shaven and had chestnut hair. He wore a blue suit. Yvan had walked off with him towards Avenue des Champs-Elysées.

Halfway up the avenue, the two had suddenly vanished, vanished inexplicably.

* * *

Meanwhile Pauline, Yvan not having returned, decided that he was already on his way to London. She started to pack her suitcase. She was going to go home; Yvan would no doubt send her a message from London.

-0-

CHAPTER EIGHT

Gestapo Prisoner

Night was falling. The sky was a molten wound. The Petiots were at home and waiting for Nézondet. He was bringing tickets for the evening's performance of the popular musical, *Ah la belle époque*, at Théâtre Bobino. Gerhardt, who had already gone to live with his uncle and aunt in Auxerre, was home for the half-term school holiday and the theatre visit was a belated birthday present for him.

Cars drew up outside Number 66 Rue de Caumartin; doors slammed, men's voices called out in German, boots scraped over cobblestones. There was banging at the Petiots' door. Leroux, the maid, ran to see what was going on. She was violently shoved against a wall by a man in a belted raincoat and fedora. Behind him stood other men dressed similarly. They held guns and rifles. She recognised them as Gestapo. One lifted his rifle and poked it into her stomach. Gerhardt was screaming from somewhere in the apartment. Georgette rushed from the bedroom: the men from the Gestapo locked her into the kitchen. Marcel, stepping from his waiting room was handcuffed and pushed into his consulting room. Two men stood guard over him. Their rifles pointed at his head. For half an hour the Gestapo men pulled drawers from desks and cupboards and emptied their contents on to the floor.

Marcel, holding his handcuffed hands over his stomach, was marched down the stairs at gunpoint to a *traction-avant*.

As Marcel reached the car, Nézondet came running down the street. The latter wanted to know from his friend what was going on. One of the Gestapo men locked handcuffs over his hands as well and he was marched up the stairs and hurled into the Petiots' living room.

"Sit!" the Gestapo man shouted at Nézondet.

He slumped, almost collapsed, into a chair.

Gerhardt was sitting on a nearby chair, crying. Georgette, having been allowed to leave the kitchen, stood a few steps from her son; she was too stunned to comfort him.

"I haven't done anything! I don't know why they've handcuffed me," mumbled Nézondet to no one in particular.

Desperately, he tried to convince the armed men that he knew nothing about Dr Petiot's affairs. He had come over to deliver theatre tickets. He begged one of the men to take the tickets from his wallet. He, too, was marched from the building and thrown into a *traction-avant*.

Mrs Denis, the concierge, having heard the commotion out on the street and in the building, had pulled down the blinds of her booth's window; she didn't want to have anything to do with what was going on, she did not even want to see what was going on.

* * *

Yodkum still had not digested the fact that Dr Eugène and Yvan had slipped through the fingers of his men on the very public Avenue des Champs-Élysées when news arrived that IV3E's *Hauptstürmführer* Friedrich Berger had arrested the doctor; real name, Marcel Petiot.

Berger, like Yodkum, used informers and he had instructed one of them, a dismissed policeman, a Charles Beretta, to discover Dr Eugène's real identity. Beretta, a man who had denounced his own Jewish wife to the Gestapo, so that his lover, a woman named Yvonne Teyssèdre, also a Gestapo informer, could move in with him, was another Bar Jobert regular.

At the bar, he had met Pintard who had not taken long to speak about an escape network run by a friend of his: a Dr Eugène.

What had followed had looked as easy and uncomplicated as a child's game.

In the barbershop Pintard had introduced Beretta to the Dr Eugène in question - Marcel - and the latter had accepted Beretta as an escapee. Marcel had decided on a departure date for Beretta and the latter had informed Berger who planned to have his men burst in at the barbershop on the scheduled day to arrest Dr Eugène, Fourrier and Pintard.

Beretta, carrying two small suitcases, had turned up at the barbershop as scheduled but had found only Fourrier and Pintard there. Dr Eugène,

242

they had told him, would not be long. Berger's men, not knowing that Dr Eugène was not yet there had burst in, shouting for everyone to put up their hands and for Dr Eugène to step forward. Shaking from head to toe, Fourrier and Pintard had blurted out that they did not know a Dr Eugène. They were handcuffed and marched to a waiting car. Beretta, his hands also up in the air, and shaking even more than Fourrier and Pintard, but with pretence, was also handcuffed and marched to a waiting car. He was biting on his lower lip in an effort not to burst out laughing: he was about to earn a neat sum of money for having led Berger's men to Dr Eugène; he had no doubt that Berger would get the doctor's address out of the old barber and the old ham actor.

Fourrier and Pintard were driven to Berger's office and after some forceful persuasion they had revealed Dr Eugène's real identity and his address. They had even given Berger the Petiots' telephone number. Beretta too was handcuffed and driven to Berger's office. He had not uttered one word of protest. He knew the procedure: once at Berger's office his grateful and generous Gestapo masters would slip him a large brown envelope stuffed with banknotes.

Before the night ended, Yodkum, knowing that the elusive Dr Eugène had been arrested along with three of his cronies was shouting over the telephone to Berger. He told him that by arresting the doctor he had foiled an excellent plan, one that would have resulted in the arrest of the entire gang of terrorists and not just a measly four involved with the escape network. Berger apologised profusely and immediately issued orders for Marcel, Fourrier, Pintard and Nézondet to be taken to Gestapo Headquarters to be handed over to Yodkum.

The four were thrown into the rear of a *Wehrmacht* truck. Half a dozen soldiers with rifles were in the rear with them.

At Rue des Saussaies, Yodkum was waiting.

For what was left of the night, he interrogated Marcel.

The *collabo* Péhu assisted enthusiastically.

In the morning, Marcel's handsome features, grotesquely swollen and his body bruised, was driven to Fourrier's barbershop. Another informer had told Yodkum that Yvan and Pauline Dreyfus had an appointment there with Marcel at 10 A.M. but the barbershop was dark.

From the barbershop Marcel was driven to Fresnes Prison. Fourrier, Pintard and Nézondet were already locked up there.

Nézondet would write in his book of his interrogation in Jodkum's office.

He wrote: 'I was asked three questions. Whether I knew the name of Petiot's girlfriend; whether I knew the addresses of the Paris buildings of which he was the owner and whether the doctor listened to the BBC.

'I could easily reply that I am not aware that Petiot was having an affair - he was not; that I did not know that he owned any apartments or buildings in Paris - here I lied because I knew that he had bought an apartment building on Rue de Reuilly.

'Of course, he listened to the English radio just as we all did. Even the Germans listened to it. But, naturally, I said that Petiot did not. The man who was asking me the questions smiled, but he accepted my answer.

'I then had to go and sit in a corridor. I sat there for a good hour and then Petiot arrived. A man dressed as badly as a *flic* was with him.

'He was taken to the office where I had been interrogated. I could hear very angry voices. Petiot was crying out with pain'.

* * *

Marcel knew life in Fresnes was going to be hell.

The prison, built at the end of the nineteenth century was Europe's largest. It consisted of a complex of three identical three storey buildings, four smaller two storey buildings and another two storey building, all around a courtyard. The buildings were connected by underground corridors. High concrete walls surrounded the complex, and German soldiers with submachine guns stood guard in watchtowers; the commanding officer was also German and so were some of the guards.

Inside, cells lined corridors. There were fifty cells on each. Marcel's was Number 440 on the fourth floor; a political detainee, he shared with three political activists, Roger Courtot, a student, an engineer named de la Teulade and a paratrooper lieutenant, Richard LHéritier, arrested on parachuting into Normandy from London. Political detainees were not allowed visitors. Neither were they allowed to receive parcels, even from the Red Cross. They also could not write or receive letters. And they lived with the knowledge their jailers, Germans or French, could shoot or guillotine them any day.

A French author would write of Fresnes: 'At the time of the

Occupation, Fresnes was to the French a place of horror, tears and of death. They called the prison 'death's antechamber' or 'the Devil's associate'.

Each morning Marcel was driven to Yodkum's office. He was put through *la danse* - the dance: German torture. He was beaten; hot slivers of metal were pushed underneath his nails; his teeth were drilled until half of his molars had been bored away. He did not break. He kept on denying he was Dr Eugène. He kept on denying he had ever run an escape network.

Later, he would describe to the Crim what he had gone through:

'I was arrested on a Friday evening and taken to the Rue des Saussaies where I was questioned. I was hit all night in an office on the fourth floor.

'The next morning the Germans took me to Fourrier's place to try to catch my accomplices as they came to get Yvan Dreyfus and his wife.

'Then I was taken to the office of the head of the Gestapo (sic) who continued with the interrogation, letting his inspectors hit me; they were apparently directed by a Frenchman who had set up the whole affair with Guélin and Péhu.

'Then I was taken to Fresnes, and, almost immediately, brought back to the Rue des Saussaies, where they continued the interrogation with their usual methods.

'I was interrogated on Sunday and Monday, and then taken back to Fresnes. After the last interrogation, I was taken one Saturday to the German army's centre of counter-espionage in Avenue Henri-Martin, where I was interrogated and tortured for three days and two nights - bath, skull-crusher, tooth-drilling, many blows, etcetera - after which I coughed up blood for about eight days and had dizzy spells for six months.

'The interrogations were prompted by the fact that Fourrier had, perhaps unintentionally, revealed my pseudonym of 'Dr Eugène'.

'When I arrived in Avenue Henri-Martin, I was shown a man close to death. He was on a stretcher and his face was covered with blood. I was told that it was a man from my group whose head had been crushed. I didn't recognise him. I was shown another man who was already dead.

'On the officer's desk in the room in which I was interrogated, there was a board with a schematic diagram of the various resistance groups.

245

The Germans apparently wanted to consider me as a Resistance leader. Among those who interrogated me in good French, I recognised men whom we had driven out and who played tennis at the Racing Club.

'They didn't get any information out of me'.

According to an unverified German report that surfaced after the Liberation of Paris, Marcel had confessed involvement with an escape network. He had allegedly given Yodkum the following statement:

'About 18 months ago, I met a man named Robert Martinetti who came to my office as a patient. I do not record my patients in any of my books. During the course of his visits for my professional services, he told me that he was a member of an organisation devoted to getting people out of Occupied France to South America. He requested me to supply him with the names of some of my patients who might be interested in becoming clients of his. Originally, the price he asked for each traveller to be taken out was 25,000 francs, but, later, he raised this amount to 50,000.

'Several months later, I told Mr Fourrier - the barber, whom I had known for some time - of the escape organisation and that if he, Fourrier, knew anyone wanting to leave Paris clandestinely, to bring them to me. Fourrier was also a regular patient of mine.

'Following this, Fourrier did return and told me he knew several people who desired to make illegal departures. Martinetti, in the meantime, kept visiting me for treatment. I therefore relayed my conversation with Fourrier.

'The departures began about six months ago. My role or participation was merely to collect the travellers and their luggage at Fourrier's and to take them to a meeting point at a time given to me by telephone one or two days before. This meeting point was usually Place de la Concorde, where I turned them over to Martinetti.

'I did not like the people recruited by Fourrier. I therefore became concerned and took it upon myself to check upon them and interview each and every one of them about the reasons for their trip. From then on, I received the right to accept or turn down the candidates for escape.

'It was always Fourrier who collected the fees from the travellers. I never had anything to do with the fees, except once when I did intervene to reduce the price asked by Fourrier. The hour of the meeting of the travellers was always the same - between 11 A.M. and noon, usually outside the Concorde Métro station on Rue de Rivoli.

'Martinetti, by the way, always had me tailed from Fourrier's place on Rue des Mathurins where I picked up the travellers. He wanted to see whether I was under surveillance'. Petiot had not said by whom.

'I must qualify what I had said of the place and the time of the meeting. Actually, there were two meeting places. This was in case the meetings drew attention. However, if Martinetti did not turn up in the agreed place and at the agreed time, a second meeting place and time was always scheduled. This was for between 4 P.M. and 5 P.M. outside the Saint-Augustin Métro station.

'I knew only Martinetti and what he told me about the escape network. At first, he told me that the clandestine apparatus was under the protection of some high-ranking personalities and that a foreign embassy supplied the passports. He mentioned the Argentinian Embassy and that the travellers had the further protection of allegedly being commercial attachés of the embassy with semi-diplomatic status. The departures, according to Martinetti, were from a seaport very close to the Franco-Spanish border, and the ultimate destination was Argentina.

'About the base or hide-out from which the travellers left Paris and where they were lodged for a period prior to their departure, I can only say that I was never told anything about the place. The only one in the network I knew, and the only one I was supposed to know, was Martinetti. And all I had to do was to deliver the travellers to him. I never again saw any of the people I turned over to him'.

The report ended by stating that Dr Petiot had acknowledged the typed testimony - it had been read to him - as an accurate transcription of his confession.

* * *

Monday, May 24, two days after Marcel's arrest, Maurice arrived in Paris. He booked into Hotel Alicot. He did not telephone Georgette to say he was in town. She was alone at the apartment as Gerhardt had already returned to Auxerre.

Early afternoon Maurice set off for the townhouse. He had the key. Returning to the hotel, he started to look for a man with a truck who could do a little moonlighting for him; he wanted goods to be collected from the townhouse and to be taken to Gare de Lyon railway station. He did not ask the truck driver his name; neither did his give his own. Getting back to the townhouse in the truck, curtains twitched behind windows. Rue le Sueur's residents watched the truck driver and his passenger carry heavy suitcases from the property. The words Avenue Daumesnil were on the truck's side panels.

In the morning, the suitcases already on a train and on their way to Auxerre, Maurice bought a ticket for the town for himself.

He went home.

* * *

Five days later, Nézondet, handcuffed and hungry, waited in a corridor at Fresnes Prison to be driven to Gestapo Headquarters for interrogation. He saw Marcel and a guard walk up. Marcel was also handcuffed and his ankles were chained together.

Nézondet would recount the incident in his book: 'They made us walk to the prison van, which was waiting in front of the prison gate. On the walk, I had a chance to speak to Petiot. He was unrecognisable with an eight-day beard and his worn-out long overcoat. He seemed to have great difficulty in moving. He had a slight stoop and constantly sponged his head with a damp handkerchief. I felt sorry for him and did my best to help him walk to the vehicle'.

In the van, Nezondét and Marcel joined other inmates, each locked into a small, windowless cell. The two were locked into adjoining cells, but they were warned not to speak to one another. Marcel's ankle chains were fastened to the floor.

A few kilometres from the prison, Nézondet noticed that the guards - they were French - were watching the passing scenery. Quickly, he pressed his mouth against the bars separating his cell from Marcel's.

"Why are they holding us?" he asked.

He had whispered.

"Clandestine departures," Marcel whispered back.

"Is it serious?"

Marcel lifted his handcuffed hands to his head.

"Twelve bullets in the head," he said.

Two days later, Nézondet saw Marcel again.

They were in the transport van again and again on their way to Gestapo Headquarters. There was no opportunity to speak; a guard, again French, stood in front of Nézondet's cell. Marcel sat with his head down; he seemed oblivious to his surroundings. At their destination the van pulled up in a courtyard. There was confusion because guards were unlocking cells and pushing inmates off the vehicle. Nézondet saw Marcel motioning with his eyes for the two of them to step aside.

"You won't be held much longer, so, when you're out, go to my wife and tell her she must go where she knows to go and she must dig up what she knows is buried there," he whispered.

Nézondet had no time to reply; Marcel was pulled aside and marched off ahead of him.

A day later, Nézondet was released.

He went straight to Gare Saint-Lazare railway station. From there he telephoned Georgette from a public phone booth. He asked her to come to the station; he had a message for her. He also asked her to bring him a sandwich; Fresnes' food was inedible. He huddled behind a pillar in the railway station's main hall and saw Georgette, her hair tousled and her face clean of make-up, rush in. Ravenous, he gobbled down the sandwich she had brought.

"Marcel asked me to tell you; you must go where you know to go and you must dig up what is buried there," he said, the sandwich having been eaten.

Georgette frowned.

"I don't have a clue what Marcel's talking about," she said.

"Well, that was exactly what he said to me."

A few days later, Georgette took the train to Auxerre.

* * *

In Auxerre, Georgette took Maurice aside. She told him that on the day of her husband's arrest, she had heard the Germans tell him that they were arresting him for having helped a man to flee France. Or he might even have murdered the man. She thought she had heard the Gestapo mention the name Yvan Dreyfus.

"Dreyfus… Yvan? But I know him! He sells electrical equipment and radios. I also know his father. But Marcel does not know them," said

249

Maurice.

Georgette was not to worry. He was going to see what he could do to get his brother freed.

It was June 12. Maurice immediately wrote a letter to Yvan's father. He told the old man that his brother, Dr Marcel Petiot, had been arrested by the Gestapo, 'because I think he helped your son get away from France; the Gestapo, though, are under the illusion that my brother murdered your son'. He described the doctor as a wonderfully kind man who had been sheltering Jews. He had seen with his own eyes how he had helped Jews to hide.

Maurice continued.

His brother earned half a million francs a year and 'his only expenses were for the purchase of art objects and books; he has always had this passion'. His brother had even been accused of being miserly.

He ended the letter: 'I know my brother as someone who is likeable and cannot even raise his voice in anger; nevertheless, he has had periods of extreme exhaustion and depression, but those he overcame, although with difficulty.

'Therefore, should you know where your son is, please go to the police and tell them.'

Yvan's father, wishing to keep a low profile because the Dreyfus family was Jewish and his son Yvan was missing, probably under Gestapo arrest, he did not go to the police.

-0-

CHAPTER NINE

Release and Destroying Evidence

It was December 1943. Nézondet's telephone rang. It was Maurice on the line; he was in Paris and staying at Hotel Alicot.

"I've got something to tell you. Can you come over?" Nézondet heard Maurice say. The two met at a nearby bistro.

"What's up? Why do you look so poorly?" Nézondet wanted to know.

Maurice was pale and thin, and his shoulders were twitching almost uncontrollably.

"I've been to the townhouse my brother has on Rue le Sueur," he began.

Nézondet would later admit that at that stage he had known that his friend Petiot had bought a townhouse and that it was on Rue le Sueur in the sixteenth *arrondissement*, but that he had not gone there.

"So? What did you find? A radio transmitter, weapons?" Nézondet asked.

Maurice sighed deeply.

"If only..."

"What did you find there, then?"

Maurice took a moment to reply.

"Something that could get us all shot. My brother's mad... most dangerously mad. I have proof of this now. The famous voyages to Argentina... for which the Gestapo got him... they began and ended on Rue le Sueur."

He had more to get off his chest.

Visiting the house soon after his brother's arrest, he said, he had found many suitcases there. All were filled with clothes. Among the clothes were German uniforms. Those he had got rid of: he had burnt them. He had also found some guns. Those he had thrown down a sewer. He had furthermore found a list with the names of fifty people. Some of the names were German. Beside each name was a date. There were also post-dated letters in the house which had been written by some of the people whose names were on the list. Some of the letters were post-dated by six months. The letter writers reported to family and friends that they were well and that they had arrived safely in Buenos Aires. He had also found sketches of a hypodermic needle. The needle could be used to inject people with poison. One could even fire the poison from a distance.

Maurice fell silent.

"And?" asked Nézonet.

"I've also found bodies. They were naked... The heads had been shaved. The bodies were stacked up in a pit in an outhouse. I filled the pit with anything I could lay my hands on... earth... coal. I also burnt the sketches and the list... and the letters."

"And?" Nézondet wanted to know again.

"That's it," said Maurice.

He sighed yet again.

"But what's come over him?" asked Nézondet.

"I don't know what's come over him. Who would have thought that he was capable of this? He was always so calm, so well behaved, and he was never away from home... not for long periods, anyway. You know... one day, he and I had to meet a relative, but he arrived late. The relative and I then asked him where he had been, and he said, 'I've just killed a *Boche*', and we laughed. He was probably speaking the truth."

"But then he's a monster..."

"No! He's sick... very sick. He's been leading a double life all these years..."

"But what if the Germans hear of this?" asked Nézondet.

Maurice sighed yet again.

"It's a miracle they haven't found out about it already..."

"What do you plan to do?" asked Nézondet.

"Hide everything and wait."

"But if he should be released from Fresnes, won't he continue killing people?"

"It's not likely he will be released soon... but should he be, then we would have to watch him... insist that he undergoes treatment in an asylum. That was why I wanted to see you. Can I count on you to help us with this?"

Nézondet gave a nervous giggle.

"You're joking!" he said. "I don't want to have anything to do with this! How do you think you can take him for treatment without the doctors finding out what's going on?"

"It won't be easy, no, but we would have to find a way. But I certainly won't let him go back into that house. I've got the only key, and I won't return it to him."

"And if he finds out that you know... that I know... his secret? Doesn't that scare you a little?"

"I'll tell him that I've taken precautions in case anything should happen to me; you should do the same. Right now, though, I want you to keep this to yourself."

Nézondet's reply was an exasperated cry.

"I recognised one of the bodies. It was Yvan Dreyfus," continued Maurice. "His body lay right on the top in the pit."

"*Merde*! How long has this been going on for?"

Sweat was pouring down Nézondet's cheeks.

"A little over a year," replied Maurice.

"Shit!" shrieked Nézondet. "Then the house must smell bad!"

"It does," admitted Maurice. Then he thought about it. "You know, strangely, it does not smell *that* bad."

He asked Nézondet not to go the police.

"You can't even tell anyone about it," he said.

Nézondet promised he would not go to the police.

"And I'll not say anything to anyone else, either," he added.

In his book, he would write that the two of them had then gone for lunch. 'We ate without appetite', he wrote.

In the evening, over dinner at a restaurant, Nézondet told Lesage and Turpault what Maurice had told him.

"Some secrets are too heavy. Oh, *merde*, some secrets are just too heavy for one man's shoulders!" he groaned, falling silent.

The wartime potato soup the three were having seemed even more tasteless than usual.

A few days later, Nézondet telephoned Georgette. He asked how she was. How Gerhardt was. How the boy was taking his father's absence.

Georgette said Gerhardt was home for a few days; she asked Nézondet and Lesage for dinner.

Georgette served a frugal dinner of soup and minced meat and she did not offer dessert or cheese or to open a bottle of wine.

After dinner Gerhardt went to his room.

The three adults remained at the table, trying to make conversation.

Not so gently, Nézondet told Georgette what Maurice had told him.

'I told her only some of what Maurice had told me', he wrote in his book.

Georgette fainted; he did not know what to do.

Lesage, the trained nurse, calmly rose and slapped Georgette lightly on both cheeks.

On their way home Lesage told her lover that she recognised a faked faint when she saw one.

Nézondet claimed in his book that he had advised Georgette to divorce her husband.

"You'll find someone else. You'll be able to rebuild your life," he said he had told her.

* * *

Within days of Nézondet and Lesage's dinner with Georgette and Gerhardt, Marcel was back in Yodkum's office. Waiting for what he thought would be another interrogation and more torture, he heard voices in an adjoining room: Yodkum was busy interrogating a woman. The door between the two rooms opened and he saw a young heavily pregnant woman sitting in an upright chair. She turned her head and looked at him and smiled encouragement. The woman's name was Germaine Barré and she was in the Resistance.

Yodkum offered Marcel his freedom against 100,000 francs.

"What the shit!" snapped a furious Petiot. "I don't care whether you release me or not. I'm not long for this world, anyway. I have stomach cancer! But pay you I will not!"

Barré overheard the conversation.

Tuesday, January 11, a bleak, bitterly cold day, Marcel was told he could go.

Maurice had paid Yodkum's asking price in full.

Yodkum would later, in his report to Massu, claim that he had released Dr Petiot because he had come to the conclusion that the doctor was stark, raving mad.

* * *

Marcel was in a dreadful condition. At home he crawled into bed. He lay shivering uncontrollably. Georgette, having been surprised by his release, held him to her to warm him: she thought he was cold. He stayed in bed for days. He wouldn't see anyone. No one went to visit him anyway. Fourrier and Pintard did not call in on him either. Nézondet, too, stayed away.

Georgette suggested the two of them should go to Maurice in Auxerre; she was certain the warmer Burgundian climate would restore her husband's health.

For the first time, Marcel and Georgette did not spend the night before their departure at Hotel Alicot. Instead on the morning of their departure, Leroux hailed a *vélo-taxi* to take the two to Gare de Lyon railway station. Leroux was overcome with emotion at what the Germans had done to her employer. She did not know what he had been accused of. Georgette had not told her.

In Auxerre, Marcel rapidly regained his strength. He went for walks along the river. At first, he leant on a walking stick, heavily, and sat down often. He and Gerhardt sometimes went sailing in a small boat; Gerhardt rowing. Mostly, he just sat upstairs in Maurice and Monique's living room and always he only looked down into Rue du Pont. Never did he look up; the steeple of the town's Saint-Pierre Church could be seen above the rooftops and, never having liked to see a church, he did not want to see that one either.

He started to put on weight.

He talked enthusiastically of going back to Paris.

One morning, he and Georgette were on the Paris-bound train.

What had been said about the townhouse the Petiots would keep to themselves.

* * *

Nézondet had heard in a *pneumatique* from Maurice that Marcel had

255

been released. He claimed in his book he was *estomaqué*. He was flabbergasted. No, more than that. It was as if his insides were being ripped out.

$$* * *$$

Back in Paris, Marcel immediately went to the townhouse. He cycled there, pulling the cart behind him. He returned to the family apartment at the end of the day without the cart.

Over the next few days, Marcel set off for the townhouse every day.

One night, back at home, he wrote a letter to Maurice. He needed quicklime, he wrote. Could Maurice get hold of some and bring it to Paris?

Maurice did not know where to find quicklime.

Robert Maxime, his young employee did; there were quicklime quarries outside a nearby village, Aisy-sur-Armançon.

Maurice asked Jean Eustache to take him to the quarries. Having bought thirty sacks of quicklime, he asked Eustache if he could drive him to Paris to drop the stuff off.

Again, on Rue le Sueur, curtains twitched behind windows. What was being delivered to the dilapidated abandoned house, the street's residents wondered?

During the following week, every morning Marcel bought coal from a *bougnat*-bistro. It was not the one on Rue le Sueur, but another. He knew the place's owner, Julia Lasserre, a former drug addict who had taken his miraculous cure for her addiction. Delighted to see him, she let him have as much coal as he wanted. On his first visit he left with 45 kilograms of it. On each of his four following visits he again bought a 45 kilogram sack. For him, Lasserre ignored rationing.

Monday, March 6, Andrée and Jacques Marçais noticed smoke pouring from the townhouse's chimney.

Saturday, March 11, Jacques summoned the police. Smoke was still pouring from the chimney; a very bad odour clung to it.

The house's terrible secret - Marcel's terrible secret - was out!

The newspapers headlined *L'affair Petiot* every day. Barefoot newspaper boys in tattered clothes - effects of the war very much in evidence - stood on street corners and shouted out the day's headlines.

256

The Mysterious Charnel House of Rue Le Sueur! The Crimes of Dr Petiot! Dr Petiot's Mysterious Suitcases! The journalists gave Marcel sobriquets: Dr Satan, The New Landru, The Liquidator, The Monster, The Mad Doctor, The Butcher of Rue le Sueur and The Murderer of 21, after the Clouzot film.

Each and every copy of each and every newspaper was sold. The Germans still gagged journalists, but they did not seem to mind them writing about Marcel; it was a good feeling to show what the French were like.

The journalists reported whatever those who had known Marcel said of him. The villagers of Villeneuve-sur-Yonne spoke of Henriette Debauve's murder, Louisette's disappearance, Frascot's sudden death. Of how Marcel had stolen the cemetery cross. Of how, as a child, he had strangled his cat to death after he had unsuccessfully tried to drown it in a pot of boiling water. One of the town hall's employees, a Léon Pinau, described Marcel as having been incapable of being honest, while another of the villagers, Clément Depond, an iron dealer, recounted how Marcel had often gone to his workshop. Every time after the doctor had been around, something was missing. "Never something big - little things like hammers or spanners. I then went straight to his house to get them back. He never seemed to mind that I did, but neither was he ever embarrassed about having stolen from me. He just laughed."

The Paris daily *Matin* claimed that one of their reporters had succeeded in interviewing Nézondet. 'My brother has killed at least fifty to sixty people, Maurice Petiot confessed to me', the paper headlined their so-called scoop. Nézondet was quoted as having told Massu that Maurice used to complain that when his brother used to stay with him in Auxerre, he had to search his pockets every day to see if he hadn't stolen something from the house.

-0-

257

100 Rue de Paris, Auxerre, the house where Petiot was born (Copyright author)

Rue Cambon in Villeneuve-sur-Yonne where the Petiots lived
(Copyright author)

The Yonne River where Petiot dumped the headless body of his first victim (Copyright author)

Auxerre (Copyright author)

Rue de Caumartin where the Petiots lived (Copyright author)

Paris's Palais de Justice where Petiot was sentenced to death (Copyright author)

The unmarked mass grave where Petiot lies buried

PART FOUR

JUSTICE

CHAPTER ONE

Slow but certain Progress

Massu put Batttut in charge of finding *corpora delicti* proving Dr Marcel Petiot was the murderer. He put another of his inspectors, a Jean Poirier, in charge of finding Marcel. He continued to question those arrested. Examining Magistrate Berry did the same. At the end of each day, the two reported the day's progress to Prefect Bussière; he forwarded the reports to the Germans.

The number arrested had risen to twelve; Malfet, the people smuggler, was the newest inmate. On his arrest at home in Nice, he had protested that he had not even heard of Petiot. No one had believed him. He had a mass of press clippings on the affair at home. Also, 315,000 francs in cash and many items of expensive jewellery; too big a cache for a *chauffeur*. He faced the same charge as Nézondet, Porchon, Pintard and Fourrier: 'concealing evidence and not reporting a crime'.

Eryane Kahan was on the run. Ginas, free because she had convincingly claimed she had never sent anyone to Marcel and had not even known the true identity of Dr Eugène, said she had no idea where Eryane had gone, but she had left her room two days after the Rue le Sueur story had broken.

Massu made breakthroughs.

The black satin evening gown with the golden swallows embroidered on the bodice, had belonged to Joséphine Aimée Pauline Grippay. The Sylvie Rosa label on the dress had helped identify her.

The L. Duplan, whose name was on the rubber name stamp and visiting cards, had died in February 1942 of natural causes. On his death, his family had handed his furniture over to an auction house. Petiot's name was on the auction house's list of buyers and he had bought Duplan's desk. It was presumed the latter had left the cards and the name stamp in a drawer.

The Wolkowitz whose birth certificate had been found was a Max Wolkowitz. He had four convictions, two were for drug dealing. It was presumed that he had been in contact with Petiot about fleeing France. The Germans had got to him before he could flee, however; he had been rounded up on February 9, 1943. He had ended up in a concentration camp.

Of the 115 shirts found in the suitcases at the Neuhausens', some were silk. Those had belonged to Adrien Estébéteguy. Henri Lafont, under lock and key in Fresnes Prison and facing the charge of 'collaboration with the enemy' - treason - had helped the Crim identify the shirts. Shown a tie that the police had taken off the neck of Gerhardt when they had questioned him about his father at Maurice's house, Lafont had also identified that as Estébéteguy's.

Another of the shirts was also identified. Mrs Braunberger picked out the light-blue hand-made shirt with the white pinstripe on a dark-blue bodice her husband had worn on the morning he had set off to keep his appointment on Rue Duret with the mystery caller. She also picked out his fedora.

Another breakthrough was the arrival at the Quay of an anonymous letter. The *corbeau* - the 'raven' as the French call poison-pen letter writers - wrote that a doctor had helped two Jewish families flee Paris for Argentina. One family consisted of three people. Mrs W was aged about sixty, Maurice W was thirty-six, and L.W. was forty-six. The other family, Family B, consisted of three couples. One couple had left in the last days of December 1942; the other two in the first days of 1943.

Massu placed an advertisement in the dailies asking the raven to come forward. He, or rather, she did. It was Ilse Gang. Taken in for questioning she didn't hesitate in identifying the Wolffs, Basch, Schonkers and Arnsbergs as the people she had mentioned in her letter.

There were more such 'lucky breaks'.

Nézondet told Massu where Marcel had bought the peephole device, a 'Lumvisor', of the triangular room. He and Marcel had each bought one on a visit to the annual *Foire de Paris* trade fair. Nézondet's was in the front door of his apartment.

Léone Arnoux admitted that she knew what were in the suitcases found at her place; Maurice had asked her to store the cases for him. She even admitted she had helped herself to some of the suitcases' contents; the dresses. She wouldn't admit she knew where the things had come from.

The Neuhausens too admitted that they knew what were in the suitcases found at their place. They too had helped themselves to some of the items; clothes in their wardrobes matched those in the suitcases. They did, though, claim that they were only airing the clothes. It had snowed heavily the previous winter, they said, and water had leaked through the roof of their attic where they had stored the suitcases and the clothes had got wet. They had had no choice but to hang the clothes out to dry. They also revealed that Georgette knew of the suitcases and their contents. She and Maurice had turned up at their shop while Marcel was in Fresnes and had asked to be shown the cases. Georgette had then taken several items of clothing for herself.

Monday, April 24, forty-five days after the discovery of the human remains at the townhouse, a Romanian-born translator, one Kurt Kunstlich, was arrested at the Food Administration Bureau, controlling rationing, based at the town hall of the eighth *arrondissement*. He was trying to renew Eryane Kahan's ration card. The police were called and he told them that he did not know Mrs Kahan personally. He said a Luftwaffe sergeant named Wesling had given him the card. The Crim questioned Wesling at the Luftwaffe's base at the Palais du Luxembourg, formerly the seat of France's Senate. He admitted knowing Kunstlich, but denied having given him the card. He also said he did not have any idea where Eryane was. Kunstlich, questioned for a second time, admitted that he had lied; a fellow translator, a man named Etienne Robert Marin, had given him the card. Marin's address, Number 21 Rue de Rémusat, was a clinic; Marin was working as an auxiliary nurse at the clinic. Scared almost witless at the sight of the Crim detective who called on him, he said a nurse had given him the card and had asked him to try to have it renewed. She had also given him 200 francs as payment for his trouble. He had passed the card on to Kunstlich, a friend. He knew the nurse only as Irène; she had a Luftwaffe lover named Wesling. The clinic's director, a Dr Louis Pierre Després said that Irene must be Irène Pascale; she no longer worked at the clinic and he did not know her whereabouts. The woman was obviously Eryane, but that was as far as Massu got.

Meanwhile, Marcel was being spotted in the Métro, in nightclubs and in brothels. A panic-stricken old lady reported he was living in the apartment next to hers. He had grown a very long beard and had put on a lot of weight, as she said, but she had, all the same, been able to recognise him. A medium reported she had seen him in a vision. He was living in Paris dressed as a woman. Another medium announced he too had seen Marcel in a vision, but the doctor was lying dead in a basement of a house in the village of Saint-Martin-du-Tertre, close to Auxerre. He had injected himself with poison. His body lay among the bodies of people he had murdered since he had fled Paris. Of all the sightings, the Crim checked out the old lady's only. Her neighbour, quite innocent, nearly jumped from the window as detectives rushed in to arrest him.

The collaborationist radio station, Radio-Paris, also claimed it knew where Dr Marcel Petiot was. 'Petiot has fled Paris to go and join the band of terrorists of the Upper Savoie to be their doctor', it announced. The band of terrorists the radio station was talking about was the Maquis of Glières - resisters. At that time they were under German and French Milice attack.

The Paris daily, L'OEuvre, too said it knew the whereabouts of Marcel. 'He was seen at the end of March on a Métro platform waiting for a train. His eyes protruded and he kept on sweeping his right hand through his long hair. He looked so much like the photograph of him that had appeared in the papers that it was impossible not to recognise him. One would have thought that he would have grown a moustache and that he would hide his eyes behind dark glasses. Or that he would be disguised as a priest, or an SNCF - French railway - worker'. A railway worker was supposed to be unsophisticated.

All that time, behind the dour, red-bricked, 2,000 square metre bulk of the Médico-Légal Institute, Dr Paul and his colleagues tried to identify the human remains. There was little they could add to what Massu already knew. The remains, they reported, were 'not talking', or they were, but they were not exceptionally *bavard* - talkative. All that they were saying was already known anyway: the victims had been eviscerated; the heads had been cut off; the faces had been disfigured; the limbs had been cut off; the hands had been severed from the arms; the fingers had been lacerated; the work had been done by someone with medical knowledge, especially of the human anatomy.

There was one small but useful bit of information Dr Paul did give

Massu. He and his team had seen tiny marks in the victims' thighs. He explained that if a pathologist had to interrupt a post-mortem he stuck his knife or scalpel into the thigh of the cadaver he was working on so that the instrument would not be mislaid. If a pathologist were right-handed, he worked from the right and vice versa. The marks on the townhouse's victims were all on the right. That meant the murderer was right-handed.

Marcel was right-handed.

At the end of May, the names on Massu's list of possible victims reached sixteen. In the chronological order of their disappearance, according to the information he had gathered, they were: Jean-Marc van Bever, Marthe Khaît, Joachim Guschinov, Dr Paul Léon Braunberger, Joséphine-Aimée - Pauline the Chinese Woman - Grippay, Adrien - the Basque - Estébétéguy, Rachel, Maurice and Lina Wolff, Gilbert and Marie-Anne Basch, Chaima and Franziska Schonker, Ludwika and Ludwik Arnsberg, and Denise - Lili– Hotin. After Lili's name, he had put a question mark despite that Jean Hotin had confirmed that Marcel, on the recommendation of Mrs Mallard, had performed an abortion on her in June 1941 and that, in June 1942, she had returned to Paris to ask him for a letter in which he was to state that he had treated her for pneumonia, and that she had not returned home from that Paris trip. Massu had verified the story with Mouron, Mallard's daughter; Mallard was dead. Mouron, indignant, had denied her mother had been an angel maker. She said that Lili, whom she described as a dear friend, had spent a few days with them, yes, and she had fallen ill with pneumonia, yes, and her mother had summoned Dr Petiot, yes, but he had not performed an abortion on her. Lili's visit had been either in June or July 1941; she could not remember which.

-0-

CHAPTER TWO

Arrest

Georges Redouté, 56, an out-of-work Belgian-born house painter had read about the townhouse like everybody else. He knew Marcel; Marcel was the kind doctor who lived in the apartment building beside La Chope du Printemps and who had treated him for various little ailments. He couldn't believe that such a good man could have murdered so many people; in fact, he was certain that the doctor did not.

Monday, March 27, early morning and 16 days of daily coverage of *L'Affair Petiot*, Redouté, with no job to go to and deep in thought, walked down Rue du Faubourg Saint-Denis where he lived on the third storey in a small two bedroom apartment at Number 83. A voice drew him out of his reverie.

"*Monsieur Redouté! Bonjour!*"

Coming towards him was Marcel.

"*Mon Dieu! Merde! Çà alors!*" Redouté called out.

Marcel grabbed his arm.

"Mr Redouté, have you been reading the papers?"

Redouté nodded slightly.

"All lies!" said Marcel. "All lies. I'm an innocent man, but I'm being hunted as if I'm a wild animal."

He said he was in the Resistance and on the run from the Gestapo and their French police lackeys; his Resistance cell had been bumping off German soldiers and French *collabos*. He needed a place to bed down.

Redouté took Marcel home with him.

"For the night. For a shower and for the night," he said.

Marcel spent the night on a mattress on Redouté's living room floor. The spare bedroom was being used by Redouté's 26-year-old niece, Marguerite Durez. Marcel had been introduced to her by her uncle as Dr

271

Henri Valeri; Marcel had told Redouté that he still had to hide his real identity and was consequently using that name.

Durez was told that she should not mention Dr Valeri to anyone.

Morning came. Marcel asked if he could not perhaps stay a little longer. Redouté agreed. It was not every day one could do something for one's motherland.

"Rest assured, you won't get into trouble because of me," said Marcel.

He would go out only once night had fallen and there was therefore no risk that he would come across someone who knew him.

Very soon the building's *concierge*, a Mrs Krabert, noticed the *monsieur* staying with Redouté. Like all *concierges*, she hung around the lobby to see who entered and left. She did not find it odd that the house painter had taken yet another boarder; she knew he was badly in need of money and the *monsieur* was probably paying him well for his board and lodging.

* * *

The BBC had been broadcasting to the Resistance in coded language throughout the Occupation. Monday, June 5, it again used coded language to warn that an Allied invasion of France was imminent, and to ask the Resistance to begin its long-planned sabotage activities. The next day - D-Day - the Allies landed on the beaches of Normandy. General de Gaulle, also via the BBC, told his compatriots, "The supreme battle has begun! After so much fighting, fury and pain, this will be the decisive shock that we have been awaiting. Let us be in no doubt; this is not just the Battle of France; it is also our battle - the battle of the French nation!" The collaborationist Pétain replied on Radio-Paris, "Do not listen to those who, exploiting your distress, will lead the country to disaster." Pierre Laval, heading Pétain's government, went a step further. "You must refuse to listen to the insidious calls of those who tell you to stop work and incite you to revolt; they are the enemies of our country. You must refuse to aggravate the foreign war on our soil by the horror of civil war."

The French chose General de Gaulle.

Thursday, August 10, railway workers in the Paris area went on strike. Five days later, told that the Germans had decided to disarm them, the Paris police did the same. Friday, August 18, all working Parisians joined in a general strike. Gunshots of defiance could be heard all over the city. Vichy-France's banner was ripped down and the *Tricolore* was hoisted; it hung over the Palais de Justice complex, taken over by the Resistance. Prefect Bussière was taken into custody. In July 1946, he would be convicted for 'collaboration' and sentenced to life imprisonment. He would be released in March 1951, and die peacefully in his bed in 1953. Count Ferdinand de Brinon, Vichy-France's Ambassador to Occupied France, was on the run to Germany. He would be arrested in May 1945 and brought back to France to be tried in a French court. He would be convicted, like Bussière, for 'collaboration'; he would be shot outside Paris in April 1947.

Saturday, August 19, the Germans began to flee Paris, as did some of those who had collaborated with them.

On that day Marcel stepped outside in broad daylight for the first time since he had moved in with Redouté. He stayed out all day. Returning, he showed Redouté and Durez a French army uniform and some French hand grenades. He had, he said, been to the Palais de Justice where heavy fighting was going on between the Parisians and the Germans. He had participated in the fighting and he was returning to the Palais de Justice in the morning to help the resisters fight the *Boches*.

Duly, in the morning, he set off.

Again, he stayed out all day.

On his return, he had yet something to show off; a drum. He didn't say where he had found it.

Friday, August 25, Paris was finally liberated. As had become his custom, Marcel had set off early in the morning and only returned late that night. He had, he said, participated in fighting for the capital. He had a rifle, a handgun and some more - German, that time - hand grenades. Four resisters fighting beside him had died, he said. He had cradled one of the dying men in his arms.

Over the following weeks a great purge of Vichy-France leaders and *collabos* took place. Those arrested were either shot immediately or imprisoned. Many of the arrests were carried out by the newly-formed French Forces of the Interior – FFI - which combined all the fighting men and women of France, including the former Resistance. FFI members - the *fifis* - wore civilian clothes with white armbands bearing the initials FFI in black. They were armed and drove around in *traction-*

avant cars with 'FFI' painted in huge white letters on the roof.

One night, Marcel returned with an FFI armband on his left arm. He told Redouté and Durez he had joined its ranks and he has been made a Captain. He showed off a British-made Webley .455 calibre pistol. It was his. A *traction-avant* with FFI painted on the roof was parked outside the apartment building. It was his too. Inducted into the 1st Infantry Regiment as its Investigation Officer, he was based at the FFI base of Caserne de Reuilly in the Reuilly district on the eastern border of Paris. He would be 'hunting *collabos*'.

He would have to remain Dr Henri Valeri for a while longer, he said. Too many collaborators were still free and they could want to do him, his wife and son terrible harm.

* * *

The Germans having fled, the Crim began receiving more letters and telephone calls from people claiming to have known Marcel. They wanted to pass on information. Some wrote or telephoned as 'ravens'. Others supplied their names and addresses. Some even dropped by to relate their stories. Many stories leaked to the press. Parisians responded with yet more calls. Massu got an idea. He was going to choose the best story he was told and plant it on the media. It might just draw Marcel out into the open.

Massu chose the story one Charles Roland from the port city of Marseilles told him. Roland claimed that in November 1937, in Marseille, a prostitute, named Solange, had offered him sex at the cut price of one hundred francs. There had been a condition; another man - Marcel - wanted to watch. After the sex, he and Marcel had had a chat and the doctor, having revealed he was dealing in drugs, had offered him the job of cocaine pusher. Times having been hard, he had accepted the job; Marcel had left the stuff for him on top of the water tanks of the toilets of bars.

His story continued that before the Occupation, both he and Marcel had moved to Paris, and the latter had started to leave drugs for him in the toilet of the chic Café de la Paix brasserie on Place de l'Opéra. He had been to Marcel's Paris apartment. His memory was a bit faulty, he said, but the apartment was either at Number 21 or 23 Rue le Sueur in the fifteenth *arrondissement*. He could though remember clearly that the building was on a corner. He had taken the Métro to the street and descended at La Motte-Picquet station. The apartment building's *concierge* had directed him to the doctor's apartment which was on a mezzanine floor. He had found the apartment strange and very quiet, and the doctor did not have any servants. The living room walls were wood panelled and a clock stood on the fireplace. A strong smell of chloroform hung over the rooms. In March, 1943, because of the shortages in Paris, he and the doctor had returned south and the doctor had joined a clandestine armed pro-Nazi group based in the village of Pont-Saint-Esprit, 48 kilometres from the town of Avignon. The group's role was to kill resisters. The doctor had worn the uniform of a German officer and had several identity cards, all identifying him as a German national.

Roland described Marcel as 1.50 metres in height, bespectacled, with a moustache and greying hair.

The last time he had seen Marcel, he told Massu, was in Pont-Saint-Esprit on June 4, 1943. On that occasion Marcel had told him that he had invented an aphrodisiac that drove women crazy for sex.

Massu knew that Roland talked rubbish, but he contacted a journalist from the Paris daily, *La Résistance*, and asked him if he would run the story. The journalist, Jacques Yonnet, who had been a resister - his code name had been Ybarne - agreed to run the story.

Tuesday, September 19, *La Résistance*, under Yonnet's by-line, published the story, headlined: 'Petiot, Soldier of the Reich'.

A couple of weeks later, *Maître* René Floriot, the lawyer who had defended Marcel in the Van Bever Drug Case, delivered a letter to the daily. The letter was handwritten and signed *Petiot*. Representing Georgette and Maurice in the Petiot Case he was not obliged to reveal how the letter had reached him.

The letter began: 'To the editor: Any accused person must be considered innocent until proven guilty. In your edition of September 19, there is an article of three columns attacking me. According to the law, I have the right to be heard and I instruct you to publish my reply. I make this demand, as a member of the Resistance for three years, to a newspaper that has bestowed on itself such a fine name. To refuse this would be cowardly. I also wish to draw your attention to the satisfaction you would receive in obtaining an interesting article at no cost to yourself. Finally, I appeal to your responsibility to repair your paper's enormous blunder by immediately demonstrating your good faith. I would like to believe that for all these reasons, you will publish my reply in full'.

Ten pages long, the letter ended: 'The members of the Resistance - some of whom hold public office - who alone have helped and still do help Doctor Petiot are seeking, as yet to no avail, a way to make the truth known without exposing themselves to pursuit, which would be prejudicial to their useful work for the country. The signatory of these lines, far from having committed dishonourable acts, far from forgiving his torturers, and still further from having helped them, did, in fact, immediately after his release from a German prison, resume his place in the Resistance with a new pseudonym, having requested a more active role, to avenge the hundreds of thousands of Frenchmen tortured and killed by the Nazis. He always kept in contact with his friends and participated as much as he could, despite the dangers of being pursued, in actions for the Liberation. He still participates as much as he can and apologises for not being able to follow the controversy. He only read the article because a friend brought him the newspaper. Having lost all except his life, he completely devotes it to the cause under an assumed name, hardly hoping that later voices and pens, freed from all present hindrances, will make known the truth that is so easy to imagine. And forget all the profound *Boche* lies that a pennyworth of French common sense would easily expose'.

Massu, because of knowledgeable references to the military and the police in the letter, wondered whether Marcel had joined the FFI. Immediately, he asked it to compare the letter writer's script with those of *fifis*. It was a long and laborious task; thousands, many of them collaborators hoping to escape justice, had joined its ranks.He also asked the *Direction des Études et de la Recherche*, the DGER - military intelligence - to check the handwriting of its members. The FFI and DGER were also to look out for someone who resembled Dr Marcel Petiot's, by then, well-known face.

Tuesday, October 31, *La Résistance* printed Marcel's letter as well as a photograph of it; someone might recognise the handwriting or the signature.

Marcel - FFR Captain Dr Henri Valeri - no longer lived with Redouté.

He had left without telling the man who had so generously housed him. In his time at the apartment he had not contributed a *sou* to his keep.

He had moved into a bedsit in the working class Saint-Mandé district in eastern Paris. The bedsit was only three Métro stations from the Caserne de Reuilly and every morning he just popped on to a train for the short ride to work.

His new abode was the property of the mother of one of his four subordinates, Corporal Jean-Richard Salvage, ex-French Army. Yvonne Salvage charged him a minimum rent. Her son would quickly be promoted to sergeant.

* * *

Marcel, when he had told Redouté he would be hunting *collabos*, he had not lied. That was exactly what he and his team - Sergeant Salvage, Lieutenant Jean Duchesne, Lieutenant Michel Dubous, also ex-French Army, and the civilian Victor Cabelguenne - did.

Very quickly Marcel and his subordinates were in trouble.

A woman named Juliette Couchoux, a bistro owner, turned up at the Caserne de Reuilly with a complaint.

Couchoux's story was that she had been robbed. She said that on Tuesday, September 12, an FFI who she was told by her patrons was Lt Dubous had burst into her bistro to interrogate her about her activities during the Occupation; a 'raven' had denounced her to the FFI as having been a *collabo*. Dubous had smashed her safe and had left with its contents; three million francs in cash and several items of rather valuable jewellery.

Marcel was ordered by his superiors to find out from Dubous what had happened. Livid at the thought that the integrity of one of his men could be in doubt, he sent Dubous to arrest Couchoux. Not even listening to her story, he had her locked up in Paris's La Roquette Prison as a *collabo*. Two months later, he released her without charge. But in her bistro she told her patrons how a fellow female inmate, also held on suspicion of collaboration with the Germans during the Occupation, had told her that she had seen a ring a *fifi* had stolen from her on her arrest, on the finger of the bearded FFI officer who had interrogated her. That bearded officer was Marcel.

Very soon afterward, Marcel and his subordinates were in trouble again.

Another woman, Virginie Bonnasseau, also under arrest for collaboration, had let slip under interrogation that a man named Baumgartner, also a collaborator, had left a priceless stamp collection behind when he fled to Germany on the Liberation of Paris.

The stamps were, as she said, with a Lucien Larrogance, 74, Mayor of the village of Tessancourt-sur-Aubette, 45 kilometres from Paris, also a suspected collaborator.

Immediately, Marcel sent Salvage, Duchesne and Cabelguenne to Larrogance's home, the Chateau Closerie des Saules, outside the village to arrest him.

The three took a fourth man, a civilian named Pierre Botelle, along. Two days before the Liberation of Paris, the Germans had shot Botelle's father after Larrogance had denounced him as an anti-Nazi. Being present at Larrogance's arrest was going to be the sweetest of revenge.

The four asked Larrogance to reveal the code to his safe. He refused. They then blew it open with a hand grenade. Inside, they found not only the stamp collection Bonnasseau had spoken of but also valuable jewellery and gold bullion. They threw all of it into a bag, and Larrogance, bound and gagged, they threw into their car. They then drove him to a nearby wood and battered his head into a pulp. Taking no chances that he might, just might, not be dead, they shot him several times in the body with a final *coup de grâce* in the back of his bleeding head. They left the body in the wood; there, a few days later horrified strollers stumbled across it.

As a car with FFI painted on the roof had been seen in the village, Marcel's superiors ordered him to investigate Larrogance's murder. He ignored the order, but hastily handed over Larrogance's valuables, including the stamps, to a Captain Crey, head of the FFI's Recuperated Funds and Goods Bureau. He did not fail to make it clear that in his opinion there should not be sympathy for a *collabo* and the whole episode should be forgotten.

The FFI did not take Marcel's advice and, when a few days later, Crey's safe was broken into and the stamp collection was stolen, a Colonel Ruaux took the investigation into the murder of Larrogance away from Marcel. As Crey pointed out to Ruaux, Marcel and his men were the only ones who knew of the stamp collection's existence.

The FFI conducted a brief investigation and charged Duchesne, Salvage, Cabelguenne and Botelle with first degree murder and theft. He did not charge Marcel who was even allowed to remain in his post.

Duchesne, Salvage, Cabelguenne and Botelle were brought in front of a military tribunal. Marcel, still furious, refused to attend it.

Duchesne was found guilty of instigating Larrogance's murder and of theft and he was sentenced to three years in prison. The other three walked free because of lack of evidence against them.

Within days, and to Marcel's delight, the FFI squashed Duchesne's sentence and he too walked free.

The four would leave the FFI and disappear into post-war France.

The stamps would never be found.

* * *

While the case was pending another FFI officer, a Captain Simonin, had started to think that there was something familiar about Captain Dr Henri Valeri's face. He started watching Marcel. He learnt where he lived. He learnt he took the Métro to and from work every day. He learnt he was a loner; no one ever visited his bedsit, and he never visited anyone.

Simonin decided that Captain Dr Henri Valeri was none other than Dr Marcel Petiot.

* * *

On Tuesday, October 31, at 7 A.M., Simonin, in a creased French Army uniform, and three plainclothes FFI men, walked on to the Paris-bound platform at Saint-Mandé Tourelle Métro station. Simonin had decided that he was going to arrest Captain Valeri.

The four waited for three and a half hours for Marcel to turn up, and tired of waiting and ready to return to Reuilly, they saw him walk on to the platform.

Captain Dr Henri Valeri, as he always did, wore a dirty overcoat. Also always wearing a fedora, he was hatless. The FFI band was around his left arm. He carried a large bag and his pockets bulged.

There were few people on the platform as one of the plainclothes men stepped up to Marcel.

"Do you have the time, please?" he asked.

Marcel shot a glance towards his gold Swiss watch.

"Ten forty-five," he replied.

Simonin stepped forward and grabbed him.

"Petiot?" he asked.

"Yes. I am Dr Petiot," replied Marcel.

He was smiling; it was a smile that said, 'Congratulations, you've got me'.

Marcel was handcuffed and marched to the station exit and towards a *traction-avant*. At the car, he tried to make a dash for it. He was thrown to the ground.

No one said a word on the drive to the Caserne de Reuilly, but Simonin pulled the FFI armband off Marcel's arm.

Back at Reuilly and in his office, Simonin unlocked Marcel's handcuffs and ripped off his overcoat. He wore an ill-fitting grey suit, white shirt and grey pullover. One of the plainclothes *fifis* removed his belt and shoes and, as if on second thought, Simonin ordered the doctor to get undressed; to take everything off. Naked, Marcel stood shivering. It was a cool, wintry day.

Simonin and the *fifis* emptied Marcel's pockets and the bag. They put the contents on a table and it was clear from what lay there that Marcel must have become suspicious of Simonin's interest in him and had decided to go back on the run. On the table lay two pistols - the FFI's Webley and a loaded 6.35mm; 31,780 francs in cash; identity cards in the names 'Henri Valeri', 'De Frutos' and 'Gilbert'; an FFI identification card in the name of Dr Henri Valeri; a French army identification card in the name of Dr François Wetterwald; a passport in the name of René Cacheux; and a Communist Party card numbered 268004 and in the name of Dr Henri Valeri of Number 83 Faubourg Saint-Denis, Redouté's address. There also lay a France-USSR Friendship Organisation membership card, also in the name of Dr Henri Valeri; a ration card in the name of Virginie Bonnasseau, the woman from whom Petiot had learnt of the stamp collection; an application in the name of Dr Henri Valeri for a position with the DGER in French Indochina; several blank application forms to search homes and to requisition property and a child's ration card in the name of René Valeri, born in Issy-les-

Moulineaux outside Paris on May 8, 1935. The ration card's number would be checked. It was that of seven-year-old René Kneller. All documents requiring photographs bore one of the bearded Marcel.

With so many identity documents, Marcel, the son of a couple who had always had a problem with names, had a name problem of his own. Each morning he had to decide who he would be that day.

Later, the Crim would succeed only in establishing that Dr François Wetterwald had, indeed, existed. Marcel, having obtained a list of French doctors being held in Germany from a journalist, he had called on Dr Wetterwald's widowed mother. He had told her he could get her son released, but he needed his army identification card. Though her maid had warned that she should not trust the visitor - Captain Dr Henri Valeri - because his eyes were weird, she had handed the card over. She was never to see her son again. He died in Mauthausen. Marcel had initially tried to obtain the identification documents of a Dr Henri Gérard, also having seen his name on the journalist's list. Dr Gérard had been freed and foiled his plan; he walked into the living room just as Marcel had started to try to draw information about him from his wife.

The Crim would find it particularly frustrating that it could not establish whether a Dr Henri Valeri had ever existed. On the documents in his name his date of birth was given as February 20, 1895, and the place of birth as Elbeuf, Normandy; had he really existed, he would have been two years older than Marcel. The Crim thought he might have been one of those who had perished at the townhouse. Another theory was that Marcel had falsified the identity card of Dr Charles Valéry, one of the doctors from whom he had bought his Paris practice. But, if so, why would he have had Dr Charles Valéry's identity card?

-0-

CHAPTER THREE

Interrogation

Marcel talked readily to Simonin. His statement, typed out, filled ten pages.

He claimed his annual income had been half a million francs a year. It had enabled him to buy the townhouse. He had planned to convert the property into a combined home and clinic; he was going to do as soon as the war ended. At the outbreak of war he was not called up because of his Great War wound. However, he had contributed to the war effort from the beginning of the Occupation; he had made it his policy to demoralise Germans who consulted him.

His resistance work had begun when he had offered the Resistance his services. It had sent him patients - Frenchmen who had returned home ill after forced labour in Germany - and from conversations with them, he had gained information about German troop movements. He had passed the information on to the Resistance. He had told them about a German secret weapon, codenamed Boomerang. The Resistance had passed the information on to the Allies.

He had become head of the Resistance cell, Fly-Tox. His undercover name had been Dr Eugène. A British army officer, parachuted into France, had trained him on how to defend himself, detect informers and use a firearm. He could not remember when he had undergone the training. Neither could he remember the British officer's name, real or undercover.

In the Resistance he had worked closely with the two prominent resisters, Pierre Brossolette and Cumuleau, real name Jean-Marie Charbonneau. Because the latter was dark-haired, the two of them had often been mistaken for each other.

He had made contact with the United States Consulate in Paris; it had been before December 1941 when Germany had declared war on the USA and diplomatic relations between the two countries had been broken and the Americans had left Paris.

His Consulate contact was named Thompson. The latter's deputy was named Muller. He had kept in touch with Muller by telephone.

He had told the Consulate about a gun he had designed. One could kill with it from a distance of thirty metres and in total silence.

Fly-Tox had specialised in hunting down collaborators and French Gestapo. He described its *modus operandi*. A Fly-Tox man would pose as a Gestapo agent to win a suspect's confidence. Once arrested, the latter was taken to the townhouse, interrogated and executed. The body was driven to a forest outside Paris. No bodies were ever left at the townhouse.

"As a matter of fact, I had stored in this property a large part of my belongings and investments in antiques, and the building represented an important part of my estate," he stated.

He refused to give the names of the people thus executed. He could not remember the names, he claimed.

"Their names had not meant anything to us anyway. Only their crimes against France did."

After contemplation, he remembered a name. "He was a *collabo*. He was a Jew named Dreyfus."

He spoke of how IVE3's Berger had arrested him and how IVB4's Yodkum had tortured him. He was proud he had not broken under the torture.

"I remained in Fresnes for eight months, and I was interrogated many times on the activities of Fly-Tox and on my secret weapon, but they got nothing out of me!" he said.

The Fly-Tox escape network had been run by a man named Robert Martinetti. The false Argentinian passports and travel documents that the latter had given the escapees had come from a man he had known only as Desaix or De C; he had been with the Argentinian Consulate. A French police commissioner whose name he had never been told, but who was based in Lyon, had supplied French travel documents.

He explained the presence of the bodies at the townhouse.

On his return from Auxerre, where his family had taken him to recuperate from his eight months in Fresnes, he had immediately gone to the townhouse.

"They were fresh and I am, therefore, certain that they were put into the pit while I was in jail. The cadavers smelt horribly, and this is the reason why I telephoned my brother in Auxerre and asked him to send me some quicklime."

He had, in fact, written to his brother.

He continued: "I did not explain to my brother why I wanted it, but I also gave my men orders to get rid of the cadavers, but all they did was cover them in a little quicklime. Most of the cadavers were then later burnt in the furnace of the burner in the basement."

He insisted he had gone to the police about the bodies. The police had shown no interest; had not even gone to the townhouse. He had even telephoned them to ask if they would ever be going to the property. A police officer had told him to forget about the bodies. Next, the officer had told him to 'disappear'.

"This was advice that I had then taken," he said.

He could not remember the police officer's name and claimed he might never have known it.

He had joined the FFI on the Liberation of Paris; to have gone to the police would have compromised his 'friends in the Resistance'.

Ending his statement, he emphasised that enemies had dumped the bodies at his townhouse. He did not say who the enemies were.

* * *

The news spread throughout the FFI that Dr Petiot has been arrested and Captain Simonin was interrogating him.

The Crim heard and demanded Marcel be handed over.

Simonin had no choice but to comply.

There were changes at the Crim. Massu was no longer Chief of Police, and Examining Magistrate Judge Berry was no longer on the case.

Massu was under house arrest, locked into an office, which had been hastily converted into a prison cell. He was being held on suspicion of collaboration. A chauffeur who had driven for Count Ferdinand de Brinon had informed the Quay that the Germans had ordered Massu not to work flat out on the investigation. Massu had obeyed. On his arrest, he had tried to commit suicide by slashing his wrists. He was rushed to

Cusco Pavilion in Hotel Dieu where, in March 1944, he had taken Georgette. The accusation of collaboration would be withdrawn and, until the end of his life, he would deny he had slowed down the investigation on German instructions. He would never get to question Marcel.

Judge Berry had been promoted. He had been put in charge of investigating collaborators. As such, he was investigating Massu.

Marcel was handed over to Massu's replacement, Commissioner Lucien Pinault, and to Berry's replacement, Judge Ferdinand Goletty, thirty-two. Only a few weeks in Paris, the latter hailed from the northern French port town of Boulogne-sur-Mer. The Petiot Case, classified as a common criminal case, would be his first in the capital. Short, thin, highly strung and aggressive, his Quay colleagues had taken an instant dislike to him and behind his back they called him the 'Goletty Case'. Nézondet would write of him in his book: 'Short; nervous; he seemed to have only one idea in his head; to bag you. He was quite capable of even looking for premeditation on the part of a tile that had plunged from a roof onto a passerby below'.

Pinault would not last long: he was to be replaced very quickly by Commissioner André Desvaux, considered the Crim's toughest interrogator.

Despite the late hour, Floriot, also by then representing Marcel along with Georgette and Maurice, rushed to the Quay to be present at Goletty's first interrogation of the doctor; he would be present at all future interrogations as well.

Goletty asked Marcel for his full name and address.

"I am Marcel André Henri Félix Petiot, and I was born on January 17, 1897 in Auxerre. I live in Rue le Sueur."

Goletty noticed the inaccuracy of the statement. He did not comment on it. Instead, he warned Marcel he might face a charge of having assassinated 27 people; he had added eleven to Massu's sixteen. The French Penal Code makes a distinction between ordinary murder - killing in a burst of sudden anger like a *crime passionnel* when a spouse kills an unfaithful partner - and premeditated murder. The second is called an *assassinat* - assassination. The other kind of murder is called a *meurtre*. Until France abolished the death sentence in 1977, as a rule assassination meant the guillotine and murder meant *perpète* - life imprisonment -

though it, too, could have meant a death sentence.

The 11 were; Kurt, Margaret and René Kneller; Francois - the Corsican - Albertini; Joseph Didoni Sidesse – Zé - Piereschi; Jo - the Boxer - Réocreux; Claudia – Lulu - Chamoux; Annette - *la Pute* - Basset; Gisèle Rossmy, Miss X - the unnamed prostitute - and Yvan Dreyfus.

A question mark still hung over the fate of the three Knellers. It would remain there until August of the following year when the French Ministry of Justice received a letter from the American Joint Distribution Committee in New York to enquire about the family's whereabouts. The Americans had received a query from a man named Siegfried Lent from La Paz, Bolivia, concerned about the family; Lent was Greta's brother. He had told the AJDC that he was aware that his sister and brother-in-law had been planning to flee to South America, and that a friend at their last known Paris address - a boarding house - had written him they had approached Dr Petiot for assistance.

Goletty read out the names of the alleged victims to Marcel and Floriot.

The two listened in silence and boredom; both looked ready to fall asleep.

"We'll continue in the morning," said Goletty.

Marcel spent the night in a cell down in the Quay's basement. He fell asleep the moment his head hit the pillow. He slept soundly all through the night.

In the morning, he was driven to La Santé Prison. It being November 1, All Saints' Day, a bank holiday, his interrogation would resume the following day.

Before its opening on August 20, 1867, La Santé in Paris's fourteenth *arrondissement* had been hailed for its creature comforts. Real beds, a steady temperature of 15 degrees Celcius and a sewage system when Parisians still had to wait until 1889 before they could enjoy one, enthused a journalist to report that it was 'without argument, the most beautiful prison in Europe', and a member of parliament to declare in a parliamentary debate that a 'majority of the inmates will find a standard of well-being there that they did not even have in their own homes'.

The jail was built in an area first urbanised in 1607 when a *maison de santé* - a hospice - was constructed on the spot to receive the victims of a pest epidemic. The hospice had evolved into a two hectare quadrilateral prison, comprising a lower and upper area. The lower, on Rue de la Santé, consisted of the administrative buildings, a large X-shaped block with a chapel in its centre, and a *cour d'honneur* - a ceremonial courtyard; it was in the courtyard that the guillotine was always set up. The upper, bordered by Boulevard Arago, Rue Jean Dolent and Rue Messier, consisted of cell blocks which housed almost five thousand inmates on Marcel's arrival. The previous July, a month before the Liberation of Paris, the inmates had rebelled briefly against their jailers. Like Fresnes, some of the warders were German, but Prison Director Jean Farge, and Maurice Couget, his second in command, were French. The inmates had hung sheets painted blue, white and red - two of the French jailers had smuggled the paint into the prison - from the cell windows and shouted *Vive la France* and sang the *La Marseillaise*. The rebellion had begun at 4 P.M. on July 14, Bastille Day, the French National Day, and ended one hour later. Although Couget - Farge was absent - had called in the police and Prefect Bussière had rushed over personally to take command, the night that followed had been disturbed only by a lone voice singing the *International*. The next day, fifty of the rebellion leaders had been brought in front of a court martial presided over by the Milice. Twenty-eight of the leaders had been sentenced to death; they were shot in groups of seven in one of the prison's courtyards. Each group had to watch the execution of the previous one.

Marcel was locked into Block 7, Cell 7 on Rue Dolent. Block 7 was Death Row. He was to be held in solitary confinement; he would be allowed neither visitors nor parcels. The cell was 2.5 metres long and two metres wide and the ceiling was at a height of three metres. The door was made of stout wood. He had a table, a stool, and a metal fold-down platform which served as his bed. The table and stool were chained to the floor and the fold-down platform to a wall. In the floor, in one corner, was a hole; it was the toilet and the washing facility that had been bragged of once. His first night he was handcuffed and chained to the floor by his ankles. That was how he was to spend every night of the time he was to remain in prison, but not for a moment did he think it would be how he would spend every night that was left of his life.

Maurice, Nézondet and Neuhausen were locked up and already well settled in cells in other blocks. Within 24 hours Redouté would join them. Like Nézondet, he would be charged with 'concealing evidence and not reporting a crime'. All of the others who had been arrested had been released, but remained *sous contrôle judiciaire sans caution* - on control order without having had to post bail. Georgette, too, had been freed. She was with Gerhardt and Monique in Auxerre.

In the morning, Marcel, again handcuffed, was driven in a police patrol van to the Quay. In the Crim's offices Goletty and Floriot were waiting. The previous day, while most Parisians had visited cemeteries to lay flowers on the graves of their departed loved ones, Goletty had been sitting in his office drawing up a list of questions to ask the prisoner.

"*Alors* Petiot? So what can you tell me?" he began.

Marcel did not reply.

As he had done two days previously, Goletty told Marcel he might be charged with the assassination of 27 people; he read out the names again.

"Error," said Marcel, impassively. "I had 63 individuals who we had judged dangerous - German officers or enemy agents - executed. They were all bastards!"

Asked to name the 63 he had executed, he reminded Goletty he had not said he had killed them.

"I won't even be able to kill a rabbit. When I was in medical school and I had to dissect a rabbit, I always took my live one to a butcher and exchanged it for a dead one," he said.

Of Guschinov's fate, he said Desaix and Martinetti had helped him to escape to Argentina.

"Guschinov, I can assure you, arrived safely in Argentina. I know because I had word from him about four or five months after he had left. All went off well for him. He's in Argentina."

He gave Goletty the names of another two people who had been involved with the escape network; André the Corsican and Lucien Romier. The latter, Goletty knew of; a director of the Paris daily, *Le Figaro*, he had, at the start of the Occupation, become one of Pétain's government ministers. As Goletty also knew, he was no longer in the world of the living; he had died of a heart attack while waiting to have dinner with Pétain at a hotel in the town of Vichy. An André the Corsican he did not know; he doubted such a person existed.

Asked about the secret weapon he had invented, Marcel said he could not speak of it.

"It can still be manufactured. It will certainly be manufactured. I will certainly not reveal the secret to people who could possibly use it one day against good Frenchmen. And, if I do tell you, you would not understand what I'm talking of anyway because you are far too uneducated to grasp such scientific details."

Asked if he would be willing to give a statement, Marcel said he would be only too willing to set the record straight. Warned it would be taken down, he said the stenographer could go ahead.

The statement read: 'I have been a member of the Resistance since the Germans first arrived in Paris. Initially my task was to issue medical certificates to prevent Frenchmen being sent to work in Germany. Or to prevent the Germans from requisitioning properties. Or to stop the Germans doing whatever else they wanted to do.

'Next I made contact with a group of anti-Franco, anti-Fascist Spaniards. They were based in Levallois-Perret. The men I knew there operated under false identities like Gomez and Alvarez. I cannot reveal what my role in the group was, because I will endanger the lives of some people. For the same reason, I cannot give you any dates, but I will give you a clue; one day while I was in Levallois-Perret my bike was stolen and I reported it to the local police.

'Also in the beginning, the Resistance had sent me Frenchmen who had been held prisoner in Germany, but whom the Germans had sent home because they had fallen ill or their wounds needed treatment. The military information I gathered from such patients I then passed on to the Resistance.

'Some major information I passed on was of a German secret weapon. The weapon was based on the principle of a boomerang, but one with a three-bladed propeller. The Germans were working on it at a weapon plant outside Berlin close to the River Elbe. It was about 72 kilometres south-west of Berlin.

'Another aspect of my Resistance activity was that I had handed some information over to the American Consulate before diplomatic relations between the United States and Germany had been severed. The information that I gave them was of a new weapon that I was working on. I gave the information to a consular secretary named Thomson and he passed it on to a man named Muller who was also with the Consulate. I had telephone conversations with this Mr Muller on the subject. He told me that the affair would be looked into.

'The work would have been minimal if we hadn't increased it with the elimination of enemies and informers who had been responsible for the situation that France had suffered for years under the heel of the German jackboot... it was because of the German police that we liquidated about 63 individuals, thirty of whom were Germans. They all deserved what they got and we should have executed more of them.

'I eliminated some of the Germans, as a trial, with a weapon similar to the one that I mentioned earlier. Two were motorcyclists. I killed one on Rue Saint-Honoré and the other on Rue Lafayette. The motorcyclists in question fell to the ground... I forgot to say that the injuries from that gun were always fatal.

'As far as the informers are concerned, we knew who they were either through our own investigations or they were denounced to us. Another method of identifying them was that some of our men went to stand outside Rue des Saussaies just before lunch time and we picked them out when they left the building. They always gave themselves away because on leaving the building to go and eat they showed the guards their Gestapo identity cards.

'How we then proceeded to arrest them was always the same. We closed in on them in the most public place possible so that they couldn't very well react violently. We always pretended that we were Gestapo. Usually they inadvertently confirmed to us that they were informers because they immediately pulled out their Gestapo cards for us to know that we were on the same side...

'We then put them into the back of a van, and, on our way to the woods in Vincennes we gave them their punishment. All we then had to do when we got to the woods was to bury them.

'Before I left, the Germans questioned me persistently about my intentions and they kept my identity papers for almost a month. They also put my apartment under surveillance and I couldn't move without being tailed by at least two people. I could of course have escaped their attentions, but I was afraid of being arrested again. This was their standard procedure. After a few days of freedom they would put you back in prison.

'I was actually ill on my release and my family took me to Auxerre where I spent several weeks. On returning to Paris I wasn't in a hurry to go to Rue le Sueur because the surveillance had started again. So I let my brother look after the house, and, thinking that my departure was imminent, either to England or on a mission, I stuck that notice about forwarding mail on the door.

'I also did not have a key to the house, but finally, having got the key from my brother and having shaken off the German tail, I went to the building for the first time around February 8. I found an indescribable mess and the very strange disappearance from the house of such objects as a large highly expensive infra-red, ultra-violet medical apparatus as well as an electric cooker.

'Several days later, I found the key to the stable, and I went in there for the first time. I saw that a very heavy and fragile marble staircase had been moved by the Germans during my imprisonment. This had been done carelessly and several steps had been broken. I also saw that two stones covering a pit in the stable had been pulled away. When I bought the house, I had the two stones sealed with cement to keep out the many rats that had got through a door and could have caused great damage to my furniture.

'After moving one of the stones with a lever, I saw that, in the pit, were a number of apparently quite recent corpses, which seemed to have been piled up haphazardly with the things that I had noticed were missing.

'I also noticed some little objects in the stable that I had taken for mouse droppings, but then realised that they were actually dead flies. I was horrified and quite stunned; the smell was strong because the place was warm because of the putrefaction and damp as water from outside had drained into the place.

'It appeared that quicklime had been scattered over some of the corpses...

'I immediately wrote to my brother asking him to get hold of quicklime to deodorise the place.

'I stress that, if I had foreseen the presence of these corpses and the need to use the quicklime, I could have loaded up a van during my stay in Auxerre and returned to Paris with it.

'Again, I emphasise that the corpses had certainly not been in the pit for the whole summer or else they would have been completely putrefied. Also I would obviously not have let the corpses of Germans or informers be put into this uninhabited house when all the buildings in the area were occupied by the Germans and I expected them to take over my building too or at least to come on a prospective visit.

'I must also mention that the building was bought in the name of Petiot and that it contained most of my worldly fortune and especially objects of great sentimental value.

'At first, I thought that it was my old comrades in the group who had continued our work in a very risky way, both for them and for me in prison. I thought that they had acted very badly towards me by providing another reason to get me shot.

'I discovered from the few comrades that I found again and also from local information that the Germans had not only visited the house during my absence, but had gone there often.

'I strongly condemned the reckless risk taking, the complete disregard for the valuable objects thrown out and the corpses cast on the pile - for there certainly were corpses on the pile...

'However, my comrades swore to me that they also did not understand why those corpses were at my house. They thought that the Germans had killed those people and had taken the corpses to the house.

'Having been removed from the pit, the corpses were treated with the quicklime that my brother had brought in far greater quantities than I had asked for. The lime was crushed and watered to increase the contact with the bodies.

'Then two of my comrades had the bizarre idea of burning the bodies.

'Having started the hot water system, which I had not yet used, they made a fire in the furnace of one of the boilers. They cut up the bodies. It was obviously necessary to keep the fire going by stoking it regularly for, because the lime had burnt the corpses only superficially, I had noticed on getting them out of the pit, that the interior of the bodies were still fresh.

'Continuing, I also noticed that the flesh was, indeed, still red, and even the heads were heavy, which proved that the brains remained. Now, the brain disappears entirely and very quickly during putrefaction.

'Contrary to what has been said, I did not see any indication that the corpses had been scalped or the eyebrows removed.

'If the bodies were found without these parts, it is most likely because the lime had burnt the skin and, when the bodies were moved, the hair had fallen off. The hair had become ginger-coloured because of the lime.

'The bones that were found burnt had been burnt on the previous days. My comrades had told me that they were expecting to finish during the night of Saturday and Sunday'.

The next part of the statement detailed what happened on the night of March 11.

He had received the police's call at 7:30 P.M. He had been told that there was a fire at the townhouse. He had rushed to the property on his bike, even though he could not have unlocked the gateway for the police; he had had six keys, but he had given five to FlyTox and the other to his brother, Maurice Petiot. Fly-Tox, he said, had only three of the keys which meant the Germans must have got hold of the other two. He had arrived at the house at around 7:45 P.M. The firefighters and police had already forced open the gateway 'with their usual brazenness'. He had identified himself to the 'swallow' in charge; he had explained that his brother normally dealt with anything concerning the property. He had told the patrolmen that he was in the Resistance and had just been released from Fresnes, where the Germans had imprisoned him. The patrolman had taken him down to the basement. 'I saw the sight so abundantly described by the Nazi press, radio and cinema. I saw the stove full of flesh burning with no coal ... and mutilated bodies'. The bodies, he had told the patrolman, must be 'part of the struggle between patriots and Germans'. He had not waited for a police officer to arrive; 'the patrolman had told me that a commissioner from the local police station was on the way; I decided to wait for him to explain what was going on. I waited for quite a time and then the patrolmen told me that since he did not know when the commissioner would be arriving, I could go. He said that he would explain the situation to him. He also asked me to telephone him the following morning at around nine. He gave me the number to call. I was to ask for a *Monsieur* William or Wilhelm. I telephoned him like we had decided. He then told me that because too many people had been present the previous night and since the firefighters would be talking anyway, he could not hush up the affair and that he was going to put in a report. He told me to flee'.

He had spent that night at the apartment of a friend. At noon the following day, Sunday, March 12, Fly-Tox had whisked him off to Redouté's place. He refused to say whether Redouté was also in the Resistance. He also repeated he had worked closely with the two resisters,

Brossolette and Cumuleau.

Goletty knew all that was correct of the statement was that the townhouse had been bought in the name of Petiot.

As for the rest...

In 1940, the year Marcel claimed the Resistance had started to send him patients who had returned ill from forced labour in Germany, no French person had as yet been sent to Germany to work. The only certificate he had ever issued to anyone had been to a man named Lechoppier, and it was to declare him in excellent health and fit to work for TODT in Germany. The Spanish anti-Franco, anti-Fascist group of Levallois-Perret had heard of him, but it was only because on December 12, 1941, the date he claimed he had been with the group and had his bike stolen, he had gone to assist with the birth of the child of a group member named Gonzalés.

Goletty also knew that no Desaix had ever worked at the Argentinian Consulate. Neither had there been a man named Muller at the American Consulate. There had been a Tyler Thomson; he had already sent an affidavit stating he had never met a Dr Marcel Petiot, and neither had he received information from anyone about a secret weapon that Dr Petiot or anyone else had designed.

As for Brossolette and Cumuleau, both were dead, but their comrades had already reported that there had been no resister codenamed Dr Eugène and neither had any of them ever met Petiot; he certainly did not resemble the fair-haired Cumuleau. Cumuleau had, in fact, died before the time Marcel claimed he had worked with him; he jumped from the roof of a building on October 4, 1943 while running away from the Gestapo. Brossolette, arrested by the Gestapo, and imprisoned and tortured in Rennes Prison in 1944, committed suicide by jumping from the window of his fifth storey cell because he feared he might crack and reveal the names of his Resistance comrades.

* * *

Marcel was taken to the Médico-Légal Institute for Dr Paul to try to get from him how he had killed his victims; Desvaux thought that Marcel would be only too eager to boast to another medical man.

Parisians lined the streets along the route; news of the visit had leaked out. Marcel sat in the rear of a *traction-avant* between two inspectors. He looked straight ahead of him. He wore a large tweed overcoat, but was still hatless; it was another cold day.

Dr Paul was waiting; so too were the Drs Piedelièvre and Dérobert, and a Prof Sanié, Head of the Quay's Identification Department.

The geographic location of the institute itself was redolent of struggle and perseverance - Place Mazas was named after Jacques François Marc - the Brave One - Mazas, who died in the Napoleonic Battle of Austerlitz - but Marcel did not find the building or the institute in the least impressive. Neither did he look impressed on being shown into a room where the four pathologists were waiting; as district surgeon, a position that he still held, he had on occasion dealt with all four. He also knew, everyone knew, Dr Paul had once 'roasted' a human head in the oven of an ordinary kitchen coal stove to see if the head could be reduced to ash. He had found it could. Consequently, his experiment had sent Landru to the guillotine. It had proved that, contrary to the assertion Landru had made that a kitchen oven heated by coal was not sufficiently hot to turn human debris into ash, it was.

Dr Paul was first to try to get Marcel to talk.

"Let's forget who your victims were. As a doctor and with a scientific interest in the matter, I ask you to tell me how you killed them?"

"I have nothing to say other than that I liquidated many enemies of our country and disposed of their bodies. The bodies at Rue le Sueur were not mine, and I never started a fire there to burn them," replied Marcel.

He added he had nothing more to say.

The four took him for a walk through the institute.

They hoped he would loosen up on seeing the remains of murder victims, some of them his own victims, displayed on shelves in large bowls or in bottles filled with alcohol.

They were right. He started to make small talk. Of his own killing frenzy he said not a word.

In the four's report to Desvaux they admitted they had been unable to get anything out of Marcel that would stick in a court. They wrote of the 'insane quality' of his eyes and of his sarcasm and cunning. He was 'extremely intelligent and extremely persuasive', and he had been 'extremely charming' when he wanted to impress them, yet they had been unable to get him to reveal exactly how he had killed. Dr Dérobert, a tiny man with a grey goatee and metal-rimmed glasses, would write of the human remains found at the townhouse in a book, The Identification of Cadavers and Human Debris: 'A very skilled hand had cut up all those bodies with the same techniques. The techniques and skills showed great and intimate knowledge of the human anatomy. All bodies were first eviscerated. Organs or entrails are the first to decompose but often the easiest to get rid of and the least dangerous with respect to identification. The hands and head were always cut off. The face was always skinned and the ends of the fingers always sliced to assure that no identification would be possible. The removal of the skin from the face was done in one operation and the scalp, hair and ears were always removed in an identical manner'.

Desvaux, dissatisfied, asked three psychiatrists, Profs Génil-Perrin, Jean Gouriou and Georges Heyer, to have a look at Marcel.

Prof Génil-Perrin, Director of Henri-Rouselle Centre at Sainte-Anne Neurological Hospital in Paris, was one of the psychiatrists who had examined Marcel in 1936 while he was institutionalised in Dr Achille-Delmas' clinic in Ivry and whom Marcel had described as a nonentity not worthy of examining him.

Prof Gouriou, Director of Villejuif Psychiatric Hospital, south of Paris, had also come across Marcel before; he was one of the psychiatrists who had assessed his mental state during the Petrol Theft Case in 1930.

Prof Heyer was an expert on alcoholism; in 1939 he had warned that France was sending an inebriated army to the Front and that it would result in a defeat.

Marcel spoke heatedly of the accusations against him. He denied having killed anyone ever. When he joined the Resistance he was, he said, prepared to make sacrifices - he had made sacrifices - yet he was being called an assassin and a monster. Also, anyone who believed he could have killed a huge, strong gangster like Jo the Boxer Réocreux needed *his* mental state evaluated.

"You don't know what it's all about!" he shouted.

Asked why, if he were in the Resistance, did he not turn himself in once the Germans had fled, he replied he had not done so because the hunt for collaborators that was going on was 'just a show to impress the Allies'.

"Those who informed for the Gestapo were the same bastards who informed for the French police. All those who are today hunting collaborators were collaborators themselves," he said.

Everyone at the FFI base in Reuilly had known he was Marcel Petiot, *the* Dr Marcel Petiot, anyway, he added.

He became even angrier recalling his Gestapo arrest.

"They locked me up and they tortured me. Then the bastards framed me by putting those bodies in my house!"

The bastards were the Germans.

He spoke of the alleged victims. All those Fourrier and Pintard had sent him including Yvan Dreyfus, were French Gestapo, or informers, he insisted.

"I did not kill them. I merely went to pick them up at Fourrier's barbershop."

He commented on his reported wealth - the newspapers had been writing he was the owner of at least fifty buildings in France worth millions of francs.

"I did not make my money from these alleged victims. I earned half a million francs a year working as a doctor. Of this sum, I didn't spend more than one hundred thousand a year - my wife is a frugal woman! And my maid did not demand a huge wage. I also made money with my second-hand and antique furniture deals. I once bought a carpet for 1,700 francs - and I sold it that same evening for 60,000 francs. I also made money on my real estate deals."

He underwent a physical examination. It was found his reflexes were a little slow and his cholesterol level was slightly above normal, but he could easily pass for someone much younger than his 47 years. He was enormously pleased when he heard that. Doctors also looked at the scar on his left foot. That pleased him as well; it pleased him even more. He did not hesitate to explain how he had been wounded.

The three psychiatrists' report to Desvaux in part repeated Dr Génil-Perrin's previous diagnosis of Marcel's mental state.

The report read: 'The accused is an intelligent, strong-willed man, clearly perverted and amoral, with no current mental disorders, but whose psychiatric past is thoroughly suspicious; his encounters with civil and military psychiatrists have always been a result of his problems with the law. We have real details on only one situation that involved his mental disorders; the affair of the theft at Librairie Gibert Joseph. However, we have seen that those disorders ceased after the charge was dismissed, and five psychiatrists noted his sudden recovery consequent to this legal decision.

'Petiot is a great illusionist, a very persuasive man, so one can quite understand his success in many of his business affairs. We thus avoided being 'indoctrinated' by him. We listened to him patiently, especially so as we immediately saw through his tactic of provoking incidents. While listening, we observed him, and noted no mental disorder worthy of the name. We became convinced that Petiot was amoral and perverted, but that is all.

'We consequently conclude that Petiot is to be considered as wholly responsible for his actions. If he is pronounced guilty, concerning the burnt bodies in Rue Le Sueur, he must be held to be entirely responsible for the murders and thefts. If he is declared innocent, the question of his responsibility is of no interest.

'No conclusion is to be drawn from our report concerning the credibility of the subject. Our point of view of responsibility is exclusively that which is defined in Article 64 of the Penal Code, and we consider that this responsibility is entire.

'In conclusion: Petiot is an energetic, strong-willed man of well-developed intelligence who presents no symptoms at all of any mental illness.

'His case history shows him to be amoral and perverted.

'He has been the object of various psychiatric decisions taken in the course of disciplinary or legal affairs in both military and civil contexts; it seems obvious, however, that the diverse and contradictory diagnoses that have been advanced should be treated with scepticism.

'The psychological anomalies that have been noted in his case - amorality and instinctive perversion - are not of a nature to mitigate his penal responsibility'.

Art. 64 of the year 1810 of the French Penal Code, still valid in 1944, and still valid today, stipulates: 'There is neither crime nor offence when the defendant was suffering from a mental disorder at the time of the act, or when constrained by a force that he/she could not resist'.

Marcel was sane. He was responsible for his crimes. He would have to stand trial.

Commissioner Desvaux told Goletty he was certain Marcel had killed more than 27 people. He thought he had probably killed two hundred.

"To be on the safe side. I'll settle on one hundred and fifty," he said.

He also told Goletty that far from having been in the Resistance, Marcel had worked for Henri Lafont's French Gestapo. He said that Lafont had known Marcel was murdering people for material gain, but, an anti-Semite Nazi supporter, he had allowed the doctor to continue, thinking that the Gestapo would sooner or later kill the Jews and informers anyway. Lafont, he said, might then have fallen out with Marcel and started to burn the human remains knowing the smoke and stink would cause alarm; he had 'smoked' Marcel out.

"It wouldn't make sense that someone who had successfully murdered so many people and who had taken such great care to cover up his crimes would leave a lit stove knowing that the smoke would be seen by the neighbours," he said.

Goletty agreed with Desvaux on the number of victims. He didn't agree with his theory about Lafont. He believed Marcel was a lone killer, one who had all his faculties and had meticulously planned his killing spree. Undoubtedly he would be found guilty of assassination; undoubtedly he would be guillotined.

* * *

Late November, Goletty put the contents of the 49 suitcases on display at the Quay. He hoped people would recognise some of it, and he would thereby be able to put more names to the human remains.

For days Parisians lined up to gape at the things; dresses, suits, fur coats, hats, shoes, purses, shirts, panties and brassieres, and a little boy's pair of pyjamas. Even the suitcases were on display.

No one stepped up to the table where a detective sat ready with pen and paper to take down the name of another victim.

A journalist with a dark sense of humour dubbed the exhibition the Exposition Petiot at the Orfèvres Gallery.

Parisians thought it the best show in town.

Also in November, a 'raven' wrote to the Crim to report that a Dr Iriane who had lived on Rue Pasquier in Paris and who had organised an escape route from France, was living in hiding in Auxerre. Graphologists said the handwriting was that of a woman. Some at the Crim said Georgette had written the letter; Eryane Kahan must have been Marcel's lover and Georgette was taking revenge. Or another female member of the Petiot or Lablais families - Monique Petiot perhaps - had written the letter, to revenge a past injustice committed by Marcel.

The letter steered the investigation back to Clinic Rémusat. Questioning staff and former patients the Crim's detectives discovered that the Irène Pascale who had worked at the clinic briefly as a nurse had lived with people named Pictin in the commune of Pecq, north-west of Paris. Detectives went to Pecq. Miss Pascale was indeed Eryane judging by the description given of her. She was no longer with the Pictins, but with a Mrs Mouroc who also lived in the commune. She was not. She had moved to the commune of Antony, south of Paris. She was lodging with a couple named Gaudry. Yet again, she was not. She had moved back to Paris. The couple said they had understood that she had been a resister and was in hiding from the Gestapo. They had heard from her after she had left and she was boarding with a Mrs Lemarchand, who lived at Number 78 Rue du Passy, near the Eiffel Tower. No, she was not. She had moved into an apartment at Number 7 Rue General-Appert. The street was close to Rue le Sueur. Detectives rushed to the apartment building. Its *concierge* told them the only person to have moved in recently was Mrs Molto; her hair was the colour of vintage champagne. Mrs Molto – Eryane - did not appear surprised to see men on her doorstep even though she instantly recognised them as Crim detectives. She was not in hiding she insisted; she had even gone to *Maître* Floriot and asked him if she should go to the police to tell them what she knew about Dr Petiot and he had advised her to do nothing.

Eryane was more forthcoming at the Quay.

She was Jewish, she said, so would she ever have betrayed a fellow Jew to Petiot? For money? As it was, she was going to take his escape route. She would have done if she had had the money that he wanted from her. In fact, he had asked her, persuaded her, to earn her escape. He had told her his Resistance cell needed someone with her linguistic talent, so she had gone to work for him, but as an interpreter, only an interpreter. She had not even known his real name until she had read in the dailies what had gone on at the townhouse. She was not a prostitute as she had read the Crim thought she was; if many men had visited her room at the boarding house it was because she had been a resister. The undercover names of her Resistance comrades she could not remember.

"Their real names I certainly would not have been told," she said.

Three days later, Eryane walked free.

Goletty had found no reason to believe she had known that the nine Jews - the Wolffs, the Basch, Schonker and Arnsberg couples - she had sent Marcel, would be murdered.

* * *

Goletty decided not to confront Marcel with Maurice, but to confront him with Nézondet, his friend.

Nézondet would write in his book that, together in La Santé's exercise yard, Marcel had warned him there was going to be a confrontation.

He wrote: 'Petiot pulled me to one side and said: "They are going to confront the two of us, and I am going to give you hell. I am going to accuse you of having spread tales about me everywhere... But remember, if they bother you, just tell them that your long stay in prison is affecting you so much that you can no longer separate truth from fantasy. But best would still be if you just claim to have been in the Resistance. Say you set alight railway wagons carrying German equipment or that you stole German post bags. You are the best of men, yet there is a 'but'. You have such an imagination that you are going to end up believing what is not true. Look, all you have to do is to say that you had only repeated what you had heard the Germans or the French police say and that you had then made up what you said my brother had told you" '.

Marcel did not give Nézondet hell. He sat in stony silence.

Nézondet recalled: 'There was never the slightest emotion on Petiot's face. He gave the impression that he could not care a damn about what was happening to him'.

Sunday, May 6, Goletty released Nézondet on control order without having to post bail. He had spent 14 months locked up. Twelve days later, he released Neuhausen. A few days later, Maurice. Both on control order without having had to post bail.

While locked up Maurice had been complaining of stomach pains. Tests which had been carried out at Hotel Dieu had showed that he was suffering from stomach cancer. The doctors thought the cancer was already in a terminal stage.

Immediately Maurice returned home to Auxerre. He hoped that without the stress of prison life and with ample rest his cancer would be cured.

For the remainder of 1945, Goletty kept trying to persuade Marcel to confess to his crimes. He even asked two men who had been resisters to question him. He hoped Marcel would confess to them. One was Jacques Yonnet, the journalist from *La Résistance* who had drawn Marcel out into the open with his article, 'Petiot, Soldier of the Reich'. The other was Lieutenant Brouard of the DGER, codenamed Brette.

Marcel stuck to the story he had already told several times.

Allowed to read Yonnet and Brouard's report, he jotted down comments in the margins: What an idiot! False! Lies! Hearsay! I never said that! Nice! Criminals and lunatics!

Yonnet and Brouard had reported that he knew nothing of the way in which the Resistance had operated, that not one resister had ever set eyes on him, and that there had been no Resistance cell codenamed Fly-Tox.

Marcel's final comment, also scribbled in a margin, was: 'On the first day of the next war, these people will be the first to be executed'.

* * *

Marcel, clean-shaven because of prison regulations, spent the long, lonely days of solitary confinement doing embroidery, writing poems and reading. He no longer read books on crime, but the French Classics; the prison library only stocked those and the Bible. The Bible he did not want to read.

At first, he was unpopular with his fellow inmates. One shouted 'vampire' each time he passed. One day, another shouted, "Petiot, if there's justice in this country, you will be condemned. You will be cut up into slices like a *saucisson sec*!" A dried sausage.

Later, allowed to exercise with the others, his unpopularity turned into harmonious camaraderie.

He was given the nickname Mégot - cigarette butt. He, the non-smoker, had started to smoke, smoke heavily, and a saliva-wet cigarette he had rolled himself, always clung to his lower lip.

One of his poems, 'Mégot sounds off, taking advantage of the slow legal system to curse his judges', he dedicated to his new buddies.

It read:

Ah! How fine it is to see, closed in conclave,
In one chamber of another quite nearby,
The dark birds of the night preparing their scheming.
Three judges, prosecutors in square formation.
It is a fine sight in this walled palace
That divine troop, fiddling away at their leisure.
Slimy with ambition, and in their ruin, bearing
All the hidden vices that consume them.
But it would be better to see the town in arms
Crying 'death to the bastards', or, without turning a hair
Sacking the palace. But more than all that,
Flaying one and hanging another.
How fine it would be to see them die a slow death?
And to see for ten pence, the hides of ten judges.

Still with time on his hands, he started to write a book, 'Le Hasard Vaincu' - Chance Defeated - on how to win at games of chance like poker, roulette, horse racing and the lottery.

* * *

Tuesday, October 30, the first anniversary of Marcel's arrest, he told Goletty he would no longer be answering questions. He wanted to, and would, explain himself only to the French nation in a court of law.

Goletty took no notice.

On Saturday, November 3, he had Marcel brought to his office for further questioning.

"On what date did you buy the Rue le Sueur house?" he began.

Floriot, as usual, was present.

"I said," replied Marcel, "that I won't reply to any of your questions anymore. I will reply to questions only in public from now on."

Goletty ignored him.

"Why did you buy the townhouse?"

"Put ditto."

"How did you pay for the house?"

"Ditto."

"Did you ever live there?" Goletty tried again.

"Ditto," replied Marcel.

Goletty, capitulating, sunk his head in his hands.

Floriot asked whether he was tired.

"I have a headache," he replied.

Floriot smiled.

"Do I dare remind you that we have a doctor right here?" he asked.

Marcel also smiled.

"Yes," he said to Floriot. "I can give him a quick injection, but, of course, he won't let me, because he is too scared!"

Goletty, too, laughed.

On Friday, December 28, Goletty had Marcel brought to his office again. He wanted to make a final effort to get him to talk. He had 48 pages filled with questions he wanted to ask him.

As before, Marcel remained silent.

* * *

Christmas arrived; it was Marcel's second behind bars.

All of that festive season, Parisians told jokes and sang songs about him.

One song became a hit in Paris's music halls.

The lyrics were:

Good people, listen without fear
to the story of Petiot, who was cold
and found the ideal way
to heat himself at less cost.
The cynical doctor of genius
had central heating at home.
This is very practical, as long as one has
a good pile of coal as well.
But alas! He only had fifty kilos
each month just like you and me.
And like that - don't you agree? -

you're just fit to snuff it.
It was then that he had the idea
of using a replacement,
a well-known substitute,
discovered one day by Landru ...
So always remember it's dangerous
to let the petiots play with fire.

The *petiots* - slang for little children - were already playing with fire. Playing 'Dr Petiot', they burnt their dolls. Thus, small fires broke out all over Paris. One little boy ended up in hospital with severe burns. One Paris daily reported that he was Jewish; he had only recently returned from the French Alps where he and his parents had spent the Occupation hiding on a farm.

Parisians also gave costume balls with 'Dr Petiot' themes.

Asked by a journalist if she thought such a theme was in good taste, one hostess replied, "Come on now! We have suffered so much, so shouldn't we relax a little now and have a good laugh?"

As the journalist knew, the hostess had been Henri Lafont's lover. She had often watched while he tortured people under interrogation. Lafont was not at his lover's ball. He was in Fresnes Prison awaiting execution by firing squad for 'collaboration with the enemy'. He would not see the end of the year. He would be shot outside Paris on December 27. Floriot had led his defence team.

The year 1946 was three days old when Goletty presented his Petiot dossier to the public prosecutor's office. He wanted a decision as to whether there was sufficient evidence for a conviction of assassination. According to normal legal procedure, the chief Prosecution Counsel, Judge Pierre Dupin, had to appoint one of his assistants to study the dossier. Each assistant he approached refused to accept the job. Finally, the most junior of the counsels, thirty-year old Judge Michel Elissalde, accepted it. Some said he had had no choice.

Elissalde took Goletty's file home and laid it out across his living room floor. He didn't return to the Palais de Justice until he knew the file almost by heart. In his report to Dupin he recommended that Goletty had gathered sufficient evidence to indict Dr Marcel Petiot for the assassination of 27 people, and for the theft of the property of 25 of them. He also recommended that all those, even Maurice Petiot, who had been arrested in connection with the case, but who had in the meantime been released on control order, should receive a final *ordonnance de non-lieu* - the charges against them ought to be dropped. It was actioned forthwith.

Of Malfet, Elissalde wrote: 'He had obviously not played any role in the killings'.

Of Porchon he wrote: 'Porchon perhaps knew more of Petiot's secret... but does not seem, as far as is known, to have been his accomplice'.

Of Georgette and Maurice: 'Their respective attitudes make it difficult to believe in their complete innocence. However, at this point in the proceedings, it would be impossible to legally prove their guilt. It is, nevertheless, certain that, if the system of justice remains so incompletely informed on their subject, the name they bear and its sorry reputation, which has affected them personally, could already cause them considerable shame, unless they have acquired Petiot's amoral lack of sensitivity'.

Goletty advised Marcel that he was to stand trial in Paris at the Assize court of the Seine for the assassination of 27 people.

Marcel did not react.

"Finally, we are going to have a laugh! I am going to kill those judges with laughter!" he told a warder when back in his cell in La Santé.

The warder was not amused.

"Oh, don't worry. I will only have them crying with laughter. This way, they will have to acquit me," said Marcel.

-0-

CHAPTER FOUR

Facing Justice

It was Monday, March 18, at half past one.

All morning, elegantly dressed men and women, several members of Europe's royal families among them, had been waiting on Boulevard du Palais outside the Palais de Justice building. Since January when news that Dr Marcel Petiot would stand trial had been released to the media, Parisians had been keeping tailors, dressmakers and milliners busy; on that morning they were showing off their new clothes.

At 1:35 P.M., the courtroom, the size of the banqueting hall of the town hall of a village, fell silent. The moment had come; the two hundred or so lucky ones, packed into the wood-panelled courtroom's public gallery, were going to see Dr Marcel Petiot for the first time.

"Sit! Sit!" voices began to shout from seats at the back.

Footsteps had been heard behind a narrow door behind the box of the accused; the diabolical killer was on his way.

Marcel stepped into the courtroom. Two policemen flanked him. It was a sunny day and the courtroom was hot; several men in the gallery had removed their jackets, many women dabbed at their foreheads with lace handkerchiefs, but Marcel wore a heavy tweed overcoat. He was handcuffed. He turned to the policemen. One nodded; Marcel must have asked to have his handcuffs removed because it was done.

His hands free, Marcel stepped into the well of the courtroom and walked slowly to his box. Reaching it, he unfastened the buttons of his overcoat and slipped out of it. For a while, he played with the coat; he folded and unfolded it, rolled it into a ball, shook it out, then, he hung it over the back of the box. He was still not finished with it; before he sat down, he tapped it. It was as if he were warning a child to behave - or else.

Over the previous two years, the media had often written of Marcel's untidiness; there was no evidence of it. Under his coat he wore a well-cut grey suit with a lilac pinstripe, a white shirt, its collar stiffly starched, and a large mauve bow tie. Large bow ties were all the fashion; in every photograph which had been published of Marcel, he had worn one. His hair was oiled and combed back; a rebel curl dropped over his forehead. He was pale and there was not a trace of a smile on his face.

The next morning, journalist Pierre Scize of *Le Figaro* would write: 'He is much younger than was expected. Also, much less satanic than has been said. He is clean-shaven, with a very white skin and he wears a suit and bow tie. If it weren't for that mouth, which, assuredly, is not good - occasionally twisting into a forced grin - there would be nothing to distinguish the greatest criminal of modern times'.

Seated, Marcel pulled sheets of paper from the inside pocket of his jacket. He put those down on the ledge in front of him.

He looked up and swept his eyes across the courtroom; crystal chandeliers hung from an ornate ceiling and large Gobelin tapestries covered sections of the wood-panelled walls. He looked down into the gallery and saw Georgette, Maurice and the 18-year-old Gerhardt. He smiled and waved. They smiled back.

Maurice's eyes were swimming in tears. He was thin and pale, even paler than his brother.The rest he had hoped he would find in Auxerre had proved elusive, and the cancer was still ravaging his body. On his arrival back in Auxerre the doctors there had agreed with those of Hotel Dieu. There was nothing that anyone could do for him: he was a dying man. He was to be a witness at the trial, but he had received special permission to be present in the courtroom. None of the other witnesses had been given such permission.

Georgette and Gerhardt would not be called to give evidence.

Next, Marcel cast his eyes over the well; a palette of white, red and black. Some of those seated there would judge him; others would defend him.

The prosecution team sat at a long table to his right. At the centre of the table sat Judge Marcel Leser, 57, a presiding judge only since the previous year. His portly figure was hidden in a red robe; strands of silver hair crept from his black and yellow toque.

Two magistrates, also dressed in red robes, sat on either side of Leser.

310

The two, Claude Meiss and Bernard Genot, would play no part in the trial until its end; then, they would deliberate with Leser and the jury to decide Marcel's innocence or guilt.

The jury sat at the table too. There were seven. Such a small jury was the product of one of Vichy-France's laws that the post-war French parliament had not had a chance to amend. Before the war there had been twelve jurors, but Vichy-France, having wished to weaken the power of the people, had reduced the number to six; one juror had been added to that number after the Liberation of Paris for the rush of post-war treason trials.

Four of the seven jurors sat at Meiss' right, the others to Genot's left.

There were three replacement jurors; they were present in the courtroom too, but because of lack of space in the well, they sat in the front row of the gallery.

Earlier in the day, the jury selection and swearing-in had taken place. By law, both the prosecution and the defence had been permitted just five challenges in total to 27 possibles. Their names had been drawn from the voter list. All were male; Parliament had also not yet debated whether to grant women the vote. The media would seize upon the bizarre coincidence of the symmetry of Marcel's 27 alleged victims and 27 possible jurors. Each juror would receive a daily fee of 57 francs. Only if two thirds agreed on Marcel's guilt could judgement be passed. By French law, the defence also had to approve the two magistrates, seeing they had been chosen by the prosecution. That, too, had been done earlier.

At Leser's left sat the leading prosecution counsel, Judge Dupin, and the junior counsel, Judge Elissalde. The latter was nervous. Not only was he new at the Quay, but the trial was his first big court case. Dupin, a tall, slim, grey-haired man, on the contrary, looked confident. He had the reputation of being humourless. He was, indeed, a man of few words, but, as all in the legal system knew, there were not many at the Paris Bar who could grasp complicated or confusing evidence as fast as he could.

A little behind Dupin and Elissalde sat the clerk of the court, the bearded Albert Wilmès, known as Old Wilmès. In his sixties, he was about to retire, and was training Jacques, his son, to take over from him. Jacques was also in the courtroom; he sat beside his father.

Like the lawyers and Elissalde, Wilmès and his son wore black robes with white cravats.

Dupin wore a red robe with an ermine border.

To Marcel's left sat the French media, while the foreign media sat at the far right of the long table. Journalists had arrived from all over the world. Among them was an American war correspondent, still in his khaki uniform.

Directly in front of Marcel, but on a lower level, sat his defence team; Floriot and his four assistants, Eugène Ayache, Pierre Jacquet, Paul Cousin and Charles Libman. The media had already given the four, young men in their twenties or early thirties, a nickname in English, 'Floriot's Boys'. Like Floriot, 'Floriot's Boys' would later speak of how fascinating they had found Dr Marcel Petiot and that they had never met such an intelligent man - one with such Baudelairian charm. Perhaps harder to impress, Floriot would agree with them, but would say, "To be truthful, I do not know how Petiot murdered or what really happened. He never once let me into his confidence."

The civil case lawyers sat to the right of the defence team. There were nine. Jacques Bernay represented the Wolff family; Jacques Archevêque, Mrs Guschinov; Claude Perlès, Mrs Braunberger; Dominique Stéfanaggi from Marseilles, the Piereschi family; Charles Henry, Paulette Grippay's family; Léon Lévy, representing the Knellers' relatives from Bolivia, Pierre Véron representing both Pauline Dreyfus and Fernand Lavie, Mrs Khaït's son; Andrée Dunant, representing Gisèle Rossmy's family, and Pierre Rein, Pauline Dreyfus's second lawyer. Pierre Véron was an old adversary of Marcel; he was the lawyer who had represented Raymonde Baudet, daughter of the missing Mrs Khaït, in her drug case. Rein was Pauline Dreyfus' brother. As the nine had assistants, it meant there were not enough seats for all in the well. Consequently, some sat with the replacement jurors in the gallery.

Between the two teams of lawyers stood glass cases filled with the prosecution's exhibits; some of Marcel's loot and some of the remains of his victims. There were umbrellas, walking sticks, spectacle cases, cigarette cases, cigar boxes, packets of cigarettes, a bicycle wheel, several books, jars filled with organs, baskets filled with bones, teeth and hair. Around the cases stood suitcases; more were piled up with trunks, hat boxes, wicker baskets, metal lunch boxes and even a Thermos flask, against the wood-panelled wall behind Wilmès and his son. Some of the trunks were padlocked; most of the suitcases were made of synthetic material and tied with straps. Each item was numbered with white chalk and from each hung a yellow label on which that item's contents were listed. Fearing the pile of luggage might collapse on top of him, Wilmès would keep a worried eye on it throughout the trial. Marcel would also often shoot a glance towards it; a sly smile would accompany each glance.

The witness box, a curved three-legged wooden railing, stood at the foot of the glass cases. In all, ninety witnesses would be called to give evidence.

In the middle of the gallery stood 12 photographers, their cameras set up. They had not moved when Marcel had walked in, but, on a nod of permission from Leser, they went down on their knees; some even lay down on the floor.

Marcel, however, did not want to be photographed. He lifted his hands and shielded his face. Yet, after a few pensive moments, he was smiling into the flashing lights.

"Come on, gentlemen! Get on with it!" he called out smilingly.

He seemed to have started to enjoy the attention.

Earlier, also as required by law, Leser had confronted Marcel in an antechamber. "You are going to be tried for the premeditated assassination of 27 people. If you are found guilty you will be executed by guillotine," he had warned.

"Not twenty-seven," Petiot had replied arrogantly. "I liquidated 63 persons, but all were enemies of France!"

"Very well," Leser, not amused, had answered. "But we will start with 27 and the verdict may do for the others, as well."

Leser gave the photographers a few minutes to take Marcel's picture; then, he called for order.

Order restored, he turned to Marcel.

"Accused, please rise. Tell the court your name and profession."

"Petiot. Marcel André Henri Félix. Medical practitioner and district surgeon."

There were cries of astonishment from the public at hearing his voice. Parisians had been wondering what the voice of a devil would sound like. It had not sounded as they had imagined it would, gruff and rough. Marcel's voice had always been gentle, passive and cultured, and so it had been again. He had also spoken so quietly many at the back of the gallery had not been able to hear him.

Leser addressed Marcel again.

"Were you born on January 17, 1897 in Auxerre, and were your father Félix Petiot and your mother Marthe Bourdon?"

"Yes, *Monsieur le Président.*"

He was looking at one of the tapestries.

"Petiot, please look at me when I speak to you and when you speak to me," reprimanded Leser.

"*Bien sur,*" replied Marcel. Of course.

"Good. You may sit down now," said Leser.

"*D'accord,*" said Marcel. OK.

Marcel sat down and put an elbow on the side of his box. He rested his chin in a cupped hand. He looked perfectly comfortable, perfectly at ease.

Wilmès rose to read the *acte d'accusation* - the indictment. His voice would quiver with fatigue. For months he had been speaking of how he could not wait to retire; he planned to leave Paris for the countryside, but he wanted *une grande sortie* - a great exit. He believed the Petiot trial would be such an exit.

The indictment was 27 pages long. Not twenty-six or twenty-eight: but twenty-seven. Elissalde had written it.

Petiot stood accused of having wilfully assassinated 27 people. Wilfully, because evidence suggested that the townhouse had been bought with the sole purpose of murder: the wall at the back of the property had been constructed to shield the courtyard from prying eyes, and the triangular room had been specially constructed and fitted with a fake door and bell, hooks and peephole, so that he could slaughter with greater efficiency.

"Petiot, Marcel André Henri Félix, you stand accused of the wilful and premeditated assassination of...," began Wilmès.

He read that sentence 27 times, once for each victim. Those were classified as 15 Jews, nine individuals of dubious character, two people who would have given evidence against Marcel in drug trials, and a young woman on whom he had performed an abortion.

Wilmès read out the names of the ninety witnesses. They were waiting in rooms adjoining the courtroom. As their names were called out, a policeman escorted each into and out of the courtroom to prove they were present. Eryane Kahan's name was read three times before she walked in. Her entrance met with an *ooh la la* from the public. She looked like a Hollywood film star: she wore a black suit with an otter-fur collar reaching to her belted waist. On her head was a matching hat and one of her white-silk gloved hands was hidden in a matching muff. The strands of hair escaping the confines of the hat were still the colour of vintage champagne, and her eyes were again hidden behind large dark glasses. Those, she did not remove and the media would report that there was something wrong with her eyes; what exactly the ailment was, they wrote they did not know.

"Present, *Monsieur le Président!*" she said, once on the witness stand.

Her guttural Romanian accent was seductive, as the media would report.

Marcel did not appear to find either Eryane or her accent seductive. He tapped Floriot on the shoulder.

"She's got a nerve!" he said.

He laughed and so did Floriot.

One of the witnesses, Colonel André Dewavrin, who had been General de Gaulle's Intelligence Chief during the Occupation, did not appear. He was to have testified with regards Marcel's claim to have been in the Resistance. Dupin rose to explain that '*Monsieur le Colonel* was away on mission'.

"I wonder's how long this mission of his will last," remarked Floriot.

"So do I," said Dupin.

"You have the means to find out," said Floriot.

"So I do," said Dupin.

At 3:15 P.M., almost ninety minutes after Wilmès had started to read the indictment, he sat down.

As French law required, Leser put his toque on to start the prosecution's interrogation of Marcel. The judge would be guided by a brief biography of Marcel which Elissalde had drawn up.

Also earlier that morning, Leser, in a meeting with the two sets of lawyers had warned them that his interrogation of Marcel could go on for up to three days.

He had also reminded them that they could intervene during the interrogation, as indeed during all of the hearing, whenever they wished. French law allowed the civil lawyers, the defence team and the prosecution counsel and his deputy to intervene at any time during the proceedings; so could the accused.

Right then the accused, waiting for Leser to begin to speak, sighed heavily as if greatly bored. He had also appeared bored while Wilmès had read the indictment. At one point he had even sketched on his sheets of paper. He had drawn cartoons depicting Leser and the two magistrates.

Marcel had not been the only one to have appeared bored, however.

In the gallery too there had been signs of boredom; some of the men had fidgeted with their bow ties while the women had played with strings of pearls hanging over their ample bossoms.

* * *

Leser began by describing Marcel as having been a mediocre scholar.

Marcel did not like that: he jumped to his feet.

"I obtained a mention of very good for my medical thesis!" he shouted.

Leser's only reaction was to remove his toque and to put it down on the table in front of him and to ask Marcel to sit down.

He continued, "You enjoyed great popularity in Villeneuve-sur-Yonne. You are, to say the least, very seductive, Petiot."

Marcel, sitting down again, beamed with satisfaction.

"Thank you very much, Mr President!" he said.

"No problem!" replied Leser.

The following day, journalists would report that some, both male and female in the gallery, had nodded in agreement with Leser. They wrote of the magnetic pull in Marcel's eyes, of his wide brow and his thick black hair.

"Not everyone in Villeneuve-sur-Yonne liked you though, Petiot," continued Leser.

Marcel grinned.

"I had political enemies. Sure I did. I do not have to make sketches, charts and diagrams for you to understand this?"

Marcel, reminded by Leser of certain things Nézondet had said of him to the police, had something to say about Nézondet in turn.

"He is a charming man, but should you have listened to him for ten minutes, you would have realised that he was batty!"

316

"Mrs Mongin also did not like you," said Leser. "She complained about you. She accused you of having stolen some things from the house you were renting from her."

"She lied," said Marcel. "She was a liar. She was going around saying that we had had sexual intercourse. I can tell you that she wanted to have sex with me - yes, certainly - but I had declined the honour!"

"Were you not your maid's lover?" asked Leser, ignoring what Marcel had said about Mrs Mongin.

"I refuse to answer that!" snapped Marcel.

"Where is she now? Where is Miss Louise Delaveau, who was also known as Louisette Delaveau, now? Do you know?"

"Ah, I see what you are getting at!" laughed Marcel. "You think that she was my first assassination! I hope you have a witness. Do you? But don't bother because I can tell you already now that she married a colleague of mine and she's very well, thank you!"

"Petiot, you were accused in Villeneuve-sur-Yonne of having stolen canisters of petrol, electricity and the cross that stood in the cemetery."

"If this is how we are going to begin ..."

Marcel tapped his fingers against the front of his box.

"I will begin however I wish," replied Leser.

"I will tell you, that all that was just gossip! But let us finish with this fable of the cross right now, so that we don't have to return to it. That was a story invented by the town's bigots and hypocrites. In fact, between us, that cross had disappeared two hundred years ago!"

"You were convicted of stealing electricity," continued Leser.

"Convicted, yes, but that does not prove me guilty!"

Leser smiled.

"Next, you are going to say that everything that will be said of you in this courtroom will be lies."

"I would not say that. No. Only eight tenths will be lies."

For the first time Dupin rose to intervene as was his right by law.

"Mr President, I protest to that remark of the accused, which I ..."

"Excuse me! I was talking! So let me talk!" Marcel interrupted him, jumping up.

Dupin slumped into his chair; he had turned red in the face with embarrassment.

"Petiot, I forbid you to speak in that tone in this courtroom. I ask you to keep your voice down and not to shout like that," Leser came to Dupin's aid.

"Fine. But I do not care to be treated like a criminal," said Marcel.

He sat down.

Leser next questioned Marcel about the advertising leaflet he had distributed on his arrival in Paris in 1933.

"It was the leaflet of a charlatan!" he stated.

Immediately, Marcel was back on his feet and shouting.

"I thank you, Mr President, for the free advertising - although I ask you to keep your opinions to yourself!"

Floriot also rose. "Mr President," he said, speaking to Leser, "a court is supposed to be impartial. I therefore ask you to withdraw the description of charlatan."

Leser nodded; Floriot was right.

"I withdraw that remark, *Maître*," he said.

To Marcel, he said, "You were district surgeon."

Marcel still on his feet lifted himself up onto his toes and for a reason only he knew he glanced contemptuously at the juror who sat nearest to him.

"I am still district surgeon!" he snarled.

The juror paled and quickly looked away and Marcel sat down.

"Petiot, you arrogantly boasted that your profession allowed you an astronomical income," Leser continued.

"Oh? Astronomical, was it?" asked Marcel. Then he said: "Fine... if you like... it was astronomical! The truth is, I had an income of between 300,000 and 500,000 francs annually."

"Of which you declared only 25,000 francs to the Receiver of Revenue on your tax return? That was, indeed, not an astronomical amount!" mocked Leser.

"If you insist... but, like all in my profession, indeed, all in France, yes, that was what I had done, because, you know, when a surgeon makes between eight to ten million a year, he declares only one hundred thousand. That's a fact, as you will also know. Had I declared all that I had earned, I would have been a real dunce. And another thing, the fact that I had not declared everything proves that I am, without doubt, French!"

Marcel winked into the public gallery and loud applause of support

318

came from it.

Leser asked Marcel about the day that he had stolen the book at Librairie Joseph Gibert and Marcel began to explain what had happened. It was raining, he said, and he had put the book under his arm so that it should not get wet and, deep in thought, he had walked from the shop without having paid. It had been an unintentional act.

"That was not what the bookshop had told the police," Leser told him.

Marcel jumped up yet again.

"Listen to me! I did not steal that book!" he snarled, and continued, "You will know that inventors are always absent-minded and are also always considered crazy. And I am an inventor!"

"On the contrary, you were the one who pleaded insanity every time you were in trouble!" responded Leser.

"Oh no, on the contrary! I was the one who always said that I was sane!" replied Marcel.

He asked Leser to define insanity to the court.

Leser ignored the request.

"Well, I'll do so myself," said Marcel, sitting down again. "One can only be insane by comparison to others."

"What did you invent, Petiot?" asked Leser.

"I invented an anti-constipation pump. It was a suction and pressure pump."

Next Marcel started a long explanation of the pump's workings and how it washed out waste matter from the body. Some of the women in the gallery dropped their eyes. The men smiled at the women's obvious embarrassement.

"I also invented a perpetual motion machine," added Marcel.

The women groaned.

"Spare the court the details, please!" urged Leser.

"Go to Rue de Caumartin, and you will see it there," suggested Marcel, looking pleased with himself.

He said that he had also invented a weapon.

"OK, tell the court about the weapon," said Leser.

"No, that I cannot do!" snapped Marcel.

If he did, he explained, the Germans 'who attacked us in 1870, in 1914, and in 1940' would certainly manufacture it to use against France in the next war.

Leser let Marcel's remark pass without comment.

Instead, he questioned him about the death of Raymonde Hanss, the young dressmaker who had collapsed and died while Marcel was treating her for toothache.

Marcel said, "The post-mortem showed that my treatment for her toothache had not caused her death. I even telephoned Dr Paul - you can ask him - about the post-mortem result, and he was quite bemused. He told me that I am too conscientious a district surgeon and, if I were going to question every post-mortem, I was going to be a very busy man. That I would have no time for anything else."

Leser listened without commenting, and said next: "We will now speak of the human remains found at your townhouse."

"Yes, do let us speak of this story about bodies..."

"Unfortunately, it is not a story," replied Leser. "It is a fact. To begin with, Petiot, explain to the court the triangular room."

Marcel grinned.

"Nothing can be easier to explain. I had it built because I was going to keep my radiotherapy machines in there. If the walls were unusually thick, it was because nowhere could I find the lead I needed to reinforce them with, and I had to use several layers of plaster instead. If the bell did not work, it was for the same reason - nowhere could I find electrical wiring. And, if one door in the room was a fake, it was to keep out damp, because that is what wood does. And, as for what the Nazi press had been writing, the hole in the wall was not there so that I could have pumped poison gas into the room. I needed the peephole to be able to keep an eye on my patients while they were receiving their radiotherapy treatment!"

"What about the bodies?" Leser wanted to know.

"I had nothing to do with them. I found them at my house on my return from Fresnes. They were fresh."

"And the pit?"

"The pit? All I can say is that I wonder who had thrown those bodies into my pit while I was in Fresnes. But it might have been my colleagues from Fly-Tox. You know - *à la guerre, comme à la guerre!*"

"Give us the names of your comrades," asked Leser.

Marcel shook his head.

"No, I won't! They are men who are not guilty of anything, just as I am not guilty. Some of them have offered to come and testify for me, that I can tell you, but I do not want them to do so, because you will put them in handcuffs for having assassinated thirty *Boches* when what you should be doing is to decorate them."

For the first time since his earlier humiliation, Dupin intervened. He jumped up and shouted, "Petiot, I will personally see that they are decorated, so name them! I guarantee them the Cross of the Liberation!"

"No!" Marcel shouted back at the top his voice, spraying Floriot with saliva. "I will not reveal their names! I will not do so while those who have sworn allegiance to Pétain and Hitler are still around, and holding positions of authority, at that!"

Marcel's outburst drew another round of applause from the public. Many of them had lost someone in the war and they knew that judges had sworn allegiance to Hitler.

Leser, exasperated, obviously embarrassed as well, did not call for order; instead, he threw his arms up in the air.

"Mr President, don't throw your arms up in the air, please," said Marcel quietly as if in a classroom and he was the teacher speaking to a pupil.

"I will do what I like," replied Leser. Turning to Dupin, he said, "I've never come across anything like this. This is a courtroom... *non*? Or am I mistaken?"

That time it was for Dupin to come to Leser's assistance. He told Marcel to tell the court about the role he had played in the Resistance.

Marcel, pleased at the request, smiled broadly.

"Certainly. I will," he said. "I joined the Resistance right at the start of the German Occupation. As for my role, I had numerous responsibilities. You can say that I had to do everything. You would be wiser to ask me what I did not have to do in the Resistance."

"Petiot, the Resistance did not exist at the start of the Occupation," Leser, having regained his composure, corrected Marcel.

Leser was right, yet the public started to boo him all the same.

It was an opportunity for Marcel to again smile: he even smiled broadly.

"Oh, it did!" he said. "There was resistance right from the arrival of the first German on French soil."

Leser turned red in the face and yet again Dupin came to his assistance. "So what did you do in the Resistance Petiot? Tell us."

"I invented a secret weapon. It could kill in total silence at thirty metres. I also laid explosives in German railway carriages. An English officer who had been parachuted into Franche-Comtè had trained me in how to handle explosives."

"What was the English officer's name?" asked Dupin.

"I can't remember."

"And what else did you do, Petiot?"

"I supplied medical certificates. I gave Intelligence information to Cumuleau..."

"Describe Cumuleau," interrupted Dupin.

"We looked alike, he and I. We were sometimes mistaken for one another."

"Would you be able to identify him on a photograph?" asked Dupin.

Marcel shook his head.

"I am not good at identifying people on photographs. I can't even identify myself on a photograph... especially not those the Nazi newspapers have been running of me."

For the first time *Maître* Véron rose.

He looked straight at Marcel.

"Explain to the court, please, how you had handled plastic explosives," he asked.

"I cannot remember," replied Marcel.

"What are plastic explosives? Tell us," urged Véron.

Marcel only shrugged.

Véron tried again.

"How does one transport plastic explosives, Petiot?"

Marcel did not reply.

"*Maître*, is this an examination my client has to pass for the École Politechnique?" asked Floriot from his chair addressing Véron.

"Yes, my dear *Maître*, this is, as you say, an examination," replied Véron.

Marcel interrupted: "Wait a minute... It is all coming back to me now! I wrapped the plastic around a hand grenade, and I then threw the grenade at German soldiers. I tried not to kill our own people, so I usually took the grenades into the Bois de Boulogne. I killed two German motorcyclists that way in the Bois. Also, another two German soldiers; one was on foot and the other on horseback. The horse also died. But some of my comrades used to pack the plastic into a suitcase, and then they detonated the grenade. Then, half an hour later, we heard the explosion."

"Half an hour later?" asked Véron and added, "Petiot, it takes plastic seven seconds to explode!"

Floriot intervened again: "Come on, *Maître*, you are putting my client through the Polytechnique examination, after all."

"I don't have to, my dear colleague. I now have the certitude that he has never handled plastic explosives in his life!" replied Véron.

"Neither have you!" came from Marcel.

"Yes, you're right Petiot! I never handled it... It only so happened that I once transported 115 kilograms of it in my car!"

"*Bravo!*" a voice in the gallery called out.

Infuriated at losing his argument with the defence laywer, Marcel shouted at him, "You have no right to question me, you Defender of Jews - of traitors!"

The remark unleashed thunderous protest - booing, hissing, whistling and stamping of feet - in the gallery. A man's voice could be heard over it. "Why didn't you bring that dead horse with you as evidence, Petiot?"

"Yes, why not?" someone else shouted.

"Go fetch the horse! We want to see the dead horse! Go fetch the horse! Fetch the horse! Fetch the horse!" the people started to chant.

It was 6:30 P.M. Leser, unable to restore order, adjourned the hearing until half past one the following day.

Marcel was handcuffed and led from the court, he turned and called out to Leser, "You're not adjourning because of me, I hope. I am not at all tired!"

He shot a glance at Maurice and smiled; the latter, as if sharing something very personal and pleasant with his beloved brother, smiled back.

In the evening, while waiting for La Santé's lights to be switched off, Petiot sat doing embroidery. Paris's *bourgeoisie* were at the same time enjoying candlelit, champagne dinners. Their conversation centred on the trial. Even the Nuremberg War Crimes trials, front paged since the previous November were forgotten. No one seemed to care in the slightest that at 10 A.M. that morning the cross examination of *Reichsmarschall* Hermann Goering, Commander-in-Chief of the Luftwaffe, had begun.

In the morning, journalists gave their views of Petiot in their newspapers.

Each described him differently.

He was calm and relaxed, furious or excited, insecure or confident, high and mighty or humble, intelligent or not very bright.

One journalist called him 'Satan Incarnate'.

To another he resembled a Hollywood cinema idol boarding a cruise liner.

They wrote of his hands. Big and ugly, the hands of a strangler, wrote one.

To another his hands were as beautiful as a pianist virtuoso playing for sentimental ladies.

Journalists would also remind their readers that if there were a great French hero, it was Véron.

The previous year when Pétain was to stand trial for treason Véron had refused to defend him.

At that moment Pétain was serving a life sentence.

* * *

Tuesday was another hot day.

Again, the gallery was packed. Some seated there had spent the night on the pavement outside the building to make sure they would get a seat. One young pretty *Parisienne*, dressed from head to toe in red, walked in, but found all the seats had been taken. It did not bother her. She sat down in Marcel's box. Walking in at 1:35 P.M., he was delighted to find her there. A policeman quickly ushered her to the back where she was to stand, but first Marcel had gallantly kissed her red-gloved hand. For the rest of the day she would shoot him admiring glances.

Leser began the day's interrogation probing Marcel's murder method.

"How did you determine who should be liquidated, and how did you liquidate them?" Leser asked.

Marcel was eager to talk. His warders had reported he had had a good night's rest; he had slept soundly.

"Fly-Tox comrades used to meet up at Drouot. It was a safe place for us because there were never any Germans there... though there were always French police, who were, well... as dangerous as the Germans," he began.

"Why were there always police at Drouot?" asked Leser, as if he did not know.

"The police knew it was a good place to grab a Jew, because that was where the Jews flogged their possessions before they quit France," explained Marcel.

Next, Marcel repeated what he had told Goletty about how he and his Fly-Tox comrades had also identified French collaborators by hanging around Gestapo Headquarters.

"This was what we did. We would walk up to a guy as he stepped from the building and say, 'German Police! Follow us'. The guy would always proudly reply, 'So am I'. We would then push him into the back of our van, where we finished him off. We did so while we were still driving to Marly Forest. It was all done very quickly!"

"And that was where you dumped the bodies - in Marly Forest?" queried Leser.

"Where we buried them. It was more prudent to bury them than just dump them under the trees."

"But you told the police that the executions had been carried out at the Rue le Sueur house," intervened Dupin, obviously a little braver that morning, from his seat.

Marcel shook his head.

"When the matter was urgent, we immediately killed them in the back of the van."

"But you had admitted to the police that the people had been executed at Number 21 Rue le Sueur, yet now you speak of a van and a forest. You had also admitted to the police that you had been present when the executions were carried out," continued Dupin.

"I may have admitted many things that were not true when I was arrested by that famous Resistance captain who, I will point out, will not be called as a witness because he used to be a *collabo*: he informed on the Resistance to the Gestapo. He is, of course, too scared to show himself here!"

"Name him, Petiot," urged Floriot.

Marcel shook his head and Floriot decided to name the man his client was referring to himself.

He looked towards the gallery.

"My client was arrested by a Captain Simonin of the FFI and DGER. Simonin had been served with papers to appear as a witness in my client's trial - just like Captain Dewarin - but they are not here." Turning to Leser, he asked, "Why do you not have Simonin brought here? Or perhaps I should call him by his real name, which is Soutif. Soutif, the former police inspector, collaborator and executioner of scores of French resisters of the town of Quimper!"

Floriot was correct. Like Marcel, Simonin a.k.a. Soutif, a notorious collaborator, had on the Liberation of Paris taken refuge in the FFI. He was on the run and would never resurface.

Leser replied to Floriot by asking Marcel if he had participated in any of the executions he had mentioned.

Marcel said, "No."

Dupin also had a question for Marcel. "Give us the names of the people who had been executed?"

"No," said Marcel.

"The names of some of them, at least?" urged Dupin.

"No!" repeated Marcel.

Floriot leant back, cupped a hand over his mouth, and whispered something to his client and Marcel nodded.

"*D'accord*," he said to Floriot.

He turned to Leser.

"Adrien Estébétéguy. Now, I've given you a name. And something else. You have no idea how brave my men and I were. We had a lot of guts!"

"But did you kill anyone personally, Petiot?" asked Leser.

"I killed two German motorcyclists with my secret weapon."

"Where? How? That was not something that could have been hidden, and the Germans never reported that a secret weapon had been used against them!" said Véron from his chair.

Marcel shot him a sarcastic smile.

"*Maître,* you're a good actor. You know just when to make your entrance and how to put on a good show for the gallery. But you can go back to sleep now, because I am not going to reveal things that must remain secret for the safety of France."

Véron rose. He did so slowly; like a cat preparing to pounce.

"Come on, Petiot; tell us of your secret weapon!"

Marcel also stood up. "No!" he shouted.

"Why not?" Véron wanted to know.

"Because of security. That's why. I know you were in the Resistance yourself, so you should, therefore, understand about secrecy and security."

"As a member of the Resistance, I will not allow you to dirty its name for your own benefit," responded Véron.

"Who says? You?" asked Marcel.

Véron did not reply.

"Yes, just shut up! You are here to defend Dreyfus, that Jew who sold himself to the Germans! So you shut up! You are nothing but a double agent yourself!" Marcel taunted him.

Véron flushed and started to walk slowly towards Marcel's box.

"If you don't take that back, Petiot, I'll smash your face in!" he hissed.

Marcel gave a loud laugh.

In front of him Floriot was fast asleep. The raised voices woke him. He asked one of his assistants what was going on. The assistant started to explain, but Leser interrupted; he said the incident was of no importance and asked the jury to disregard it. Floriot, still looking drowsy, whispered something to Marcel; the latter nodded and sat down.

Véron returned to his seat and he too sat down.

Leser again asked Marcel to give the court the names of the people Fly-Tox had executed.

"*D'accord*, I'll give you another name. I can remember the name Joseph Réocreux. He was known as Jo the Boxer. He had the look of a... well, he looked like a mackerel."

The public screamed with laughter again. Some clapped their hands. The word 'mackerel' was the nickname for a pimp - but also for a policeman.

Marcel said he would reveal no more names.

"I will give you all the names you want once I am acquitted," he said.

"You, acquitted!" muttered Dupin from his chair.

Marcel leaned over to glare at him.

"These gentlemen here," he pointed in the direction of the jurors closest to him, "they will judge me, and they will acquit me," he said.

He turned and looked at the jurors.

"Gentlemen of the jury," he said, "I trust you."

"That's enough, Petiot!" snapped Dupin.

Marcel looked away from the jurors and to Dupin.

"Mr Chief Prosecutor," he said, "I will not allow you to judge me. I saw my comrades die in Fresnes after having been tortured by the Germans. I took tremendous chances then, and, when I fought in the street battles for the freedom of Paris, I had done so yet again. So my acquittal by the jurors is certain!"

"Petiot, I rather doubt that you will be acquitted," replied Leser, speaking hardly above a whisper.

Suddenly, Marcel started to cry.

He dropped his head into his hands and cried quietly into a large, white handkerchief. He cried until Floriot tapped him on the arm and asked him to pull himself together.

It was 4:30 P.M. The repartee had been going on for three hours. All in the courtroom were hot and tired. Leser called a break of a quarter of an hour.

No one had noticed, Floriot included, that by having expressed his opinion on Marcel's guilt, Leser had committed a *faux pas*.

Floriot could have called for a mistrial.

When the court reconvened, Leser questioned Marcel about his other alleged victims. He started with Denise Hotin. He wanted to know what Marcel could tell the court about her. Despite that his missing wife had not yet been declared deceased, Jean had remarried. He was waiting in an antechamber because he was to give evidence. His new wife had stayed at home on the farm.

Marcel dismissed Leser's question with a wave of the hand.

"I've never even heard the name."

Asked about the death of Raymonde Baudet, he said: "You know what addicts are like. They lie, they cheat, they steal, and they cannot be trusted or believed."

He said he had treated Baudet for her addiction because she was quite nice looking.

Véron intervened.

"She was plain. Quite plain!"

"*Maître*, you didn't know her at the right time! When you met her, her best years were behind her," Marcel corrected him.

"She was very plain!" insisted Véron.

"Well, she was past her prime when you saw her."

"Petiot, you sound like a character in a bad novel!" said Véron.

Véron was right. Baudet had been a large, big-breasted, overweight woman.

Asked by Véron about the disappearance of Mrs Khaït, Baudet's mother, Marcel denied that he had ever given her any kind of injection.

"Just answer yes or no. Did you give Mrs Khaït saline injections?" insisted Véron.

Marcel grinned.

"You are a very talented lawyer... I shall have to send you some clients," he said.

Véron retorted: "It is certainly less dangerous for you to send me clients than for me to send them to you!"

"I sent you Raymonde Baudet, remember! And I was the one who paid you!" replied Marcel.

The letters Mrs Khaït had written to her husband and son were passed around. Floriot took them, read them and handed them to Marcel.

"I've never seen these before," Marcel mumbled.

Leser asked Marcel about his arrest by the Gestapo and Marcel started to cry again. Almost immediately though he pulled himself together; loudly he blew his nose into a white handkerchief.

"They crushed my head ...," he said through his tears. "They filed my teeth. Do I have to go into it all?"

"Why did the Gestapo release you?" Leser wanted to know.

"My brother paid them 100,000 francs, that's why," was Marcel's reply.

"What about the bodies at Rue Le Sueur?"

"I saw a large heap of them when I went to the house. I was very angry. I didn't want that kind of thing in my house," replied Marcel.

"Is that why you asked your brother to bring you quicklime?" asked Leser.

Marcel shook his head.

"The quicklime was for doing away with some cockroaches, but, because my comrades had a problem with carting the bodies away, I had the idea of putting the bodies into the lime. That did not work so well. So my comrades thought of burning them in the furnace of the burner in the basement. I had already lit the furnace to burn a rug that was infested with bugs. So they went ahead and burnt the bodies in the furnace."

Asked about the various identities he had used while on the run, Marcel claimed that it was the Resistance that had given him the identity of Captain Henri Valeri. He had however 'borrowed' the identity papers of Dr Wetterwald. "He was only thirty-three and here I am - almost fifty!" he bragged, pushing his chest out, his thumbs under his arms.

"You're lying, Petiot. You did not borrow Dr Wetterwald's identity papers, you stole them!" said Leser.

"That's irrelevant. The FFI had known that I was Dr Marcel Petiot, the resister. They had known all along," said Marcel.

Someone from the FFI had betrayed him, he added.

Having stopped crying, he started yet again.

"It means that the Resistance had also betrayed me, because the man who had betrayed me represented the Resistance," he told Leser.

Then, not addressing anyone in particular, Marcel said: "But was there not a Judas even among the 12 Apostles to denounce Jesus?"

While Marcel cried, Floriot and Dupin started to argue. Floriot accused Dupin of being vague in that he was not giving the court precise dates and times.

Marcel broke up the argument.

"May I say something?" he asked, rubbing his hands together.

"Why? Are you getting bored? Or do you not like being ignored?" asked Véron.

"This is my trial!" he shouted.

Like a spiteful child, he kicked his box.

It was 5:45 P.M.

Quickly, Leser adjourned the day's session.

The third session would commence at half past one the following day.

The *New York Herald Tribune* journalist, David Perham, stopped Leser on his way from the courtroom and asked what he thought of Dr Petiot.

"He is a demon, an unbelievable demon. He is a terrifying monster! He is an appalling murderer!" replied Leser.

Perham asked two members of the jury the same question.

One replied: "He is mad; of course, he is mad. He is intelligent,

330

though. He has a terrible intelligence. He is guilty, and the guillotine is too swift for such a monster!"

The other said: "We are only hearing of the bodies that were found, but how many more he killed and how many bodies he hid, we shall never know."

In the morning, the remarks would appear in the paper and a furious Floriot would demand that the two jurors be dismissed. They were and two of the replacement jurors took their place.

No action was though taken against Leser.

Floriot could again have called for a mistrial; again he did not.

* * *

On the third day of the trial, Leser again wanted to question Marcel about his alleged victims.

He began with Van Bever.

Of Van Bever Marcel said: "He was a drug addict, *par excellence!*"

So was Jeanette Gaul, he added.

He gave a detailed description of the damage the drugs had done to Gaul's body.

"She was covered in sores. It couldn't have been pleasant for Van Bever to have sex with her," he added.

Shivers of disgust ran down the bodies of some of the women in the gallery.

Asked about Guschinov, Marcel admitted he had helped him flee to Argentina.

"Where is he now?" Dupin wanted to know.

"In Argentina."

"We haven't been able to find him there," said Dupin.

"You won't. Argentina is a big country. It is also a German colony, or almost. You won't find him," said Marcel.

Floriot asked Dupin if anyone had actually tried to find Guschinov.

"Inquiries were made, yes," replied Dupin.

"I have copies of the so-called enquiries here. Mrs Guschinov wrote to two people in Buenos Aires to ask them if they had perhaps seen her husband. They wrote back that they had not. Of course, they hadn't seen him anymore than you would know the names of 99 per cent of the people of Paris you see. This is ridiculous!" snapped Floriot.

"Did you receive money from Guschinov for helping him?" Leser asked Marcel.

"No," Marcel replied.

He changed his mind. He had received something from Guschinov, yes.

"He was a furrier. I asked him if he had any ermine for my wife. I love ermine because of the colour. Instead of ermine, he brought me three mink pelts. I did not know anything about furs, so I thought they were worth about ten thousand, but I've since been told that they were worth something like one hundred thousand. That really moved me. I was really touched at such a kind gesture on his part."

Questioned by *Maître* Archevêque, Renée Guschinov's lawyer, about the identity and travel documents he had given her husband, Marcel bragged: "They were excellent. It was as if Hitler himself had issued them!"

No one in the gallery laughed.

"Why did you tell Guschinov to remove labels and monograms from his clothes?" asked Archevêque.

"That is elementary. That was the first thing we were taught in the Resistance."

Dupin intervened: "I knew the Resistance better than you."

"Yes, but we were on opposing sides," retorted Marcel.

Again, the public refrained from laughter. Marcel had yet again referred to the fact that judges had sworn allegiance to Hitler; it was sensitive ground.

Leser questioned Marcel about Dr Braunberger and Marcel claimed he had seen Dr Braunberger only once and that was for ten minutes. It had been at a First Communion; he did not say whose First Communion and was not asked to explain.

Maître Perlès, lawyer of Mrs Braunberger, stood up and intervened for the first time.

"Why were his shirt and hat found at your house?" he asked Marcel.

"We will come to that later," replied Marcel.

"You are an anti-Semite, Petiot!" murmured Perlès.

Marcel yawned.

"Petiot, listen when you're being spoken to," reprimanded Leser.

"I am listening, but what he is saying does not interest me."

"Petiot, what I say interests the jury," said Perlès.

"And that is all you want from life, is it?" Marcel wanted to know.

"Petiot, you are indeed an anti-Semite, do you know!" was the reply.

"No!" said Marcel. "Before the war, I wasn't an anti-Semite. During the Occupation, I wasn't one, either. But, after what I had gone through in Fresnes at the hands of the Gestapo, and what I'm going through now… after all that I've done for the Jews… and seeing all these Jews against me… now, I am beginning to become an anti-Semite!"

Questioned by Leser about the gangsters and their women, Marcel admitted having been present at the execution of two or three of them; he could not remember the exact number.

He described the arrest of François Albertini.

"Ten of us approached him on a street. We went through the usual thing about being German police. He immediately said he was with Lafont. So… we executed him!"

"Describe how that was done," Leser requested.

Marcel again started to rub his hands together.

"My, but you are sadistic!" he said and added, "What am I to tell you? I wasn't there personally, but what I can tell you is that he was beaten with a truncheon. The truncheon had been doctored. It was filled with sand and lead, and bicycle spokes stuck from it."

Joseph Réocreux, Marcel said, had arrived with a girlfriend, a large German woman.

"That was really a distressing scene. Jo went on about how he had spent his childhood in borstal. He made out that his life had been very hard and that he was just an unlucky sod. He said his real name was something like Grosjean or Granjean - I can't remember which. He tried to make a deal with us. He said he would give us Lafont. He even offered to join our group. Then he offered us 400,000 francs to let him go."

"Did you participate in his execution?" Leser wanted to know.

"I did," confirmed Marcel.

"Tell us about it?" ordered Leser.

Marcel nodded.

"We were a bit frightened of him. He was a big, strong man. But… he… when his time came, he was down on his knees begging for mercy. The German woman with him pulled a gun on us. She gave us a hard time," he said.

He continued that Adrien Estébéteguy had been afraid of being tortured and had confessed he was a Gestapo informer so fast that it had not even been necessary to interrogate him. He had though resisted arrest so that they had to stick a gun into his back before he would get into their van.

"Then we drove him to Rue le Sueur, and there he started to scream. But he had a knife on him, and he managed to get hold of it. He wounded one of my men. There was blood all over the place. It was a real slaughter! But one only had to look at his face to know what kind of person he was. If you want to circulate his photograph, everyone can see exactly what he was."

Asked by Leser why the gangsters' women had also been executed, Marcel replied, "What would you have had me do with them?"

"Petiot, that kind of reasoning will not take you far," observed Dupin from his chair.

"They were whores. They slept with Germans. If we had let them go, they would have denounced us to their German lovers," argued Marcel.

"Have you no respect for life?" asked Dupin.

"For the lives of Gestapo members? No. No, I do not!" replied Marcel.

Floriot intervened and asked Dupin if he had respected the life of Gestapo members. Dupin did not reply; instead he asked Marcel what right he had to judge and execute people.

"If there had been a proper court of justice at the time, we would gladly have let it do the work, but there wasn't. It wasn't very pleasant work, you know," Petiot told him.

"How much did you make out of all these people?" asked Dupin.

"Nothing. Not a *sou*."

"What about the women's jewellery?" Dupin asked next.

"We didn't touch it... I don't know anything about their jewellery."

Dupin tried again.

"What of the four million francs Estébéteguy's friends said he had taken with him and some of which he had hidden in the linings of his clothes?"

Marcel pointed to the pile of baggage behind Wilmès.

"Why ask me? You must have his stuff over there. Have a look!"

Leser ordered one of the policemen standing guard behind Marcel to help Wilmès look for Estébéteguy's suitcases. The two tried to pull one of the suitcases free and the entire pile began to wobble so that those sitting in front of it began to jump for cover. Even Leser looked as if he were going to make a run to safety. The public thought the upheaval very funny and began to scream with laughter. The jurors also could not help laughing.

Hastily, Leser, red in the face with embarrassment, called for a recess.

Marcel, being escorted from the room, again handcuffed, shouted to him over his shoulder, "Put guards at the doors. I don't want to be accused of theft should there be anything missing on the court's return!"

While waiting in an adjoining room, Marcel felt unwell. He asked a policeman standing guard if he could have some black coffee. Handed a cup, he emptied it with one gulp. Almost immediately he complained of feeling even worse. Back in the courtroom, asked by Floriot how he felt, he assured him that he felt fine again.

A light-yellow suitcase stood open on a small table in the well. Estébéteguy's name was written on the label hanging from it. Leser ordered Marcel to step up to the table. Doing so, Marcel asked the judge if any money had been found in the suitcase, whether he could have ten per cent of it. The public laughed again.

A policeman started to take men's clothing from the suitcase.

Leser wanted each item examined for a torn lining.

The policeman held up an evening jacket for the prosecution to see. A smell of cheap Eau de Cologne clung to it.

Suddenly, Marcel leaped at the policeman and grabbed the evening jacket.

"Look! Look!" he shouted excitedly, holding the jacket up towards the gallery. "The lining wasn't touched!" He prodded the shoulder pads. "Neither were these!"

Floriot jumped up and rushed to Marcel's side.

"Go and sit down, Petiot, and allow me to do my work!" he reprimanded in a raised voice.

Marcel, a sarcastic grin on his face, did as he was told.

It took Leser a few minutes to restore order, then, he told Wilmès he could put the suitcase back where he had found it. The clerk of the court did not however attempt to do so; the pile of baggage looked too unstable. He put the suitcase down beside his chair.

Leser began questioning Marcel again. He wanted to know about his alleged Jewish victims. Marcel admitted that his group had killed the three Wolffs and the Basch couple.

"They were German spies. I didn't know they were Jews! But what is important, as you will agree, Mr President, is that they had to be eliminated."

"Petiot, how can you call the Wolffs spies?" asked Dupin from his chair.

"Eryane Kahan brought them to me. She was Gestapo; they, like her, were spies," stated Marcel.

Maître Bernay, representing the Wolffs' family, stood up to support Dupin.

"The family fled Holland on July 12, 1942 and were in constant fear of the Germans and of arrest, so how can you describe them as German spies?" he asked Marcel.

"They were Germans - they came from Berlin," stated Marcel.

Floriot quickly stood up to support him.

"I have a report here written by Inspector Battut, and it says that the Wolffs entered France with passports issued in Berlin, and which were perfectly in order. Frightened Jews would not have asked the German government for passports so that they could leave Germany. Another thing - when they arrived in France, they 'hid' in a hotel the Germans had requisitioned. Therefore, there were German officers staying in that hotel."

Marcel rose to his feet, beaming with satisfaction at Floriot's support.

"Oh yes, they were hiding from the Germans! They were hiding from the Germans the way I hid from my wife in bed when I was a newlywed. I would get under the sheet naked and call out to her 'try to find me!' "

The public roared with laughter again, and Leser reached for the judge's hammer on the table in front of him and started banging for order.

"What about the Basch couple's parents, the Schonkers?" asked Dupin when the gallery was silent.

"I've never heard of them, but, if it will make you happy, put them down on my bill," replied Marcel.

"Why didn't you kill Eryane Kahan, too?" asked Dupin.

"If she had brought me a hundred Jews or a hundred Gentiles, I would have killed them all. Then, she would have been the one hundred and first," replied Marcel.

At that the public began to boo Marcel, and Leser, sensing the moment was right, adjourned the court for the day.

It was 5:45 P.M.

While one of his guards slipped the handcuffs back over Marcel's wrists, a well-dressed woman called out from the gallery, "Petiot, I have not enjoyed myself so much for a long time as I did today! Thank you!"

Shocked, a ghostly, emaciated man dressed in a worn-out suit and frazzled shirt jumped up and grabbed the woman by the throat.

"Bitch!" he hissed.

As the newspapers would report in the morning, the man had been deported to Auschwitz.

His parents, wife and children too had been deported. They had not survived.

* * *

Back in his cell, Marcel worked on his book. Georgette would have it published in its handwritten version. It was to become a best seller - though no one would claim they had actually understood what Marcel had written.

Marcel dedicated the book to: 'You who have allowed me this free time'.

In a foreword he wrote that the research had been carried out by 'Doctor Eugène', Ex-chief of the Resistance Group, Fly-Tox, and that the columns of figures had been aligned under the command of Captain Valeri of the 1st Army, 1st Regiment of Paris, but that the errors in the calculations were those of Doctor Marcel Petiot.

He continued: 'This is a serious book that I wrote for my amusement. In reading it seriously, it will amuse you. And you will certainly gain something thereby. I am one of those twisted people who are amused by work. All the better for you if you read it seriously - it will amuse you.

'Man was created to play... To play at tinkering around, at love making, at fighting... But he has lost the rules, and, at the same time, the appetite for the game, and, as he didn't play enough, he was forced to

337

play. The tinkering was called *work* with the obligatory sweat; love making became *produce children* and fighting became *war*.

'So he started cheating... and losing. I am not going to teach you to cheat; I am going to teach you to win, when possible, at the games miscalled the games of chance.

'We will know one day what magnificent influence, volcanic or astronomical, directs the Gulf Stream against the resistance of the mass of the oceanic waters. We will be able to forecast the exact moment when the neighbour will be cuckolded and, less amusing, the exact second of our own deaths... where we will at last escape from all the laws of human probabilities... to find ourselves subject to other laws that will - I assure you - be no more elastic than the first ones.

'After a whole life when our grandchildren will know, will see all the strings that pull the human puppets, they will choose with joy - if they can - a happy *Nirvana* to deliver them. Imagine the mocking eye of the privileged, the Cherubim, products of the *back street abortionists*, and the redeemed, doddering Pygmies - deaf, dumb and senseless - that this state - of grace - makes incapable of committing the least sin...

'Imagine an eternal *Heaven* where, for all time you will be pulled in opposite directions - on the right by a God who would pay you for all the good due to your instincts, who would punish you for all the evil that you had committed; and on the left pulled also by a devil who would pay you for the evil that you had done, and who would eternally reproach you for all the good that you were guilty of, and for the evil that by forgetfulness or by laziness, you had neglected to commit.

'I propose to give you the exact laws that rule chance. The knowledge of these laws will allow you to either use them to your profit or to avoid chancing the slightest sum - which is also a way of profiting.

'I am astonished that this study has as yet never been undertaken seriously. It is true that I would not have applied myself to it if a certain God had not given me a completely free spirit as well as sufficient free time... *haec otia fecit...*

'Look at what the human sciences would have lost if... but I will finish my sentence later. I have already studied in depth other *games* - notably war, politics, Bridge, Chess etc. Unfortunately, this work has disappeared as a result of several thefts and break-ins that I have suffered. If I ever recover them, I will publish them. Otherwise, I will never have the courage or the inclination to start again…

'To avoid any similar disappearances in the future, I have decided to publish this despite the danger of providing the public with arms, which, although good in themselves, may turn against the user if he does not know them in depth'.

-0-

CHAPTER FIVE

The Trial Continues

It was March 21, officially, the first day of spring.

At the Palais de Justice it was the fourth day of Marcel's trial. All night, Parisians had camped outside. It had been announced that only those with an invitation issued and signed by Leser would be allowed to attend the trial in future, and, as a policeman standing at the complex' gate would hand those out, everyone had wanted to be first in line in the morning. The atmosphere had been carnavalesque; musicians had entertained with accordion music, music hall performers were eating fire and walking on coals, and vendors had set up stalls and sold grilled sausages, baguette sandwiches, pancakes, and even *barbe à papa* - candy floss. The bistros in the area had stayed open and despite that the night had been cool, their terraces had remained packed.

The invitation system was not a success; the moment the courtroom's door opened, a horde, most without invitations, ran for seats. Women in hats and gloves lashed out with handbags at seated elderly, moustachioed gentlemen. Two of the latter became engaged in a punch-up with one another. One was led, not just from the courtroom, but from the complex; he was a venerable American in Paris for the conference of Allied leaders being held at the nearby Palais du Luxembourg which had served as the Luftwaffe's headquarters during the Occupation.

Leser's interrogation of Marcel had been scheduled to end the previous day already, but Marcel had yet to be questioned about Yvan Dreyfus and the Knellers. Accordingly, as soon as Marcel was seated in his box, Leser asked him about Dreyfus.

"Oh! Dreyfus! Bah!" retorted Marcel.

His mind began to wander.

"There was a certain general - Victor was his name, I believe," he

341

began. "He was parachuted to the Lyon area. To capture him, the Germans mobilised four hundred prostitutes, and then..."

Leser held up a hand.

"Petiot, we are not here to listen to war stories, but to discuss the case of Yvan Dreyfus."

"Dreyfus, yes, of course, " continued Marcel. "He was sent to me by two shabby individuals... Guélin and Chantin. Guélin got in touch with the barber Fourrier. It was at Fourrier's barbershop that I was to have been introduced to Dreyfus. Fourrier said that Dreyfus had just been released from Compiègne camp and that he had to get out of the country as quickly as possible. At that time, I didn't have too many men under my command. They had all gone to Lyon to do some cleaning up. As for Dreyfus... it was obvious he was a Jew. He told me that he was in the radio business, and he did have some knowledge of radios. Guélin was a lawyer. I said to myself, this man - I was thinking of Dreyfus - is a different kind of person to Jo the Boxer, and we have to get him out of the country."

"Did you ask him for money?" Leser wanted to know.

"I never asked for money from anyone!" snapped Marcel. "It was Fourrier who did. But, to get back to Dreyfus... it was the same scenario as before. We took Dreyfus in the van to the Place de la Concorde, and there Robert Martinetti waited for us, as usual. We saw him walk off with Dreyfus. The two walked off towards the naval ministry. In the morning, I was arrested. It had been a race between two Gestapo heads to lay their hands on me. Each used an informer - Beretta and Guélin. It was Beretta who got me taken. I managed to let my comrades know that I had been taken so that they could get out of the way."

He took a long and loud breath and continued: "Mr President, I was tortured. My life was at risk!"

He started to swallow as if he were trying not to cry.

"Petiot, we are not interested in that. Instead, tell us what happened to Dreyfus," said Leser quickly.

"I don't know what happened to him. He had probably left the country," replied Marcel, still swallowing saliva.

"Your brother was worried about his disappearance," said Leser.

"Yes," confirmed Marcel. "He tried to find him. He also wrote to Yvan Dreyfus's father because he wanted him to intervene on my behalf so that I could be released."

Floriot turned to Leser.

"There exists a 1943 Gestapo document that proves that Dreyfus had informed for them, so there is no cause to become soft over his fate."

Véron jumped up.

"*Maître*, that document is in copy form only, and its authenticity has not been established."

Marcel chipped in: "The Germans pretended to me that Guélin and Beretta were also under arrest, but I quickly understood that those two were traitors. They, the Germans, also wanted to know from me what had happened to Dreyfus. I said to them, 'if he is a Jew, what difference does it make to you that he has disappeared, and, if he's an informer, you will find another'. I had quite a bit of fun!"

Leser held up a hand. "Petiot, we are not interested in the fun that you had or in your idea of what fun is!"

He asked Véron if he had anything else to ask about Dreyfus. Véron said he had something to say about Dreyfus, yes. He gave the court a short, but moving, summary of Yvan Dreyfus's career. He spoke of how Dreyfus had rushed back to France from safety in the USA to fight for his country. How he had tried to reach General de Gaulle in London. How the Gestapo had arrested him. How he had planned to make another dash for London, but had instead made the acquaintance of Dr Petiot. Comparing Dr Petiot to Dreyfus, he said that unlike Dreyfus, Dr Petiot had taken no part in defending France. He called Dreyfus a hero.

Listening, Marcel started to rub his hands together.

"Dreyfus was a traitor four times over," he mumbled. "Traitor to his race. Traitor to his religion. Traitor to his country. Traitor…"

"Don't moralise, Petiot. It does not become you," interrupted Leser.

"Neither does it become you!" snapped Marcel.

In the morning, journalists would write that it was a pity that Leser had not allowed Marcel to finish his sentence. It would have been interesting to have known what or who the fourth ideal or person was that Dreyfus was supposed to have betrayed.

Asked about the Knellers, Marcel admitted he had helped them to flee France. Kurt Kneller he described as a patient who he had been treating for an embarrassing affliction.

"Kneller told me he was desperate to go to the free zone - they were staying in a house that was infested with Germans. Because I knew that he didn't possess a fortune, I wasn't going to charge him much for processing the necessary documents, yet he haggled over the fee. I had to pay two thousand out of my own pocket in the end. And he already owed me money. He had been borrowing from me for some time. I proposed to him that he should leave his furniture with me as collateral and that he could pay me later."

"So you charged him?" asked Leser.

"He had to refund my expenses," replied Marcel.

"You took his furniture to Rue le Sueur?"

"Listen…," said Petiot, "I'm not all too proud of this, but the Knellers were Germans, and, after all, in the next war… one can't be too certain…"

"Oh, Petiot, do spare us this thing about a next war!" snapped Leser.

"As things are going, Mr President, it won't be long before there is another!" said Marcel all the same.

He spoke of the Knellers some more.

"They left - him, his wife and the child - for Bordeaux. I had given him Belgian nationality papers and Alsatian ones to her. I got them train tickets to get them to Bordeaux. I recommended that they should take two bottles of cognac to give to the people smuggler who was going to escort them. They spent a night at Rue le Sueur. Despite all I had done for them, I only received a postcard from her … Mrs Kneller… about two or three months after they'd left. She wrote just one word - *bonjour*. Not a word about whether they had arrived safely. A while later, I had another postcard from her. She wrote that her husband was ill, and she asked advice about treatment."

"And the child?" asked Leser.

"Ah, yes… the child! He was quite a cute little boy!"

Marcel smiled and the public groaned.

"There was not even mercy in your heart for a child of seven?" asked Leser.

Marcel did not reply. Several women in the gallery dabbed at their eyes. A man loudly blew his nose into a handkerchief.

"Petiot, how do you explain that the boy's pyjamas were found at your house in a suitcase of the Knellers?" asked Dupin from his seat.

Marcel shrugged and pulled a face.

"It must have been the pyjamas he had worn the night they had spent at my house. They didn't want to take dirty clothes with them - that, I know. Or anything that bore a KK monogram. Would you have taken your dirty clothes with you, or something that bore your monogram, had you fled to the free zone? But, tell me, why do you think I would have wanted to keep the kid's pyjamas?"

That time it was Dupin who chose not to reply.

Marcel took up where he had left off.

"The pyjamas might have been with the stuff I'd picked up at their apartment. The *concierge* made such a fuss when I arrived to take the furniture Kneller had told me I should take, that I only took some linen. The pyjamas could have been with it."

"That pair of pyjamas is your undoing, Petiot," said Dupin. "It is the death of this seven-year-old boy that totally breaks down your line of defence that your Resistance cell had eliminated traitors, and you know that this is so and that was why, during the police's interrogation of you, you stopped replying to their questions. They wanted to know about the Knellers, and you refused to reply."

Marcel shook his head.

"Not true! I answered all their questions!"

Floriot intervened, "As a matter of fact, we never even received an inventory of what had allegedly been found in the suitcases and ..."

Dupin interrupted, "That is not correct, *Maître*. Judge Goletty did offer you the inventory... and he had done so frequently... but Petiot had not wanted to see it."

"That's not true!" snapped Marcel. "Like everything else you are saying, it is not true! Anyone could have gone through the suitcases - even Lafont. He... they... the police, could have put whatever they wanted into them."

"That's certainly so," agreed Floriot.

"And I replied to all the questions," insisted Marcel. "I only refused when I was requested to sign a list of 362 answers I was supposedly to have given to 362 questions - questions I had never been asked!"

"Why give the court incorrect information?" Floriot asked, turning to Dupin. "You seem to say whatever comes into your head. Have you even read the file?"

"Judge Goletty confirmed to me just this morning that Petiot had been offered the inventory of the contents of the suitcases and he had refused to look at it," Dupin told him.

"So, call Mr Goletty to the stand!" ordered Floriot.

Marcel shook a fist in the air.

"No one showed me that list!"

Floriot insisted that Goletty should be called.

"But where is Mr Goletty?" he cried out, exasperated. "Call him to the stand! If he can give me proof that my client had seen the inventory list then I will stop practising law right now!"

Leser adjourned the court for a quarter of an hour.

Fifteen minutes later, the court having reconvened, there was no further mention of the inventory list because during the break Goletty had been found and he had confirmed to Leser that he had offered Dr Petiot the inventory list on several occasions, but each time the latter had refused to look at it. That was sufficient proof to Leser that Marcel had seen the list and he had told Floriot so.

* * *

Commissioner Massu, having recovered from his suicide attempt and apparently enjoying early retirement, was to give evidence and waiting in an antechamber to be called, but the first witness of the hearing was his initial replacement, Commissioner Lucian Pinault.

Pinault was extremely nervous; he perspired freely and a facial twitch was out of control.

Marcel, no doubt because of experience gained in practising medicine, sensed the commissioner's nervousness instantly.

"Tell me, Commissioner," he began, yet again grinning and his dark eyes flashing like those of a dangerous animal coming in for the kill, "was I someone who was known to frequent seedy places or someone who associated with criminals or loose women?"

"Ah... Well, no... no," stuttered Pinault.

Immediately, Marcel hurled another question at him.

"Did anyone ever say to you that I was a greedy man, one who was just after money?"

"Ah... Well, no. You... you... seem to have left rather the opposite impression... I must say."

346

"Thank you, Mr Commissioner! That will be all. I thank you dearly," said Petiot.

Pleased with himself, he was smiling broadly.

Leser also had questions he wanted to ask Pinault. He wanted to know what the latter had discovered about Marcel's Resistance claims.

Pinault, his face still distorted with twitching, shook his head. No one he had questioned - resister, French Gestapo member or informer, no collaborator and that included Lafont - had had any recollection of ever having dealt with a Marcel.

"Not as Dr Eugène. Not as Dr Petiot."

Marcel intervened.

"You just misunderstood what they'd said! But don't worry! It's not your fault. Believe me... I understand how things are... with the police..."

Pinault turned red in the face and Marcel grinned from ear to ear. The public nodded in agreement; they had a low opinion of their police because of how they had collaborated with the Germans.

Floriot also wanted to question Pinault.

"Didn't your investigation show that Guélin was working for the Gestapo?"

"He was an informer. Correct," confirmed Pinault.

"Two bodies were found in Marly Forest. They were identified as Germans. Correct?"

"Ah... correct... but that was not my jurisdiction. I only happened to have learnt that two bodies found buried in Marly Forest had been identified as those of two Gestapo agents."

The public laughed Pinault off the witness stand.

Inspector Jean Poirier - he was the inspector Massu had put in charge of finding Marcel - took the stand next.

Looking as uncomfortable and nervous as Pinault had done, his voice was hardly above a whisper. He recalled that he had questioned Lafont and the latter had not recognised Marcel as either one of his informers or as a member of the Resistance from the photographs which he had shown him. Lafont had, he added, recognised both Estébétéguy and Réocreux as having been his informers, but said that they had suddenly disappeared. He had also shown a photograph of Eryane Kahan to Lafont, he said, and the latter had not recognised her either as having been among his informers.

"Did you question her?" Floriot wanted to know from his seat.

"I did, *Maître*."

"And what do you think of her?" Floriot wanted to know. "Is she a woman of the world, as one says, or is she just an adventuress?"

"I lean more towards the description of adventuress," replied Poirier, pulling at his tie like he was a schoolboy embarrassed at the word 'adventuress'.

The inspector, asked by Leser, what those he had questioned had said about Marcel, he replied that all had spoken of his staring eyes; those eyes had scared them.

Marcel threw his hands up in the air.

"Oh, here we go again! Now I'm going to be called crazy again!"

He started to laugh. Floriot and his 'boys' laughed, too. It encouraged Marcel to laugh louder; he laughed until tears ran over his cheeks.

Calm restored, Leser asked Poirier about Georges Redouté, the man who had taken Marcel in. Poirier said that Redouté had genuinely believed that Marcel was a member of the Resistance.

Floriot asked about Dr Braunberger.

He produced a 1942 police report of an investigation the Crim had carried out on the doctor's disappearance. He asserted it exemplified a police habit of making unproven assertions. The report stated that Dr Braunberger had returned home two days after he had set off for the 10 A.M. meeting on Rue Duret in the sixteenth *arrondissement* and, as a consequence, the Crim had closed their missing person investigation.

Why, therefore, he wanted to know from Poirier, was Dr Braunberger's name among his client's victims?

Poirier did not have an answer.

On that note of confusion, Leser adjourned the day's session.

* * *

On Friday afternoon, at half past one, March 22, the public gallery was almost deserted; the Parisians had gone somewhere else - to Rue le Sueur. With Marcel's agreement, Floriot had asked Leser if the jurors could be taken to the townhouse because by seeing the place they would realise that there was nothing sinister about it, and, despite that one could

348

commit murder anywhere, the house did not have any special features that would have made it a perfect place for killing.

The visit to the house would be for the afternoon.

The Quay's Prof Charles Sanié was to orchestrate the visit.

The professor began the day's proceedings on the stand.

His first act was to pass diagrams of the property around the well. No one showed much interest in those.

Next he began describing what the police and firefighters had found. He described the pit and the stinking, bubbling quicklime; the rotting, half-devoured flesh; the bones; the eyeless, toothless skulls. Several jurors wiped sweat from their pale brows.

Half an hour later, Sanié having finished his gruesome testimony, Leser announced that the court would set off for Rue le Sueur.

In a few minutes the gallery emptied; all there ran for their cars or to the nearest Métro station. The journalists also ran; they hitchhiked rides from the photographers. Groaning and cursing, they squeezed into the sidecars of motorcycles already packed with camera equipment.

Those in the well also hastily gathered their coats, hats and briefcases and rushed out. They squeezed into 15 vehicles. Leser, in his red robe and toque was in the lead car, a black *traction-avant*. Marcel was in the fifth car, also a black *traction-avant*. He sat in the rear between two detectives. He wore his grey tweed overcoat, the collar of which was turned up. It was a cool, windy, rainy day, but he also wanted to hide his face.

The convoy, escorted by police motorcyclists, crossed over Pont Neuf Bridge to Paris's Right Bank. It took Quay des Tuileries and passed the Louvre Museum on its way to Place de la Concorde. From there it raced down the length of Avenue des Champs-Elysées to Place de l'Étoile. At Place de l'Étoile it turned into Avenue Foch and, moving against the normal flow of traffic, ascended the Rue le Sueur. Some two hundred 'swallows' had been brought to Paris in case the Parisians became unruly or rioted, but, although the entire route had been lined with people and more had leant from windows or stood on balconies, there had been no trouble.

Rue le Sueur was closed to normal vehicle traffic, yet, the pavements were packed with people. Jacques and Andrée Marçais were among them. Le Crocodile was the busiest it had ever been in its existence; patrons stood four deep at the zinc-topped bar. Le Rendez-vous des Chauffeurs was also open and packed, and no one had gone there to buy coal. In both, the street's residents were amusing non-residents with stories about the townhouse. They told of the smoke that had poured from the chimney for at least a fortnight; of the stench; of the loaded cart; of the screams that had come from the house almost every night for two years; of how frightened they had all been of the 'house of horrors'.

Leser stepped from the car and the Parisians cheered.

"Bravo!" someone called out.

He disappeared through the gateway; it had not yet been repaired and was being held in place with planks.

The car with Marcel drove up. Shouts of 'assassin', 'death to you' and 'rot in Hell' rang out. He kept his head down.

"What a homecoming!" he murmured to one of Floriot's 'boys' waiting for him in the front courtyard.

Leser, Prof Sanié, Dupin, the magistrates, the jury, Wilmès and his son, and the lawyers waited in the back courtyard. So did some of the journalists and the photographers; their colleagues had chosen to go into the house itself. They were hanging from the windows.

"Keep the gateway open!" Leser called out to a 'swallow'.

Outside, the crowd, having heard Leser's order, surged forward. Fists started to fly as those at the back pushed to the front. Barriers at both the Avenue Foch and Avenue de la Grande-Armée ends of the street collapsed as more surged forward. Several 'swallows' jumped aside to avoid being trampled. A woman in high-heeled shoes shouted abuse at one of them for stopping her going into the second courtyard. Although she claimed to be one of the lawyers' wives, she was led away to a 'salad basket'. Legally speaking, while the court was at the townhouse, the property was to be considered as a courtroom. As such, the public could not be barred from it.

In the second courtyard, Floriot's 'boys' started to pose for pictures. One of them had found a femur; he was holding it up for the cameras. Marcel was called over to be photographed as well. He was ashen and looked bewildered, and small and thin.

Leser led the jury into the outhouse that Marcel had converted into a consulting room. After the police's investigation had ended at the property, the electricity had again been disconnected and as no one had thought of reconnecting it for the court's visit, there was suddenly a frantic search for some source of light. A carton of candles was found; fortunately Marcel, the compulsive collector, had, at some stage, found a carton of candles irresistible. A 'swallow' rushed the candles down from the house to Leser.

In the gloom that the candles provided, the group saw that thick, black dust covered everything in the consulting room. The furniture was shabby. It was hard to believe that Marcel could have envisaged receiving patients in such a place. On his desk lay several prescription forms. Those quickly disappeared into the pockets of the journalists. Later, the forms would be sold as collector items at ridiculously high prices.

Holding up a flickering candle, Leser led the group into the corridor that led to the triangular room. Addressing the jurors, Dupin, right behind him, explained, "In reality, *Messieurs*, those who walked this way were under the impression that this corridor led to their freedom."

It was very cramped in the triangular room despite that only Dupin, Leser, Marcel, Floriot and two jurors had been able to squeeze in. In the morning, Pierre Scize would, in *Le Figaro*, describe the room as *un quart de Brie* - a triangular-shaped slice of Brie cheese.

In the room, Dupin continued his explanation.

"They found this padded door. They tried to open it. They realised that it was a fake, but, at that moment, the door behind them closed. The door with the chain and latch, but which did not have a knob on the room side. They saw that the fake door had a bell. They pressed it. The bell did not ring."

Dupin had lifted his voice so that the jurors who had remained in the corridor could have heard him as well.

There was a gaping hole in the wall where the peephole had been. Floriot wanted to know what had happened to the peephole.

"Where is the viewer? Where is the viewer?" he asked.

His voice boomed; it carried to the courtyard.

No one seemed to know what had happened to it.

"I would have wanted it to be here so that I could have explained to the gentlemen of the jury how it worked," grumbled Marcel.

A face, pulled into a grotesque grimace, appeared behind the hole; a journalist was trying to ease the tensity of the moment. No one was amused. Least of all Marcel: he started to sway.

"I am not feeling all that well, *Maître*," he said to Floriot.

The lawyer shot him an anxious glance.

Marcel asked Leser whether he could sit down for a moment. Without being given such permission, he sank down onto the edge of the small metal bed.

Floriot again asked why the viewer was missing. He wanted the jury to see it. Someone said it had been left behind in the courtroom.

"It wasn't stolen or lost, was it? Because, if you're going to start losing stuff that should be under seal...," said Marcel from the bed.

He asked one of the two jurors in the room whether he knew what was meant by a 'viewer'. The juror turned pale; so addressed by a murderer, he was unable to get a single word out. His fear amused Marcel. It even seemed to make him feel better. He got to his feet.

"I will explain to you what it is, and then you can tell your colleagues," he told the juror.

He was grinning from ear to ear; he was enjoying the juror's discomfort.

"I bought the viewer directly from the manufacturer. It was not a periscope, as had been reported in the Nazi press, but a kind of telescope. It allowed me to see only part of the room. To see that area there where Mr President is standing now."

He pointed towards Leser. The latter suddenly looked as uneasy as the juror; he shifted his weight from one foot to another.

Marcel continued: "I was going to put my radiotherapy apparatus there, and I would have been able to monitor my patients without having to step into the room, which would have disturbed them."

"But the viewer was covered under wallpaper," observed the other juror, who had also been able to squeeze into the room.

"That was a mistake the builders had made," replied Marcel.

He smiled at the juror.

"This room could have served as a prison cell," observed the juror, encouraged by the smile.

"If you know anything of construction, you will see that the walls are simple plaster ones. One can put one's fist right through such a wall," replied Marcel. He turned to Leser. "Mr President, tell me how I could have killed in this room; come on, tell me?"

The juror though was not finished with Marcel yet. "But you told us that you killed in the back of a van," he said.

Marcel's smile vanished.

"Look here, one can kill anywhere!" he snapped.

The juror stepped back quickly and did not stop until he was against the wall behind him.

Having finished with the juror, Marcel turned back to Leser.

"If I had said that I had never killed I can understand your obstinacy. But I admitted willingly to having executed several people. But whether I'd done it here or elsewhere, what's the difference? This business is going to make us look like a bunch of imbeciles to the rest of the world."

The group set off towards the stable to see the pit. There, a journalist, sweating profusely, lit a pipe to calm his nerves.

Leser reprimanded him: "It is forbidden to smoke in a courtroom, and I must remind you that this is a court of law."

Photographers wanted to take photographs of Leser, Marcel and Floriot at the pit. Leser asked Marcel if he minded and he said that he did not, but again he complained of not feeling well. Once the photographs had been taken, he began to reel. All but Floriot, who shot him a worried glance, ignored him.

"May I step outside for a while?" asked Marcel of Floriot.

The lawyer said that he could.

Soon, Marcel was back.

"I feel better again now - though I felt very bad a minute ago," he explained.

Only Floriot seemed to have heard him; the lawyer patted him on the shoulder.

Leser asked Marcel about the quicklime.

"The quicklime was only to clean up the pit. That's all!" snapped Marcel.

The group stepped out into the courtyard. It had started to rain heavily. No one had brought an umbrella. Soon, all were soaked.

"Why did you have this wall built, Petiot?" asked Leser, ignoring the rain. He pointed at the high back wall.

"Children threw all sorts of stuff into the courtyard... peach stones... cherry stones," replied Marcel.

Everyone looked up at the wall. All that was visible above it was the top floor of one of the buildings on Rue Duret behind Rue le Sueur.

Going down the stone steps to the front basement, Marcel yet again complained of feeling unwell. That time even Floriot ignored him.

In the corridor, Sanié stepped forward.

"Here lay many morsels of flesh. And there, in the last room on the corridor, was half of a human corpse. It had been cut lengthwise," he said.

He stepped into the room. So did Leser and a juror. A 'swallow' held up a candle.

"The corpse was there next to the two burners," continued Sanié. "Only the larger was lit. There were some human remains sizzling in there."

No one seemed to want to be in the basement. Not even Marcel; he motioned to Floriot he might throw up. Going up the steps he clung to the railing as if he were trying not to collapse. In the courtyard, he started to sway. Floriot called over a 'swallow' and the two rushed to his side. Marcel smiled his gratitude. In the morning, journalists would report what had been amiss with him. Unlike what everyone had thought - the realisation of what he had done had got the better of him - he had just been hungry. He had had a problem eating since the beginning of the trial; the only food he had been able to keep down had been the bowls of watery broth that passed for breakfast in La Santé.

It was 4 P.M.

Leser ordered the return to the Palais de Justice.

He also wanted the gateway to be closed and boarded up again.

It could not be done; too many people were still milling about.

When it was finally done at the end of the day the property would look as if a tornado had hit it. It had been ransacked; anything not too heavy had been grabbed as a souvenir and carried off. One man had even carried a stack of Prof Locart's books out on his head.

Back at the Palais de Justice, Sanié took the stand again. Floriot rose to ask him if Marcel's fingerprints had been found on any of the items the police had removed from the townhouse. Sanié admitted that Marcel's fingerprints had not been found anywhere in the house or the outhouses or down in the basement. Fingerprints which had been found had remained unidentified.

Maître Bernay, representing the Wolffs' relatives, also had a question for Sanié. He wanted to know whether it was plausible that the triangular room could have been used for radiotherapy treatment.

"As you would have seen for yourself, there was hardly space in the room for the bed, so how could a table for the radiotherapy equipment still have fitted in there?" replied Sanié.

Marcel, colour having returned to his face, also had a question for Sanié.

"Did you see if the bag that had contained a body was a German *Feldpost* one?"

"Petiot, I don't know what kind of bag it was!" snapped Sanié.

He added that Marcel's question was out of place.

Floriot did not agree. He demanded the bag should be fetched; the jury should see it because it had, indeed, been a German Post Office bag, and it proved that the killings had been the work of the Gestapo.

"My client is innocent," he stated firmly.

Like with the viewer, no one knew where the bag was. It sent Floriot into a fury.

"First the viewer is lost, and now we hear that the bag is also lost! This is ridiculous!"

He wanted Massu to be brought to the courtroom to clarify the issue of the bag. Massu was fetched from the antechamber and walking to the witness stand, he kept his eyes to the ground; he might have been enjoying retirement but he had not yet put the humiliation of having been accused of 'collaboration' behind him. He swore in a shaky voice to tell the truth and nothing but the truth and for God to help him to do so. He had held the Bible with his left hand and all had seen that it was still bandaged from his suicide attempt. Having been questioned twice by Goletty in the month after Marcel's arrest, he had admitted his handling of the investigation had lacked vision, but he had denied he had ever collaborated with the Germans in covering up the case. "I never received any orders or advice from the occupational authorities on how to investigate the Petiot Case. I am most adamant about this. All that I did was that I reported daily to the authorities, as all did at the time. I never even heard back about my reports," he had told Goletty.

He had slashed his wrist, he had added, because 'a young inspector, then under my orders, had accused me of having lacked courage during two of my investigations. But those two investigations had nothing to do with the Petiot Case. I have nothing to reproach myself with in the Petiot Case'.

On the first day of the trial he had walked around Place Dauphine nostalgically to see whether its horse chestnut trees had yet again bloomed before those of Avenue des Champs-Elysées. They had.

"Try to remember the bag," said Floriot addressing him. "Can you remember any detail about it?"

Massu blinked and mumbled something incomprehensible.

"Think! Was it a *Feldpost* bag?" urged Floriot.

"Well, it had looked like an ordinary bag to me... Like a bag in which potatoes are kept ..."

"Where is it now?" asked Floriot.

"I think Chief Inspector Battut handled that..."

Massu shrugged his shoulders and the public sniggered.

"Commissioner, tell me," asked Floriot, "what did you do as Chief of Police?"

"I directed criminal investigations," mumbled Massu.

"*Did* you now, Commissioner!" said Floriot and winked into the gallery.

Before there could be another burst of laughter there in the gallery, Leser announced that the court was to adjourn for the day.

* * *

In the morning, Pierre Scize would comment on how pathetic the police were and how incompetent the prosecution team was.

Of the police he would write: 'Why, nine times out of ten do these civil servants cut such pathetic figures? The least important question from the defence have them stuttering. They hesitate; they become evasive; the one hides behind the other, and they even contradict each other. Commissioner Massu was out of his depth faced with Floriot's questions. Since yesterday the expression *coup de Massu* has lost its meaning as far as I am concerned'.

Coup de Massu was a play on the expression *coup de massue*, a staggering blow.

Of the prosecution team he would write that after five days, the court had yet to establish the means by which Marcel had killed. He wrote that they had provided several possibilities, yet it was possible to argue the feasibility of each. (1) Marcel had pumped poison gas into the triangular

356

room: that could not have been because the room was not airtight. (2) Pretending that he was vaccinating them for their trip to Argentina, Marcel had instead injected them with poison: that too could not have been because they had been able to write letters he had dictated to them. (3) They had poisoned themselves on pressing the fake doorbell, but that too could not have been because the police had taken the bell apart, and there had been no syringe hidden inside, or space in which to hide one.

The columnist Georges Ravon, also with *Le Figaro*, wrote that Marcel was being given too much attention; the Nuremberg War Crimes trials were of vastly greater importance.

He called Marcel 'the little quack of Rue de Caumartin'.

* * *

On Saturday the trial resumed at one o'clock.

The public gallery was again packed. Many Brits had taken the boat train over to Paris for the weekend. There were also members of Europe's royalty in the gallery: right at the back, on a comfortable chair that had been brought in especially for him, sat the 23-year-old Prince Rainier, heir to the throne of Monaco. The wife of Félix Gouin, France's interim president was also in the gallery. Two 'swallows' had escorted her to her front row seat.

All in the well looked tired; they had bags under their eyes. Leser sat slumped, resting his chin in his hands. Several jurors sat with closed eyes. Marcel's face was damp, his skin was yellow and he had dark circles under his eyes. He leant against his box and smiled only on catching the eyes of his family. Maurice fiddled with a handkerchief and pressed it against his lips. Gerhardt smiled back at his father. Georgette pulled her pretty face into a frown, but still tried to smile; she grabbed one of Gerhardt's hands and pressed it against her bosom.

Inspector Battut was first to be called to the stand. Journalists would write of how physically strong a man he looked. They would especially admire his large neck and broken nose. The nose, they would write, gave him the appearance of a boxer, but a *boxeur bienfaisant* - a kind hearted, considerate boxer, one who did not like to hurt his opponents.

Battut readily admitted that the Germans had been interested in the Crim's investigation. He knocked down Marcel's justification for the killings that the murdered ones had been *collabos*. He said that Eryane Kahan could not have been a Gestapo informer because the Germans had made it clear that they wanted her arrested; they would not have done had she worked for them. He also testified that the Wollfs and the Basch couple and their relatives hadn't been Gestapo informers either.

"I can positively swear under oath that they were not," he said.

Asked by Véron what he knew of Yvan Dreyfus, he said: "I only know what I had read in the police file."

"What of Guélin?" asked Véron.

"Guélin has been charged with 'intelligence with the enemy'," he stated.

"Can Petiot's testimony that Dreyfus worked with the Germans be believed?" Véron wanted to know next.

"I don't think so," replied Battut.

Floriot intervened.

"Did Dreyfus not agree to do a certain job for the Germans?"

"I would have to say that, yes, he did, but he was just a poor unfortunate, like the rest of them. To be released from Compiègne, he had agreed to furnish the Gestapo with some information. When he had agreed, he had not known what kind of information they would want from him."

"So he worked for the Germans!" stated Floriot.

Marcel nodded vigorously.

The lawyer accused Battut of having no clear grasp of the case.

"I did not have four assistants and twelve secretaries like some people present here," Battut retorted.

"But you had twelve inspectors!" was Floriot's reply.

He wanted to know whether the Crim had shown the contents of the suitcases to the relatives of those Marcel stood accused of having murdered.

"I don't think so," admitted Battut.

"Why didn't they?" asked Floriot.

"*Maître*," said Battut, "we're talking of something that had happened during the Occupation, unless you have forgotten."

Marcel rose and asked Battut how many French men and women the police had arrested during the Occupation and had turned over to the Germans.

The question flustered Battut; he could only shrug.

"Yes, of course there were too many to count," remarked Marcel.

Véron tried to come to Battut's assistance. "Petiot," he said, "remember, you are the murderer on trial here!"

Two Crim inspectors, Pascaud and Casanova, testified next.

Inspector Pascaud was a tall, lean man with little hair. Journalists would describe him as a man who looked like a scholar who had fallen on hard times. In a quiet voice he admitted that the police had lost, or at least mislaid, not only the viewer and the sack in which there had been a body, but also Dr Braunberger's shirt and hat.

Floriot asked: "Weren't the shirt and hat in a suitcase?"

"I don't know," he replied.

Floriot shook his head.

"Are you lot, policemen or magicians? Things seem to be vanishing all the time."

"Some of the suitcases had been opened," said Pascaud.

"Who opened them?" asked Floriot.

"I don't know," was the reply.

Inspector Casanova was extremely nervous; his voice kept on breaking like a teenager's. His unease was further intensified when, while he was taking his oath, the actress Paulette Dubost - at the time one of France's most popular film stars - entered. She glided into the courtroom like a grande dame and hoisted her skirt to her knees to sit down quite nonchalantly on some steps; all seats had been taken.

Casanova told the court that the Crim had established that two bodies found buried in Marly Forest had been those of two French Gestapo agents named Fauvel and d'Auger. The two had fallen foul of IVE3's Berger who had had them shot. Marcel's claim that he was the one who had ordered them shot was idle boasting, or, rather, a total lie.

Next on the stand was a Captain Henri Boris. He had been at Compiègne with Yvan Dreyfus. Not having befriended Yvan during their shared imprisonment, he had almost nothing of significance to say. Questioned by Floriot all the same and asked whether in his opinion Yvan had willingly agreed to spy on the Resistance, he replied, "I would have signed such a paper myself if I had been given a chance to escape to England and fight the Germans with General de Gaulle."

Jean Hotin was called to testify.

Marcel threw his head back and yawned loudly when Hotin walked in.

"Mr Hotin, when did your wife discover she was pregnant?" Floriot asked.

"I don't know," replied Hotin.

He was not under oath; bound to request compensation from Marcel for the loss of Lili, his first wife, he had not been asked to take the oath.

Marcel eased himself into his chair as if preparing to doze off.

"Well, when did she have her last period?" asked Floriot.

"I don't know," replied Hotin.

"You know what I am talking of? You know what a period is?" asked Floriot.

Hotin turned red as beetroot and looked down at his shoes.

"Look, man," said Floriot angrily, "surely you must know when she fell pregnant. You had something to do with it, after all!"

"Ah... no... I mean... Ah... Yes," Hotin began to stutter.

"Look man, when were you married?" asked Floriot, emphasising every word.

"Ah... on... ah ...it was... Ah..."

An exasperated Leser intervened.

"Oh *Maître*," he said. "Do let's forget about this, please!"

Captain Urbain Coureau, retired from the Villeneuve-sur-Yonne Gendarmerie, was next to be called.

After having taken oath, he fixed his eyes on Marcel.

"Petiot is an unscrupulous adventurer," he stated in full voice.

Floriot wanted to know from him about Louisette Delaveau.

"Her head is lying at the bottom of some abandoned well somewhere," said Coureau.

Asked to tell the court about Marcel's other crimes, he told of how *Monsieur le maire* had parked his car wherever he wanted; how he had driven around the village in the dark without switching on his headlights; that he had also driven too fast, and how he had blocked the pavement outside his house because that was where he used to work on his car.

"I gave him seven traffic tickets - and he murdered Mrs Debauve!" he stated.

"There's only one problem here, gentlemen of the jury," said Floriot. "Before Captain Coureau had accused my client of having murdered Mrs Debauve, he had already accused nine other villagers of having murdered the woman. If the case had not been closed, he would have accused everyone in the village - one after the other!"

The public slow-clapped Coureau from the stand and Leser adjourned the session until Monday.

* * *

The Sunday newspapers would conduct an editorial post-mortem of the week's events. Dissatisfied with how the case was going, the journalists agreed that the only thing the prosecution had yet been able to establish was that human remains had been found at a townhouse belonging to Dr Petiot.

As if time was short, Marcel spent all that Sunday working on his book.

He was devoting many pages to a battle that had raged between God and the Devil.

On one of the pages he wrote: 'After the memorable dispute between God the Father and Lucifer, there was an armistice... negotiations and statutes were drawn up for an Eternal Peace based on the equal number of souls to be attributed to the two Greats...

'Lucifer had the better hand, because he didn't even have the bother of creating them, like a broom seller who steals them ready made, while his rival had to steal the broom branches, the handle and the wire...'

'... A friend of mine even claims that, in the battle, God took one hell of a hiding and that now there only remains a few atoms of infinite goodness and divine providence. This over-pessimistic view of Fresnes was expressed after six months of being tortured by the *Boches*...'

'... I have a more optimistic belief. By the peace treaty, God and Satan - Lucifer had changed his alias - shared half and half. But how to distinguish between the chosen and the damned?'

'... As the Bible tells us, God had not noticed while doing his accounts that Satan had populated his whole kingdom and had a largely sufficient workforce - whereas Paradise seemed quite empty'.

-0-

CHAPTER SIX

Innocent or Guilty

On Monday, March 25, 2 P.M. sharp, the second week of the trial began.

Eyes were bright; everyone seemed to have had a good rest. Even Marcel looked better. Walking into the courtroom, the yellow colour had gone from his face.

Renée Guschinov was first on the witness stand. She was dressed from head to foot in black and she pulled nervously at her hair; the hair cascaded onto her shoulders from underneath a small black hat. She spoke of how Marcel had told her husband that he would see to everything with regard his flight from France. They had to buy some very expensive jewellery he was to take with him to Argentina. On the doctor's recommendation her husband had also taken three mink pelts with him; the doctor had suggested those could be sold to finance a new fur shop. Joachim had been worried about having to be vaccinated.

"Worried?" scoffed Marcel from his box. "I'd been injecting him for two years! Did he ever tell you what his ailment was?"

Maître Archevêque, Renée's lawyer, duly objected.

"Oh come on!" shouted Marcel. "Guschinov had no reason to be worried about me injecting him! But these stories of injections are newspaper inventions. There are no vaccination requirements for travelling to Argentina. In any case, the witness is lying!"

Leser pointed out that Renée was under oath: she was not allowed to lie.

"No! She is not under oath! She's an interested party in this trial, and she can't take the oath!" Marcel corrected him.

Marcel was right. Renée, also bound to request compensation for the loss of her husband - her livelihood - had also not been asked to take the oath. Neither would any of the other relatives still to give evidence.

Leser, embarrassed, turned red in the face.

Renée went on to explain that Marcel had also told her husband that he would have to wait for three days somewhere in Paris in a safe house before he could set off. She would dearly have loved to have stayed there with him, but the doctor would not hear of it.

"Having to stay somewhere safe for three days seems illogical. He lived across the street from your practice, and could have seen you whenever necessary," said Archevêque to Marcel.

"On the contrary, it was quite logical. I could not have taken care of him at Rue de Caumartin. I was too busy. And my wife was there and my child. And my maid. And patients were always in my waiting room. I can invite the jurors to come see my apartment for themselves, but I won't, not after the mess I understand that had been made on Friday at my Rue le Sueur house. Never will I allow anyone into a property of mine again!" replied Marcel.

Archevêque questioned Marcel about Guschinov's suitcase found at the townhouse.

"I was the one who showed the police the suitcase!" Marcel pointed out angrily. "It showed that I had nothing to hide from the police!"

The suitcase, he explained, would have been far too big and heavy for the furrier to have carried on such a long journey; he had given him a smaller one and his had remained at the townhouse.

Archevêque smiled.

"You are, indeed, an intelligent fellow, Petiot!" he said.

Petiot too smiled.

"*Maître*," he said, "intelligence is a matter of comparison!"

Archevêque asked Marcel about the letter Guschinov had supposedly written to him on the letterhead paper of the Buenos Aires hotel, Alvaer Palace.

"I gave her that letter and all the others," said Marcel.

He pointed at Renée.

"He did not," she said.

"There she goes again - lying!" retorted Marcel.

"Yes, she's lying. In fact, everyone's been lying," said Floriot.

Turning to Renée, he asked why she had not gone to Argentina.

"I was… not well. I also had the business…"

"What she had was a lover! That's what!" snapped Petiot.

"But you had faith in Dr Petiot?" Floriot asked.

"I had faith in him, yes."

"You told the police you did not go with your husband because you did not have faith in Dr Petiot."

There was an awkward silence, but Renée gathered her wits.

"I was not well, *Maître*, so I could not go," she replied quietly.

Floriot returned to the subject of the Alvear Hotel. He asked Dupin whether the Crim had contacted the hotel.

"Mrs Guschinov telegraphed the hotel," replied Dupin.

"But were police inspectors sent to Buenos Aires to search for Guschinov?" he insisted.

"As I said, Mrs Guschinov telegraphed ..."

Floriot interrupted him: "Was a photograph sent to the hotel for the staff to see if they could identify Guschinov as a client?"

"It's all in the dossier, *Maître*," said Dupin.

"There is nothing on it in the dossier," insisted Floriot, and added, "You had plenty of time since October 1944 to look for Guschinov," referring to Marcel's October 1944 arrest.

"You are trying to impress the jury again, *Maître*," reprimanded Dupin.

"I am only trying to establish if any effort had been made to find Guschinov," responded Floriot.

"Well, *Maître*," said Dupin, "I do not have to answer your questions. I am not the one who is in the dock here."

"So, I will answer my question myself! No, you have not done a damn thing to look for Guschinov!"

Weakly, Leser intervened: "Let us send a telegram."

There were more roars of laughter from the gallery and Leser had to call for order.

When calm was restored, Floriot continued: "In any case, no one is dead or missing..."

An audible gasp from the gallery silenced him.

"*Maître*, you were saying," said Leser, mischievously. "You were interrupted, but do please finish your sentence. The court would like to know what you mean."

"I was saying that no one is dead or missing..."

That time a voice shouting from the gallery silenced him.

"Shame on you!"

Leser called for order.

"*Maître*, please finish your sentence," he said again.

Floriot held up a hand to show that he wished the public not to interrupt him again.

"What I meant was that, as the court had not looked for Mr Guschinov, it cannot declare him dead, or even missing. But do please send your telegram to Argentina so that we can see what reply you will receive."

He sat down.

Gilberte Mouron, Mrs Mallard's daughter was the next witness. She said she could not understand why she had been called as a witness because this was a case that had nothing to do with her. Haltingly, she explained that her mother had not sent Lili to Marcel for an abortion; Lili, a friend, had fallen ill with pneumonia while staying over and her mother had called a doctor - Dr Petiot.

"I don't know anything of my mother having carried out abortions. She was in her eighties... You don't really think that she... a woman in her eighties... would have had the strength for something like that, do you?" she wanted to know.

Michel Cadoret de L'Epinguen - he was the man who had handed half of a 150,000 francs fee over to Marcel - was the next witness.

"Was the money returned to you?" Marcel asked him immediately.

"My wife and I thought that a real Resistance hero would not have asked for money in the first place!" he replied.

"But was the money returned to you?" Marcel insisted.

"Eryane Kahan returned the money."

"So what's your problem? How much was it by the way?"

"I can't remember."

"Well, think about it, because this is important. It was what had saved your life!"

The public groaned. Some people hissed.

Marcel began to try to explain what he had meant.

He looked into the gallery.

"I suspected that Cadoret was Gestapo - he'd come to me via Kahan. But then he squabbled over the fee, and I knew that he couldn't be Gestapo. They would have given him whatever he needed! Knowing he was not Gestapo, I called his execution off."

Cadoret turned to Leser.

"Mr President, he told us that he was going to give us injections that would make us invisible to the eyes of the world."

Hearing that Marcel screamed with laughter; he slapped the sides of his box.

"Invisible to the eyes of the world! That's something to dream of!"

The public laughed with him.

"I hope that we will be seeing Mrs Cadoret. How is she?" Marcel asked Cadoret, before the latter, without replying, left the witness stand.

A Joseph Scarella, a restaurant chef, was next to step up to the witness stand. He had been scheduled to be transported to Germany for forced labour, but a certificate from Marcel certifying that he had syphilis had prevented him going. He started by explaining he had sought guidance from Floriot on what to say in the witness box and that Floriot had replied, "Just let your conscience guide you."

Marcel was nodding.

"That certificate I gave you was a fake, was it not?" he asked Scarella.

Scarella turned scarlet.

"I certainly hope so!"

Some women in the gallery giggled.

"And I saved your life," observed Marcel.

Scarella said that Marcel had, indeed. He recounted how Marcel had offered to help him and his wife leave France at a fee of 100,000 francs and some jewellery.

"Petiot said that I should make sure I brought my wife along or, as he said to me, 'she might just bother me'. I wanted to take up the doctor's offer, but my wife wouldn't allow me to do so."

A Mr Masseur, 83, a retired teacher from La Neuville-Garnier, the Hotins' village, was next.

"I know everything that goes on in the village. I've been living there for 23 years, you know. I was there when little Lili was born. I've known her all her life," he began.

"Do you mean Denise?" Dupin asked him.

Masseur nodded.

"We all called her Lili. She was such a cute little thing. She was bareheaded when she left... She didn't take anything with her. If you heard all the rumours in the town ..."

"It must be a very nice town - La Neuville-Garnier!" observed Leser, well aware that Lili Hotin had gone to live in the village only after she had become a Hotin.

"Very nice it was," agreed Mr Masseur.

As he kept on staring at Marcel, Leser asked him not to do so.

"Look at the court, please, *Monsieur*, when you reply to a question," said Leser.

"The court? What court?" queried the old man.

"Don't worry about it, *Monsieur*," said Leser kindly.

"*Bon!*" replied he.

Leser asked if there was anything else that Masseur wanted to say.

"Yes," he replied. "I can tell you whatever you like. Twenty-three years I've lived in the village. I know the Hotins... They insulted my son."

"But is there anything else you want to tell us that concerns the Petiot Case?"

"Yes, whatever you wish me to say, I'll say," he replied.

Leser had obviously had enough of that particular witness.

"Oh, remove the witness from the stand!" he ordered.

Exasperated, he announced a recess until the next afternoon.

* * *

The newspapers of Tuesday, March 26 promised that the day would be fascinating; the experts - Dr Paul, the Drs Piedelièvre and Dérobert, the Prof Henri Grippon of the Quay's Department of Toxicology, Edouard de Rougemont, France's most prominent graphologists who had also analysed the handwriting of murderer Eugène Wiedmann, as well as several psychiatrists were to give evidence.

The gallery was packed. Many had had to argue their way into the courtroom; they had bought invalid invitations from touts. Some had even tried to enter with invitations that a *clochard* – tramp - had forged. So perfect was his imitation of Leser's signature that journalists would describe him as 'as good a forger as Petiot'.

Dr Paul, in a grey tweed suit, a white handkerchief in his top pocket, was first to take the stand. In front of him lay a report of five hundred pages he, and the Drs Piedelièvre and Dérobert with Prof Grippon had drawn up. He read out a list of the human remains found at the townhouse. One of the policemen guarding Marcel began to swallow air, as if trying not to vomit. The CME noticed the man's discomfort; indifferent, he continued with his testimony. He described how the victims' heads had been scalped. How the facial skin had been ripped off with one movement and in one piece, from the chin to the hairline. How the lips, noses and ears had been cut off.

"Petiot dissected perfectly," he observed casually.

Marcel beamed on hearing the compliment.

So did Floriot.

"I would like to point out that Dr Petiot never took a dissection course at medical school," said Floriot.

He was pleased that someone had at last said something flattering about his client.

"What a pity that he had never taken a dissection course, because, even without it, he had dissected perfectly," continued Dr Paul.

"I beg your pardon, Doctor, but you should say 'the dissector dissected perfectly'," Floriot rebuked Dr Paul.

Dupin asked Dr Paul how many bodies there had been.

"Who knows, but we were able to reconstruct ten bodies. But, taking into consideration the smaller bones and the hair, there had been many, many more victims."

"Were you able to determine the sex of the victims?"

"We found an equal number of males and females. The tallest of the males was 1.80 metres tall. The shortest of the females, one metre three."

"Their ages?"

"We could not establish that, but there was no grey hair."

"Were you able to determine the dates of the death of the victims?"

"We had not been able to do so because of the quicklime and the burning."

"What about the cause of death?" asked Floriot. "Were you able to determine the cause of death?"

"No. I am afraid we were not able to determine the cause of death. We did eliminate a fatal blow to the head as a cause of death, because the skulls were not fractured. But we could not exclude stabbing, strangulation or asphyxiation. Or poison. Or they might have been injected. But there was no way that we could determine how the victims had died and I am not in the habit of revelling in hypotheses. But we did find small puncture marks in the victims' thighs. When a post-mortem is performed on a body, one sticks the scalpel into the thigh to be able to find it quickly again. That is what I teach all my students. One used the thigh as a pincushion, so to speak," explained Dr Paul.

Floriot continued: "Weren't similar cadavers found in the Seine in the course of 1942?"

"Yes, indeed. Between May 1942 and January 1943, thirteen cadavers similarly dissected had been fished from the Seine. Those cadavers had been carved up most skillfully. I said to myself at the time that only a medical person could have done it. I'd even wondered whether one of my students might be the killer."

Marcel was scribbling in a notepad; he seemed to have no interest in Dr Paul's testimony.

Drs Dérobert and Piedelièvre would confirm their colleague's testimony.

"The bodies were so putrefied and damaged by the quicklime and the burning that it was impossible to establish the time of death," said Piedelièvre.

Marcel stopped scribbling and looked up at Piedelièvre.

"But isn't there a method of using insect larvae during a post-mortem?" he asked.

"Yes, there is. The size of the diptera on the remains gives one a fairly accurate idea of how long they had been feasting on the flesh. But, in this particular case, the quicklime and the fire had destroyed the diptera as well."

"I would like, if I may, to drop by at your place after the trial to discuss this further," came from Petiot.

Dr Piedelièvre did not reply; but he grinned.

Prof Grippon gave evidence next. He said tests that had been carried out on the human remains had failed to find poison.

"But this does not mean that the victims had not been poisoned - poisoned with gas, because the triangular room might have been a gas chamber."

Floriot jumped up.

"I wish to point out that there was a large gap under the door of the triangular room."

"It could have been stopped up with a rug or something," argued Grippon.

"That is a hypothesis, unless you can produce the rug," replied Floriot.

Dupin asked what kind of gas could have been used.

"Any kind could have been used, but not domestic gas. In that case, there should have been a gas outlet in the room, and there wasn't."

He pointed out that the police had found 504 phials of morphine at the Rue de Caumartin apartment.

Petiot interrupted him: "Hey, I used morphine for painless childbirth!"

"Did you find any poison at the apartment?" Floriot wanted to know from Grippon.

"Only the morphine," he replied

"Morphine is not a poison," stated Floriot.

"*Maître*, that depends on the dose," replied the professor.

"Was there any morphine at Rue le Sueur?" was Floriot's next question.

Prof Grippon said that there was not.

"Interesting," mused Floriot. "No morphine at Rue le Sueur. No poison at Rue le Sueur. Nothing to block that opening under the door of the triangular room. Nothing at all!"

Prof Jean Gouriou, Director of Villejuif Psychiatric Hospital and one of the three psychiatrists who had examined Marcel on Commissioner Desvaux's request, was next to take the stand.

"Petiot is not a madman. He is perverse, amoral and a simulator," he stated.

"He was a brilliant student," said Floriot in a sing-song voice.

"I have it here in the dossier, yes, that he was a good doctor. But it is known that mental disorders in doctors make them become extremely devoted to their patients - which Petiot was."

"Did he try to pretend to be insane when you examined him?" asked Floriot.

"No, but he lied on several points. But not on that one, I must say."

"In your report on my client, you expressed the view that there was something mysterious about how he had completed his medical studies. Do you know the grades he had received?"

"As I'd said," said Gouriou, "he was not mediocre as a doctor. And

371

there remains a mystery about where he had studied medicine."

"Mediocre in dissection, was it?" asked Floriot.

The public roared with laughter.

"He received a notation of very good for his thesis, but I must point out that one can buy a thesis any day anywhere. He did not sit for any examination anywhere, and another thing, a thesis is based on memorisation from text. It does not testify to the true value of a man of medicine."

"You are making many insinuations, Professor. Of all what you had said there, you have no proof. But did you examine Petiot's family? Did you examine his sister? And how did you find her?"

"She is quite normal," replied Prof Gouriou.

"Are you certain?" asked Floriot.

"As certain as anyone could be after a brief psychiatric examination of a subject," confirmed the professor.

Floriot chuckled. "Professor," he said. "Petiot does not have a sister."

Gales of laughter chased Prof Gouriou from the witness stand - and the courtroom.

Edouard de Rougemont, the graphologist, took the stand. A tall man with an untidy grey beard, he explained about his study of the handwriting in the letters Van Bever, Mrs Khaït, Lili Hotin and Dr Braunberger had written.

"All were written under extreme agitation. The letters were either dictated or the writer was under some kind of constraint. Or the writer could have been drugged," were his first words.

"And you could tell that just from the handwriting?" asked Floriot.

"A good graphologist can delve into a man's soul," stated de Rougemont.

"Really?" asked Floriot.

The people giggled.

De Rougemont, unperturbed, continued, "A good graphologist can even tell whether the writer was lying or telling the truth."

"Read this and tell me what it tells you," demanded Floriot.

He wrote something on a sheet of paper and passed it to the graphologist who started to read what he had written.

"Read it out loud so that the jury can hear it," instructed Floriot.

De Rougemont blushed.

He read out: "Mr de Rougemont is a great scholar who never makes a mistake."

"Now, what I wrote there, would you say it's the truth or a lie from my handwriting?" asked Floriot.

De Rougemont failed to reply; he too was laughed from the witness stand.

"We should have got my client to write his life story, and then Mr de Rougemont could have told us what was true and what was false, and we could have dispensed with this trial," muttered Floriot.

* * *

The experts, having given their testimonies, the day's last witnesses were to be the three resisters - Yonnet and Brouard who had interrogated Marcel shortly after his arrest, and a Mr Vandeuille, standing in for the absent Colonel André Dewavrin.

All three confirmed Marcel had not been in the Resistance and that Fly-Tox had never existed.

The three's testimony gave Véron another opportunity to ask Marcel to tell the court how he had killed his 63 victims.

"That's none of your damn business!" snapped Marcel.

"What did you do with the bodies?" Véron tried again.

"I did not commit those killings!" shouted Marcel in reply.

Véron still would not let Marcel go.

"Petiot, give us details of where you buried the bodies," he asked.

"Go to hell!" shouted Marcel. "But ... you and I will talk of this when I am acquitted!"

Véron tried again.

"Why did the Gestapo let you go when you confessed to having smuggled people from France?"

"The Germans would have shot anyone instantly who had made such a confession," observed Yonnet from the witness stand.

"Mr Yonnet, would you like me to reveal where I'd seen you?" asked Marcel.

"You never saw me anywhere, Petiot! But what place was this? Tell the court. Let us hear it!"

"You played tennis at the Racing Club," said Marcel, nodding with a conceited grin.

"I don't play tennis. And I've never been to the Racing Club," replied Yonnet.

At the mention of Paris's Racing Club those in the gallery looked at one another: all knew that *collabos* used to hang out there.

The next morning newspapers would report that it had not been the trial's longest session, but it had been the most riveting. They would also report some good news for Paris's male population. Charles Luiset, the capital's new prefect, had decided that brothels could remain open despite that the French parliament had voted that they should close on March 31; in other words in six days.

* * *

On days nine and ten of the trial, Marcel's cronies were to give evidence. Had the charges against them not been dropped they would not have been able to do so.

Fourrier was first to take the stand. He insisted he had not sent anyone to Marcel. It was Pintard who had done so. Asked whether he and Pintard had made money from Marcel's escape network, he said no.

"You introduced them to Petiot out of the goodness of your heart?" asked Leser.

"Of course. We only asked each 25,000 francs."

"That's what you call the goodness of your heart?" quipped Leser.

Pintard wore his beret as always; he was asked to remove it. He was hardly more talkative than his friend Fourrier, or rather his former friend. The Petiot Case had ended the friendship.

"I can only say I am deeply sorry I sent those travellers to Petiot," said Pintard.

"I sincerely hope so," responded Leser.

Asked if he had been curious to know whether those he had sent Marcel had arrived safely in Argentina, Pintard said that yes, he had been curious, but the doctor had shown him a letter '*Monsieur* Jo' had sent. The letter had been sufficient proof that all had arrived safely in Buenos Aires.

"Mr Jo had made quite a few grammatical errors. Petiot said that it was obvious that he was not very cultured," said he.

Marcel smiled broadly.

"I wrote that letter myself so that the Gestapo would not become suspicious. I imitated his writing and signature very well," he said.

Neuhausen was next. He was as taciturn as Fourrier and Pintard, but he claimed he had no knowledge of Marcel's activities.

Porchon followed. Asked to take the oath, he explained that he was forbidden to do so. Since Elissalde had released him, he had been convicted in another case; it had robbed him of his civil rights. He also had little to say apart from insisting on his innocence. He also insisted that he was an *entrepreneur*. It drew more laughter from the gallery.

Dressed in a black overcoat, despite the heat in the courtroom, Nézondet was next. Floriot ignored him assiduously. Commenting on that, Nézondet would write in his book: 'Considering me barmy; the defence asked me no questions'.

Nézondet told of how Maurice had confessed to him that he had seen bodies at his brother's townhouse. Maurice had told him about it in July 1943; as all in the well with the Petiot dossier open in front of them realised, his story had changed; he had told Massu that Maurice had told him in December 1943. The discrepancy, accidental or deliberate, was ignored.

He continued speaking.

"I told Maurice 'your brother is a monster', and he said 'no, my brother is ill and he must receive treatment'. He told me that I must keep quiet about what he had told me because we could all be shot. Now he is denying he had ever told me about the bodies."

Maurice was called to the stand. He struggled to rise from his chair; walking to the stand, he dragged his feet. Standing beside Nézondet, the latter towered over him. Marcel's brother wore a grey suit and a black shirt, with a striped beige and blue tie. The suit hung loose.

"Poor fellow," whispered Marcel to Floriot. "I'm not doing so well, but look at him!"

Journalist Albert Palle of the Paris daily *Combat* would describe Maurice: 'He appeared calm but sad, and there was a degree of finesse about his features. Whereas there was a flamboyant, if not diabolical, look on the face of the accused, Maurice Petiot's was without expression. Yet there was in him something savage and cruel. He was an electrician and had obviously not reached the same social level as his brother'.

Leser questioned Maurice about whether he had told Nézondet about the bodies.

"No, I did not tell him anything. The stories he tells he has made up. He never recovered from having been arrested by the Gestapo. He's a good type, though, and he means well."

Maurice had spoken so quietly that Leser had asked him to speak up.

"I can't. I'm sorry. I won't be able to," he had apologised.

'Maurice, facing me, persisted in his denial that he had told me that he had found bodies at Marcel's house. I understood why he did so. He wanted to save the life of his big brother. Who can reproach him? I let it go. I did not have it in me to argue with him', Nézondet would write in his book.

Maître Charles Henry, representing the family of Paulette Grippay, asked Maurice to explain the German uniforms that he had told Nézondet and Massu he had found at the townhouse.

"Did you not find it strange that there should be German uniforms at your brother's house?"

"No," he replied. "I concluded that my brother had eliminated some *Wehrmacht* soldiers. He was in the Resistance. He was a brave man."

"What about the other clothes at the house? What conclusion did you draw about those?" asked the lawyer.

"None."

With that one word reply Maurice walked back to his seat. Almost there, he turned and gave his brother a long, loving look. Marcel lowered his gaze.

Aimée Lesage and Marie Turpault were called next to take the witness stand. Both confirmed Maurice had told Nézondet of the bodies at the townhouse. Lesage also told of how she had accompanied Nézondet to the Petiots' apartment on the night he had told Georgette that her husband had been killing people.

"Mrs Petiot fainted three times, but I could tell she was acting. I am a trained nurse, you see," she said.

René Marie, who, like the Cadoret de L'Epinguen couple, had also planned to take Marcel's escape route, but had decided not to do so, was the day's last witness. He told of how he and his wife had heard that Marcel was a drug trafficker and had decided not to have anything to do with him.

Marcel dismissed Marie with a wave of his right hand.

"I don't remember him and his wife. In any case, what he's been saying is completely uninteresting. But the further we go with this trial, the worse it gets!" he said.

"*Voilà!*" agreed Leser.

He adjourned the session.

* * *

The next afternoon, Eryane Kahan, again in dark glasses, was first to give evidence.

With the same firm, confident gait, she strode across the gallery. She wore the same outfit she had worn on the first day of the trial, but, instead of carrying a muff, she had a large black leather handbag. She hung it over the edge of the witness stand and, like a stripper in a Pigalle nightclub, slowly rolled her white, silk glove off her right hand. She rose the hand, a large red stone in a ring on her pinky, flashing, and took the oath to tell the truth and nothing but the truth.

"I must point out that I am also Petiot's victim," she began.

She had, she said, worshipped Marcel - worshipped Dr Eugène. She had not known his true identity. When she did find out he was *the* Dr Petiot, it had been too late; too late for what she did not stipulate. The Basch couple had also worshiped him; they thought he was God.

"They used to speak of how amazing Petiot was. They used to say, 'This Frenchman comes to the assistance of foreign Jews he does not even know'," she said.

She drew a handkerchief from her purse, lifted her dark glasses and dabbed at her eyes.

Marcel, in his box, wept.

She had more to say once she had recomposed herself.

"I am a Jewess. I also wanted to leave. I had asked Petiot to allow me to leave, but he said I was too valuable to the Resistance. After the Liberation of Paris, I felt hunted like I was a wild beast. I was arrested. I was called a collaborator. A Gestapo informer. I was accused of having recruited victims for Petiot. The most ignoble accusations were made against me."

Journalists would again write of her very sensuous accent.

Dupin, untouched by Marcel's weeping and seemingly un-aroused by

Eryane's accent, asked her if she had received money from the doctor for sending him clients.

"No!" Eryane gasped.

Floriot asked her if she had had a German lover during the Occupation.

"He was Austrian!" she protested.

"So was Hitler, Madame!" retorted Floriot.

The public sniggered.

Dupin had another question; he asked if the Wolffs had been German spies.

"They were Jews. They lived in fear of their lives. They were nice people. They were very scared," she replied.

"In one police document, you are described as a Gestapo informer," said Floriot, remaining seated.

Dupin protested: "*Maître*, the prosecution has a more recent document that proves that the witness had given information to the Resistance. It was information she had received from her German lover."

"Mrs Kahan, did you ever visit the Gestapo's offices?" Floriot asked Eryane, ignoring Dupin's protest.

"It's possible that I might have," she replied.

"Did you walk around Paris in the company of German soldiers?"

"Only when my boyfriend was with them. But *Maître*, I want to say that I do not know of a document identifying me as a Gestapo informer."

"The document's number is 16582. It bears the date, April 3, 1945. Please find it," said Floriot to Leser.

Dupin sighed.

"This is irrelevant, *Maître*, as there are no charges against the witness. If there were, she would not be allowed to give evidence," he said to Floriot.

"It is document 16582, and I think it ought to be found," insisted Floriot.

Dupin scribbled down the number.

Leser told Eryane she could leave the witness stand.

Eryane Kahan's exit from the courtroom was less dramatic than her entrance; she walked fast and kept her head down. Marcel watched her walk away. The three Petiots in the gallery did not; they found something or someone more interesting to look at at the other end of the courtroom.

Dupin said that he had to draw the jurors' attention to a correction Inspector Poirier had filed with regard to the evidence he had given.

"I ought to mention that Inspector Poirier had come to see me after he had given evidence. Something that he had said was not quite correct," he said.

"What nonsense! We have all the facts we need. Whatever he wants to say won't change the facts," snapped Floriot.

"I don't allow myself to speak to you using the tone you have just used when you spoke to me. I might just answer you, *Maître*. And remember, your role is quite different from mine," replied Dupin.

"Obviously! I am your adversary," said Floriot.

Dupin was ready with a response.

"*Maître* Floriot," he said, "your role has no honour whatsoever!"

Floriot jumped up, ready for an argument, but Leser hastily announced a recess of a quarter of an hour.

"No," shouted Floriot. "I want to reply to Dupin's attack on me first!" Leser ignored him.

On reconvening, Dupin was the first to speak. He said he wished to apologise to *Maître* Floriot for what he had said to him. Floriot waved the apology away. Nothing more was said about Inspector Poirier.

* * *

Leser again called Eryane to the witness stand and her second entrance of the day was as humble as her exit had been.

The moment she was on the stand, Marcel jumped up. He held his hands out towards her.

"Tell me, were my hands ever dirty? Did you ever see me with dirty hands?" he hurled at her.

She dropped her eyes and did not reply.

"Maybe that day when I went to Rue Pasquier to meet the Basch couple my hands were not all that clean. My bike had broken down that day. I'd worked on it earlier in the day so that I could go really fast in case I needed to escape. But at least my hands were not dirty because I had raised them to swear allegiance to Pétain!" said Marcel, speaking not to Eryane, but to the judge.

"You are insolent, Petiot!" was the judge's response.

"Towards whom - Pétain?" asked Marcel.

"You are again referring to the fact that judges had to swear allegiance to Pétain. You know very well they had been obliged to do so," said Leser.

"One judge did not! One had refused to do so!" snapped Marcel, hitting the front of his box with the flat of his right hand.

"We will not discuss that now, Petiot," said Leser calmly.

Hastily, he told Eryane that she could leave the witness stand: she had not uttered a word while on it.

* * *

The name of Mrs Gingold, the Romanian dentist who had introduced the Wolffs to Eryane, had been on the list of witnesses, but she had disappeared two months previously.

Ilse Gang and Ginas were present.

Both confirmed Eryane's testimony; the Jewish couples who had gone to Marcel for help to leave France had all been petrified of the Germans.

The two, having little more to say, were dismissed.

A policeman escorted the next witness, Charles Beretta, the stool pigeon, to the witness stand. He had been brought from Fresnes Prison; so had Jean Guélin and Pierre Paul Péhu. The three were being held on the charge of 'intelligence with the enemy' - treason. Guélin and Péhu's two co-informers, Marcel Chantin and Marcel Dequeker, were on the run. As for Jodkum, he had disappeared; presumably he had fled to Germany on the Liberation of Paris. Berger had certainly fled. He would be arrested in Milan in May 1948, but, having lost none of his Gestapo cunning, he was to escape from prison. Having been condemned to death in absentia in France for 'crimes against humanity', he is believed to have died peacefully in Germany in February 1960. Heinz Röthke, Jodkum's superior, had also fled to Germany. Although he had sent 40,000 Jews to Auschwitz between August 1942 and June 1943, the French would not request his extradition; after the war he would practise law in the Bavarian town of Wolfsberg: there he would die in 1966, aged fifty-three.

Beretta, questioned on his role in the disappearance and presumed death of Yvan Dreyfus, claimed innocence. White knuckled, he gripped the witness stand.

"I was caught in the middle," he said.

"Relax, *mon vieux*," said Floriot sarcastically. "We understand exactly how it was!"

Guélin vehemently denied he had been a Gestapo informer. On the contrary; he had been a great resister.

"I had my actors sing *La Marseillaise* in the theatre every night!" he said.

He also claimed that he had tried to save Dreyfus' life by putting him in touch with Marcel.

"I have been looking forward every day to this opportunity to explain my actions to the French people," he said.

"Guélin, you are a traitor!" shouted Marcel, his palor gone and his face the colour of an overripe tomato.

The former theatre director broke down and wept.

"*Bof!*" scoffed Marcel.

Guélin, on leaving the witness stand, said accusingly to Floriot, "You are a lawyer for collaborators and for Germans!"

"Is that why you asked me to represent you in your treason trial?" asked Floriot calmly.

Péhu was next to take the stand. Like Guélin he denied that he had ever been a Gestapo informer; on the contrary, he had been a resister.

"Liar!" shouted Marcel.

Turning to the jurors, he said: "This man broke my nose with his fist at Gestapo headquarters on Rue des Saussaies. He's a traitor!"

Guélin was led away to such hissing and stamping of feet, Leser felt it necessary to adjourn the trial until the next day.

* * *

Friday, at half past one, Péhu took the stand.

He described himself as a great patriot; he had, he said, nothing to say about the Petiot Affair. He was quickly dismissed.

Pauline Dreyfus took the stand. She wore a plain black suit, white blouse and large dark curls of hair were partly hidden under a black woollen hat. Apart from her gold wedding band, her only piece of jewellery was a single string of pink pearls.

"We planned to leave Paris together - Yvan and I. However, Guélin came to fetch Yvan because there was some last formality at Rue des Saussaies. Yvan was going to return immediately, but he did not come back. I never saw him again," she began her testimony.

She denied accusations hurled at her from Floriot and Marcel that her husband had been a Gestapo spy.

She admitted she couldn't remember everything that had happened during those fateful days.

"I was just so happy to have my husband back," she said.

She started to cry; so did many women in the gallery.

"What were those two pledges your husband had to sign? One was that he would not take up arms against Germany again, but what was the other?" asked Floriot, pretending he did not know.

"He had to find out information of a group of people, or of a Resistance organisation that was helping people to flee Occupied France. That was the second condition. Yvan would never have done such a thing. And he was assured that he would be able to tear the two documents up. As for me I was horrified, because his liberation, as I then learnt, was not to be without some conditions. But we were assured those two pledges he had to sign would never be given to the Germans," she said.

"What did it all cost you, Madame?" asked Leser tenderly.

"Four million francs... but that is not important," she said and continued, "Yvan and I - we wanted to go to England. We were going to go to England together, but then Guélin came... and I never saw my husband again."

She again started to cry and again some women in the gallery wept with her.

Maître Véron rose. He had a telegram he wanted the prosecution to read. It had arrived in the morning. It was from Pierre Mendès-France, the French politician; he had been with General de Gaulle in London. 'I have learnt with regret that Petiot dared to vilify the memory of Yvan Dreyfus. Petiot's insinuations are unacceptable to those of us who knew the courage, patriotism and goodness of heart of Yvan Dreyfus.' Pierre Mendès-France had written.

On entering the courtroom, Pauline Dreyfus had ignored the group of Petiots sitting in the gallery, and, leaving the courtroom, she did so again.

She also did not look at Marcel; she had not looked at him while she was giving evidence. Not even once.

Fernand Lavie, Mrs Khaît's son, was the next witness. He said that his mother had never told them she wanted to leave Occupied France; her disappearance was inexplicable.

Floriot asked him about his half-sister, Raymonde Baudet.

"Where is she now?" asked Floriot.

"I don't know. I've lost touch with her," replied Lavie.

"Where's your stepfather?" asked Floriot.

"I don't know," replied Lavie.

"Do you know that your mother was seen in Vichy-France a year after she was supposed to have disappeared?" was Floriot's next question.

"I did not know that, no," replied Lavie.

Marcel turned to Leser.

"Oh, those are a whole lot of witnesses you won't be able to call! Are we to conclude that they are dead? Were they murdered, do you think?" he asked sarcastically.

Leser ignored him.

Dupin did so too, but he asked Lavie: "Do you know…? Do you think your sister is in Paris?"

"I have no idea where she is," said Lavie.

"She must surely know what is going on here in the Assize court and that her presence would be welcomed," said Dupin.

Lavie shrugged.

"I don't know where she is. I can't help you there," said Lavie apologetically.

On that tone, the eleventh day of Marcel's trial ended.

* * *

It was Saturday again.

Like the previous Saturday, many Brits were in the courtroom.

Mrs Braunberger, a large woman with a double chin and stiffly-curled grey hair, was to be first to give evidence. Extremely short-sighted, she allowed a policeman to guide her to the witness stand.

She told how she had identified her husband's shirt and hat; the two items, having been missing, had been found and lay on the small table in the well where Estébétéguy's suitcase had stood a few days previously.

Leser ordered a policeman to hand the shirt and hat to her; she lovingly pressed them against her.

"This was the shirt and the hat my husband wore that morning I had seen him for the last time," she said.

Her voice was thick with emotion.

Maître Perlès, representing her, asked Marcel how the shirt and hat had ended up at his townhouse.

"The moment had come for me to ask you that question," he said.

"It might have, but the moment has not come for me to reply to it," replied Marcel.

Leser turned to Marcel.

"Petiot, I suggest that you reply."

"When all the other witnesses have been heard, yes, then I will reply," Marcel told him.

"Petiot, I order you to reply now!" insisted Leser, raising his voice.

Marcel shook his head.

"Petiot, your refusal to reply proves your guilt," intervened Dupin.

Marcel laughed.

"I will reply. I told you I will reply. I will do so in half an hour. I'm not bound to go anywhere now, am I?" he said.

He insisted on being allowed to study the two items for himself. After he had done so, he said quietly, as if speaking to himself, "I had no earthly reason for killing that old Jew. He had no money on him when he set off, so the prosecution's theory I had done him in for financial gain collapses."

Floriot took the shirt and hat from Marcel. He studied both. He pointed out that from what Mrs Braunberger had told Massu, her husband wore a hat, two sizes smaller, than the hat he was holding. He said the milliner, who, according to her, had made all her husband's hats, had not made that particular hat. That that milliner's label was always in all the hats he made. He held up the hat.

"No label!"

Marcel, suddenly in a fury, jumped up, grabbed the shirt and hat from Floriot and threw them on to Wilmès' lap.

"No hat! No shirt! Case dismissed!" he shouted.

The public jeered and Leser ordered Marcel to sit down; he ignored the order.

"Sit down, Petiot! I'm telling you to sit down!" shouted Leser.

The public jeered louder.

"You had better sit down," one of the policemen standing behind Marcel warned.

Marcel swung round.

The policeman had used the familiar *tu;* that, he had not liked.

"I forbid you to address me as *tu*!" he snarled.

"*Assieds-toi!*" said the policeman. Sit down!

He had yet again used the familiar *tu*.

"Fuck you!" murmured Marcel.

Leser told the policeman who had helped Mrs Braunberger to the witness stand to take her back to the antechamber.

Next he told Marcel to sit down.

Marcel did as he was told.

Mrs Callède, the Braunbergers' maid was next to give evidence. After her it would be Raymond Vallée.

Callède testified Dr Braunberger had not liked Raymond Vallée; it was inexplicable that the doctor would have written to him for him to give a message to Mrs Braunberger.

Vallée disagreed that Dr Braunberger had not liked him; he admitted that they had never really become friends and had never employed the familiar *tu*, but the doctor had not disliked him. He agreed it was inexplicable, in fact, unthinkable, that the doctor would have used *tu* in the letters he had written to him. He said he could not even understand why Dr Braunberger would have written to him in the first place.

"To be exact - we weren't friendly! We weren't that friendly!" he said.

Leser adjourned the court until Monday, April 1 - April Fools' Day.

It was to be the thirteenth day of the trial.

Tarot readers did not fail to notice. They told journalists that they had drawn cards for Marcel. Those predicted a dark day for him.

Floriot hoped it would be the exact opposite; the defence witnesses would be heard.

* * *

Floriot had, since the trial's commencement claimed that he had

385

affidavits from two thousand of Marcel's patients and friends. According to him, all had praised Marcel. They had done so not only for his capability as a medical man, but for his competence as a politician, and his compassion as a human being.

A François Comte, retired Villeneuve-sur-Yonne shopkeeper, and once Marcel's patient, was first to step into the witness stand. He wore his best suit and a beret: he was not requested to remove the beret.

"Petiot was the doctor of the poor. His devotion to us was legendary. Mr President, you do not know Villeneuve-sur-Yonne... There are good people in our village, but bad people, as well, and you can be the one, to one person, and the other, to another. One can just make it clear you support this or that politician, and to someone you will be one of the bad ones. This Petiot Case, if you ask my opinion... it is just a political plot against the doctor. He was a brave soldier in 1914-18. He fought in the Battle of the Dardanelles. He was awarded eighteen medals - one, the Cross of the Orient," he said.

Second on the witness stand was a Claude Pathier, retired from his job as clerk at Villeneuve-sur-Yonne town hall.

"Dr Petiot did amazing things for Villeneuve-sur-Yonne. No one had done anything like it for us before him or since he has left. He gave us a sewage system. He had a school built for our children - and he had the old school fumigated because tuberculosis had broken out there in the past."

"Why was he dismissed, then, as Mayor?" asked Dupin.

"Mr Prosecutor, you are asking me a political question now, and I will give you a political reply. Villeneuve-sur-Yonne is a political hotbed. The most lukewarm radical is called a communist there!"

"For 45 months, he treated one of the villagers who had fallen from a poplar tree without having charged the man a *sou*!" said a Mrs Davy; she had worked in the Villeneuve-sur-Yonne post office.

Another of the villagers testified that Marcel had been his family doctor since 1920.

"My son, who is 16 today, is alive only because of him."

No one asked him what his son had suffered from.

Jeanne Husson, another villager, said Marcel had saved the life of a little boy who had a large growth on his head. The boy's parents had been told by Paris doctors that they should take their son home, he was dying. Back in the village they had taken the boy to Marcel and he had put an ointment on the growth, an ointment he had made. Three hours later the growth had gone. It never returned.

Another villager, a Jacques Fritsch, said a neighbour of his had been sent home from hospital to die. Marcel had gone to see the dying man.

"With his usual brusque manner, the doctor told my neighbour's wife 'a day more or a day less; what does it matter? I've got something new to give him. It can carry him off in a second, but it might just cure him. You choose'. My neighbour's wife had chosen to try Dr Petiot's medication. He had then given my neighbour several injections and far from dying - he recovered!"

A Paris witness said that, when poverty prevented him from accepting the treatment Marcel had offered him, the doctor had told him, 'who is talking of money here'. Marcel had then treated him free of charge.

The most valuable witnesses were Lt Richard LHéritier and Roger Courtot, the two resisters who had shared Marcel's cell in Fresnes, and Miss Germaine Barré who had witnessed his outburst when offered his freedom by Yodkum.

Lhéritier - from Fresnes he had gone to Ravensbruck - cut a dashing figure in the black uniform of a French paratrooper.

"Dr Petiot was both courageous and witty," he said.

"You who have spent very many months with my client; do you think he could have hidden his true nature?" asked Floriot.

"I don't think that someone could have been fooled through five months by a cellmate," he replied.

Asked what he made of Marcel's current situation, he said: "If you want to know my opinion? One - I believe that he did not act alone. I also believe he is perfectly capable of sacrificing himself for a cause. Two - I believe he was with some French political group - not the Resistance, but some other political group. Three - I believe he carried out their orders as he had understood them. Four - I believe the political group is now refusing to come forward to support him because it fears voters' reaction."

"Do you think that I worked for the Gestapo?" Marcel asked him.

"Absolutely not! Never!" replied LHéritier.

Turning to the jury, he said, "Gentlemen, no matter what the outcome of this trial, I will always be honoured that I have shared a cell with the doctor."

Floriot also asked Roger Courtot if he thought that Marcel could have disguised his real character.

"No! One cannot lie for 78 days and 78 nights. Besides, Dr Petiot hated the Germans," replied Courtot.

Barré, pretty and elegantly dressed in a suit and frilly blouse and bonnet, made it clear she had volunteered to give evidence for the defence.

"I've read in certain newspapers that Petiot was being accused of having collaborated with the Germans, and I've come to tell you this could not have been. When Jodkum asked him if he would be willing to pay 100,000 francs to be released, he replied angrily, 'I don't give a shit whether you condemn me or not. I have stomach cancer and I'm not going to live very long anyway. So do with me whatever you wish. But don't do me any favours'," she said.

She added that she had overheard Jodkum telephone Maurice to ask whether he would pay 100,000 francs to secure his brother's release.

"Do you remember if Jodkum asked me to promise that I would not fight against Germany again?" Marcel asked her.

"Doctor," she said, smiling dazzlingly at Marcel. "I can remember everything I heard in that office. You refused to make any deal with the Germans."

Turning to the jury, she added: "The doctor was insolent... very arrogant in his dealings with Jodkum. He made Jodkum understand what a low opinion he had of him."

Leaving the witness stand, she gave Marcel another smile and the thumbs-up sign. It was too much for him; he burst into tears. Even Floriot was moved. He blinked behind the thick lenses of his glasses.

Tuesday, the public gallery was almost deserted. Journalists had reported that the civil suit lawyers would be endeavouring to establish Marcel's guilt so that their clients could claim restitution and no one wanted to hear what they would be saying. Even Marcel seemed to lack interest; no sooner did the first of the lawyers, *Maître* Archevêque - representing Renée Guschinov - start to speak than he leant his head against the back of his box and closed his eyes. Floriot also prepared for a nap. He took his glasses off, put them on his lap and closed his eyes.

Archevêque said that he did not believe Joachim Guschinov was in

388

Argentina; the furrier had never reached that country, or any other. He was murdered at Rue le Sueur. Sitting up abruptly, Floriot wanted to know if, as he had requested, the prosecution had sent the telegram to Hotel Alvear Palace in Buenos Aires to enquire about Guschinov's whereabouts. Dupin admitted the telegram had not been sent.

Véron was next to speak on behalf of Fernand Lavie; he would also still speak on behalf of Pauline Dreyfus.

He accused Marcel of having brutally slaughtered Mrs Khaît to silence her.

"It was but a banal case, but Mrs Khaît was a threat, so he murdered her," he said.

Floriot closed his eyes again. Marcel's were still closed.

Defending Mrs Braunberger, Perlès spoke next. He called for Marcel's execution because there wasn't the least doubt that he had murdered Dr Braunberger. Floriot opened his eyes slightly and peeped at Perlès. Marcel continued to sleep, or to pretend to.

Leser recessed the court for twenty minutes.

Maître Stefanaggi, representing the Piereschi family, was the first to speak on the court reconvening. Marcel and Floriot closed their eyes yet again. Stefanaggi said there was no doubt Marcel had killed Piereschi; he did not try to defend Piereschi's criminal activities.

Next, *Maître* Andrée Dunant, dark-haired, slim and attractive, was to speak on behalf of Gisèle Rossmy's family.

Marcel and Floriot opened their eyes and straightened up. The men in the gallery were already sitting up straight at the sight of an attractive young woman.

"There is no justifiable cause for the murder of Miss Rossmy. As we had heard Petiot say, there was nothing else he could have done with her but kill her. That's assassination!" she said.

Next to speak was *Maître* Charles Henry, representing the family of Paulette Grippay. Henry, a man with black-dyed hair, pushed out his chest.

"I am here today," he began, "to shed light on this affair. No one has understood this trial... not the prosecution, or the public. Petiot is even guiltier than any of you think!"

He spoke with the rolled 'r' regional accent of his native Marseilles; the public giggled at it and even Marcel smiled.

Leser called for order.

"Get on with it, *Maître*!" he ordered.

Henry described Marcel as having been part of a 'Nazified faunae that inhabited the outskirts of the Gestapo'.

"Nazified faunae?" queried Floriot from his seat.

"But what about your client, *Maître* Henry?" asked a bemused Leser.

Henry rambled on.

"Petiot worked for an anti-French organism operating on the fringe of the Gestapo to defend the interests opposed to this latter entity."

"Meaning, *Maître*?" asked Floriot.

"Seen in this light, of course, the whole trial becomes perfectly clear," replied Henry.

"Meaning, *Maître*?" Floriot asked yet again.

The public laughed. Marcel, Floriot and his 'boys' laughed, too. Elissalde was doubled up trying to disguise a fit of laughter as uncontrollable coughing, and Leser turned bright red in the face trying to suppress his laughter.

"I am explaining what no one has until now explained," said Henry.

Tears of laughter ran down Floriot's face.

"Are you enjoying this spectacle, *Maître*?" asked Henry.

"Leave *Maître* Floriot alone. Rather, finish your summary," cautioned Leser.

"I am finished, Mr President. I have tried amid general incomprehension to explain what no one has explained. I can only ask that the gentlemen of the jury condemn Petiot with full comprehension rather than through not comprehending at all. But I will not insist, Mr President," replied Henry.

It was 7 P.M. Leser adjourned the trial until the next afternoon.

Pierre Scize would describe Marcel Petiot in the morning's *Le Figaro* as having been 'silent, worn out and beaten down', and as having 'the eyes of a night bird', which he said 'were sunken into deep sockets'.

* * *

Wednesday, April 3, was scheduled as the penultimate day of the trial.

On that day Dupin was to summarise the prosecution's case, but four civil lawyers, Bernay, Gachkel, Léon Lévy and Véron, the latter in his capacity as Pauline Dreyfus's lawyer, still had to speak.

They would do so first.

At 1 P.M. Marcel was back in his box.

As on every day, Georgette, Gerhardt and Maurice were in the gallery. It was yet again hot in the courtroom, but Georgette wore a long-sleeved dark-blue winter dress with a matching jacket and hat. Gerhardt wore a light-grey suit and a dark-blue tie. Maurice, also in a light-grey suit, sat slumped in his chair. His arms were folded over his stomach. He was in pain. Georgette had suggested he should miss the session, but he had insisted on accompanying her and his nephew.

Maître Bernay spoke first.

Extra chairs had been brought in, so many had turned up for the day's hearing, but there seemed little interest in what Bernay was saying; many walked out.

Next, *Maître* Gachkel spoke.

Then, *Maître* Léon Lévy.

There was also little interest in what they said.

Even the prosecution's attention wandered. Elissalde fiddled with papers on the table in front of him; Leser stared at the tapestries on the walls as if he had not seen them before.

The jury also fiddled with papers; one kept on wiping his brow with the back of his hand.

Marcel and Floriot dozed off.

Shortly after 4 P.M. Véron rose to speak.

The prosecution straightened up, those in the public who had walked out ran back; they did not want to miss hearing what he had to say.

The commotion woke Marcel and Floriot.

Véron did not dwell long on Yvan Dreyfus' fate; he spoke of what Marcel's fate should be. He began by telling the story of the 'ship wreckers of legend' who had placed lanterns on the cliffs to lure ships ashore in order to rob the seafarers.

"Petiot was just like that. The ship wreckers filled their coffers with the spoils of their foul deeds. He filled his coffers with the spoils of his foul deeds. He lured the desperate, the frightened, the already hunted to his lair, and there, he profited from mankind's natural instinct of self-preservation, and murdered them. No, Petiot was never connected to the Resistance. You condemn him to death! Death must be his end!" he said.

He ended by speaking of the Nazis' death camps.

"I do not know if some of Petiot's victims did work for the Gestapo, but, if they did, he did not know it. Therefore, their ashes will join those of the dead of Auschwitz and Dachau. The smoke from Rue le Sueur has joined those of the crematoriums of the Nazis' death camps."

He returned to his seat amid applause.

Marcel, his eyes bulging, jumped to his feet.

"Yob!" he shouted at Véron.

"Petiot, I will be at your execution," said Véron calmly from his seat.

Floriot touched Marcel's arm and told him firmly to sit down and to keep quiet.

Dupin rose to begin his summary.

It was nearing 5 P.M.

Marcel sat slumped in his chair; Floriot in his. Floriot's 'boys' kept their eyes down. Maurice coughed into his cupped hands. Gerhardt was looking at his mother; she stared straight ahead of her.

"Not for a hundred years has there been recorded in the archives of the Assize court of the Seine a case more horrible than this one. Even the horrendous crimes of Landru have been surpassed. Petiot was not in the Resistance. He was a gangster, a simulator, an illusionist, an impostor, a liar. He is a criminal and an assassin. Landru killed seven. Petiot killed twenty-seven. He killed men ... women... a child... to rob them. It will take me five minutes to show that everything he has said is a web of lies. His cover story that he had passed those who had gone to him on to others and that he did not know what had happened to them afterwards does not carry any weight," said Dupin.

At 7 P.M, some two hours later, he was still talking.

"Eryane Kahan," he said. "She was a member of the Gestapo…"

Eryane was in court. Yet again dressed as on her two previous appearances, and again wearing dark glasses, she jumped up and protested loudly.

"I was in the Resistance! The Resistance! The Resistance!"

She wanted Dupin to withdraw what he had said. He did.

"That was merely an assumption, because, contrary to the accusations of the defence counsel, Mrs Kahan has never been subject to any charges of collaboration. There also exists no file on her, as the defence counsel had claimed. The file the defence had mentioned has been found. This is all that has been noted in it: 'The authorities hereby certify that Eryane Kahan is not sought under any charge by the Department of Justice'."

She would still not sit down. Stamping her feet, she demanded Dupin offer her an official apology. He refused. She insisted. He refused yet again. Exasperated, Leser called a recess.

On the court's return, Dupin immediately returned to the subject of Eryane.

"Why did Petiot not kill her? Why did he not kill her when he was certain she was a Gestapo spy and all the people she brought him were so, too? There is only one answer. Kahan brought him such wealthy clients that he wanted her to continue to do so. She took him nine in the fifteen days from December 15, 1942 to December 30, 1942. Fifteen days! Nine innocents!"

Eryane did not respond. After Marcel's trial, she would disappear. It would be presumed that she had left France, that having grown up in Vienna, she had returned there.

Dupin continued.

He said that he was going to go over the deaths of those nine innocents. Leser held up a hand: he said it was late and could they continue the next afternoon. Dupin shook his head. He would prefer to finish his summary. Leser adjourned the court anyway.

In the middle of Dupin and Eryane's heated exchange, Marcel had busied himself drawing caricatures of the members of the prosecution. The caricatures he had passed from Floriot to each of the lawyer's 'boys'. None had shown interest. Angry, he had hurled the drawings to the floor.

The following day, journalists would report that not only had the defence lawyers been boring, but the courtroom had been too hot. And, they wrote, the women's perfume was too strong. The ladies of Paris should be less generous with the Chanel No. 5.

* * *

The next day, Wednesday, April 4, at one o'clock sharp, Marcel stepped into the courtroom. It was to be his sixteenth and, if the jurors did not take their time deciding his fate, final day of trial.

As on the first day of the trial, Marcel wore his grey suit and large purple bow tie. His hair, cut the previous evening, was again heavily oiled and combed back.

Sitting down, he gripped the front ledge of his box.

Anxiously, he sought out his family. Seeing them, he smiled.

Georgette wore a charcoal-coloured suit, a blue floral blouse and the same dark blue hat of the previous day. Earlier, in the corridor outside the courtroom, she had sat down on a bench with Floriot. Twice she had nodded at what she heard him say; she had not spoken herself. Gerhardt and Maurice had stood in thoughtful silence at the other end of the corridor. As female Parisians had not failed to notice, Gerhardt was a handsome young man; he looked like his father - and his uncle. He wore a suit and tie.

The session began with Dupin's continued summary. Marcel had killed for personal gain, he said. Although he stood accused of the assassination of 27 people, he had probably killed many, many more; more even than the 63 he had at one stage of his police interrogation admitted he had ordered his men to execute.

"Rue le Sueur was a murder factory!" he stated.

He continued that Marcel was not insane; three eminent psychiatrists had found him completely sane and responsible for his deeds.

Finally, Dupin turned to Marcel.

"Petiot, no, we will not let you soil the sacred memory of the French Resistance. Your blasphemy has lasted long enough! The hour of judgement rings!"

"Signed - Prosecutor of the Vichy regime!" shouted Marcel from his seat.

"The role of judge does not suit you, Petiot!" murmured Dupin.

"Nor you," retorted Marcel.

He held up one of the caricatures he had drawn the previous day. It was of Dupin. No one laughed.

Neither did Dupin laugh; instead, he swept his eyes over the faces of the jurors.

"Gentlemen of the jury, your conscience and mine are protected. Petiot, the great liquidator of Occupied Paris, the monster of Rue le Sueur, is entirely responsible for his deeds. In the past, I have often hesitated before demanding the death penalty. I do not hesitate to do so today. Let justice follow its proper course. Let Petiot join his victims!"

He sat down. Beads of perspiration had broken out all over his face.

"Thank God that's over," mumbled Marcel. He was ashen, but grinning.

Leser nodded to Floriot; he could begin his plea for his client's life. It was 3 P.M.

That morning, extra chairs had been brought into the courtroom and had been squeezed into the well. On them sat several dignitaries and celebrities; French as well as foreign politicians, French as well as foreign film stars, the writer Colette who was reporting the trial, countesses and counts, princesses and princes. Prince Rainier of Monaco had also turned up again. All wanted to be able to say that they had seen Marcel Petiot in the flesh; seen Marcel Petiot being sentenced to death. As for Marcel, he gave each a long, stern look. Next, he looked towards where his family sat. Georgette sat stiffly in her chair. She clutched a white handkerchief. So did Maurice. He had dark circles under his eyes. Gerhardt's eyes were red. It looked as if he had been crying.

The prosecution's file on Marcel weighed thirty kilograms. Floriot's 'boys' had carried their copy into the courtroom, as they had their own files; those weighed almost as much. Each also had a copy of Floriot's summary and plea for Marcel's life. The document was typed out in single spacing and filled 339 pages. Each page had a left-hand margin of two centimetres.

Floriot was known for his plain speaking; he did not disappoint.

"My adversaries have just spent 15 hours by the clock. I repeat, 15 hours, trying to convince you of Petiot's guilt. Obviously, this case is neither simple nor very clear, but I will not take up that much of your time, rest assured."

He had the habit of drinking a glass of champagne - only ever just one single glass - before he started to plea; he had indulged his habit before he had entered the courtroom.

"Let us return to the Liberation," he continued. "We have the charnel house on Rue le Sueur. Several of the victims were Jews and, therefore, the newspapers insinuated that Petiot was a Gestapo agent. *Voilà* - it was so very simple! Petiot could not of course have been a member of the Resistance, because it would have dirtied the name of the Resistance. Therefore, he had to be the rogue. He had to be accused of every vice on earth. But these accusations crumble when studied against the true facts.

"My client stands accused of having murdered 27 people. Of these 27, he admits having ordered the execution of nine, but he categorically denies having had anything to do with the disappearance of eight. If the prosecution can prove that he killed even just one of those eight people, he should be condemned. As for the other 19, it was for Petiot to prove he had executed members of the Gestapo or Gestapo collaborators. If he had failed to prove this for even one of the 19, then I again say he should be condemned. But remember, by our law, there is no crime or wrongdoing where the crime or wrongdoing has been committed in the interest of France. We will start with the cases that Petiot denies."

He said those were Lili Hotin, Van Bever, Mrs Khaît, Guschinov, Dr Braunberger and the three Knellers. Lili Hotin, an unhappy wife, had one morning set off for Paris. There was no proof of a connection between her and Dr Petiot. As for Van Bever. It was a simple presumption that Dr Petiot had killed him; Van Bever had, in fact, already been assaulted by the brother of one of his former lovers who might finally have done him in. Mrs Khaît? Her own family had manifested no alarm at her disappearance so why should anyone else? Joachim Guschinov? He had safely arrived in Buenos Aires and had written several times from there. Dr Braunberger? The Germans had probably grabbed him off the street, and he had ended up and died in one of the Nazi camps. And Mrs Braunberger, being three quarters blind had made a mistake when she identified a shirt and hat as her husband's. The hat was too large and would have hung over her husband's nose.

"As for the shirt, the moment Mrs Braunberger had been told that a shirt made by 'David from Avenue de l'Opéra' had been found at the townhouse, she said that it was her husband's. She had not even seen the shirt at that stage. She had showed the police shirt cuffs, which she said her husband had always worn with that particular shirt. Because there were four or five buttons on the shirt sleeve and four or five button holes on the cuffs, the police had immediately agreed with her. But the cuffs and the shirt were of different colours."

As for the Knellers, they, too, had written to report the success of their flight.

"My client had risked his life for them. He accompanied them to a photographer to have their photographs taken. They had no money. They were, in fact, in dire straits when Petiot had helped them. The child's pair of pyjamas was at the townhouse only because the family had brought too much for people who had to travel light. And, if Petiot had one of the Knellers' rationing cards, it was because he had given them other identity papers. Those identify papers had, in fact, saved their lives."

The body of a boy of about seven or eight, which had been found in the Seine soon after the Knellers had set off, could have been that of any of 20,000 boys who had disappeared during the War and the Occupation. He said there were also still 60,000 unsolved missing persons cases for Paris alone left over from the dark years.

As for the other 19 cases for which Dr Petiot stood accused, those had been executions and not assassinations. All 19 had been traitors - the Gestapo's valets. Their survival had threatened France.

He went over Marcel's past. He had been a brilliant scholar and medical student, he said. He had been heroic as a Bearded One. He had enjoyed, and justly so, the confidence of the people of Villeneuve-sur-Yonne who had elected him as their mayor and as their regional councillor.

"The accusations that had been made against him in the village had been due to countryside pettiness. Stealing electricity, cans of petrol, and a cross from a cemetery; those were laughable charges."

He did not mention the disappearance of Louisette Delaveau, the murder of Henriette Debauve and the mysterious sudden death of Frascot, and he evinced Marcel's two drug dealing convictions as minor, which the small fines had proved. However, Dr Petiot, he said, had conceded the triangular room had served as a prison cell for some of the executed, but it should be remembered that the executed had been German spies and collaborators. As for Yvan Dreyfus. It had been proved he had agreed to work for the Gestapo.

"Regarding the Basch and Arnsberg couples, I have four receipts from the Wagons-Lits/Cook travel company that show the two couples had twice travelled from Nice to Paris on night trains. This means they had to cross the demarcation line between Vichy and Occupied France twice, and in the most unsafe way possible - fast asleep in train couchettes. So, one cannot really say they were in hiding!"

The clock on the wall ticked over to 9 P.M.

Floriot had been speaking for six and a half hours. His usually loud, bombastic voice had gradually diminished into a croak. He had been able to sit down only twice; each time only for a few minutes during recesses. One of the recesses had been called because a young man in the public gallery had fainted.

Yet, Floriot had not yet said all he wanted to say.

Slowly, he removed his glasses, wiped them, wiped his eyes and his brow; put his glasses back on and turned towards the jurors.

"The truth is that Marcel Petiot was in the Resistance. It has been proved undeniably that he was anti-German. He issued false health certificates to keep French workers from being sent to Germany. He warned his Jewish patients when he had heard there were going to be selections of Jews destined for the camps. There were different ways of having resisted the Germans during the Occupation - official, semi-official, unofficial. Having resisted the Occupation through one's patriotism alone was also a form of Resistance. And, say that this was how it had been with Petiot, who can reproach him for not having joined the official Resistance? Remember that Lt. LHéritier, a patriot, a hero, a survivor of a German concentration camp, swore to you that no matter what your decision would be, he would remain proud for the rest of his life of having been a prison cell companion and friend of Dr Marcel Petiot.

"I also, and despite what your decision is going to be, tell you I will forever remain proud of having defended Dr Petiot before you.

"Gentlemen of the jury, I place him and his future in your hands. Gentlemen of the jury, I ask you to consider the facts and only the facts. Whatever you have been told by the prosecution have been lies. Just lies. All lies. But I do not blame anyone for that being so. I blame the extraordinary epoch we had lived through. Dr Petiot is not a murderer. Ah! He is not an ordinary man. I admit it readily. No, this is not a normal man with normal qualities and normal defaults. No, he brought down his enemies. Our enemies! But do not say he is an assassin. Do not say he is a greedy man. His entire life and every aspect of his behaviour proved the contrary. I place Petiot in your hands, and I have full confidence in you. I know that you will acquit him."

Finally, Floriot had said all he wanted to say. He walked back to his seat. The public gave him a standing ovation. Sensing or imagining hope, Georgette, Gerhardt and Maurice also stood and clapped.

Marcel sat slumped in his chair.

He was crying.

"Petiot, rise please," ordered Leser.

Marcel rose. He tried to stop crying; he swallowed deeply and wiped his eyes against his sleeve.

"Petiot, do you have anything to say to add to your defence?" asked Leser.

"*Non, rien du tout,*" replied Marcel. No, nothing at all.

He looked from Leser to the jurors. He wanted to say something, after all - to the jurors.

Leser nodded his agreement.

"Gentlemen, you are Frenchmen. It has been proved to you that I eliminated agents of the Gestapo. You know what is left for you to do," said Marcel.

He had spoken slowly and softly.

He slumped back into his chair.

His eyes were perfectly empty.

Leser explained to the jurors they were to reply yes or no to five questions for each of the 27 charges of assassination against Marcel Petiot. This meant they would have to deliberate on a total of 135 questions.

The original five questions were:

(1) Is the accused guilty of the murder in Paris or any other place in France of X?

(2) Was the murder of X committed with premeditation, making it an assassination?

(3) Did ambush and confinement accompany the assassination of X?

(4) Did theft of property accompany the assassination of X?

(5) Was there concomitance of (3) and (4) in the assassination of X?

He further explained that the prosecution would need a two-thirds majority of guilty in order to pronounce a death sentence.

* * *

Leser, Meiss and Genot followed the jurors to an antechamber. They would remain with them until they had finished their deliberation.

The door of the antechamber closed; a clock on a wall stood at 9:30 P.M.

Almost immediately, the door swung open again.

Leser stood in the doorway; one of the jurors had complained of feeling hungry. He called over a policeman standing guard; the latter was to go and find food for ten people.

Quickly, a chef at a nearby restaurant threw a meal of *sauerkraut* together. The waiter who brought the food handed the restaurant bill to Leser. He refused to pay.

"The courthouse will settle with you later," he told the waiter.

"*Non, Monsieur. Tout de suite, Monsieur,*" the waiter replied.

He wanted Leser to settle the bill there and then; Leser obliged.

Eighteen months later, he would complain that he still had not been reimbursed.

Journalists, in their morning reports, would not overlook the irony of the jury having enjoyed a German dish.

They would also comment on what Marcel had looked like at the commencement of Floriot's plea for his life. 'Petiot looked as if he could not continue. He looked exhausted. For the first time, there was fear on his face. His face was lined. His skin had a greenish hue'.

They would further report that the relatives of Marcel's victims were displeased at Dupin's remark that Marcel should go join his victims; their murdered relatives were in Heaven.

Dr Marcel Petiot was going to go to Hell.

* * *

Marcel waited for the verdict in a small room down the corridor. Floriot set off to stretch his legs; his 'boys' took turns sitting with Marcel. Georgette, Gerhardt and Maurice set off to a nearby bistro; the bistros had put up signs to say that they would remain open throughout the night.

Half an hour passed. It seemed like a month.

A policeman's head appeared around the door of the room in which Marcel sat. Would he like something to eat? He said no. Although the 'boys' tried to persuade him to change his mind, he said he was not hungry.

A few minutes later, the policeman's head popped around the door again. Would Dr Petiot mind stepping into the corridor to autograph copies of his book?

Yes, he would be delighted to was the reply.

In the week before the trial, Marcel had finished writing his book and Georgette had taken it to a Paris printer, Roger Amiard. The book had been published in its original handwritten form and had appeared on March 18, the opening day of the trial. It was a best seller. It was 350 pages long. It was incomprehensible. It was likened to the Bible; there was one in every home, yet no one could say that they had read all of it or had understood all of it.

Page 137 read: 'I used to tell my son that one had to help unhappy people.

'Taking advantage of my teaching, he would never omit, when we went to a certain town square, to ask me for a *sou* to give to a poor young woman who sold barley sugar.

'Today, barley sugar no longer costs a *sou*, and my son is interested in other young people... but, as Kipling would have said, that is another story.

'One day, I explained that his exchange of a *sou* for a stick of barley sugar wasn't exactly charity, and that he should not really take the barley sugar.

'My son replied quite logically that, if everyone did that, the same barley sugar, which was already not very fresh with all the dust sticking to it, would soon be so disgusting that people would no longer want to go near her. Well, I replied, to bring the conversation to a close, tell her to eat it.

'I forgot the incident and, the next time, my son asked for the usual *sou* and took it to the woman. Unexpectedly, he repeated my exact reply and returned the sugar to the poor woman, who did not understand. 'But keep it, as you've bought it', she said. And I really liked what she said next. 'It's for selling, not for eating...' But as my son insisted, and so as not to displease a customer, she finally bit on the sugar, taking just a small bit that she pretended to enjoy tremendously as if she had never tasted any before... I suspected that she had quite different reasons for her tact, and that she knew perfectly well how and from what they were made. Then she took a few steps away and put the remains of the stick in her pocket.

'On leaving the square half an hour later, the poor young woman was still there. In her basket, there was one stick of barley sugar that was a bit shorter than the others and the end had been refashioned by licking.

'But excuse me for this diversion on 'charity'. I will make no allusion to the self-interested way in which some important personalities practise 'charity' on such women, and I will return to the matter in hand - horse racing'.

Petiot autographed each book pressed into his hands. Even the policemen on duty in the building rushed over with copies. Dr Paul stood nearby. Displeased at Marcel's fame he told journalists that the doctor was France's greatest criminal ever.

At 11 A.M. Marcel told Floriot's 'boys' that he wanted to return to the courtroom; he wanted to await the verdict there.

The courtroom was crowded and had become noisy; although policemen had asked the public to leave, the people had remained seated fearing that should they relinquish their seats, those would be grabbed by others. They were dining from picnic baskets, drinking beer and despite the non-smoking rule, smoking large cigars or puffing on pipes. Marcel ignored it all. He put his head down on the ledge in front of him; within a minute, he was sound asleep.

At 11:50 P.M. word swept through the building that the jury had agreed on a verdict.

Members of the prosecution and the two teams of lawyers hurried back to the courtroom.

Floriot broke with tradition; he drank a second glass of champagne.

Marcel remained sleeping.

Floriot shook him by the arm.

"Petiot, wake up. The verdict's in," he said.

Five minutes later, the jurors filed back in. They did not look at Marcel. They looked at their feet. They had been out for just under three hours. It meant they had spent approximately one minute and 33 seconds on each of the 135 questions. But not even. They had spent some time eating their *sauerkraut*.

Wilmès rose as soon as all were seated. He accepted a roll of paper tied with red ribbon from a member of the jury; the jurors' verdict was written on it. The courtroom was silent. Marcel leant towards the right and slightly to the back to see Wilmès.

Georgette, Gerhardt and Maurice stared at Marcel. Gerhardt held his mother's hand.

The jurors had replied yes to 132 of the 135 questions. The questions they had replied no to concerned Van Bever, Mrs Khaït and Lili Hotin; Petiot had not robbed the first two and he had not wilfully murdered – assassinated - Lili. Therefore, he had been found guilty of the assassination of 26 people.

Leser asked Marcel to rise. He did. His face betrayed not a trace of emotion.

It was thirty-five minutes past midnight; already Thursday, April 5.

Marcel grabbed hold of the side of his box. He fixed his black eyes on Leser. He was ashen. Before the jurors' return, he had slipped back into his grey tweed coat; he had buttoned all of the buttons.

Floriot turned slightly towards Marcel and put his arm on the ledge of the box. He was as ashen as his client.

"Marcel Petiot," said Leser, "you are condemned to die and, as French law demands, your head will be severed from your body."

Marcel was as motionless as a statue.

There was a single gasp in the public gallery. Later, journalists would speculate whether it had come from Georgette, Gerhardt or Maurice.

The photographers burst from their place in the centre of the gallery. Lights started to flash. Leser did not call the photographers to order. It did not seem necessary to do so; the condemned man seemed unaware of their presence.

Floriot announced that he was to appeal the sentence. He had already prepared the necessary papers. He gave them to Marcel to sign. Marcel did so.

What was to happen next?

Marcel frowned; he appeared not to know.

A policeman stepped up to him and whispered something; he nodded and offered his wrists to be handcuffed. The policeman pointed to the door through which he had each day entered the court; the time had come for him to walk through it for a final time.

At the door, Marcel swung around.

"I must be avenged!" he shouted.

Who had he addressed? What had he meant? Journalists would not even try to speculate.

Leser recessed the court. He, Meiss and Genot were to deliberate the amount of restitution the Petiot estate was to pay the victims' families. People in the gallery remained in their seats.

On the three's return - it had taken them only a few minutes to decide - Wilmès read out the amounts; those were based on the victims' estimated financial worth to their families.

"Piereschi - 10,000 francs; Mrs Khaït and Gisèle Rossmy - 50,000 francs; the Arnsberg couple - 80,000 francs; Paulette Grippay and Joachim Guschinov - 100,000 francs; Dr Braunberger - 700,000 francs, and Yvan Dreyfus - 880,000 francs."

The Wollfs' and the Knellers' relatives were to receive nothing.

The Petiot estate was, furthermore, ordered to pay the court costs; those came to 312,361 francs and 50 centimes. Of that amount, the amount of 250 francs was for official stamp duties.

The total amount the Petiot estate - Georgette and Gerhardt - would have to pay out was F2,282,316 francs and 50 centimes. They would pay only a fraction.

Despite the fact that the prosecution had been able to decide the financial worth of Marcel's victims, it had not even attempted to establish how much he had made from those victims.

* * *

As Marcel was being driven back to his cell on La Santé's death row, the cleaners of the Palais de Justice threatened to go on strike unless they were paid extra for the 16 days of Marcel's trial. They complained that because there were so few toilets in the building, people - both men and women - had relieved themselves in the corridors.

* * *

Thursday, May 16, Marcel lost his appeal. Floriot immediately sued Mrs Braunberger and Callède, her maid, for false testimony. He also sued the two jurors who had spoken to the *New York Herald Tribune* for 'defamation of character'.

Thursday, May 23, Marcel lost those cases as well.

There was only one thing left for him to do; wait for *Monsieur Paris* to pay him a visit. He asked Floriot on which day he could expect the visit.

"Promise me you will come and tell me," he requested.

"I will," promised Floriot. "You can trust me."

The condemned were not supposed to know when they were to die.

The following day, early afternoon, Paul Cousin, one of the 'boys', walked into Marcel's cell. Marcel, not allowed visitors - not even Georgette - was glad to see him.

"Sit down," he said to Cousin.

He swept some papers off the bed to make space.

Cousin sat down, his eyes on the floor; he could not look Marcel in the face. He cursed himself for his weakness. He had driven around the prison twice before he had found the courage to pull up.

"You've come... because...?" asked Marcel.

"It's for tomorrow," Cousin blurted out.

Finally, their eyes met.

"Very well," said Marcel. "Now let's drop the subject!"

'If *Maître* Floriot had been able to plead each of the 27 cases separately and each time to a different jury, he would have succeeded in having Petiot acquitted. It was only the numbers of victims that brought Petiot down', a journalist would write.

* * *

Once Cousin had left, Marcel lay down on his bed.

He started reading.

Next, he did some embroidery.

Then, he packed away the embroidery materials and books that were lying around. Because he tidied up his cell every night - he, the man with the reputation of being untidy - the warders did not suspect he knew of his imminent death.

Marcel slept well that night. The warders looked in on him several times. Each time they saw that he was, or appeared to be, lost in sleep. He had worked out a way how he could be as comfortable as possible despite the handcuffs and the leg irons by lying on his back, his legs stretched out and his arms crossed.

He had written in 'Chance Defeated':

'Not one of all the creations is happy with its lot. The stone is sad thinking of the oak that grows in the sun. The oak is sad when it thinks of the animals that it sees running in the shade of the woods. The animals are sad dreaming of the eagle soaring into the sky. And man is unhappy because he cannot understand why he has been put here... He is aware of all his imperfections.'

-0-

CHAPTER SEVEN

Death

At 3 A.M. on Saturday, May 25, several police vehicles - several black or grey *traction-avant* Citroën cars, a red ambulance and a grey Citroën box-shaped police van drove towards Rue de la Santè.

At the same hour, other such police vehicles, their sirens tearing up the silence of the night, sped in the direction of the commune of Kremlin-Bicêtre. There, just south of the capital, on April 15, 1792, in a basement room of a hospice, the guillotine, a more practical version of the thirteenth century Halifax Gibbet, the wooden structure into which men were strapped so that their heads could be chopped off in payment of their crimes, had been put to work for the first time. It had been tested on three cadavers, the victims of syphilis. One had been a woman. The shortest route between La Santé Prison and Ivry where the guillotined were buried - and where in 1936 Marcel had been institutionalised - cut through the commune.

On Rue de la Santé, policemen set up barriers at each end of the street. On Saturdays there was an open-air food market on the tree-lined Boulevard Port Royal from which the street led, and traders, arriving to set up their stalls and fearing they might not be allowed to do business that day, angrily shouted at the policemen. The traders wanted to know what was going on; they were told to 'circulate'; they were waking up the neighbourhood.

The neighbourhood was already awake.

The residents were at their windows and Parisians from all over the capital came walking up; news had leaked out that Dr Petiot was living his last hours on earth and they had come to watch. If they were not to actually assist the execution - that was no longer allowed by law - they would at least be in the vicinity.

407

A small black car pulling what looked like a black horsebox was waved through a barrier. Four men were in the car. They wore dark suits and hats. The first thing they would do, once they had driven through the prison gate, would be to change into *bleu de travail*. Chopping off a man's head could be a bloody business and suits were expensive in post-war Paris. Jules-Henri Desfourneaux, 65 - *Monsieur Paris* - and his three assistants were about to chop off Marcel's.

Dupin, Meiss representing Leser, and Goletty, as well as a man named Schweich, Goletty's assistant, also drove up to the prison. They were to witness the execution. Other witnesses arrived; the commissioners Desveaux and Pinault; Dr Paul; Floriot and Eugène Ayache, another of his 'boys'. Saying he would not be able to take seeing Marcel die, Paul Cousin had begged to be excused.

Inside the prison, Abbé Berger, La Santé's chaplain, was waiting. With him were the prison's director and several police dignitaries.

At 4:45 A.M. the witnesses approached Marcel's cell. He lay on his back. His handcuffed hands rested on his chest. His chained legs were crossed. He wore a pair of black prison pyjamas. He was fast asleep. The witnesses squeezed into the cell.

"Petiot, wake up," called Dupin.

Marcel stirred.

"Have courage. Be brave. The time has come," said Dupin.

Those were words tradition required him to say.

Marcel opened his eyes. He glared at Dupin.

"You're a pain in the arse!" he hissed.

The warders removed the handcuffs and the chains. Marcel dressed. He put on the suit and shirt he had worn on the first and last days of his trial. Knowing what was to come, he left the collar and the purple bow tie lying on the bed.

Dupin asked if he had a special request.

"Yes," he replied.

He wanted to write letters to Georgette, Gerhardt and Maurice.

Experienced in such matters and moments, Floriot had had the foresight to bring a writing block, envelopes, pen and ink.

Marcel began to write. When he still had not finished after twenty minutes, one of the witnesses whispered something to Dr Paul; he wanted to know how much time a condemned man should be given to write letters.

"They can take as long as they like… provided, of course… Once, a condemned man sat writing letters for four hours, and we all had to stand and wait," whispered Dr Paul.

Overhearing him, Goletty said he might have to leave the cell. He was not feeling well. He had turned white. By contrast, Marcel was calm. It would be remembered his hands had not trembled at any time.

Marcel, half an hour after he had started writing his letters, put the pen down, folded the letters and slipped them into envelopes. He wrote the name of the recipient on each and handed it to Floriot.

In his letter to Maurice, he had written: 'See you soon in Heaven or Hell, whichever it will be'. Gerhardt's letter he had ended: 'Be a good son to your dear mother and never forget your surname is Petiot. Also never forget you are the son of an honest man and a good doctor'. Georgette's letter, he had started: 'I did not confess, my darling, and die an innocent man'.

Abbé Berger stepped forward and offered Marcel the Last Rites.

"No. I do not need your services. I am an infidel," said Marcel.

"Your wife wants you to have them, and I therefore ask you to accept them for the love of your wife," said the Abbé.

"In that case, go ahead," replied Marcel.

It was Dupin's turn to feel unwell. He went as white as Goletty and swayed.

"Oops!" said Marcel, "Someone should better look after *Monsieur* Dupin. I fear he is going to faint."

Offered a glass of rum, another of France's guillotine traditions, Marcel turned it down. He would die without ever having drunk alcohol. Instead, he asked if he could smoke a cigarette. Floriot quickly offered him one of his own.

Marcel inhaled deeply and blew rings into the stale air.

Finished, he swept his eyes over the men in the cell with him.

"Gentlemen," he said. "I am ready."

He was again handcuffed, and his night chain was swung around his ankles.

Without wasting any more time, the group started walking down the corridor of Block 7 - Death Row. Other inmates kicked and banged violently on the doors of their cells.

"*Adieu* Mégot!" a voice called out.

It was a long walk down the many corridors and across two yards to the ceremonial courtyard where the guillotine was waiting. Marcel, because of the chains, lost his balance and stumbled several times; to steady his gait, he lifted his handcuffed hands over his chest.

Close to the courtyard, he was pulled into a small room. He was to have his neck shaved, and his shirt had to be cut open so that his neck would be exposed for the guillotine's kiss. He seemed familiar with the routine. The room was in semi-darkness; whenever there was an execution in the courtyard the blind in front of the window was to be pulled down because sometime somewhere someone had decided it would be too cruel for the condemned to see the instrument of death.

His shirt cut, and his neck smoothly shaved, Marcel asked for another cigarette. Again, Floriot gave him one of his.

While Marcel smoked, some of the witnesses stepped outside to wait in the courtyard. They were silent. And they tried not to look at the guillotine.

The cigarette, smoked, Marcel's handcuffs were removed. Those had been on very tightly and they had left red marks across his wrists. He was still shaking his arms to return their blood circulation when he was asked to take off his jacket and to put his hands behind his back. He shot a glance at the handcuffs lying on a table as if implying they weren't needed anymore; would not be needed in future - not for him. He must surely have read in the books found at the townhouse, but must have forgotten, that the condemned did not go to the guillotine handcuffed; their hands were tied with ordinary domestic cord. So were his.

They were tied behind his back.

The chain around his ankles was removed.

His blood was free to rush.

At a minute before 5 A.M. he stepped out into the courtyard. He looked small and frail beside the four metre high wooden guillotine.

'In all cases where the law imposes the death penalty on an accused person, the punishment shall be the same, whatever the nature of the offence of which he is guilty; the criminal shall be decapitated; this will be done solely by means of a simple mechanism'.

Those were the words of Art. 2 of the proposition concerning the death sentence, which Dr Guillotine had submitted for debate in the

French parliament in 1789. In honour of Dr Antoine Louis, who had drawn up the blueprints for the apparatus, Dr Guillotine's machine would be nicknamed 'Louisette'.

Dr Marcel Petiot's killing spree had started in 1926 with a girl named Louisette. Twenty years later, it was to end with another.

Marcel embraced Ayache.

He turned to Floriot.

"Maître, mon chèr ami, if anyone publishes something on my case after my death, please ask them to include photographs of those I have been accused of killing. Maybe someone somewhere will then remember that they had seen them after the dates on which I was supposed to have done them to death. Then my innocence will be proved," he said.

He kissed Floriot three times on the cheeks.

"Petiot, do you have anything you wish to say?" asked Dupin, standing a few steps away.

"No," replied Marcel, firmly. "I am one traveller who is taking all his baggage with him."

Non. Je suis un voyageur qui emporte tous ses bagages avec lui.

* * *

It was always preferable that death should come quickly to the condemned. Therefore, Desfourneaux and his three assistants worked fast. They pulled Marcel towards the guillotine; they did not look left or right. They did not even seem to waste time to breathe.

"Don't look, gentlemen; this won't be pretty," said Marcel, looking over his shoulder at those who had come to see him die. He was smiling.

The 'gentlemen' stood well away. They wore their best suits. Those too had been expensive and blood could splatter.

Desfourneaux took Marcel by the arm and pushed him against the *bascule*, the guillotine's vertically-positioned tilting board. Rapidly, two of his assistants swung wide leather belts around Marcel's torso and legs and tied him to the board. They pushed the *bascule* down into a horizontal position until it was level with the *lunette*, the device that kept the condemned's head in position. Desfourneaux was waiting and as the *bascule* came to a halt, he grabbed Marcel's head and pushed it through the lunette. Suddenly, Marcel began to thrash about as if he wanted to get

411

up and run away. With ease that came from years of experience, Desfourneaux, with both hands, held him down by the shoulders. Marcel calmed and became still; the reflex had passed, the storm had ended; he had accepted the abyss. He turned his head and looked and smiled at Desfourneaux. The latter's face betrayed not a trace of emotion, but his left hand was moving towards the *déclic* that, when pushed down, would release the blade that would rob Marcel of his life. The blade was oblique. Such a blade had been found to be far more effective than a straight-edged one. A straight blade was inclined to crush the neck rather than to severe it. It made guillotining an altogether messier procedure.

Desfourneaux's third assistant was standing directly in front of the *lunette*, but behind a wooden shield that would protect him from Marcel's blood. Between the *lunette* and the shield stood a wicker basket. As Marcel's head appeared through the *lunette*, he grabbed it by the hair; it was imperative that a condemned's head should not move. Had Marcel been bald, he would have grabbed him around the top of his head.

Desfourneaux pressed the *déclic*. The guillotine's blade was attached to a metal block known as the *mouton*. Its purpose was to add speed and force to the blade. The *mouton* weighed thirty kilograms; the blade seven. Three bolts that kept the blade in place weighed a kilogram each. That was a total of forty kilograms: it hit Petiot's neck with a dull and very sharp thud.

It was 5:05 A.M.

Marcel's head fell into the wicker basket. It was the kind of basket as might be found in any office, but this one was lined with lead so that blood could not seep out. Marcel's body, as lifeless as it was headless, laid stock-still on the bascule. Hastily, the two assistants, one on each side of it, pushed it into another wicker basket, this one long. It was also lead-lined and was large enough to hold four adult bodies.

Dr Paul stepped up to the long basket. He had to establish death had taken place. He had always found that procedure such a ridiculous formality. He looked into the basket and nodded heavily. Marcel lay on his back. His arms were underneath his body. His legs were bent.

Dr Paul would later say, "For the first time in my life, I saw a man leaving death row if not dancing, at least showing perfect calm. Most people about to be executed do their best to be courageous, but one senses that it is a stiff and forced courage. Petiot moved with ease, as

412

though he was walking into his consulting room where a patient was waiting."

Those who had witnessed guillotine executions, used to say that after decapitation, the eyelids and lips of the guillotined had continued to contract for five or six seconds. Rumour has it that Marcel had continued to smile and flutter his eyelids for at least twenty or thirty seconds after his head had been severed from his body.

Some of the witnesses left the courtyard, got into their cars and drove off.

Desfourneaux and his three assistants still had work to do before they too could go. They transferred Marcel's body and head to a plain wooden coffin. They hosed down the guillotine, the basket into which Marcel's head had tumbled and the basket into which his body had been pushed. They hosed the courtyard. All part of the service.

Monsieur de Paris and his three assistants had nearly not turned up for Marcel's execution. They had gone on strike for an increase to their 65,000 francs annual salary, and the 50 francs bonus they received for each execution. Since the increase had been promised, but had been slow in coming, Desfourneaux had threatened he would not be able to guillotine Dr Petiot; threatened with dismissal in return, he had said his machine was not in working order; it had been damaged during Allied bombing. In fact, Desfourneaux had efficiently guillotined Germany's enemies - mostly resisters, some of them women - throughout the War. It was something that would sully his name until the day he died in 1951 of a heart attack, probably caused by the alcoholism and depression of his last years, years he had spent repairing bicycles. Just like Maurice Petiot.

Desfourneaux had not become an executioner by chance; no one in France ever had done so; it was a profession that had run in families. Father to son; grandfather to grandson; uncle to nephew. He had two executioners in his family; his great uncle, Edouard Mathieu and an uncle Leopold.

* * *

A 'swallow' arrived at the prison on a bike to sign a certificate stating the body in the coffin was, indeed, Marcel Petiot's.

Afterwards, the coffin was closed and sealed with red wax.

Next, it was slid into the grey Citroën box-shaped police van, which had arrived at the prison earlier in the morning for transportation to Ivry cemetery. The vehicle had a motorcycle and *traction-avant* escort. Floriot, Ayache, Meiss, Dr Paul, and Abbé Berger rode in the two *traction-avants*.

The four-vehicle convoy turned south down Boulevard August Blanqui to Place de l'Italie, from where it rode down Avenue d'Italie to Porte d'Italie. It was not only the shortest route to the cemetery; it was also the road to Auxerre. At Porte d'Italie, the southern border of Paris, it entered the commune of Kremlin-Bicêtre. Slowly, it descended the length of Route de Fontainebleau and turned left down a short, tree-lined street to the cemetery gate. The cemetery formed the border between Kremlin-Bicêtre and Ivry.

Just after 6:30 A.M. the convoy reached the cemetery. Barriers erected in front of the gate by the police earlier in the morning had alerted locals to the fact that it was the morning that Dr Petiot would be guillotined. Many, therefore, gathered; they wanted to watch his burial.

As soon as the convoy had passed, the cemetery watchman slammed the gate shut. Next, he jumped onto the police van's front bumper to direct the driver to the place where Marcel would be buried. The public would not be allowed to enter the cemetery until it was all over.

At the graveside, Marcel's coffin was lifted from the van and placed on top of the rope which would cradle it into the hole that had been dug by gravediggers during the night. They stood waiting impatiently to lower the coffin into their nice new hole. They could then go home. It was forbidden to bury people in France at the weekend; therefore, because it was Saturday they were working overtime.

The Ivry police chief also waited at the graveside. He would have to sign the papers necessary for the Paris town hall to confirm that Dr Marcel Petiot had been buried.

Georgette had asked to attend her husband's funeral. Though Dr Guillotine had stipulated: 'The corpse of an executed man shall be handed over to his family on their request. In every case, he shall be allowed normal burial and no reference shall be made on the register to the nature of his death', she had been told that it would not be possible.

Abbé Berger said a short prayer over the coffin and made the sign of the cross.

The moment he dropped his arm, the gravediggers started to lower the coffin. Not sure they were going to be paid for the overtime they were putting in, they worked fast.

Not one person waited to watch the coffin finally disappear.

In the afternoon, Georgette, Gerhardt and Maurice arrived at the cemetery. The watchman had gone off duty: he, too, had put in extra time in the morning and like the gravediggers, he was not sure he would be paid. Earlier, in a telephone call Floriot had told Georgette where to find the grave. She, her son and Maurice, the two men in dark suits, walked straight to it: Marcel lay underneath a low heap of fresh earth near the gate on the Ivry side of the cemetery. They stayed for a few minutes, standing silently, their heads bowed; each made the sign of the cross. After a couple of minutes, they walked away. All three were crying.

* * *

For nineteen years Marcel lay under a flat slab of cement on which a number had been painted. The number meant nothing to anyone. Only the official in the Paris Hotel de Ville - city hall - who kept a record of all Parisian burials, knew it was Dr Petiot's grave.

In 1965, Marcel's remains were moved to a mass grave on the Kremlin-Bicêtre side of the cemetery. Georgette was dead and Gerhardt was living in Brazil: the Paris municipal authorities did not ask him whether he would like to claim his father's remains as they should have done.

Marcel Petiot still lies in the mass grave; he lies with other nameless victims of the guillotine.

It is a calm, shady spot.

The End

BIBLIOGRAPHY

Amouroux, Henri. *Les Beaux Jours des Collabos*. Éditions Robert Laffont, France (1978)

Joies et Douleurs du Peuple Libéré. Éditions Robert Laffont, France (1988).

Aziz, Philippe. *Tu Trahiras Sans Vergogne*. Librarie Arthème Fayard, France (1970).

Barroco, Michel. *Les Tueurs en Séries*. Le Cavalier Blue, France (2006).

Bayac, J. Deperrie de. *Histoire de la Milice*. Series 'Les Grandes Études Contemporaines' , France (1969).

Beevor, Antony with Cooper, Artemis. *Paris After the Liberation*. Hamish Hamilton, UK. (1994).

Berlière, Jean-Marc. *Policiers français sous l'Occupation*. Librairie Académique Perrin, France (2009).

Bertin, Claude (Editor) *Les Grands Procès de l'Histoire*. Éditions Famot, Geneva, Switzerland (1976).

Birnie, Renée Jardin. *Le Cahier Rouge d'Eugène Weidmann*. Éditions Gallimard, France (1968)

Boterf le, Hervé. *La Vie parisienne sous l'Occupation*. Diffusion F.Beauval, France. (1978).

Césaire, Frédérique. *L'Affaire Petiot*. Édition De Vecchi. Series 'Grands Procès de l'Histoire' France (1999).

Chambot Albert. *Quand la France était occupée* – 1940-1945. Empire, France. (1998).

Closet, René. *L'Aumonier de l'Enfer.* Éditions Salvator, France (1964).

Collard, Gilbert Maître. *L'Affaire Petiot, le docteur Satan.* Éditions Tallandier, France (1997).

Dominique, Jean-François. *L'Affaire Petiot.* Éditions Ramsay, France (1980).

Elliott, Catherine. *French Criminal Law.* Willan Publishing, UK (2001).

Excelsior (Paris Newspaper). *L'Execution de Landru à Versailles.* (No. 4694 26 February 1922).

Ferracci-Porri, Michel. *Beaux Ténèbres.* Éditions Normant, France (2008).

Ferro, Marc. *Pétain.* Librairie Arthème Fayard, France (1987).

Fontaine, Jean-Pierre. *Les Nouveaux Mystère de l'Yonne.* Éditions De Borée, France (2007).

Fontenelle, Sébastien. *La France des Mouchards.* Éditions Belfond, France (1997).

Grombach, John V. *The Great Liquidator.* Doubleday, USA (1980).

Halimi, André. *La Délation sous l'Occupation.* Éditions Alain Moreau, France (1983).

Hany-Lefèvre, Noémie. *Six mois à Fresnes.* Flammarion, France (1946).

Historia Magazine , *Petiot, Médecin de Satan.* France (June 1982).

Hoobler, Dorothy and Thomas. *The Crimes of Paris.* Little, Brown and Company, USA (2009).

Jacquemard, Serge. Petiot, docteur Satan. Fleuve noir, France (1993).

Jullian, Marcel. *Le Mystère Petiot*. Édition No 1, France (1980).

Maeder, Thomas. *The Unspeakable Crimes of Dr. Petiot*. Little, Brown & Company, France (1980).

Massu, Commissaire Georges-Victor. *L'Enquête Petiot*. Librairie Arthème Fayard, France (1959).

Monestier, Martin. *Peines de Mort*. Le Cherche Midi, France (1994).

Montagnon, Pierre. *42 Rue de la Santé*. Pygmalion, France (1996).

Montarron, Marcel. *Les Grands Procès d'Assises*. Bibliothèque Marabout, France (1967).

Murder Casebook No 50. Marshall Cavendish Ltd., UK (1990).

Murder In Mind No 29. Marshall Cavendish Ltd., UK (1990).

Nézondet, René. *Petiot, Le Posséde*. Privately Published, France (1950).

Paris Jour. (Quaterly) No. 1. France (1977).

Perry, Jacques with Chabert, Jane. *L'Affaire Petiot*. Gallimard, France (1957).

Petiot, Marcel. *Le Hasard Vaincu* (Chance Defeated) self-published in hand-written form in Paris, France by Georgette. Printer: Roger Amiard, France (1945).

Thèse: Le Doctorat en Médecine, l'Etude de la Paralysie Ascendante Aiguë par Marcel Petiot. Printer Ollier-Henry, France (1921)

Popot, Abbé Jean. *J'étais Aumonier à Fresnes*. Librairie Académique Perrin, France (1962).

Pottecher, Frédéric. Les Grands Procès de l'Histoire. Fayard, France

(1981).

Rais, Gilles de. *Les Grands Procès de l'Histoire*. Édition Famot, Switzerland (1976).

Real-Life Crimes No 69. Eaglemoss Publications Ltd., UK (1994).

Rousso, Henry. *Le régime de Vichy*. Presse Universitaires de France. (2007).

Seth, Ronald. *Victim of Chance*. Hutchinson & Co, UK (1963).

Sigot, Jacques. 1946, Le Procès de Marcel Petiot, le bon docteur de le rue Le Sueur. Éditions CMD, France (1995).

Varaut, Jean-Marc. *L'Abominable Dr. Petiot*. Balland, France (1974).

Weitz, Margaret Collins. *Sisters in the Resistance*. John Wiley & Sons, U.S.A. (1995).

I wish to thank Dave Lyons, publisher with Raven Crest Books. A great big thank you, Dave!

CONTACT DETAILS

Visit Marilyn's website:
www.marilynztomlins.com

Follow Marilyn on Twitter:
www.twitter.com/MarilynZTomlins

Like or join Marilyn on Facebook:
www.facebook.com/marilyn.tomlins

Cover designed by: Raven Crest Books

Published by: Raven Crest Books
www.ravencrestbooks.com

Follow us on Twitter:
www.twitter.com/lyons_dave

Like us on Facebook:
www.facebook.com/RavenCrestBooksClub

CPSIA information can be obtained at www.ICGtesting.com
Printed in the USA
LVOW10s1723210514

386773LV00005B/220/P